# Edson's Raiders

# Edson's Raiders

The 1st Marine Raider Battalion
in World War II

Joseph H. Alexander

NAVAL INSTITUTE PRESS
*Annapolis, Maryland*

Naval Institute Press
291 Wood Road
Annapolis, MD 21402

ISBN 1-55750-020-7

Printed in the United States of America

All photographs and illustrations are courtesy of the Edson's Raiders
Association, with the exception of the illustrations by Carl Fox and
Larry Klatt, or as otherwise noted.

To the 2,800 Marines and Navy medical personnel and chaplains
who served in the ranks of the 1st Marine Raider Battalion
during the period 16 February 1942 to 1 February 1944
...and most especially to the 312 members of
Edson's Raiders who were killed in action,
died of their wounds, or who were missing in action
and eventually presumed dead.

# Contents

# Foreword

THOSE WHO WOULD DIMINISH THE VALUE of small, specialized combat units have made a point of saying, "They're just strong enough to get into trouble but not strong enough to get out of it." Nobody ever said that about the 1st Marine Raider Battalion.

Activated shortly after Pearl Harbor, selectively manned at every level, armed with the best weaponry available, and conditioned and trained under the merciless direction of Colonel Merritt A. Edson, the battalion was ready and able for the first combat actions of the war. What it may have lacked in deep support was more than compensated by superb conditioning and high individual and small unit attainment in the area of close combat effectiveness. In a corps long renowned for battlefield performance, it was second to none.

In America's first offensive at Guadalcanal no one was more aware of this than General Vandegrift, who assigned to the 1st Raiders the post of honor in the initial assault—the seizure of Tulagi. The hard-won success of Edson's battle-minded force at Tulagi caused the division commander to proclaim that the enemy "was driven from every place he held by the resolute attack of men who were not afraid to die." Those men were Raiders.

Tasimboko, which followed, will long stand as the classic seaborne raid of the Pacific War. Cold calculation and cool judgment were needed here when the unforeseen necessity of landing two successive echelons exposed the first to defeat in detail. Again the Raiders pulled it off. They "singed" General Kawaguchi's beard like Drake did to Philip of Spain at Cadiz in 1587.

It is difficult to exaggerate the importance of the Raider victory during the three-day battle for Edson's Ridge in mid-September of 1942. The 1st Raiders got in deep trouble not of their own making and fought their way out of it. On the afternoon of 13 September I visited their command post and found all hands utterly exhausted after three days of unremitting combat, but there was not the slightest sign of faltering in their determination to prevail. They talked eagerly of their plans for the forthcoming night and of changes to be made in light of lessons learned the night before. These men would not be licked.

The Raiders left their indelible mark from Tulagi to the Dragon's Peninsula in New Georgia, accepting every mission in good grace and fighting with unrivaled ferocity against some of the best troops in the Japanese empire.

This book records a brilliant chapter in our national history. It will live to inspire generations of Marines yet unborn in battles yet undreamed of.

General Merrill B. Twining, USMC (Ret.)

# Acknowledgments

THIS IS A NARRATIVE HISTORY of a unique organization of remarkable men, the 1st Marine Raider Battalion, known then and now by the name of its founding commander, Merritt A. ("Red Mike") Edson. Edson's Raiders fought seven critical battles in the canopied rain forests of the Solomon Islands during the darkest years of the Pacific War. Their battles have names that with the passage of time sound increasingly exotic to newer generations—Tulagi, Tasimboko, Edson's Ridge, the Matanikau River, Enogai, and Bairoko Harbor—but they were desperate, frightfully bloody affairs. While victory did not crown every endeavor, the Raiders fought with singular savagery against some of the most experienced jungle fighters in the Japanese empire.

Surely the best measure of their valor in those long-ago battles is embedded in the fact that twenty-four U.S. Navy ships were named in honor of individual members of Edson's Raiders—all but one posthumously. Eighteen enlisted Raiders and corpsmen garnered this unusual honor. Their achievements form colorful strands in the tapestry of modern Marine Corps history and traditions.

This book represents the culmination of a number of earlier attempts to tell the whole story, beginning in the 1950s with "Pete" Pettus, and continuing through the 1990s with Colonel Thomas Mullahey, USMC (Ret.), Colonel John B. Sweeney, USMC (Ret.), and Lieutenant Colonel Jon T. Hoffman, USMCR. I have benefited from the hard work of each of these predecessors, and many of the endnotes acknowledge their earlier research and interviews. In more recent years, the archival collection started by Pettus and enhanced by Mullahey was carefully nurtured by Sweeney, by Captain Frank Guidone, USMC (Ret.), and by Joseph Murphy. The final obstacles were bridged by the Book Committee, chaired by Duke Vierling, assisted by Robert Addison, Fred Serral, James "Horse"

Smith (he stopped being "Horse Collar" after the war), and Gerry West, each a former president of the Edson's Raiders Association and all frequent contributors to my research. Brigadier General Edwin H. Simmons, USMC (Ret.), the Director Emeritus of Marine Corps History, contributed significantly to my project, as did Dr. Lee Minier, the nephew and namesake of Raider Lee Minier, whose upbeat letters appear often in this narrative.

Raider Carl Fox designed all of the maps and provided a sketch of the principal firearms used in the fighting in the Solomons. Former World War II SeaBee Larry Klatt provided sketches of special weapons and equipment employed by the Raiders and their Japanese opponents. John Sweeney provided copies of original sketches by Raiders Houston "Tex" Stiff and Doug Greenbowe.

Bunichi Ohtsuka provided translations of Japanese accounts of the fighting on the Dragon's Peninsula and a detailed biography of General Kawaguchi. Researcher Scott Anderson found many invaluable original accounts in the National Archives. Robert Aquilina, Dan Crawford, David Crist, and Evelyn Englander provided biographies, oral histories, and unit reports from the Marine Corps Historical Center in Washington. Raider Horse Smith provided many documents from the Griffith Papers, including Kawaguchi's Guadalcanal memoir, as well as the original Casualty Cards for the 1st Raider Battalion. Raiders Frank Guidone and John Sweeney provided me with frequent insights on each campaign from the squad and rifle company perspective.

In the process of my research I received specific assistance from a number of other well-informed veterans and historians. Kenneth Smith-Christmas of the Marine Corps Museum provided photographs and information on 1941-vintage rubber boat training. Dr. Carl Boyd educated me on the role of Japanese submarines in the Kula Gulf; my brother, U.S. Navy Captain William Alexander, USNR (Ret.) provided detailed information on troop submarines in the Pacific War. Ordnance specialists Bruce Canfield and Lieutenant Colonel James Hitz provided details on the Reising Gun and the Boys antitank rifle; Eric Mailander shared his knowledge of Japanese field pieces and machine guns; Homer Brett did the same concerning the bayonets and fighting knives used by the Raiders and their enemy. Doctor Mike Keleher shared little known facts about his former commanding officer, the colorful "Jumping Joe" Chambers. Collector Leonard Hancock kept me honest about the Raider patch. Colonel Richard Poore, USMC (Ret.) helped with the loan of out-of-print books from his wondrous library. Raider Robert O'Neal provided a cassette recording of the Singing Eight Balls from the Library of Congress master disk. Accomplished authors Richard Frank and Matthew Stevens kindly shared insights about Guadalcanal, then and now.

Special thanks, as well, to Raider James Childs for his collection of muster rolls; retired Major Rick Spooner for his copy of General Breckenridge's last letter; Sloan McCarthy for his technical details on the P-39 Airacobras of the Cactus Air Force; and Lieutenant Colonel Jon Hoffman for frequent oversight and careful editing.

Regarding the Naval Institute edition, I am very much obliged to Robert Krick and James Hitz for diligent proofreading, and to the Institute's Paul Wilderson, Rebecca Hinds, Karen White-Doody, Kimberley VanDerveer, and Barbara DeGennaro for their exceptional assistance.

Finally, heartfelt thanks to my wife, Gale, who patiently shared a year of our life together with 350 different accounts of Red Mike Edson's extraordinary Raiders.

# Edson's Raiders

# Prologue

## Those Men in Burlap Hats

GUADALCANAL, BRITISH SOLOMON ISLANDS
30–31 AUGUST 1942

During the fourth week of the battle for Guadalcanal, two opposing rein-forcement commanders splashed ashore on the island's north coast with all the confidence of champion prize fighters entering the ring for the main event. Both were savvy, proven veterans, impatiently seeking deci-sive action and greater renown.

One wore a white star centered on yellow tabs along both sides of the open collar of his tropical olive-drab uniform. Mature, mustachioed, and peremptory, Major General Kiyotake Kawaguchi, Imperial Japanese Army, had arrived on Guadalcanal at the head of his 35th Infantry Brigade.

Kawaguchi's counterpart conveyed a much less imposing appearance. He was short and wiry, his small head dwarfed by his steel helmet and its unique burlap covering, his silver eagle rank insignia hidden under-neath the collar of his faded herringbone utility jacket. There was little about the man that identified him as a legendary jungle fighter until you noticed his eyes—pale blue, unsmiling—the eyes of a professional marks-man, the unblinking eyes of an assassin. Colonel Merritt Austin ("Red Mike") Edson had arrived on the island from nearby Tulagi at the head of his 1st Marine Raider Battalion.

Kawaguchi's own jungle fighters were the victors of Borneo, the suc-cessful executors of a series of assault landings the previous December that had captured untold oil resources for the Emperor. Three months later, Imperial General Headquarters had selected Kawaguchi's brigade to spearhead the planned assault on American Samoa and Fiji—a plan that abruptly died with the Japanese naval defeat at Midway. Cooling his

1

heels in the Palau Islands for the summer had been aggravating for Kawaguchi. Now came the opportunity to restore Guadalcanal and its invaluable bomber strip to Imperial ownership.

Edson's Raiders, barely a half-year in existence, had prevailed convincingly in the bloody seizure of Tulagi during 7–10 August 1942 against a battalion of die-hard *rikusentai,* the Japanese Special Naval Landing Forces. The Raiders sustained abundant casualties in their first combat operation, but they sought out and killed the defending garrison virtually to the last man. Now Major General Alexander A. Vandegrift needed them to reinforce his critically undermanned 1st Marine Division in defending Henderson Field, the strategic prize of the southern Solomons.

Edson's Raiders represented the vanguard of a limited, four-battalion experiment by the U.S. Marine Corps with special, lightly-armed, mobile "commando" units (though their commandant forbade the use of the British term). Hand-picked volunteers, the Raiders considered themselves elite, much to the ire of all conventional Marine outfits. Yet their swagger and spirit comprised a welcome offensive spark in the woeful early days in the South Pacific.

A full year before the Marine Corps would adopt the now-traditional camouflaged helmet cover, Edson's Raiders stormed ashore on Tulagi wearing improvised burlap rags atop their steel pots. Before long, the native Solomon Islanders who scouted the Japanese reported that the enemy had placed a bounty on "those men in burlap hats."

The Japanese were dismayed to realize that Edson and others like him could so swiftly transform raw-boned American youngsters into professional, first-class fighting men, into Marine Raiders. But for the people of the United States, with virtually everything on the line in the Solomons, the 1st Marine Raider Battalion—short on firepower, long on valor—kindled an incandescent blaze of hope and confidence.

Within the next two weeks, Edson's "men in burlap hats" would sting and stymie Kawaguchi's large force three times, once at the tail, twice in the teeth.

# 1

## The Roots of the Raiders, 1937–1941

*It is not enough that the troops be skilled infantrymen, jungle fighters, or artillerymen of high morale; they must be skilled water men and jungle men who know it can be done.*

Major Earl H. ("Pete") Ellis, USMC
"Advanced Base Operations in Micronesia," 1921[1]

THIS IS THE OPERATIONAL HISTORY of the 1st Marine Raider Battalion, commonly known as "Edson's Raiders," during World War II.

The battalion existed for two years, distinguished itself in eighteen weeks of violent combat in the British Solomon Islands, fought seven major battles, and left a legacy of audacity, grit, and lethality that will outlive all its survivors. Yet the outfit was conceived in desperation and born amid controversy, both circumstances a reflection of America's lack of military preparedness.

The United States essentially fought two different wars against Japan. The first, waged principally in the South Pacific between December 1941 and November 1943, featured desperate holding actions and limited offensives, both handicapped by severely restricted manpower, weapons, and strategic reach. "Operation Shoestring," the troops' cynical nickname for the Guadalcanal campaign, could easily characterize the entire era.

The "second war," waged between November 1943 and August 1945, differed from the first as sharply as day from night. Enormous fleets, preceded by far-ranging carrier task forces, swept inexorably across the Pacific, isolating island objectives and projecting powerful landing forces ashore to overwhelm the Japanese garrisons. This phase commenced

3

with a division-sized assault landing against Betio Island, Tarawa Atoll, and ended with the combined Third and Fifth Fleets preparing to land the U.S. Sixth Army on southern Kyushu in the Japanese homeland.

Assault forces in the second phase had to overcome larger, better led, more heavily armed, and much more intensely fortified enemy defenders—conditions that would have proven suicidal for the under-strength Raiders in the early years. On the other hand, the Raiders and their contemporaries fought against Imperial Japan's "First Team" in terms of veteran aviators, soldiers, and sailors. The arena for each of their pitched battles was always the sub-equatorial jungle, itself a formidable enemy. Edson's Raiders by no means won every battle. Yet the fact that they prevailed in five of their seven engagements against such veteran troops in close-quarters jungle fighting—and with control of the air and sea literally up for grabs hour by hour—reflects exceptional leadership, training, and esprit.

Appreciating the differences between these two contrasting stages of the Pacific War is key to understanding why the Raiders were terminated in early 1944 despite their combat record. The Raiders were relevant throughout 1942–43, a "force-multiplier" in today's parlance. By 1944 they (as well as the parachutists, glider troops, and all other special units) had become superfluous. The demise of the Raiders had little to do with their military effectiveness and everything to do with the drastic change in the nation's global war-fighting capability.

The midwife of the birth of the Marine Raiders, then, was the nation's chronic unpreparedness in 1942 to wage a two-ocean, offensive amphibious war against such formidable opponents as Nazi Germany and Imperial Japan. Despite all the undeniable warnings and indicators in the years preceding Pearl Harbor, it still took the nation two years to gear up for the job. The Raiders flourished in this prolonged vacuum.

Everyone, it seemed, developed strong feelings about the Raiders. One either loved, envied, or loathed them.

Regardless of their opinion about the Raiders themselves, few Leathernecks questioned whether the raiding mission was an appropriate role for Marines. After all, raids from the sea had been an adjunct tactic of the increasingly amphibious corps for much of its history, beginning with the Revolutionary War. The real issue, hotly debated at headquarters and within each barracks, concerned whether the Marines should invest their meager resources in elite, special units for arguably temporary missions or should the raiding role be executed by standard infantry battalions with a bit of workup training? By 1944, most Marines, including Edson and his successor, Samuel B. Griffith, concluded that the second option made more sense.

Edson never let the controversy distract him from his ingrained responsibility for transforming his uneven mixture of veterans, newly-activated reservists, and untrained volunteers into a finely-honed instrument of operational usefulness. Edson's indomitable personality infused the 1st Raider Battalion with both a craftsman's professionalism and an aggressive desire for close combat.

## War Begins in the Far Pacific

The Pacific War began four years before Pearl Harbor with Imperial Japan's decision to seize strategic objectives in mainland China by force of arms.

The year 1937 was pivotal to many people whose lives had not yet intersected. In early July of that year Major Merritt Edson arrived in Shanghai, China, for duty as regimental operations and training officer of the 4th Marines. One day later, the Japanese launched their invasion of north China. A month later, Japanese Special Naval Landing units came ashore and the fight for Shanghai began. The city fell to the Japanese by November. Edson had a front-row seat throughout this period from which to observe the Japanese forces and study their tactics, weapons, and aggressiveness. So did Captain Samuel Griffith, a gifted linguist, studying Chinese in Peking in 1937. After the war erupted he became an official observer with the Japanese army, an invaluable learning experience. Second Lieutenant Lewis W. Walt, a fresh graduate of The Basic School in Philadelphia, served as a platoon commander under Edson.

It is certainly possible that Edson, Griffith, or Walt in their many contacts with the Imperial Army may have encountered newly-promoted Colonel Kiyotake Kawaguchi, their future opponent on Guadalcanal, who in 1937 served as a staff officer with the North China Area Army.

A Japanese area army in 1937 was several times larger than the entire prewar United States Marine Corps. During that fiscal year, the major general commandant reported his enlisted end strength to be 16,500 men. Operationally, the Corps had 3,953 men in the fledgling Fleet Marine Forces at Quantico and San Diego as well as 2,526 men serving as Marine Detachments on board forty-eight warships around the world. The Navy Transportation Service listed two serviceable troop transports, including the beloved USS *Henderson,* already long in the tooth after twenty-one years service and not configured as a tactical vessel.[2]

By 1937 some Marines had grown concerned with the nearly total lack of attack transports and suitable ship-to-shore assault craft with which to wage amphibious war. Brigadier General James J. Meade, USMC, a veteran of the 1914 Veracruz landing, observed these acute shortfalls during several weeks of fleet landing exercises with his 1st Marine Brigade. In Meade's view, the few cargo ships chartered by the navy for temporary use as transports were too slow, too deep in draft, and deficient in boat davits and antiaircraft weapons. Nor was Meade encouraged by the navy's offer to scatter the landing force among the cruisers and battleships of the fleet. To Meade, this practice sacrificed unit integrity and made the landing force mission hostage to whatever exigencies of fleet action the warships might encounter in the objective area. His practical solution in February 1937 would have a lasting impact on the 1st Marine Raider Battalion of 1942: "I recommend we equip destroyers as attack transports from which troops could move closely into shore and disembark under the protection of the ships' guns." The first "four-stacker" destroyer transport would appear in the next year's training exercise.[3]

The year 1937 included several other amphibious breakthroughs. The Navy Department invited New Orleans boat builder Andrew Jackson Higgins to Washington to discuss production of his successful Eureka boat, valued throughout the Mississippi delta for its shallow draft, protected propeller, and spoon-bill bow. Five years later, militarized versions of Higgins' Eureka boat would deliver the 1st Raider Battalion to Tulagi and Tasimboko. And *Life* magazine in its 4 October 1937 issue featured a Florida engineer named Donald Roebling with the strange-looking, swamp-loving tracked vehicle he called "The Alligator." The Marines were immediately interested.[4]

In 1937 Colonel Holland M. Smith ("Hoke" to his friends; he would not be known by his signature nick-name of "Howlin' Mad" until the 1940s) served as Director of Operations and Training at Headquarters Marine Corps. On the other side of the world, First Lieutenant Robert S. Brown, a 1931 graduate of the Naval Academy, served as guard officer, public relations officer, and PX officer at Marine Barracks, Guam. Second Lieutenant Kenneth Dillon Bailey, an experienced platoon commander in the 5th Marines, participated in the ragged landing exercises in the Caribbean.

Most future Raiders in 1937 were happily involved in peaceable pursuits. Frank Guidone was a junior tailback on the Wellsville (Ohio) High School varsity football team. During the summer he toured the small steel towns along the Ohio River Valley as an amateur boxer. Richard

Capt. Ken Bailey, commanding C Company, 1st Battalion, 5th Marines, spring 1941, Quantico, before Edson's arrival and well before the unit's conversion to Raiders.

"Red" Sullivan tired of life as a dairy farmer in North Carolina and at age twenty enlisted in the Marines. Joe Murphy, a Marine Reservist in Boston, underwent two-week training camp. Harold "Pappy" Holden served in the Civilian Conservation Corps in New York and Oregon. Jim Thomas, then seventeen, dropped out of high school to help his parents cope with the Depression and worked as a 75-cents-per-hour grocery clerk in Chester, Pennsylvania. Robert Addison, fourteen, worked as a caddy at the local country club in Alliance, Ohio, and played baseball throughout the summer. Jack Tracy, fifteen, was another ballplayer in a church league in Lancaster, Pennsylvania. In upstate New York, Gerald West graduated from high school, worked in a grocery store, and played amateur baseball.

In 1937, Clint Haines was a corporal in the 4th Marines, stationed in Shanghai and closely watching the Japanese occupation forces along with Major Edson. Private First Class Angus R. Goss, already a veteran of seven years' service, was winding up a tour at Cavite Naval Station in the Philippines and anticipating orders to China and a corporal's warrant. Bill Stevenson was a sophomore at Dartmouth; Houston "Tex" Stiff, a junior at North Texas; George Herring, and Tony Antonelli were plebes at Annapolis. Art Haake had entered his first year at Harvard Law School. Ed Dupras was a freshman at Providence College where he worked part-time as a soda-jerk. Gene Martin was a junior at Culver Military Academy.

In Millburn, New Jersey, Harold Smith graduated from high school where he had been captain of the Millers' football team and prepared to join his father on the local police force. In Jacksonville, Florida, Herschel Sterling played high-school sports and worked part-time in construction. In New York City, George "Ken" Peters commuted from his family's summer home on Long Island's South Shore to work for Socony-Vacuum Company, the forerunner of Mobil Corporation. Near Yuba City, Arizona, George Taylor loaded hay on a ranch and rode broncos on the local rodeo circuit to earn a few extra bucks. Meanwhile, Harvard graduate Bob Skinner worked on a farm to earn enough money to return to the University of Pennsylvania Medical School.[5]

## The Plank Owners

Marines take their relative longevity in an outfit with deadly seriousness. True graybeards who can authenticate their membership in the elusive "Old Corps" value their standing more than their rank stripes or hashmarks. Two old-timers will meet and invariably try to seize the high ground of history. Says one: "I've been in this outfit since John the Baptist was a Mess Cook!" Replies the other: "That's nothing—I was Right Guide for the Three Wise Men!!" The navy uses the term "Plank Owners," referring to the original crew of a newly commissioned man-of-war.

The "Plank Owners" of Edson's Raiders can trace their lineage back through their preliminary designations as 1st Separate Battalion to the old 1st Battalion, 5th Marines ("1/5"). Even then, one could not call oneself "Old Corps" unless one could speak of the primitive landing exercises in the Caribbean using ship's whaleboats, the first experiments with rubber boats, and the lengthy deployment in 1940–41 to hardscrabble Camp Garavella Point in Guantanamo Bay ("Gitmo"), Cuba. *"Were you at Gitmo, wise guy??"*

The first wave of newcomers came to the 1st Battalion, 5th Marines in autumn of 1940 when President Franklin D. Roosevelt, concerned with the outbreak of war in both theaters, declared a "limited national emergency" and activated the Marine Corps Reserve. A number of trained Reservists from Boston and Brooklyn joined the 1/5, including not only John Apergis and Joe Murphy, but also Second Lieutenant William E. Sperling III who arrived in Quantico on 8 November 1940. Sperling became a platoon leader in Baker Company, commanded by Captain Robert S. Brown, by now well-seasoned following his tour on Guam and sea duty on board the carrier *Ranger*. "Sergeant Clinton F. Haines was my platoon sergeant," recalled Sperling, "and he certainly took a green 2d Lt. under his wing and had me shadow him while on maneuvers at Culebra. In that first platoon I ever had in the Corps were superb current and future NCOs like Clifford McGlocklin, Thomas D. Pollard, Joseph Buntin, Frank Guidone, and Joe Connally."[6]

Not all of the activated reservists were rookies. Gunnery Sergeant Anthony Yelanich returned to active duty in his mid-thirties, a veteran Leatherneck who had received the Navy Cross as a PFC "for extraordinary heroism, courage, and coolness" in a firefight near Ililihuas, Nicaragua, in 1928 when most of his new battalion-mates were still in grammar school. Yelanich, a runner entrusted with a critical message from Captain Merritt Edson, fought his way through two onrushing bandits with cool marksmanship and fancy footwork.

Gunnery Sergeant Yelanich brought a wealth of field experience and disciplined leadership to the task of training the forerunners of Edson's Raiders. Many considered him a father figure. "My father took twenty-one years to straighten me out and he did not succeed," said Raider Nazario J. DiSalvia. "Tony took only nine months to make me into the man that I am today....He made Marines out of bums and smart alecks like me."[7]

While not a reservist, Frederick A. Serral from Ambler, Pennsylvania, exemplified another source of volunteers who wound up in 1/5 ahead of Red Mike Edson. This group enlisted for two major motives: the growing clouds of world war spreading over Europe and the Far East, and the lingering economic depression at home. Serral could neither afford the tuition at Temple University nor find a decent job. A recruiting billboard that depicted a Marine in dress blues standing at present arms (captioned "If you're going to join up, why not join the very best?") caught his eye, sparked his decision. He enlisted on 16 September 1940. He was eighteen years old and weighed 116 pounds. After Parris Island, Serral attended Radio School in Quantico with Duke

Vierling and Joe Szakovics. All three joined 1/5 in early 1941.[8]

If Gunnery Sergeant Tony Yelanich was a father figure for the mass of young Marines swelling the ranks of 1/5, Sergeant Angus R. Goss was more like an "uncle." Goss was thirty-one when he joined 1/5, a Marine since 1930. Tall, with rugged good looks, he was the first of his family to graduate from high school, but the only job he could find was to stand outside the Publix Theater in Tampa in a fancy uniform and hawk the current movie. The Marines provided the same discipline and work ethic he had learned as a youngster, helping his father, Jacob Goss, operate the family grocery store. Young Goss flourished in the Corps. He served in the Philippines, China, and at sea on board the battleship *Maryland*. He had strong mechanical skills and an innate curiosity about all things, attributes which as a Marine led him to become a foremost weapons authority, equally adept at mortars, machine guns, and explosives. "I had six months' experience in mortars when I joined 1/5," said Private Gerald V. West, "but I soon found I had a lot to learn from Sergeant Goss." Under the NCO's tutelage, West became the first in the battalion to qualify for Fifth Class Specialty Pay as a gunner ("when you're making $21 a month, getting an extra $6 a month was a big deal—like making PFC!" said West). James "Horse Collar" Smith found Goss to be uncommonly "wise and possessed of a remarkable intellectual curiosity for an old, hard-bitten Marine." No Marine would better reflect both the glory and the anguish of Edson's Raiders than Goss. "He was the greatest Marine I ever knew," said Gerry West. Added Smith, "Like Mother Nature, no one screwed around with Angus Goss."[9]

In later months Red Mike Edson would inspire many hard-charging young officers and non-commissioned officers to volunteer for duty with his Raider battalion. Each would benefit immensely from the cadre of seasoned leaders already on the ground in 1/5—gifted NCOs like Yelanich, Goss, and Haines.

### Howlin' Mad Smith

One of the intriguing ironies of the military profession is the frequency with which small decisions lead to momentous consequences. When Major General Commandant Thomas Holcomb assigned his Assistant Commandant and long-time friend Brigadier General Holland Smith to Quantico in the autumn of 1939 he probably regarded the decision as routine. Quantico, the small Marine outpost along the Potomac thirty miles south of Washington, had been a beehive of professional activity earlier in the decade. There the students and faculty of Marine Corps Schools had developed a revolutionary new doctrine for offensive amphibious warfare. But the follow-up work of transforming ideas into reality had languished due to the paucity of resources and lack of interest from the other services. Holland Smith, like Holcomb, a combat veteran of the fighting in France in 1918, had a reputation for strategic vision and hard-nosed training.

Holcomb could not have made a more fortuitous choice. Smith took command of the small 1st Marine Brigade, then barely more than a single regiment. Within a year he took his brigade to Gitmo for extended field and amphibious training. When the "limited national emergency" enabled the Corps to expand sufficiently to create the first division-sized organizations in its history, Smith assumed command of the new 1st Marine Division. Later he took command of the amphibious forces, Atlantic Fleet, and provided corps-sized amphibious training to tens of thousands of Marines, soldiers, and sailors. Many would go on to execute the nation's first amphibious landings in North Africa, the Solomons, and the Aleutians. In addition, Smith would lay the groundwork for the eventual creation of Marine Raider and force reconnaissance battalions. None of this came easily.

The revolutionary essence of the new doctrine developed in Quantico and encapsulated in the unimposing *Tentative Manual for Landing Operations* in 1935 was the assertion that modern weaponry had not relegated amphibious warfare to the dustbin of history, as many sages alleged. Taking the contrary view, the Quantico Marines argued that with certain specified preparations and conditions it was still entirely feasible to launch an amphibious assault against a fortified enemy coastline. Not many senior officers in any service fully accepted this theory. Most watched Holland Smith's initial training experiments with a jaundiced eye.

Smith, for his part, became frustrated that the fleet lacked the amphibious resources to allow him to convince the skeptics. This scarcity of landing ships and craft, assault vehicles, naval gunfire assets, and training areas persisted for years, further delaying the true validation of the new doctrine (it was then that *Time* magazine began calling Smith "Howlin' Mad"). Within this protracted drought the concept of Marine Raiders emerged as one of several alternate roles of the Corps.

A world of difference exists between an amphibious assault and a raid. The former is an attack launched from the sea by naval and landing forces, embarked in specialized ships and craft, against a hostile shore.

To succeed, an amphibious task force requires at least temporary naval supremacy against enemy surface and submarine forces, preponderant air superiority, a substantial superiority over enemy forces ashore, sufficient preparatory naval gunfire and close air support against beach defenses, and adequate means of transporting assault forces ashore for rapid buildup of combat power to full-striking capability. The absence of these preconditions—and this was categorically the case in the first two years of the Pacific War—is very often a prescription for disaster.

Operational alternatives in such circumstances include the use of the fleet's mobility to conduct surprise landings against relatively undefended beaches (examples: Guadalcanal, New Guinea, Rendova), or to use deception and audacity to launch short-term amphibious raids against enemy facilities to distract the enemy and divert his resources (Makin, Tasimboko, Choiseul).

The *Tentative Manual,* with its focus on major, full-scale amphibious operations, paid little attention to seaborne raids. The first chapter, under Objectives of Landing Operations, contained this short paragraph:

> Landing raids are generally made for the purpose of destroying enemy facilities and establishments, such as batteries, bridges, docks, supplies, aircraft, etc. Such operations depend largely for success upon rapidity of movement and surprise, and normally involve relatively small forces, a limited penetration inland, and a quick withdrawal.[10]

Holland Smith's first concern was amphibious readiness. He and Admiral Ernest J. King, commanding the Atlantic Fleet (soon to become the commander in chief of the U.S. Fleet), may have been the only senior officers in the nation who truly foresaw the enormous amphibious campaigns to come in both theaters of war. The two commanders were made from the same mold—King was rumored to shave with a blow torch; Smith's blasphemous temper outbursts were legendary. Such leadership traits would be essential to shattering the inertia surrounding amphibious training.

Here is where Holcomb's selection of Smith began to bear real fruit. Smith, nearly sixty years old when war erupted, spent endless hours stalking up and down one cluttered landing beach after another. Everything that could go wrong in those early "FLEXs" (Fleet Landing Exercises) did so, maddeningly. Boats landed on the wrong beach or capsized in the surf. Experimental tank lighters foundered and sank. Senior generals and admirals squabbled incessantly. Infantry platoon sergeants and boat coxswains came to blows. Shipboard gunners missed their target islands. Strike aircraft showed up too early, or not at all. Communications failed famously. As one early observer succinctly described a fouled up landing exercise: "Chaos reigned."[11]

Throughout the chaos Holland Smith thundered and swore. Smith was particularly critical of certain Marine commanders, field grade officers, who took little interest, never got wet in the surf zone with their troops, and remained in their well-appointed command posts. Smith had seen enough of war to know these aristocratic dinosaurs would be of little use in the coming amphibious campaigns. He began casting his eye about for younger, hungrier, field commanders.

Smith was as much a realist as he was a visionary. When the Navy Department promised that all the amphibious ships and landing craft he would ever need were "in the pipeline," he knew better. Neither the Marine Corps nor the nation could afford to wait for that illusory delivery date. The fleet would have to develop interim measures of stinging the enemy from the sea.

Other far-thinking Marines, struck by both the likelihood of amphibious warfare as a major role for the Corps in the coming war and the critical shortage of "amphibious wherewithal," began to suggest the use of raids. Captain Alpha L. Bowser (who in the Korean War would serve admirably as the 1st Marine Division's operations officer for Inchon, Seoul, and the Chosin Reservoir) published a 1941 essay in the *Marine Corps Gazette* recommending the use of lightly-equipped assault battalions, armed with short-range automatic weapons to seize and clear defended beachheads in advance of the main landing to follow.[12]

Smith may have differed with Bowser in the details, but he certainly shared the vision of special, highly mobile troops for use as an amphibious spearhead. For this he would need three ingredients: a designated unit for test and evaluation, a hard-charging commander, and—to attain amphibious mobility—a squadron of fast transports earmarked for this unique line of work.

## The Able-Peter-Dogs

If ever there were a marriage made in heaven it was the union between the 1st Marine Raider Battalion (including its predecessors 1/5 and 1st Separate Battalion) and the first six converted high-speed transports, known as APDs ("Able Peter Dogs" in the phonetic alphabet of the time). Rarely has a single Marine outfit been so closely identified with the same squadron of ships for such an extended period. For more than two years the same APDs provided a seagoing home for Edson's Raiders. The small ships first provided experimental amphibious raid training along the Atlantic coast and in the Caribbean, then launched the Raiders in their initial combat action on Tulagi, transferred them to Guadalcanal, delivered them to their night landing at Rice Anchorage, New Georgia, and then returned two months later to extract the emaciated survivors back to "civilization."

The Marines came to love the APDs—ship, captain, and crew. General Merrill Twining described them as "those heroic little ships."[13]

The APDs were originally destroyers built to fight the German U-boat threat to Allied convoys during World War I. Displacing 1,200 tons and originally capable of thirty-five knots, the "flush decks" or "four-stackers" were standardized for mass production during the crisis of 1917–18. One shipyard reportedly completed a vessel only seventeen days after laying her keel. The expedient new ships saw limited convoy escort duty in the last months of the war, then went into mothballs. The realities of World War II led to their activation. President Roosevelt tendered fifty of the four-stackers to Great Britain in 1940. Others became high-speed minesweepers or seaplane tenders. Thirty-two received a conversion to high-speed transports, very likely a result of General Meade's 1937 blunt suggestions.

As far as the economy-minded Navy Department was concerned, converting the four-stackers into high-speed transports merely involved the removal of two boilers and two stacks to provide a troop stowage space between decks, plus the installation of four davits to handle, first, the unpopular 30-foot landing boats, then—at Holland Smith's irate insistence—the new 36-foot boats built by Andrew Higgins. Loss of two boilers reduced the APDs speed to 25 knots, but that would suffice for the Marines. The converted ships lost their torpedo tubes but retained a residual armament of three 3-inch guns and two 40mm antiaircraft guns, skimpy but adequate for close-in work.

Under the most spartan of conditions the converted APDs could accommodate 135 officers and men of the landing force, barely half a standard rifle company. There would only be space left over for a minimum of crew-served weapons and equipment—certainly no room for light tanks, half-tracks, large trucks with towed artillery, or very much ammo. As such, the APDs were generally useless for conventional Marine infantry outfits—but ideal for the Raiders.[14]

This early and lasting marriage with the APDs shaped every fiber of the 1st Marine Raider Battalion. Their rifle companies eventually numbered five officers and 130 Marines, no more, no less, the precise number of troop "berthing spaces" on board each ship. Moreover, the battalion would intentionally go to war armed only with their small arms and a few light machine guns and mortars. They would fight their amphibious battles solely with the weapons and equipment they could carry aboard these small ships in their packs or slung from their shoulders. These limitations would in turn determine the way Edson's Raiders trained and fought—the tactics they used, the special leadership they developed.

The first converted APD appeared in the 1938 FLEX. Able Company of 1/5 ran some of the initial ship-to-shore experiments. In 1941, Holland Smith assigned three companies of the 7th Marines to conduct experimental rubber boat landings from three fresh conversions, the ships *Colhoun, Gregory,* and *Little* (APDs 2, 3, and 4). To this point only *Little* had a modest claim to fame: after World War I, she had escorted President Woodrow Wilson to Europe for the Paris Peace Talks. These same three ships would share a common and tragic fate while working with Edson's Raiders in the Solomons in the summer of 1942. All three would be lost to Japanese air and surface attacks within a week's span. Indeed, one in every three APDs would be lost in the Pacific War, eight to Japanese aircraft, two in surface action, one in a collision off Peleliu.

Holland Smith, in another routine high-level decision with significant low-level consequences, reassigned the responsibility for training with the APDs from the 7th Marines back to the 1st Battalion, 5th Marines after the 1941 fleet exercise.

Although the APDs now featured four davit-mounted landing craft, the Marines considered their engines too noisy for stealthy raiding missions and began experimenting with inflatable rubber boats. By 1941 the Leathernecks had adopted the LCPR (Landing Craft Personnel, Rubber, although no one but staff pogues used either the name or the acronym). According to a wartime report, "the Marines developed the LCPR from the navy's old inflatable life raft, and rubber boat companies landing silently by night were a...forerunner of the raider and commando tactics of the war." The Marines' bare-bones research and development capabilities produced few major breakthroughs for the Pacific War, but they included these rubber boats, the tracked landing vehicles or LVTs (now AAVs), the army's old 75mm pack howitzer, and the Johnson light machine gun. Each paid dividends.[15]

The 1st Battalion, 5th Marines' amphibious training with their APDs soon followed a distinct pattern. Troops would inflate the boats, lower them over the gunwale with rope lines, secure them alongside with a sea painter, then dispatch the troops down the rope cargo net into the waiting boat. This last evolution, usually executed at night, was invariably a hair-raising experience. Although the APD's freeboard measured less than nine feet, a running sea could create havoc with the debarkation. At one point the rubber boat would be almost level with the main deck, then, abruptly, far below. Said Joseph L. Murphy: "It was tricky to get aboard."[16]

Sometimes it proved safer to position a sturdier Higgins boat alongside the APD with a rubber boat rigged to the outboard side. Recalled Frank Guidone of those early tests: "Sometimes we would debark into Higgins boats, pull away from the APD, then scramble into the rubber boats. The Higgins boat would then tow three or four rubber boats in line and, as we approached the beach, cut us loose."[17]

Ordinarily, ten Raiders would embark in each rubber boat. Experiments proved that the outboard motors available in the early 1940s would not work reliably in salt water. Propulsion then devolved into paddle power, or the use of Higgins boats to tow the rubber boats to a site seaward of the surf zone, thence paddle power through the surf to the beach. Typically, eight Raiders would paddle, four to each side; the ninth served as helmsman in the stern. Contemporary photographs usually portrayed the tenth man determinedly cradling a light machine gun or Browning Automatic Rifle (BAR) in the bow, but this was mainly for public consumption. In practice, the tenth man had the responsibility of tending the tow line and protecting the team's weapons, stowed along the centerline.

The Navy Department, understandably obsessed with a crash program of building large combatants for a two-ocean war, gave short shrift to amphibious requirements. While the APD program provided a welcome infusion of small transports, the conversion program stopped decidedly short of providing even the most fundamental facilities for troop comfort and sanitation. Removing the two boilers created a small cargo hold, nothing more. The first APDs contained no bunks, heads, showers, vent fans, galleys, or fresh-water evaporators to support 130 troops embarked for weeks at a time. These were intolerable conditions even for tough-as-nails Raiders.

Joe Murphy recalled trying to sleep on the crowded main deck as his APD headed down the Potomac River to the sea. "The navy failed to warn us sleeping Marines when we entered the ocean swells. When the bow first went below the waves we were suddenly awash and lost part of our equipment over the side." Things got worse. "Trying to keep clean and find a toilet facility was a lesson in frustration. Sea sickness added to our problems."[18]

Frank Guidone recalled how the troops struggled to find a place to sleep over a period of several weeks in the rough Atlantic. "We slept on thin mattresses that were rolled up in a canvas protector and stored during the day. Sleeping on deck was cooler but you always ran the risk of getting soaked by rain or spray."[19]

The troops vented their frustration with these conditions. When the APDs pulled into Charleston, Holland Smith sent Colonel Graves B. Erskine to investigate. Erskine (who would later command the 3d Marine Division at Iwo Jima) found troop living conditions appalling. The navy simply had not envisioned Marines embarking aboard these small ships for extended periods. Erskine's report created waves. In time bunks appeared, then a few wash basins, a tiny troop galley, and other amenities. Conditions were still rough ("bunks so close together there was barely enough room to turn over," said Irvin H. Reynolds[20]), but the "can-do" spirit of the APD crews made up for most of the shortcomings. The bonding began here. Surviving Raiders attending the unit's fifty-first annual reunion still became tearful in recalling the loss of so many of those faithful ships and their good-hearted crewmen. They had been shipmates in the age-old bond of the sea.

In late August 1941 the 1st Marine Division moved from Quantico to New River in Onslow County, North Carolina, to build a training camp. The movement order fatefully exempted the 1st Battalion, 5th Marines. Instead, 1/5 would "remain at Quantico and continue training as an APD Battalion." By then Holland Smith had taken steps to place command of 1/5 in new and capable hands.[21]

### "Red Mike"

Lieutenant Colonel Merritt Austin Edson was neither a protégé nor a personal friend of Major General Holland Smith in the late spring of 1941, but Smith knew enough of Edson's professional reputation to ask for his assignment to command 1/5 in Quantico. Smith certainly knew of Edson's widely heralded achievements as a long-range patrol leader in the Nicaraguan jungles, as captain of the national champion Marine Corps rifle and pistol teams, and as analytical author of the Corps' *Small Wars Manual*. According to Jon T. Hoffman, Edson's definitive biographer, Smith saw Edson as "a noted tactical thinker...one of the top

**Merritt A. ("Red Mike") Edson in the field as a brigadier general, 1946.**

weapons experts in the Corps...and a proven leader who could get the most out of men when the going was rough."[22]

Up to this point—before his crowning glory at Lunga Ridge—the defining moment in Edson's life was his series of three long patrols in pursuit of Augusto Sandino's guerrillas along the Coco River in Nicaragua during 1928-30. Captain Edson, then commanding officer of the Marine detachment on board the cruiser *Denver,* flourished in the previously impenetrable jungle, successfully driving the Sandanista forces out of their sanctuaries and prevailing in dozens of sharp skirmishes. Marines, then and now, have long considered this performance to be among the most astounding in a Corps known for its audacity.

For these sustained forays Edson received a Navy Cross, an enviable field reputation, and the lasting nickname "Red Mike," based on the color of his jungle-bred beard. More importantly, he learned invaluable lessons about jungle warfare, small-unit leadership, terrain recognition, advance planning, and rigorous physical training. Each would prove extremely useful in the Solomons in 1942. And while no man is without fear in close combat, Edson learned to manage his fear by meticulous preparation for every expedition. Few combat leaders ever spent more preliminary time on such mundane topics as communications, logistics, supporting arms, and emergency reaction options.[23]

Yet the Coco River had occurred nearly a dozen years earlier. Edson arrived at Quantico on Saturday, 7 June 1941, somewhat the worse for wear following a frustrating tour at Headquarters Marine Corps. He was forty-four years old, stale, overweight, and out of shape. Leaving pretentious Washington to take command of field Marines gave Edson new life.

His new troops did not know what to make of Edson at first. Most of his officers and NCOs knew of his reputation and viewed his arrival with a mixture of curiosity and unease. Edson conveyed a misleading first impression. Unlike some of the tall, raw-boned, athletic officers he was soon to inherit (Ken Bailey, Sam Griffith, Lew Walt, and Joe Chambers come to mind), Edson was undersized, stoop-shouldered, and soft-spoken. A pair of pale blue eyes that could stab holes through a bulkhead represented his only remarkable feature. Veteran combat correspondent Richard Tregaskis assessed "Red Mike" Edson in this fashion:

> He usually spoke in a hoarse whisper that had you leaning forward to hear him. But though he never raised his voice, his men trembled when he was displeased. He could wither a man with his China-blue, gimlet eyes....I thought of Edson's eyes as being as purposeful as a killer's and as unemotional as a shark's....But, although he did not look the part, he was the bravest, the most effective killing machine I met in fifteen years as a war correspondent.[24]

An apt one-word adjective for Merritt Edson is "cool." If his inter-personal relationships lacked warmth, he more than compensated for this deficiency by his invariable coolness under fire. Observed Captain Henry "Hank" Adams, the former FBI agent selected by Edson to serve as battalion intelligence officer, "He was absolutely fearless. I've seen a lot of bank-robbers and ex-cons, but I've never seen a guy as cool as that fellow. I don't believe he was ever scared."[25]

Edson's first order of business in June 1941 involved a protracted deployment with the APDs. Although no stranger to sea duty, Edson was a newcomer to the emerging practice of launching raid missions in rubber boats from destroyer transports. He maintained a low profile, observed carefully, and took notes. The fact that Holland Smith had been promoted to major general and reassigned to command the new headquarters that would become known as Amphibious Force, Atlantic Fleet (AFAF) was a boon to Edson. Smith soon established AFAF headquarters at Quantico in a building across Barnett Avenue from 1/5's barracks. Thus, while Edson in mid-1941 still had to honor a chain of command through his regimental and division commanders down in New River, he enjoyed direct access to the force commander. Smith obviously had greater things on his mind than just the "rubber-boat/APD battalion," but he now knew he had at hand a kindred spirit already working hard to evaluate the potential and the problems of such an organization.

Edson's first APD deployment lasted eight weeks and produced unremarkable results. The landings were ragged, the troops often miserable in rough seas and stormy weather; many could not complete a nominal twelve-mile hike once ashore. Edson saw how much work needed to be done but kept his patience. He met often with his officers, listened to their views, and mixed it up with his troops. He greeted Gunnery Sergeant Yelanich fondly. Yelanich had been his runner on the first Coco River patrol and in fact had snapped off a quick shot that saved Edson's life when his own pistol misfired in a point-blank exchange with a guerrilla. Edson learned a lot about his new battalion from the handful of unflappable old-timers in the NCO ranks like Tony Yelanich, Sergeant Major Edwin C. ("Parson") Clarke, tall and courtly, and the loquacious First Sergeant Pearly A. Stone.

Edson returned to Quantico engrossed in thought about the role and configuration of his "APD Battalion." He reflected on what he knew, what he had just seen in the confused and often chaotic landing exercises, what his officers and senior NCOs had told him, and what Holland Smith desired. He drafted a detailed twenty-seven-page report that would provide the basis for the raider battalion to come.

Edson's comments and recommendations ranged from roles and missions to rifles and boat compasses. The nub of his analysis, however, concerned the organization and equipment of the 1st Battalion, 5th Marines. If the Marine Corps desired 1/5 simply to maintain proficiency with APD deployments as an adjunct mission, then the standard configuration for an infantry battalion would suffice. The unit would simply reconfigure to embark the small ships whenever directed, then revert to the authorized standard afterwards. But how, Edson asked, would the battalion fight in conventional combat without the balance of its weapons, vehicles, and equipment? It would be a bastard outfit, a tactical and logistical drain on the parent regiment once the initial raid missions ended. The regiment would always be at a disadvantage.

On the other hand, Edson argued, if the Corps truly wanted to commit a battalion to permanent duty as an APD-based, rubber-boat raiding outfit—he used the term "Mobile Landing Group"—then it should be an independent, specialized, light battalion, responsive to division or corps headquarters, and reconfigured to fit precisely within the narrow lift and delivery capabilities of the "Able Peter Dogs." This meant smaller rifle companies, severely limited crew-served weapons, less overall firepower, and zero tactical mobility once ashore. The issue required a major, top-level decision. The Mobile Landing Group would be excellent for surprise, hit-and-run raids, using the mobility and modest firepower of the APDs. But the special battalion would be in great jeopardy if it had to launch a conventional attack on its own against a well-fortified and fully-alerted enemy—exactly the fate of the Raiders at Bairoko two years later.[26]

Edson also called for more night amphibious training. "Any organization that can make a satisfactory night landing can land effectively under extremely adverse conditions during daylight hours," he asserted. Not even Holland Smith fully accepted this wisdom, but Edson would always emphasize night operations in his training programs. The Raiders would pay him back ten months after he left them, executing a critical and complex night landing at Rice Anchorage in the Kula Gulf.[27]

Edson had served at higher headquarters long enough to realize that definitive responses to his recommendations would be a long time coming. Meanwhile, he had plenty to do in whipping his battalion into shape for whatever missions would finally be assigned. Field training was one of Red Mike's characteristic strong points. His troops were in for a heavy emphasis on field work, physical fitness, map reading and terrain appreciation, combat marksmanship, and night operations. As a reflection of the importance Edson placed on first-rate field training, he reassigned his most experienced company commander, Captain Robert Brown, as the battalion plans and training officer. Brown would prove invaluable in this capacity, but the training would forever bear the imprint of the commander. As much as the troops may have cursed Red Mike for making them sweat during extended field exercises, they would grudgingly admit that "The Old Man" shared every moment of their discomfort.

Doctor Bob Skinner had been a member of 1/5 for several months before Edson arrived. "Things got tougher when Edson took over," he recalled, adding succinctly, "Lots of hiking."[28]

Everyone would later recall with a bit of marvel how Edson, during a halt in a long march, would walk down the length of the battalion column, checking each man. Then, as the troops saddled up their packs and lurched forward again, he would nonchalantly *jog* past them all to reclaim his position in the front. They knew him to be easily twice their age.[29]

Sergeant Major John H. Carson recalled an incident during one of the battalion's earliest conditioning hikes that reflected the spirit of the future Raiders. "We were on a forced march out of Quantico. Edson came back down the column and spotted my squad leader, the unforgettable Joe Connolly. 'How's it going, Joe?' Connolly growled, 'the sonofabitch who thought up this hike ought to be strung up by the balls!' I was in shock. But Edson only laughed."[30]

Sometimes it was tough for the young Marines to appreciate the professional benefits of conditioning hikes. On one occasion Red Mike led the battalion on an extended overnight march to Manassas battlefield and back. Nearing Quantico on the return leg, Edson directed his runner, the popular Corporal Walter Burak from Greensburg, Pennsylvania, to assign road guards with semaphore flags to protect the battalion in its crossing of U.S. Highway One. Burak picked fellow communicators Duke Vierling and Fred Serral. The two Marines dutifully flagged down traffic while the battalion hustled across on the run. With the job done, and the column already a half-mile ahead, Vierling turned to Serral and suggested, "Let's get a beer!" They had just enough money for two cold beers apiece plus a taxi back to the base, hunkering down in the back seat to avoid being spotted by any of their peers or—God forbid—Red Mike Edson.[31]

Purposeful field training appealed to some of the young men, particularly Floridian Thomas Pollard who could hardly wait to leave high school and enlist. This upset his mother, who tearfully sent him on his way to recruit training at Parris Island with the rejoinder, "Watch your table manners and be nice to the instructors!" Pollard would soon become a consummate field Marine and would flourish under Edson's rigorous training.[32]

Red Mike Edson had the combat credentials to convince his troops that there might be a method to his training madness. At first, Boston reservist Joe Murphy and his squadmates thought Edson was sadistic. "We naturally assumed the CO was crazy, trying so hard to kill us....Many times we did double-time from the main gate on Highway One to Barracks A just to show the rest of the base how tough we were. But we ourselves were not impressed; our utilities were soaked with sweat." Yet Murphy soon took note of a grudging appreciation: "Edson's training began to separate the men from the boys. Each day became tougher than the last and each march longer than the last, usually with added equipment. If a man had a weakness it soon surfaced. The men began to feel the importance of the whole team."[33]

Rough as it was, life at Quantico retained a special flavor. For those whose blistered feet would still allow some after-hours adventures, liberty in Washington or even nearby Quantico Town was incomparably superior to that available at the division's isolated "Tent City" in the piney woods of coastal North Carolina. Washington, D.C., with its growing legions of unmarried female secretaries, lay within easy reach via the Richmond, Fredericksburg, and Potomac Railroad. The men favored the Mayfair Hotel or Thompson's Restaurant as advance outposts, often partying all night with the stamina of youth, then catching the "Reveille Special" to make it back to Quantico.

Then came news of Pearl Harbor, and their world changed abruptly, irrevocably.

## Notes

1. Jeter A. Isely and Philip A. Crowl, *The U.S. Marines and Amphibious War* (Princeton, New Jersey: Princeton University Press, 1951), 27.
2. *Annual Report of the Secretary of the Navy,* FY 1937, 9, 17.
3. CG, 1st Marine Brigade "FLEX Three Report" 28 February 1937, cited in Isely and Crowl, *Amphibious War,* 55. The authors incorrectly list 1936 as the date of the first fleet experimental use of the future APD USS *Manley* as a high-speed transport (page 57). The actual year was 1938.
4. Kenneth J. Clifford, *Progress and Purpose: A Developmental History of the United States Marine Corps* (Washington, D.C.: HQMC, 1973), 50–55.
5. The author is indebted to Thomas J. Mullahey for his earlier collection of these 1937 vignettes from his fellow Raiders.
6. William Sperling to Thomas Mullahey, 5 February 1992.
7. Nazario J. DiSalvia, "A Tribute to Anthony 'Tony' Yelanich," *The Dope Sheet* [newsletter of the Edson's Raiders Association], July 1987, 1–3.
8. Frederick A. Serral to author, 23 November 1998.
9. Gerald V. West to author, 10 March 1999; James Smith to author, 24 January 1999; Leroy B. Edwards to Irvin H. Reynolds, 20 November 1988; "Marine Gunner Angus R. Goss," news release written 26 June 1943 by combat correspondent T.Sgt. Frank J. McDevitt for the Tampa papers (author's possession).
10. *Tentative Manual for Landing Operations, 1935.* (Washington, D.C.: HQMC), 4. Nor did subsequent experience with raids result in more specific doctrinal

guidance. The navy's version, *Landing Operations Doctrine, 1938,* added only a single phrase to the list of raid objectives: "...for harassing defense forces, diverting attention from operations in other localities, and effecting division of enemy forces." The navy manual became the bible for amphibious operations in the Pacific War, yet despite three significant updates, no additional changes were made to this brief section on raids. The navy and Marines (and the army, as well, in its derived 1941 Field Manual 31-5, *Landing Operations on Hostile Shores*) fought World War II without any additional doctrinal authority concerning the use of amphibious raiders.

11. "Chaos reigned," said Brig. Gen. Eli Cole, USMC of the 1924 Fleet Landing Exercise, quoted by Isley and Crowl, *Amphibious Warfare,* 30–31.

12. Capt. Alpha L. Bowser, Jr., USMC, "Lightweight Assault Troops," *Marine Corps Gazette,* March 1941, 19–20.

13. Merrill B. Twining, *No Bended Knee: the Battle for Guadalcanal* (Novato: The Presidio Press, 1996), 93.

14. Details on the APDs derived from Nathan Miller, *The U.S. Navy: A History,* 3d Edition (Annapolis: Naval Institute Press, 1998), 186; Paul H. Silverstone, *U.S. Warships of World War II* (New York: Doubleday, 1968), 103, 112, 276; and *Dictionary of American Naval Fighting Ships*, Volumes II, IV, and VI (Washington, D.C.: Department of the Navy, 1963–76). The spartan APDs reflect the contrasts between the "two wars" the United States fought in the Pacific. By 1944 the navy had constructed scores of new attack transports, or APAs, that would dwarf the APDs. The *Haskell*-class APA could transport up to 1,500 embarked troops—a reinforced battalion landing team with all its combat equipment—and deliver them ashore with its complement of thirty-two Higgins boats and four LCM-3 tank lighters. Still, few amphibs ever matched the fighting spirit of the APD crews in 1942–43.

15. R.T. Vance, HQMC (AO-775), to Col. David M. Shoup, "Development of Special Equipment for Amphibious Warfare," 11 December 1944, Shoup Papers, Hoover Institute Archives.

16. Joseph Murphy to Thomas Mullahey, 29 September 1992, 3.

17. Frank Guidone to Thomas Mullahey, n.d.

18. Murphy to Mullahey, 29 September 1992, 3.

19. Guidone to Mullahey, 1992.

20. Irvin H. Reynolds interview with Jon T. Hoffman, 1993.

21. CG, 1st Marine Division Warning Order 2-41, 27 August 1941, Box 1786, RG 127, National Archives.

22. Jon T. Hoffman, *Once a Legend: "Red Mike" Edson of the Marine Raiders* (Novato: Presidio Press, 1994), 130–31 [Hoffman, *Legend*]; Hoffman to author, 20 April 1999.

23. For a detailed account of the Coco River patrols, see Hoffman, *Legend,* chapters 4 and 5; also see Hoffman, "Edson's First Raiders," *Naval History,* Fall

1991, 20–25; and Joseph H. Alexander, *A Fellowship of Valor* (New York: HarperCollins, 1997), 59–61.

24. Richard Tregaskis, "The Best Soldier I Ever Knew," *Saga* XIX (February 1960), 18.

25. Capt. Henry Adams, quoted in *Ibid.*, 18–19.

26. CO, 1st Battalion, 5th Marines to CG, 1st Marine Division, "Report on New River Exercises, August 1941," 23 August 1941, Amphibious Force Atlantic Fleet files, Box 1, Series 63A-2535, Washington National Records Center (WNRC). See also Hoffman, *Legend,* Chapter 8.

27. Hoffman, *Legend,* 26.

28. Dr. Robert Skinner interview with Jon T. Hoffman, 1993.

29. Among many who recalled Edson's stamina on the march: James F. Thomas, Jr. to Jon T. Hoffman, 25 July 1991, and Edward C. Roche to Jon T. Hoffman, July 1991. Wrote Roche, twenty years old at the time of the forced marches, "I said to myself, if that old man in his late forties could jog to the head of the column, nothing was going to stop me."

30. John A. Carson to Frank Guidone, 26 July 1991.

31. Frank C. Vierling to author, 5 December 1998.

32. Thomas Pollard to John B. Sweeney, 11 March 1996.

33. Joseph L. Murphy to Thomas Mullahey, 29 September 1992; Murphy, "The Birth of the Raiders," unpublished manuscript, n.d.

## 2

# Commandos or Raiders?
# December 1941–March 1942

*At that particular time the British commandos were very much in the
headlines. There was considerable thought that my outfit should be
organized and trained to do just the same things they did....I did not
agree with this thinking....I recommended a battalion so organized and
equipped that it could easily take its place as part of a division in a
major offensive, while still being perfectly capable of carrying out special raiding operations.*

> Major General Merritt A. Edson, USMC
> 22 April 1952[1]

THE UNITED STATES seemed utterly incapable of striking a blow against
its fascist enemies throughout much of the first half-year of the war.
Each dire report seemed to generate more demands for the nation to
establish special commando forces akin to British or Chinese models.

The commando mystique held an "enormous psychological and polit-
ical appeal in the dark days of defeat and retreat," observed historian
John W. Gordon. The Marine Corps, with its light infantry tradition and
uncertain mission for the new war, became a likely candidate to recast
itself into some form of commando force. Gordon discerned a "pro-
found psychological need to 'out-tough' a militaristic foe."[2]

Certain retired Marine generals gnashed their teeth at the seeming
impotence of the nation's military in the face of German and Japanese
aggression. Major General James C. Breckenridge, one of the earlier legends in the Corps, wrote the commandant offering to take command of
a group of condemned felons, whom Breckenridge would train "in the
old-fashioned way," then lead them in a suicidal raiding operation

against the Japanese homeland. Breckenridge died three days later, well before his letter reached the commandant, and by then Holcomb had dealt with the issue by more conventional means.[3]

Holcomb found himself at the epicenter of swirling pressures to commit the Corps to the commando mission throughout several months in the winter of 1941–42. President Roosevelt, prodded by British Prime Minister Winston Churchill, urged his military advisors to establish a commando force along the lines of the United Kingdom. The president also gave serious consideration to a top secret proposal by highly-decorated World War I army veteran Colonel William J. Donovan to form a guerrilla corps independent of the army and navy. This raised the likelihood that the Marine Corps would receive this major mission, along with the further possibility that Donovan would be appointed to the Marines as a brigadier general to command it. Holcomb was not happy with any part of this proposal. As an expedient, however, he agreed to dispatch two company grade officers, Captains Samuel B. Griffith and Wallace M. Greene, Jr., to Great Britain for direct observation of commando training and tactics.[4]

Another distraction surfaced. Captain James Roosevelt, son of the president and protégé of guerrilla zealot Major Evans Carlson, wrote a letter to General Holcomb on the subject of "Development Within the Marine Corps of a Unit for Purposes Similar to the British Commandos and the Chinese Guerrillas." Young Roosevelt suggested such units be deployed against the Japanese "mandate Islands" (the Marshalls, Marianas, and Carolines) as well as northern Japan. Holcomb recognized Carlson's influence on the letter, but also recognized the obvious connection with the president.

Holcomb answered Captain Roosevelt with polite disinterest. The standard infantry battalion, suitably trained—and especially the APD/rubber-boat battalion being developed in the Atlantic Fleet—should suffice, said Holcomb. It was obvious the name "commando" rankled the general. "The term 'Marine' is sufficient to indicate a man ready for any duty at any time," he wrote, "and the injection of a special name, such as 'Commando,' would be undesirable and superfluous."[5]

These were hectic times for Edson and his Marines. On 6 January 1942, Holland Smith requested that Holcomb redesignate 1/5 as the 1st Special Battalion, assigned directly under the amphibious force commander, and create a replacement battalion under the 5th Marines at New River. Holcomb did so promptly (although a number of old-timers in the battalion resented giving up membership in the historic regiment and the loss of their distinctive World War I fourragère award). Holcomb also created a 2d Separate Battalion in California to be commanded by Evans Carlson. This clarified the chain of command that worried Edson but did little to resolve the "Commando Issue."

In fairness, General Holcomb was swamped with more immediate concerns—the critical decisions needed to address manpower, weaponry, facilities, and leadership for a Corps about to triple in size almost overnight. Every week another emergency deployment seemed to arise. Some proved to be false alarms, like the planned preemptive landings in Martinique and the Azores. Others involved actual commitments of Marines to Iceland and Samoa and a dozen smaller outposts.

Worried about frittering away his resources in this fashion, Holcomb believed the last thing he needed was a lot of uninvited "experts" kibitzing with the role of the Corps. As far as Holcomb was concerned, the Marine Corps had one sure and unique thing to offer the nation, a new capability of waging offensive amphibious warfare. His principal means of undertaking such a mission would be his two new divisions, each composed of nine trained infantry battalions supported by artillery, tanks, amphibian tractors, combat engineers, and special weapons (anti-tank, anti-air) components. He also sought to integrate these forces as combined arms teams with his equally new Marine aircraft wings.

Holcomb was willing to invest in a pair of lightly-armed separate battalions for hit-and-run raids or diversions during the prolonged defensive phase, but he insisted they be linked to the amphibious mission, launched from the sea to enhance or facilitate an amphibious operation. Any other missions—especially the creation of a large-scale, elite commando force—that diluted or distracted from this primary role would be decidedly unwelcome.

Holcomb would insist throughout the remaining years of his commandancy that the standard Marine infantry battalion, with sufficient work-up training, could execute any mission associated with British commandos or Chinese guerrillas.

During this period of turmoil, Holcomb remained extremely grateful for the pioneering work already accomplished by Holland Smith and Merritt Edson. Amid all the proposals and pipedreams, Holcomb could point to the actual existence at Quantico of a special Marine battalion, trained and configured for amphibious raiding missions. And, while Holcomb knew in his heart the establishment of elite special-mission units would create resentment within his elite Corps, the alternative of losing the amphibious mission altogether was much worse.

A new urgency entered the debate in late January when Admiral Chester Nimitz, newly assigned to command the Pacific Fleet, submitted an operational request for "commando units" for "speedy and surprise" demolition raids against "lightly defended island bases."[6]

In private correspondence with his top generals, Holcomb urged quick action "to prepare ourselves particularly for one of our most important missions, the execution of amphibious raids." Major General C. F. B. Price, commanding the 2d Marine Division in Camp Elliot, California, proposed the name "commando," suggesting that prospective troops be recruited from lumber jacks, miners, cowhands, or professional athletes. Edson weighed in, via Holland Smith, decrying the current name "Separate Battalion" as nondescript, and suggesting "First Destroyer Battalion." Edson further stated the requirement for an all-volunteer outfit, with each man "physically fit to sustain long marches at above average rates; a qualified swimmer; and not susceptible to sea sickness." Holland Smith offered a more dynamic name, the "1st Shock Battalion."[7]

But it was Holcomb the commandant who selected "Raiders" and, having done so, he broke the logjam of indecision in Washington. Within a week he created two Marine Raider Battalions, the 1st under Merritt Edson, and the 2d, in California, under Evans Carlson. Edson's battalion was activated first. February 16th, 1942, became the birthdate of the 1st Marine Raider Battalion—"Edson's Raiders."

There was little time to celebrate. When Admiral King reinforced Admiral Nimitz's earlier call for "commando-type" units with emphatic guidance to Holcomb to accord "first priority for the units on the West Coast (Pacific Fleet)," the Commandant had no choice but to rob Peter (Edson) to pay Paul (Carlson). He ordered Smith to detach a reinforced company—a wholesale slice, seven officers and 190 men—from Edson's outfit to serve as a cadre for Carlson's battalion. In a surprise move, Holcomb even offered General Clayton B. Vogel, senior Marine officer in the Pacific, the services of Lieutenant Colonel Edson to command and train the new outfit, in lieu of Carlson. Vogel declined the offer.[8]

Rampant personnel turmoil rocked Edson's Raiders immediately. The battalion reported twenty-nine officers and 667 enlisted Marines on the rolls on 1 February. Within the next sixteen days, Edson transferred Able Company, reinforced by a machine-gun platoon and a mortar section, to Carlson's outfit, dispatched one officer and five NCOs to Great Britain for extended training with the Royal Commandos, and reconfigured the battalion from three rifle companies to four. In effect he had to create two new rifle companies out of whole cloth.[9]

A natural rivalry emerged between the 1st and 2d Raider Battalions, but an unfortunate enmity also developed and festered, a resentment that stemmed almost entirely from the mandated transfer of the reinforced rifle company from Edson to Carlson during February 1942.

Most commanders, faced with the task of giving up nearly a third of their command, would be tempted to use the opportunity to cleanse the unit of misfits and malcontents. There is no evidence Edson did so—the muster rolls reflect no flurry of last minute transfers into Able Company. The unit was as well-led and trained as any other in the battalion. Edson hated to give them up, saw them off with a heavy heart. The detached company exulted at the chance to be the cadre for a new raider outfit destined, by hearsay, to lead the first offensive in the Pacific War.

But Evans Carlson cast a cold eye on the easterners, screened them methodically, and rejected half the officers and most of the troops, who were then scattered among the newly forming 9th Marines. Carlson allegedly said bad things about the quality of troops received from Edson.[10]

Word of this unexpected situation sent Edson into a cold fury. His response to Major General Price's warning that "the angel of wrath was abroad," blistered the envelope that carried it. There was nothing he could do, but he never forgave Carlson for what he considered a cheap and unwarranted shot. Nor was Edson's mood improved a month later when twenty-seven former members of Able Company, each rejected by Carlson, sent a petition requesting their return to the unit in Quantico.

In truth, some members of this detachment gained acceptance by Carlson and served him with distinction. Captain John Apergis became a company commander. Lieutenant Richard Washburn would eventually rise in rank and combat experience to command the 2d Raiders. Sergeant Chester Goll (formerly Golaszewski) would become the battalion sergeant major. Corporals Robert V. Allard and Dallas H. Cook would receive posthumous Navy Crosses for conspicuous gallantry on Butaritari Island in Makin Atoll. But for the time being there was hell to pay back in Quantico.[11]

## The 1st Marine Raider Battalion

Fortunately, Edson had no time available to pursue his grudge against Carlson or attempt to retrieve his lost company. The late winter of 1942 was a period of intense organizational turmoil for Marine commanders stationed on the east coast. Many conventional units, still seething over the loss of "volunteers" to such fancy new units as raiders, parachutists, and "air-infantry" (glider troops), suddenly had to sacrifice more of their best junior officers and NCOs to flesh out the 7th Marines, soon to deploy to Samoa with the 3d Marine Brigade. While many 1st Marine Division officers would forever blame Edson for "raiding" their assets, such losses paled in comparison to the toll exacted by the new brigade.

Although Edson's suddenly decimated unit was spared from contributing to the 3d Brigade, the vacuum thus created made it virtually impossible for the Raiders to establish two new rifle companies with trained Marines. Instead, Edson had to settle for "pot luck" like all the other depleted units, accepting new troops directly from recruit training.

All of this posed a major challenge for Edson. He had to rebuild his battalion, remotivate the old-timers who had been rocked by all these changes, initiate another comprehensive training program, and ensure that each new man was properly screened. Time was suddenly precious. Barely a month remained before the Raiders would deploy to the South Pacific.

The turmoil continued. Baker Company, as one February example, gave up two lieutenants, Arthur Haake and William Sperling, plus Gunnery Sergeant Anthony Yelanich and forty-seven other men to provide the nucleus for the new Able Company, then struggled to absorb seventy-nine new privates.[12]

Edson considered it critical that all his new men be volunteers for the Raiders' hazardous mission. He sent two officers to Parris Island to solicit volunteers, which netted such future combat leaders as Jack Tracy and Irving Reynolds, but a fortuitous development allowed the Raiders to recruit closer to home. With Parris Island figuratively bulging at the seams, the two-week rifle-range qualification session had to be farmed out, in part, to Quantico. There most of the line coaches came from the only infantry outfit on the base, the 1st Marine Raider Battalion. This provided the coaches an excellent opportunity to observe likely candidates and proselytize them to volunteer. Edson helped create the mystique, showing up at the 500-yard line one afternoon and, according to an astonished "Jinx" Powers, nailing five straight bulls-eyes from the offhand position.[13]

Marlin F. Groft was one recruit attending rifle qualification at Quantico who became intrigued with the Raider legend displayed by his coaches. He volunteered. Shortly he found himself being interviewed by the head Raider himself, Lieutentant Colonel Edson. Groft said Edson admired his German-Irish roots but had to reject him because he could not swim. Days later he was abruptly assigned to the Raiders, non-swimmer or not. When Herbert L. Coffin volunteered and was asked by Lieutenant John W. Antonelli whether he could swim, he equivocated and said yes, an outright fib. He was accepted.[14]

Bob Addison, whose nineteenth birthday had coincided with the Japanese attack on Pearl Harbor, went to see the Marine recruiter in his hometown of Alliance, Ohio, within a week. He and Serephine "Buddy" Smith, also nineteen, from Canton, went through recruit training at Parris Island together. They were among the boots farmed out to Quantico for the rifle qualification course. Both were encouraged to volunteer for the Raiders by their line coach. Captain Bailey interviewed Addison, telling him the outfit would be "the cream of the Marine Corps," and also warning him that their likely mission would be "first in, last out." Addison and Smith were hooked. Following a brief graduation ceremony at the Quantico rifle range (where Lejeune Hall now stands), Addison and Smith simply marched west to "A" Barracks. "I was assigned to PFC Erland Coombs' 81mm mortar squad," said Addison, "and the rest is history."[15]

Ken Peters of New York City had to have a hernia operation in order to qualify for the Marines. He and Harold Smith, the Millburn, New Jersey, police officer, decided to volunteer together for the 1st Raiders. Part of their screening process required them to "parade in our birthday suits" before the scrutiny of Lieutenant Colonel Edson and Doctor Ed McLarney, the battalion's senior surgeon. Edson noticed Peters' hernia scar: "What the hell is that?" Peters told him he had voluntarily undergone surgery to join the Marines. Said Edson, grinning, "You are now a Marine Raider."[16]

Not all recruits on the range detail volunteered, despite the appeal of Raider mystique. New Yorker Carl Fox declined the solicitation, soon regretted it, then made amends by volunteering for the battalion in 1943 before the New Georgia campaign. Likewise, James E. Vittitoe considered the opportunity and decided to pass. He was surprised when the battalion commander called him in to inquire why. Vittitoe gave Edson his reasons. Edson then flashed his crooked grin and asked him to reconsider. Vittitoe, flattered, agreed to volunteer. The ranks slowly began to refill, and there seemed no degradation in quality.[17]

Aware of sagging morale among his veterans (the "Plank-owners") Edson took the screening process a step farther. He asked each of his original members to *volunteer* for hazardous duty with the new Raider outfit, or be transferred back to the 5th Marines with no questions asked. Some left; most stayed, and of these Edson was convinced their motivation would sustain them during the trying times ahead.

"Tools of the Trade" by Raider Doug Greenbowe, reflecting the Raiders' Springfield Rifle, APD fast transport, F-4F Wildcat fighter support, and the prototype, rampless Higgins boats of the Tulagi-Guadalcanal campaigns.

Satisfied that the enlisted replacement recruiting and screening program was well underway, Edson turned quickly to the subject of officers. The new battalion began its existence with but twenty-one on hand of the thirty-five it rated. The newly-commissioned lieutenants displayed encouraging potential, but Red Mike was very concerned with the shortfall of senior officers. With no certainty or precedence as to how or where his battalion would be employed in combat, Edson had to prepare for the contingency that some missions would involve individual companies operating independently or apportioned as task forces. Such missions would demand, in Edson's view, a strong battalion executive officer and proven company commanders.

Like many other regular officers of his generation, Edson held a prejudice against reserve officers. In two revealing letters to Holland Smith written immediately after the creation of the 1st Marine Raider Battalion, Edson asked for regular officers to replace his reservists in critical billets. He specifically asked that his current executive officer, a reserve lieutenant colonel, be replaced with "a younger, more active officer, well grounded in infantry tactics"—namely Major Joseph H. Berry, then serving at The Basic School. The second letter discussed his need for captains. Edson praised his three regulars, his operations and training officer Bob Brown, charismatic Kenneth Bailey, commanding Charlie Company, and Henry Cain, the capable but frail commander of newly formed Dog Company. Red Mike assessed his reserve captains, including the versatile Ira J. Irwin, as lacking force, vigor, and tactical background (Captain Irwin would prove himself, however, and eventually commanded the battalion for four months). Regular officers, Edson argued, had the advantage of previous sea duty, an invaluable asset in dealing with APD captains on independent assignments.[18]

Edson suggested likely candidates, described as "volunteers," indicating some advance solicitation. He would shortly ask for such highly regarded captains as Victor ("Brute") Krulak (a forlorn hope, "Brute" was Smith's aide-de-camp), Homer Litzenberg, and Herman Nickerson. He also asked for an increase in the number of surgeons assigned the battalion from two to five to support independent company-level missions.[19]

Edson's luck had faded. Only one of his "volunteer" captains appeared, a hulking former college athlete named Lewis B. Walt. But Headquarters Marine Corps disapproved his request for additional surgeons and said Litzenberg and Krulak were unavailable. The personnel bureaucrats fumbled the request for Herman Nickerson, assigning instead Captain Lloyd Nickerson, a reservist with little experience and somewhat long in the tooth. Then tragedy struck. During a forced march on an overly warm first day of spring, Captain Henry Cain, thirty-three, toppled and died of thrombosis of his coronary artery, leaving a wife and six-week-old son grieving in their quarters at Quantico.[20]

Edson kept looking, asking, dealing. Now his preference for regular officers became irrelevant. Captain Jake Irwin would remain and take over Cain's company. Edson then pulled a coup in soliciting the assignment of the dynamic adjutant of the 1st Marine Division, Captain Justice M. ("Jumping Joe") Chambers—much to the fury of the commanding general. Edson also asked for the assignment of two gifted second lieutenants, Thomas F. Mullahey and Clay A. Boyd. Edson had known Mullahey for years, made a special effort to take him out to lunch when Mullahey was still a senior at Georgetown University, and discerned the young man's native leadership abilities. Boyd, twenty-eight, was a 1934 graduate of New Mexico Military Institute, where he had been a conference middleweight boxing champion. He had then served a four-year tour as an enlisted Marine that included plenty of sea duty. Both officers would distinguish themselves in combat; both would become superb company commanders during the New Georgia campaign the following year.[21]

The hectic shake-up produced in time a solid group of company commanders, anchored around the experienced Ken Bailey, Charlie Company. Bailey, thirty-one, a native of Pawnee, Oklahoma, initially served three years with the 130th Infantry, Illinois National Guard, then accepted a Marine Corps commission in 1935. He was a true "Plank-Owner," having already served many years in the 5th Marines, plus a tour on board the battleship *Pennsylvania*. Of Bailey, John Sweeney would later recall: "He was the Hollywood version of a Marine officer: tall, six-foot-three or so, handsome, with...broad shoulders and lean of hip. His men loved him, and every junior officer in the outfit wanted to be just like Captain Bailey."[22]

Lew Walt, twenty-nine, arrived on 19 March to command the newly reincarnated Able Company. He was a 1936 honors graduate of Colorado State, where he was a chemistry major, president of the student body, and captain of his football and wrestling teams. Walt had enlisted in the Colorado National Guard at seventeen, but resigned his army commission upon graduation to become a second lieutenant of Marines. Following service in Shanghai and Guam, he was a company commander at Officers' Candidate Class in Quantico when Edson's solicitation found him. Walt's birthdate, the 16th of February, coincided with the

"birth" date of the 1st Marine Raider Battalion, a coincidental mani-
festation of what would become a life-long affinity between the Raiders
and the exuberant Kansan with the blazing blue eyes.[23]

Captain Jumping Joe Chambers' tour as a Raider was destined to be
short but memorable. He joined the battalion on 23 March. Edson
assigned him first to command Easy Company, the weapons outfit, but
would give him Jake Irwin's rifle company just before the Tulagi assault.
Chambers' wild and woolly nature may have had its origins in his ances-
try: he was related on his mother's side to Valentine Hatfield, notorious
patriarch of the Hatfield clan in their long feud with the McCoys. Chambers, thirty-four, began his military service as an enlisted man, first in
the Navy Reserve, then the Marine Reserve in the early 1930s. By the
time of Pearl Harbor he had a law degree, a captain's commission, and
a reputation for headstrong initiative.[24]

The exceptional leadership resident in these three captains—Bailey,
Walt, and Chambers—is evident in their World War II record. The three
officers would account for two Medals of Honor, two Navy Crosses, three
Silver Stars, and seven Purple Hearts.

Captains Lloyd Nickerson and Jake Irwin would serve competently,
if fairly briefly, in command of Baker and Dog Companies, respectively.
Nickerson arrived late, barely in time to catch the train west, and would
have to earn his spurs that spring and summer in the South Pacific. Irwin
temporarily fell out of favor with Edson when he admitted in a staff
meeting he could not swim but expressed no concern with his deficiency
because "anyone who fell out of a rubber boat carrying all the gear
assigned to the Raiders would drown anyway." Jake Irwin's laid-back atti-
tude would prevent him from holding a rifle company command for
long, but he proved himself a competent staff officer in the Solomons
and a solid battalion commander.

One missing link in the Raiders' top leadership remained. Edson still
needed a hard-charging executive officer. When his repeated efforts
failed to extract Nicaragua veteran and Fort Benning Infantry School
graduate Major Joe Berry from The Basic School staff, Edson quickly went
after another candidate with impeccable qualifications, newly-promoted
Major Samuel B. Griffith. His choice was serendipitous. The battalion
would benefit more from this one decision than any other Edson would
ever make.

Sam Griffith, thirty-five, joined the Raiders the second week in March
following his five-month assignment to England and Scotland to observe
Royal Commando training and techniques. This experience was a nat-

ural boon, but the real benefit to the battalion came from Griffith's ability to provide both a backstop and a counter-foil to the enigmatic Edson. The two represented a perfect "odd-couple" match in both appearance and demeanor. As one young corporal wrote his parents, "Where Edson is able and courageous, he looks small and sort of shriveled up; Griffith is big, rugged, a real fighter."[25]

Griffith, a native of Lewistown, Pennsylvania, graduated from the U.S. Naval Academy in 1929. Captain Edson had been his tactics instructor at The Basic School. He served in the second Nicaraguan campaign, as well as in Cuba and China. He would survive the war, retire as a brigadier general, then pursue a doctoral degree in Chinese military history at Oxford (in his fifties, he was the oldest history student in the school). A prolific writer, his after-action reports became collectors' items, and his published accounts of Guadalcanal and Enogai remain among the best eye-witness accounts of those campaigns.[26]

John "Tiger" Erskine provided a nice thumbnail portrayal of Griffith: "He could communicate at all levels from buck private to general. He was physically fit for the field and he knew his craft. He was a professional in every sense of the word." Added New Georgia veteran Frank Kemp, "We were most fortunate in the 1st Marine Raider Battalion to have had two of the Marine Corps' finest combat officers, General Edson and Samuel B. Griffith as our leaders." Edson would command the battalion for seven months; Griffith would take command on two occasions, first for six days, then—following his recuperation from a sniper's round in the shoulder—for eight months. The Raiders were twice-blessed.[27]

## Making Up for Lost Time

Red Mike Edson seemed to spend each night pondering the special needs his Raiders might face in their coming deployment. Recalling Admiral Nimitz's request for "speedy and surprise" demolition raids against "lightly defended island bases," he began making plans to establish a special demolitions platoon. He also realized he needed someone with advanced technological training to help him identify and either dismantle or capture Japanese electronic equipment, such as the hush-hush radar systems on which he had been briefed. His request for "a young, fit, unmarried Marine knowledgeable of such systems" resulted in the reassignment of Sergeant James "Horse Collar" Smith from the highly classified Bellevue Center at the Naval Research Laboratory in Washington. Smith had served two years in the Fleet Marine Force with the

5th Marines and now was looking forward to improving his education. One of only two Leathernecks to be selected for special training at Belle-vue, he had anticipated a long, intriguing tour as a radar specialist. Abruptly, he was a Raider. When a training injury forced him to sick bay instead of participating in one of the battalion's infamous forced marches, Edson eyed him in silent accusation. Smith wouldn't shed that stare until he nearly got killed in a boxing smoker in Samoa. Lying flat on the grass, gasping for air after the match, Smith felt someone kick his foot, saw Edson standing over him, grinning. "Thought you'd won!" He'd made the team.[28]

More newcomers poured in. Second Lieutenant John E. D. Peacock wrote in his diary, "I joined the 1st Marine Raider Battalion today....It is a very unique outfit, patterned after the British Commandos." Like many other candidates, Peacock had been screened by Edson himself. Peacock described his new battalion commander as a tough soldier of fortune. "He warned me that when the outfit went into action there would be no quarter asked and no quarter given....and when we pulled out after a raid if a man couldn't make it he would probably have to be left on the beach." (Jumping Joe Chambers used more graphic methods in screening candidates: "Do you have the nerve to slit a Jap's throat with a knife?") Another newcomer, Private Joseph R. Baricko, retained a dif-ferent first impression of Edson. Baricko had wanted to become a Marine since he was eight years old. He enlisted in 1939, served in two defense battalions, and in the winter of 1942 left the 2d Battalion, 5th Marines to volunteer for the 1st Raiders. Red Mike Edson personally presented Baricko with his promotion warrant to private first class just after he arrived, a nice touch, long remembered.[29]

On 23 February 1942, Private Lee Minier wrote his parents that he had completed recruit training and had his new assignment: "I volun-teered for service with the 1st Marine Raider Battalion and was accepted. This outfit...is a spearhead for landing parties. We operate from destroy-ers and land in rubber boats. I am in E Company. That's a machine gun and special weapons company." Minier revealed both pride and concern about his unique new unit. "I only hope this outfit is as good as they say it is. They call it a suicide outfit, but I notice a lot of Marines try to get into it." He assessed his chances for promotion as limited. "The non-coms here are veterans and there are plenty of them. Some of them saw action in Nicaragua and the Philippines."[30]

Sam Griffith was as impressed with the profusion of veterans among the NCO ranks as young Minier. "They knew they were tough and they knew they were good," Griffith would later write. "They could live on jerked goat, the strong black coffee they called 'boiler compound,' and hash cooked in a tin hat."[31]

Not the least of these colorful old-timers was Gunnery Sergeant Gerald B. Stackpole, capably filling the billet peculiar to the raider battalions as rubber-boat maintenance specialist. Stackpole, an old China Hand, took a decidedly professional view of his job. The inflatable rubber boats, he believed, represented as much the tools of the Raiders' trade as their stilettos and submachine guns. Sloppy maintenance or careless handling of the boats, Stackpole vehemently warned, would jeopardize the raid mission and cost lives. So protective was Stackpole of his precious rubber boats that he quickly became known as "The Admiral," and—not to his face— "The Admiral of the Condom Fleet."[32]

Right in the middle of all the reshuffling within the battalion, Edson received an irksome requirement to provide nearly half the unit for a parade in New York City. This was a Navy Relief Society event to commemorate the doomed garrison of Wake Island, which had fallen exactly three months earlier, and the commitment proved to be just the boost to morale Edson sought. There was little time to spare for the men to prepare their winter green uniforms and get last-minute haircuts. Private First Class Grover Don Penn spotted with alarm the battalion being formed on the parade ground across from the barracks. Dashing out of the barber's chair to race upstairs for his blouse and rifle, Penn bowled over the battalion commander in the stairwell. *Damn! I'm dead,* Penn thought, too flustered to speak. But Edson simply steadied him and said, "Take it easy, son, you've plenty of time."[33]

Edson led a contingent of ten officers and 244 troops by train to New York City. Approached by the "Plank-owners" with a request to wear the distinctive fourragére of the 5th Marines one last time, Edson wisely compromised—not in the parade, but okay for liberty afterwards. The parade was an uplifting event for the Raiders and the people of New York. The Marine Band played, the crowds cheered, the Leathernecks threw back their shoulders in pride as they marched up Fifth Avenue to Rockefeller Center. Overnight liberty in the Big Apple constituted a special treat. The men stayed in the St. Regis Hotel, went to a hockey game at Madison Square Garden, and partied late. Recalled John Sweeney, "we were given a warm welcome wherever the Marines went; it was difficult to buy our own libations such was the patriotic outpouring of the people." For the first time, the new battalion felt like a unit, something unique.[34]

Heavily loaded Raiders practice rubber boat landings off New River, North Carolina, during 1941–42. Note the light machine gun mounted in the bow.

Earlier the battalion officers convened to select a distinctive insignia. Most agreed the design should include a four-stacker destroyer and the old Sandinista battle flag from the Nicaraguan campaigns, a white skull on a red background. The combination proved unwieldy. Edson showed up and in typical fashion suggested something simpler and more distinctive: delete the ship, retain the skull, change the background from red to blue. Someone else would add the five principal stars of the Southern Cross after the battalion deployed to the South Pacific, but the design was essentially in place before the unit ever left Quantico.[35]

Returning from New York, Edson resumed his special brand of combat training with a will. The Raiders would later describe their last six weeks in Quantico as a "preparatory course in physical endurance and deliberate mayhem." Edson stressed weapons competence and confidence, seeking to make all hands familiar with all weapons fielded by the battalion. While he would also emphasize "the more intimate tools for killing—knives, machetes, bayonets"—his principal intent was to make every Marine proficient in every form of firearm, from the Colt .45 automatic pistol to the enormous Boys .55 caliber bolt-action anti-tank rifle (quickly named "The Elephant Gun"). Recalled Gunnery Sergeant Robert Jesse Jernigan, "We spent so much time working with weapons we actually felt naked without 'em."[36]

Training was intense. Said Lieutenant Ed Dupras, a new platoon commander in Lew Walt's Able Company, "It was mostly a blur; I have vague recollections of moving pell-mell over the old Pipeline Trail, of some rubber-boat work in the very chilly Potomac, and some bivouacs out along the Chopawamsic Creek." Similarly, Private First Class James V. Mallamas of Baker Company observed that "training intensified....lots of hiking with heavy packs and full combat gear...and in garrison we would begin every day with a run from the barracks out to the main gate and back." Lieutenant Foster "Frosty" LaHue of Charlie Company recalled: "Training was rigorous....Emphasis on physical conditioning, marksmanship, stealth, camouflage, small unit tactics."[37]

Edson strove to attain a march rate of seven miles an hour, impossible to achieve by walking alone, and the command "double-time, MARCH!" frequently rang out from the head of the column.[38]

Two days after joining the Raiders, Lieutenant Peacock reported in his diary that his machine gun platoon "had to fire in the rain just as we hiked in the rain this morning." He admired his troops: "They have to be plenty good to march as fast as we do and still carry those [machine guns]." Doctor Bob Skinner recalled one hike of twenty-five miles in five hours, followed by a mock battle. Edson led them back to base after midnight. As they re-entered mainside about 0200, the troops began singing—loud enough to wake the dead. The base commander lambasted Edson the next day, but Red Mike knew morale was coming back strong.[39]

Edson's "madness" had its obvious method. With each march, each field bivouac, he tried to teach his men the essential survival skills they would need. Private First Class Jack F. Tracy admired Edson's compass marches. "Sometimes we would go over the terrain in daylight, then return again at night to appreciate how everything always changed in darkness." Private First Class Anthony Massar liked Edson's idea of having an aircraft take photographs of their camouflaged bivouac. "The aerial photos showed a nice neat row of dark blotches under the trees; they were shelter-halves, heavily covered with branches, and supposedly camouflaged; instead they were perfectly outlined, a giveaway." Nor did Massar find Edson unduly harsh. "One evening," he recalled, "we returned from a long, cold, wet hike, and Edson had our galley serve hot coffee with a slug of sickbay alcohol in each mug—what a morale booster!"[40]

Edson's hot-blooded young men rose to the challenge and still tried to burn the candle at both ends. Private First Class Frank J. Guidone of Able Company recalled many nights when the footsore troops would return bone-tired to the barracks but revive with a shower and a visit to their favorite table at the Privates Club for rounds of cold beer and platefulls of pig's feet. "Joe Connolly was the chief counselor of our group. He was older than most and therefore wiser. We were often short of cash, but he knew several of the managers of the club and they would extend us 'jawbone' until payday." After closing, Connolly and Guidone would smuggle beer into the barracks, making a long night still longer. "It was very difficult to make the morning formation," Guidone admitted, but Joe Connolly saved the day when he discovered how perfectly cans of beer would fit inside his mortar tube, thereby providing a welcome "hair of the dog" at the first break in the inevitable march.[41]

Despite the distractions of the Privates Club, the young Raiders responded well to Edson's challenge. Private First Class Lee Minier was now a machine gunner and proud of it. As he reported to his parents in a 7 March letter: "Wednesday we were in the hills all day and covered about twenty miles. Thursday we had a maneuver...covered another fifteen miles. Friday we were on the Potomac River all morning in rubber boats firing machine guns and getting wet....And about a fourth of the distance we run like the devil himself was after us....We also have gun drill every day. That is learning to put the gun into action quickly."[42]

Edson demanded effective communications in training and operations. This put the onus on the headquarters "comm" platoon, led by First Lieutenant William D. Stevenson and featuring such colorful radio operators as Duke Vierling, Fred Serral, and Horse Collar Smith. Marine Corps radios and field telephone systems in 1942 were bulky and famously unreliable. The troops struggled to lug the heavy components through the Virginia boondocks, just as their counterparts in the weapons platoons stumbled along on the march with their mortar baseplates and machine guns. On many occasions, the radiomen recall Private First Class Walter Burak lending a helping hand, relieving an overloaded and overheated Marine of his radio for a couple of miles, carrying two loads.

Walter Burak had both the physique and the disposition for such acts of mercy. Standing nearly six-feet tall and weighing 195 pounds, Burak had been a star football player in his Greensburg, Pennsylvania, high school. Devoutly Catholic, studiously unprofane, and totally unselfish, Burak impressed all Marines with whom he had contact. Edson recognized the youngster's unique qualities and made him his runner. Burak never let his elevated standing go to his head. Time and again, while panting up and down the marching column to deliver some message from the colonel, Burak would pause to lift a load from the back of one of his struggling former squadmates. Nor would Walter Burak ever go empty-handed in combat. In every firefight he would be seen delivering messages while simultaneously delivering a fresh box of grenades or a reel of comm wire. If Major Sam Griffith is remembered today as "a special breed of cat" among the Raider officers, Walter Burak fits that same rarefied category among all the enlisted Raiders.[43]

Edson knew from his experience fighting Sandinistas along the Coco River how difficult it always was to teach American troops aggressive hand-to-hand fighting techniques. In this most extreme version of combat, the objective is brutally simple—kill or be killed. While the preferred option was a well-aimed rifle shot in the opponent's "center of mass," that choice would not always be available to Raiders. On a stealthy mission, each Raider would have to be capable of coldbloodedly killing enemy sentries with either his bayonet, his stiletto, a make-shift piano-wire garrote, or his bare hands. Additionally, once surprise was forfeited, the Raiders could expect the enemy to come after them in close quarters. The Japanese were especially gifted blade fighters, and the jungle environment in which the Raiders would soon face them would lend itself to such close encounters.

Red Mike Edson therefore requested the services of sixty-five-year-old retired Marine colonel Anthony Biddle, a World War I veteran and legendary master of close combat. "I know of no one else as capable as you," Edson wrote Biddle, "to put this sort of instruction across as it should be done." Biddle acceded, came to Quantico, and provided an amazing demonstration for the Raiders. Biddle, said Jumping Joe Chambers, crouched barehanded and nimble-footed within a circle of Raiders engaging him with bare bayonets—and disarmed them all. Although Edson discouraged his troops from sparring with each other thereafter with unsheathed blades, he did acquire fencing foils and face masks for a safer application of Biddle's principles. Edson also revoked the temporary orders of Private First Class Robert S. Youngdeer, a native American of the Eastern Cherokees, scheduled to compete in the 1st Marine Division boxing matches in North Carolina. Youngdeer had previously claimed the regimental middleweight crown, but he also was one of the most accomplished instructors in individual combat in the battalion. Boxing could wait. Edson needed Youngdeer to further train the Raiders after Biddle's bravura demonstration.[44]

Edson and Griffith knew it would soon be time to respond to Nimitz's call for Raiders in the South Pacific. Indeed, events were already on the move. On 27 March Admiral King sent a hand-written note to Lieutenant General Holcomb asking, "What is status—and equipment—of your special battalions (raider) (via APDs) which are your 'commando' organization?" Holcomb had just been working this issue. Most of the 1st Marine Raider Battalion would be dispatched initially to Samoa, not yet a combat zone, but a key island base of strategic importance to the sea lanes to New Zealand and Australia, and an outpost very much threatened by the seemingly invincible Japanese advance. Holcomb's response to King on 31 March reported the imminent deployment: "The 1st Marine Raider Battalion (less Rear Echelon) of twenty-nine officers and 638 enlisted...leaves Quantico with full equipment on 1 April for San Diego for transfer to duty in Samoa. The Rear Echelon, consisting of nine officers and 233 men remains at Quantico for employment with the Amphibious Corps, Atlantic Fleet."[45]

Details of the deployment order caused Edson to scowl. Leaving a third of his battalion behind and sailing to a backwater outpost was hardly the meaningful mission he anticipated, but at least there would be time for more advanced training. And, at last, his Raiders would enter the theater of operations. It was a significant step, if a bit half-baked.

Edson issued Battalion Operations Order 4-42, the movement order for his main body, directing his Raiders to "be prepared in all respects for combat duty beyond the seas." Private First Class Lee Minier had time for a quick final note home: "We have drawn full equipment and have our bayonets sharpened and heavy marching packs ready."[46]

## Combat Readiness

The split deployment of Edson's Raiders to Samoa could have led to a dangerous, piecemeal combat commitment. Having so carefully tailored the 1st Raider Battalion's organization and equipment to fit precisely within the limited lift capacity of a squadron of destroyer transports, the Marine Corps then dispatched the battalion to the South Pacific months before there were sufficient APDs in that theater even to handle the truncated outfit. On 23 April, with both the 1st and 2d Raider Battalions underway for the Pacific, Admiral Nimitz apprised Admiral King he only had three APDs in the Pacific, a number "insufficient not only for the simultaneous employment of two Raider Battalions, but even for the employment of one complete battalion."[47]

Here was the danger. The Raiders, as organized and trained, would be more than capable of conducting stealthy strikes against lightly defended Japanese island installations (further assuming APDs or other ships were available). Yet Edson's Raiders would in practice perform this mission only once, at Tasimboko. Each of their other six engagements featured stand-up battles against large, well-armed forces. The fact that the 1st Raiders won most of these battles is a tribute to their leadership and spirit. The fact that they did not win them all is a reflection that, by design, the Raiders were usually outnumbered and always outgunned.

Comparing the D-series tables of organization and equipment in effect in 1942 demonstrates the differences between a conventional infantry battalion and a raider battalion. While aggregate numbers for the former were only percentage points larger than the latter, the key difference lay in their rifle companies. A raider company reflected its commitment to the APD: 137 officers, Marines, and navy corpsmen, as compared to 183 in an infantry company. In another comparison, the Raider battalion rated eighteen light, air-cooled .30 caliber guns, about a quarter of the total number of machine guns of all calibers fielded by an infantry battalion. In terms of tactical mobility, the infantry battalion could rely on fifty-five jeeps and eight 4x4 one-ton trucks. The Raider battalion in comparison rated sixteen jeeps, plus two 6x6 2.5-ton trucks—meaningless assets because they wouldn't fit on the APDs. In truth, the Raiders' tactical mobility was restricted to the destroyer transports and a bunch of inflatable rubber boats, none of whose outboard motors worked reliably in salt water.[48]

By the same token, the Corps had still not fully shaken out the wrinkles in the Raiders organization. The commandant had re-inserted the 81mm mortar platoon that Edson wanted deleted. No one could argue the welcome punch the big mortars would contribute in a conventional firefight, but the reality of the Raiders' limited mobility created major headaches. The problem wasn't the heavy weight of the weapons themselves—Edson could always find in his ranks some stalwart like Walter Burak strong enough to hump the forty-six-pound baseplate through a jungle swamp. The critical factor was the 81mm ammunition. The Raiders did not travel lightly. Adding, say, three 81mm rounds per man would have dangerously slowed this supposedly fast-moving outfit.

The issue of the 81mm mortar platoon demanded resolution, and there is evidence that Edson spent a lot of time pondering it during the train ride across the continent.

The related issue of command relations also remained unresolved as the Raiders began to deploy. Edson was right to a certain extent—the Raider battalion did not belong within a division, certainly not within an infantry regiment. The Raiders would spend most of their overseas years assigned to the 1st Marine Amphibious Corps, reasonably enough, but their most significant relationship occurred throughout the Guadalcanal campaign when they were attached to the 1st Marine Division. There they were free to land at Tulagi and Tasimboko from APDs, but when things grew critical during their stand-and-deliver battles on Edson's Ridge, they were most capably supported by the hot-shooting howitzers of the 11th Marines, the division's artillery regiment. Lacking this relationship with the 1st Marine Division at Bairoko the following year, the 1st Raiders attacked fixed fortifications with no artillery support whatsoever.

These loose ends were perhaps inevitable in the wake of the hasty establishment of a new and frankly experimental unit. The plus side of the equation is the fact that the 1st Marine Raider Battalion left the United States in a superb state of physical condition and combat readiness. They were superbly led from top to bottom, and their *esprit de corps* was both infectious and universal. Given the grace of a few more months in Samoa to shake-down all the last-minute transfers, the battalion would represent a small but lethally effective instrument in the nation's first counteroffensive in the Pacific.

As early as January 1942, a field grade officer from The Basic School, assigned as the chief umpire for Edson's battalion during a cold and confused amphibious landing exercise, reported the unit to be a well-trained and efficient organization. "The men showed evidence of a thorough grounding in combat principles," he wrote, "and it was particularly noted that they always acted as though they were facing a real enemy. Their morale was of the highest, and they were at all times possessed of a strong initiative." Similarly, Holland Smith's chief of staff, Colonel Graves Erskine, remembered observing a huge and hapless landing near Virginia Beach where "only one battalion hit the beach when it was supposed to, and it was Edson's battalion, the Raiders."[49]

Edson and the "Plank-owners" had done their initial job well. Now would come the post-graduate training. For Private First Class Hugh Davis the weeks at Quantico had been a blur following his screening by Red Mike Edson and Sergeant Major "Parson" Clarke, who asked him why he wanted to volunteer. "I must have given the right answer," said Davis. "The next thing I knew I was on that train heading west, calling myself a 'Raider." It was sorta like getting married. Changed my life forever!"[50]

# Notes

1. Maj. Gen. Merritt A. Edson to Herbert R. Edson, "The Do or Die Men: The Development and History of the First Marine Raider Battalion," unpublished manuscript, 1954, Chapter II, 4–5.

2. Dr. John W. Gordon, PhD, "The U.S. Marine Corps and an Experiment in Military Elitism: A Reassessment of the Special Warfare Impetus, 1937–43," paper presented at the Third U.S. Naval Academy Symposium on Naval History, 1977.

3. The author is indebted to retired Maj. Richard T. Spooner, USMC, owner of the popular Globe & Laurel restaurant in Triangle, Virginia, for providing the author a copy of Gen. Breckenridge's 15 February 1942 letter to the commandant. Give me some life-term convicts, said Breckenridge, "and a lonely and simple place in which to train them, and about six months in which to work: and then, under my friend Nimitz who I expect to land us somewhere on the beach of Japan—with nothing but ammunition and a light lunch—I will not stop until all of us are either in Tokyo or dead."

4. R. M. Mattingly, "The Worst Slap in the Face," *Marine Corps Gazette*, March 1983, 58–66. Lt. Col. Mattingly earned the 1983 Robert D. Heinl Award in Marine Corps History for this well-researched essay.

5. Capt. James Roosevelt, USMCR to Holcomb, 13 January 1942, Raider Battalion Correspondence Files, Archives Section, Marine Corps Historical Center (MCHC); Holcomb to Capt. Roosevelt, 20 January 1942, Box 3, Series 63A-2535, WNRC.

6. CINCPACFLT to CG, 2d Joint Training Force, "Organization of 'Commando' Units," 24 January 1942, Box 3, Series 63A-2535, WNRC.

7. Edson to Smith, "Designation of and Replacements for the First Separate Battalion, Fleet Marine Force," 6 February 1942, Box 3, Series 63A-2535, WNRC. See also Hoffman, *Legend*, 150–154.

8. Holcomb to Vogel, personal, 10 February 1942, Raider Battalion Correspondence Files, Archives Section, MCHC.

9. James Childs to John Sweeney, 15 March 1993. Childs, a first sergeant during this period, became the battalion's field sergeant major during the Guadalcanal Campaign. His collection (and interpretation) of the unit's monthly muster rolls proved invaluable to this project.

10. John Apergis to Thomas Mullahey, 19 January 1992, 31 January 1992, 3 January 1993; Hugh Gilman to Thomas Mullahey, 23 August 1992.

11. Oscar F. Peatross, *Bless 'em All: The Raider Marines of World War II* (Irvine, California: Review Publications, 1995), 14.

12. James Childs to John Sweeney, 15 March 1993, based on unit muster rolls.

13. Thomas "Jinx" Powers interview with Jon T. Hoffman, 24 August 1991.

14. Marlin Groft and Herbert Coffin interviews with Jon T. Hoffman, 1993.

15. Robert Addison to John Sweeney, 3 December 1993.

16. George K. Peters to John Sweeney, 7 June 1993.

17. Carl Fox to author, 24 January 1999; James Vittitoe interview with Jon T. Hoffman, 1993.

18. Edson to CG, AFAF, 16 February 1942, re: Maj. Berry, Box 4, Edson's Papers, Library of Congress. Edson to CG, AFAF, 17 February 1942, re: replacement officers, Box 4, Edson's Papers, Library of Congress.

19. Edson to CMC, 9 March 1942, requesting additional surgeons ("casualties as high as 25 percent may be anticipated"), Raider Battalion Correspondence Files, Archives Section, MCHC. Request denied 21 March.

20. Casualty Card, Capt. Herbert B. Cain, USMC.

21. Edson requested the assignment of Lieutenants Mullahey and Boyd in his 17 February 1942 letter to CG, AFAF, cited above; Thomas Mullahey to Jon T. Hoffman, 12 September 1991. Col. Boyd's biographical information provided by Reference Section, MCHC. See also Boyd obituary in *Fortitudine XI* (Fall 1981–Winter 1982), 28.

22. Maj. Bailey's official biography provided by Reference Section, MCHC; John Sweeney unpublished memoir, ca. 1995, provided to author 1998.

23. Gen. Walt's official biography provided by Reference Section, MCHC.

24. Paul H. Chambers, ed., *The Third Battalion, 25th Marines: An Oral History of Col. Justice Marion Chambers, USMCR (Ret.)*, unpublished manuscript, 1987, vi, copy provided author by Dr. Michael F. Keleher, MD, former battalion surgeon, 3/25, during Marshalls, Marianas, and Iwo Jima; Col. Chambers' official biography provided by Reference Section, MCHC.

25. Cpl. Lee N. Minier to parents, 15 April 1943; Lee N. Minier, *Raider*, unpublished manuscript, 1989. Doctor Minier is the nephew and namesake of Corporal Minier.

26. Gen. Griffith's official biography provided by Reference Section, MCHC; Griffith obituary, *Washington Post*, 7 April 1983, B-4.

27. John Erskine and Frank Kemp quoted in "Sam Griffith: A Rare Breed of Cat," in *The Dope Sheet*, November 1983, 2, 8.

28. James Smith interview with author, 8 April 1999. Smith to author, 14 August 1999.

29. John Peacock diary entry, 19 March 1942, copy transmitted to Thomas Mullahey, 15 February 1993; Chambers vignette from Ira Irvin interview with Jon T. Hoffman, 1992; Joseph R. Baricko to author, 12 February 1999.

30. Lee Minier to parents, 23 February 1942, Minier, *Raider*, 70–72.

31. Samuel B. Griffith, *The Battle for Guadalcanal* (Philadelphia: Lippincott, 1963), 23–24

32. Among many sources on the colorful Gy. Sgt. Stackpole, see Peatross, *Bless 'em All*, 11–12. Maj. William K. Jones, who commanded the 1st Battalion, 6th Marines at Tarawa, also proudly bore the nickname "The Admiral of the Condom Fleet."

33. Grover Don Penn to Thomas Mullahey, 1992.

34. James Childs to Thomas Mullahey, 29 April 1992, including February muster roll reports indicating the New York contingent numbered ten officers and 244 enlisted; *New York Times*, 25 February 1942; John Sweeney to Thomas Mullahey, 18 May 1993, 2.

35. Arthur Haake to Thomas Mullahey, 23 July 1992.

36. All quotes from George Doying, "Red Mike and His Do or Die Men," *Leatherneck*, March 1944, 15–17.

37. Edward Dupras to Thomas Mullahey, 1 June 1992; James V. Mallamas interview with Jon T. Hoffman, 1991; Lt. Gen. Foster C. LaHue to Jon T. Hoffman, December 1991.

38. Hoffman, *Legend*, 159; James Childs interview with Jon T. Hoffman, 1992.

39. Peacock diary entry, Saturday, 21 March 1942; Robert Skinner interview with Jon T. Hoffman, 1992.

40. Jack Tracy interview with Jon T. Hoffman, 1992; Anthony Massar to Jon T. Hoffman, 1992.

41. Frank Guidone to Pete Pettus, 28 September 1956; to Thomas Mullahey, 26 September 1992; to author, 22 January 1999.

42. Lee Minier to parents, 7 March 1942, in Minier, *Raider*, 72–73.

43. Burak's exemplary character has been attested to by countless Raider survivors; the best summary comes from Fred Serral to author, 5 December 1998.

44. Edson to Col. Anthony J. D. Biddle, USMC (Ret.), 21 January 1942, Box 4, Edson Papers, Library of Congress; Col. J. M. Chambers, USMC (Ret.) Oral Memoir, Marine Corps Oral History Collection [MCOHC], MCHC, 263; Edson to Col. Miller, 1st Marine Division, 30 January 1942, Box 4, Edson Papers, Library of Congress.

45. COMINCH memo to CMC, 27 March 1942; CMC to COMINCH, "Status of Marine Raider Battalions," 31 March 1942, both in Box 1806, RG 127, WNRC. Holland Smith's command changed its name (again) on 3 March 1942 from Amphibious Force to Amphibious Command, Atlantic Fleet.

46. 1st Marine Raider Battalion OpOrder 4-42, "Movement Order," 29 March 1942, Box 1, Series 63A-2535, WNRC; Lee Minier to parents, 27 March 1942, in Minier, *Raider*, 75–76.

47. CINCPACFLT to COMINCH, 23 April 1942, copy held in Marine Raider Files, Reference Section, MCHC.

48. Raider Battalion organization and equipment figures from D-series to #D-175 and #D-169, both in author's possession. Comparative figures from Benis M. Frank and Henry I. Shaw, *Victory and Occupation: Volume V of The History of U.S. Marine Corps Operations in World War II* (Washington: Headquarters Marine Corps, 1968), Appendixes I, J, and K, 843–51.

49. Lt. Col. John W. Beckett, USMC, chief umpire to CO, The Basic School, 21 January 1942, Box 1, Series 1277694, WNRC; Lt. Gen. Graves Erskine Oral Memoir, MCOHC, MCHC, 261.

50. Hugh Davis to John Sweeney, 22 April 1995.

# 3

## Combat Duty Beyond the Seas, April–August 1942

*The Marine Corps throughout its history has specialized in brush war-fare and amphibious operations.*

Major General Commandant Thomas Holcomb, USMC
11 February 1942[1]

"BRUSH WARFARE AND AMPHIBIOUS OPERATIONS" would character-ize the mission environment of the 1st Marine Raider Battalion. Edson's Raiders would execute three difficult landings in their two campaigns in the British Solomon Islands, and each of their seven engagements would be fought in heavy brush, ranging from the thick *kunai* grass of "The Ridge" to the nearly-impenetrable jungle of Dragon's Peninsula. Yet no Raider in the spring of 1942 could envision the alien conditions that lay ahead, nor for that matter could they imagine such exotic names as Pua Pua, Nouméa, Tulagi, Tasimboko, the Matanikau, Enogai, or Bairoko.

The men had volunteered for enlistment in the Marine Corps—and volunteered again for combat service with Edson's Raiders—for a variety of extremely personal reasons. Of these, the search for adventure surely ranked high as a universal incentive. These young men crossed the threshold of real adventure when they awoke on April Fool's Day 1942 and beheld a long line of passenger cars parked on the nearby railroad siding—their troop train. And although their journey to combat on Tulagi would still take a dizzying four months, the first step—boarding their train—was nonetheless memorable. Very few of the Raiders had ever crossed the Mississippi before. No troops knew their destination, but all knew their adventure had begun.

Meanwhile, ten thousand miles away Imperial Japanese forces of significant future importance to the Raiders were already on the move. On 23 January, when the Raiders were still the orphan 1st Separate Battalion at Quantico, Japanese Special Naval Landing Forces of the Fourth Fleet seized Rabaul with its airfields and priceless deep-water harbors. In short order the Japanese would develop Rabaul into the predominant fortress of the South Pacific, as lethal and formidable as a den of rabid foxes. From Rabaul for the next two years would emerge Imperial warships, bombers, and reinforcement troops that would make life miserable for Edson's Raiders.

On 15 February the Japanese captured the British fortress at Singapore following an incredible march through the surrounding jungles. During the final two days of the month the Allies lost their Far East Fleet in the Battle of the Java Sea, an unmitigated disaster that spelled doom for the besieged defenders of the Philippines. General MacArthur and his family departed by PT boat on 11 March; Bataan fell on 9 April, Corregidor on 6 May.

On 3 May, during Edson's Raiders' first week ashore in Samoa, Commander Masaaki Suzuki led his 3d Kure Special Naval Landing Forces ashore unopposed on Tulagi Island, the former center of the British colonial administration for the Solomons. The Japanese viewed Tulagi as the first step in Operation MO, which would bypass the balance of the southern Solomons to capture Port Moresby on the southeast coast of New Guinea, a potentially fatal blow for nearby Australia. The Allies reversed this drive in the costly Battle of the Coral Sea (4–10 May), but the Japanese retained their prize of Tulagi. Swiftly, a float-plane reconnaissance base became operational there. Japanese planners then began looking around the area for a suitable place for a bomber strip. The large island of Guadalcanal, some twenty miles south across Sea Lark Channel, looked promising.

Meanwhile, an enormous armada of Japanese warships and an invasion force began to assemble for a thrust into the Central Pacific. One objective was Midway, from which Japanese bombers could render Pearl Harbor untenable as a fleet base. The main objective, however, was destruction of the remnants of the U.S. Pacific Fleet in decisive battle, just as the Japanese had whipped the Russian Far East Fleet in the 1905 Battle of Tsushima.

This was the Pacific Theater as the 1st Raiders boarded their troop train and began chugging west towards their unknown destination.

### Pua Pua

Merritt Edson began the journey to the South Pacific with mixed emotions. The four-week excursion would crimp his training programs and derail his physical conditioning regimen. On the other hand, he would need every bit of the three-month grace period that lay ahead in Samoa and New Caledonia for advanced combat training and resolution of unfinished business. Chief among the latter considerations remained the unit's still undefined mission. Would the battalion fight as hit-and-run sea raiders or as long-haul, behind-the-lines guerrillas? Would their main purpose be deception, diversion, and demolition—or would they be training indigenous forces in the Philippines to fight as partisans against the occupying Japanese? Would they fight as a battalion, individual companies, or small patrols? With only three APDs in the entire Pacific, what were they going to use as transports? And what about the three troop transport submarines available in this theater? These would be ideal for certain missions, but Edson's Raiders had never trained with subs and few knew anything about their configuration or employment.

Edson knew the grace period would also provide simple unit stability, a condition impossible to attain amid all the personnel turmoil at Quantico. His company commanders badly needed time to shape and train their men as a team. Samoa would provide the necessary seclusion and focus.

The fate of the rear echelon remained of concern to Edson. Mere numerical replacements would not do. Each man in the rear echelon had been screened, selected, and trained by Edson and his assistants. They were, to Edson, virtually irreplaceable.

Edson had further concerns with the organization, weapons, and special equipment of his battalion, but his men hardly noticed his preoccupation. All eyes were on the troop train; all ears alert for the "scuttlebutt" rumors about their destination.

"This morning [1 April 1942] is rather dark and dreary," begins the diary of Private First Class Henry C. ("Popeye") Poppell, a radio operator in Able Company who would chronicle his observations throughout the deployment of the 1st Raiders. "We look across the Parade Ground to see the long line of cars on the railroad we will board in a few hours." As they embarked, Poppell noted, they were headed for "parts unknown. Maybe the War front or maybe Florida to train." He commented on all the secrecy, noting as they left that, "unlike other troop trains, we had no one to say goodbye or cheer us on."[2]

**Raiders hit the beach during amphibious training in Samoa in 1942.**

The possibility of Florida as a destination, or as a jumping off site for some Caribbean adventure, remained a viable rumor until the next day. Then the train took a right turn. Poppell recorded, "To our amazement we have left the Florida route and are headed in the direction of western Georgia." By the third day the train had passed through Birmingham and the initial mystery appeared solved. "We now realize that we are going to the West Coast, although our destination remains a secret."[3]

The battalion reached San Diego and established a temporary tent camp at the recruit depot. By now the troops had discerned that their time in California would be fleeting, and they took full advantage of the various amenities offered by that friendly, sea-faring city. Edson meanwhile recruited two more officers for his main body, the former FBI agent and trick-shot artist, First Lieutenant Henry Adams, who would teach combat marksmanship to the Raiders in Samoa, and a Japanese language specialist, Second Lieutenant John Erskine.[4]

John Erskine was the least likely of all Raiders. Rejected by Marine recruiters in early 1941 because he failed to meet minimum physical standards—too short, too skinny, too myopic—the twenty-five-year-old graduate student became of interest to the Marine Corps as war with Japan loomed closer. Erskine, the son of missionary parents, had spent the first sixteen years of his life in Japan and could speak and read Japanese with great fluency. The Marine Corps gave him a commission and sent him to advance training at the University of Hawaii. He was there when the Japanese struck Pearl Harbor, and his first combat duty was to scurry around the parade deck at Marine Barracks, Pearl, reminding the Leathernecks to shoot only at the planes with "the red meatball" on the sides. As Tom Bartlett would later write, Erskine missed both OCS and The Basic School: "He knew nothing of Marine Corps history and traditions. He did not know how to salute, couldn't erect a shelter half, and couldn't find the safety on a .45 pistol or field strip an '03'." But, as the Raiders would discover, Erskine had a fighting heart and an abiding sense of humor. In time he would become one of their most distinguished alumni.[5]

Edson also took this opportunity to compose three thoughtful letters to higher headquarters concerning the configuration of his battalion on the verge of combat deployment. To the commandant he proposed further modifications to the battalion's tables of organization and basic allowances. He requested quite a laundry list, including collapsible bicycles, air compressors (to inflate rubber boats), individual scaling ropes, camouflage helmet netting, Bangalore torpedoes, and stilettos with six-inch blades. Since the army had first claim to the new M1 Garand semi-automatic rifle and its carbine version (as well as the old faithful Thompson submachine gun), Edson asked for temporary provision of the controversial Reising submachine gun, plus more M1903 Springfields with scopes. Edson further requested a field test of the Johnson "light machine rifle" for consideration as a replacement for the reliable but hefty Browning Automatic Rifle (BAR). The BARs could then be substituted for the battalion's Browning M1919A4 .30 caliber air-cooled light machine guns. Edson figured these exchanges could save the battalion an aggregate of 1,000 pounds of man-packed weight.

In the same letter, Edson resurrected the issue of the 81mm mortar platoon which the commandant had incorporated into the Raider battalions. Edson politely reminded Holcomb of the requirement to tailor the battalion to fit aboard its APD transports. More importantly, Edson argued, the weapons were too heavy and the ammunition too awkward "for fast-moving operations."[6]

General Holcomb was still a busy man, up to his neck in appeals for men and equipment from every major commander in the Corps. Edson

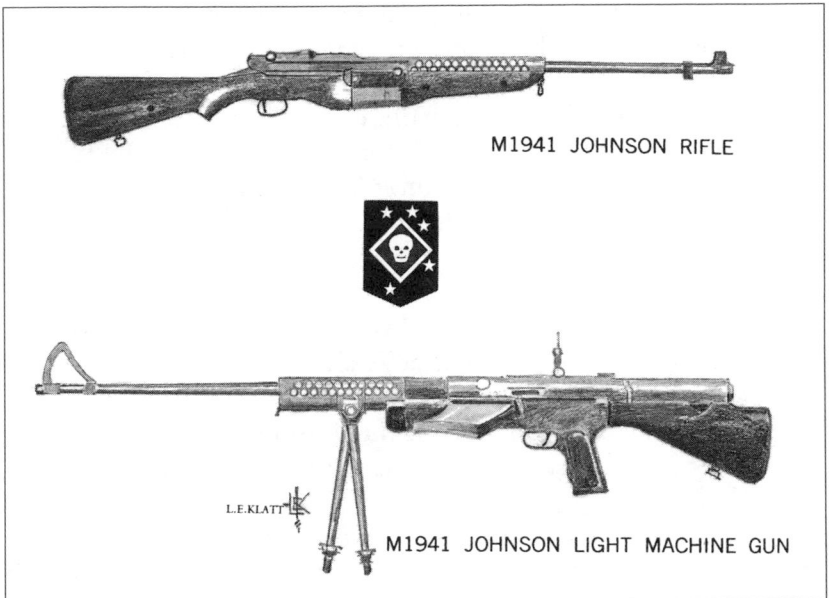

M1941 JOHNSON RIFLE

L.E.KLATT

M1941 JOHNSON LIGHT MACHINE GUN

"The Johnson Weapons" by Larry E. Klatt. It was said of those Raiders fortunate to carry either of the experimental firearms in combat: "No man wanted to give them up."

was a mere battalion commander, and the Raiders and other special units had already occupied too much of the commandant's time. Yet Holcomb respected Edson's combat savvy and his professional reasoning. He did what he could with Edson's request. The 81mm mortar platoon would soon be erased from the table of organization. There would be no field test of the Johnson rifle, no collapsible bikes, and no (or few at best) Bangalore torpedoes, a regrettable shortfall in view of the fortified caves awaiting at Tulagi. But Holcomb would ensure that enough Reising submachine guns would be on hand in plenty of time in Samoa so that Edson's officers and senior NCOs would not have to storm ashore armed only with the 1911 automatic pistol (often described as "a short-range revenge weapon").

Edson's second letter went to the commanding general of the Pacific Fleet Amphibious Corps, into whose bailiwick the Raiders were now entering. Here Edson expressed his concerns about his rear echelon. While admitting he no longer believed the 81mm platoon essential for his mission, Edson emphatically requested that the balance of his battalion be deployed rapidly. He predicted combat casualties up to 25 percent of his manning level; the best source of quality replacements would be the trained Raiders in his fourth rifle company. He needed a full-time executive officer. The current "double-hatting" of Major Bob Brown as battalion XO and operations/training officer would work in transit, but not in the forthcoming field training and combat deployments. Edson spoke out for his incumbent exec: "The return of Major Samuel B. Griffith is especially desirable because of his recent experience as an observer with the British Commandos and other combat units in Great Britain." The last thing Edson wanted to do at this late date was have to break in a new XO, likely overage, over-weight, or overly ambitious.[7]

Edson's final letter before leaving the United States was a polite but insistent request to the commandant to expedite the deployment of the rear echelon.

While Edson thus probed the upper stratosphere of the Corps for the additional men and equipment he deemed essential for combat duty, his men formed working parties to load such gear as they had on board their assigned transport at the San Diego Naval Station. She was USS *Zeilin* (AP 9), the twenty-two-year-old former SS *President Jackson,* acquired by the navy in 1940 and renamed for Brigadier General Jacob Zeilin, the sixth commandant of the Corps. The old salts among the Raiders eyed her appraisingly. Compared to their familiar APD destroyer transports, *Zeilin* appeared to be huge (she had, in fact, ten times the displacement weight), of similar vintage, and with perhaps half the speed. A ship destined for yeoman service throughout the Solomons, Gilberts, and Aleutians, *Zeilin*'s great asset throughout the war proved to be the abiding can-do spirit of captain and crew. The Raiders were in good hands in their initial journey deep into the Pacific.[8]

The Raiders often compensated for their shortcomings in equipment (and food!) by their light-fingered "appropriations." When some self-important but naive staff officer left his jeep parked unattended on the dock, the Raiders quickly rolled it into a cargo net and hoisted it aboard *Zeilin,* the sailors grinning approvingly. The ship would sail before the investigation got underway.[9]

The battalion enjoyed one final night on the town, keenly aware of yet another threshold awaiting on the morrow, and the men toasted their fortunes in a dozen bars and bistros. Reveille came, excruciatingly, at 0400. The troops marched up *Zeilin*'s gangway, hungover and subdued. It was a gray Monday, the 13th of April. The ship eased into the channel, proceeded slowly along Shelter Island, then hit the first great Pacific rollers as she passed Ballast Point, the final, outstretched arm of the United States.

Some men became seasick, but for the most part the Raiders disappointed the sailors, watching with wicked anticipation for the usual epidemic of *mal de mer* to convulse the landlubbers. The Raiders had plenty of experience on the smaller, rough-riding APDs—not to mention their bouncing cork-like rubber boats. Soon, hangovers suppressed and sea legs regained, the men began to enjoy the ride. Once underway the officers apprised the men that their destination was Pago Pago, Samoa. In the meantime, here was adventure galore—"millions of flying fish," other warships in accompaniment, and then the bizarre ceremonies of Davy Jones' Court as the ship crossed the Equator, painfully converting Lowly Polliwogs into Trusty Shellbacks.[10]

Edson continued to squeeze every possible moment afloat into constructive improvement of his command. No longer willing to wait for Marine Corps Headquarters to act on his recommendations for replacing the 81mm platoon in Easy Company with a more useful demolitions unit, Red Mike created his own out of whole cloth. While still afloat, he converted his fifteen-man "casual" platoon in the headquarters company (until then his emergency replacement pool) into a provisional demo unit. Lieutenant James E. Blessing became the platoon commander. Edson and Blessing endeavored to teach demolitions to their captive audience aboard ship, but the vessel's captain did not warm to the idea of practical application, even by tossing the explosives off the fantail. Edson appointed weapons-wise Gunnery Sergeant Angus Goss as Blessing's platoon sergeant and arranged for Goss and his protégé Corporal Gerald West to attend demolition school upon arrival in Samoa. In view of the possibility of small unit deployments, Edson also designated an NCO in each eight-man rifle squad as a demolitions man, each to be trained subsequently by Goss and West. For newly assigned guide Frank Guidone, the requirement to carry a demolition pack with detonator caps and blocks of TNT atop his own knapsack proved both onerous and dangerous. Edson later agreed, reverting to the attachment of demo teams to the platoon or company in greatest need.[11]

While Edson endeavored to make the most of his voyage to the South Pacific, Major Sam Griffith continued to train his rear echelon on the East Coast. During 21–30 April 1942, Dog Company and the unwanted 81mm mortar platoon conducted amphibious training with two APDs of Transport Division Eleven. The Atlantic Fleet no longer conducted its landing exercises in the Caribbean due to the German U-Boat menace. The Raiders and APDs therefore executed rubber-boat landings at Solomon's Island within Chesapeake Bay. A Washington-based newspaper team came along for the story. Their subsequent five-photograph spread handsomely portrayed the Raiders inflating their rubber boats, climbing down a cargo net, paddling clear of the transport, and—the climax—a lively but staged shot of a dozen grinning Raiders storming the beach, bayoneted Springfields held high, their leader brandishing an automatic pistol. Stated one caption: "The commando type of surprise attack is nothing new to the United States Marines. They've been at it ever since they were organized in 1775."[12]

Things went well at Solomon's Island. The ships had become so proficient at this stage they could launch, load, and dispatch all rubber boats within nine minutes after arrival at the designated splash point. Experienced sailors and Raiders alike quickly acknowledged the artificiality of the Chesapeake's calm seas and modest "surf." The South Pacific, they knew, would be quite different.[13]

Curiously, Sam Griffith did not accompany his command during this important training. Captain Jake Irwin led the detachment and signed the after-action report. Griffith instead left Quantico the day after Edson sailed on *Zeilin* and traveled to southern California to spend two weeks observing the 2d Raider Battalion as a guest of Lieutenant Colonel Evans Carlson. There is no evidence of Griffith asking Edson's permission, which likely would have been refused. Griffith, who did not share Edson's animosity towards Carlson, took the opportunity to learn what he could of Carlson's unique organizational and training ideas. He had sense enough, events would prove, to rule out those that would be inapplicable, but the Carlson influence would be quite evident, as one example, in Griffith's 1943 experimental use of fire-teams.[14]

In any case, Griffith's expectations for the rear echelon in April 1942 differed decidedly from Edson's. In Griffith's words: "The deal was that the second echelon of the battalion which I commanded was to form the nucleus of a third Raider battalion, which I would command....to be formed at Quantico." This may have been the case at first. Holcomb's response to Edson's request of 9 April for prompt deployment of the balance of the battalion was guarded at best, a stiff note advising Red Mike that the "disposition of the rear echelon...is under consideration. You will be advised if it is found practicable to transfer this unit to your command."[15]

Like a bulldog, Edson kept up the pressure. Shortly after arrival in

Samoa, he convinced the island defense force commander to send an urgent message to the commandant (copy to Nimitz) stating "early employment 1st Raider Battalion demands men to bring organization to strength be sent this area first opportunity. Order rear echelon at Quantico or equal number selected volunteers with basic special Raider training."[16]

Holcomb had already changed his mind. The four-week period between the Battle of the Coral Sea and the Battle of Midway was one of great tension in Washington. Holcomb knew every Marine unit in the Pacific was now in jeopardy, especially those in Midway, Palmyra, and Samoa. When staff officers called his attention to space unexpectedly available on the transport *Heywood* (AP-12), sailing from San Diego in June for Samoa, Holcomb asked Admiral Ernest King for authority to embark the Raiders' rear echelon of nine officers and 250 men on board. King agreed. Abruptly, Sam Griffith and his "orphans" had their sailing orders. They would remain Edson's Raiders[17]

In the South Pacific, the USS *Zeilin* arrived in Pago Pago, Samoa, late in the day on a very rainy 28th of April. The Raiders, all astir at landfall, could see nothing of their new training base. But the next day, Henry

Last liberty in San Diego for Griffith's echelon of Raiders. Left to right: Sgt. George Simon, Cpl. Gerald West, PFC Kenneth Champlin, PFC Finlay Foden, Sgt. John Combs (KIA Enogai), and Cpl. Arthur Edmonds.

Poppell recorded: "We awake early to see one of the most beautiful harbors in the world...we disembark to establish a camp site. After covering eighteen miles we pitch camp near the village of Leone."[18]

The Raiders called the place Pua Pua, and they would never forget it.

## Post-Graduate Training

Lovely as the tropical island was, beguiling as the graceful native women appeared, the Raiders would have scant opportunity for sight-seeing or making whoopee. Edson's "Post-graduate Training" began with a vengeance.

Samoa's high humidity, rugged hills, and pounding surf would provide an excellent training arena for the Raiders. Here, for example, would be the perfect opportunity to apply certain principles of British Commando training learned by the six members of the 1st Raiders who had undergone special cross-training in the United Kingdom. First Lieutenant Russell Duncan had led the detachment to Scotland in February. They were in exotic company. Recalled Corporal Sterling W. Schaar, the trainees included "Free French, Dutch, Belgians, Poles, Checks, Norwegians—you name it." Yet the training proved overly exotic as far as the Raiders were concerned. Useful as the curriculum surely was for the European Theater, the Raiders would find little application in the Pacific for mine warfare, anti-tank tactics, cliff-scaling, Molotov cocktails, escape and evasion, or acts of sabotage. The most appropriate training for the Raiders proved to be the same activities they had been taught by Red Mike Edson at Quantico—physical fitness, night operations, marksmanship, and small-unit tactics. Similarly, Sam Griffith returned from his earlier sojourn with the commandos impressed by their emphasis on realistic training. "It was very rugged," he reported, "Cross-country hikes, night exercises, very realistic, live ammunition." Yet these themes were vintage Edson. And in his remote Samoan camp, Edson would be free to conduct much more training under live-fire conditions.[19]

Private First Class Jim Mallamas found the training on Samoa to be "particularly tough—lots of mountain climbing, constant hiking, several mock attacks on native villages." Private First Class Tony Massar recalled the "hot, muggy weather, the muddy, slippery trails along the steep ridges." Jinks Powers described the frequent rains that made the footing along mountain trails treacherous—"yet the native women moved easily over those same trails, barefoot, carrying heavy loads on their heads." Powers was one of those archetypical Marines like Joe Connolly who tested the disciplinary system in garrison but proved to be lionhearted in battle. With the energetic Captain Chambers pushing his weapons company harder and harder on these frequent mountain hikes, Powers and company began to omit the machine gun and mortar rounds from their prescribed load, secretly carrying empty containers uphill and back. This worked until Chambers surprised his men by ordering a mid-hike live-firing exercise. Powers, caught empty-handed by a wrathful Jumping Joe Chambers, had to repeat the hike the next day, this time carrying a double load of live rounds.[20]

Edson liked what he saw of Chambers' energetic training. Having placed a wager with the island defense commander that his Raiders could sneak up and "capture" the island's most heavily guarded, top secret, mountaintop radar site, Edson challenged his Raiders, being sure to include Chambers' weaponeers. The Raiders took three days to make their stealthy ascent. Then, in the darkest hour before dawn, they fell on the surprised defenders like a Biblical horde. Edson won the bet, rewarded the battalion with his rare, lop-sided grin, and promised Chambers his own rifle company in the near future. Private First Class Poppell was elated with the feat: "We return with long tales of success....Every place we go we are welcome."[21]

Defense of the radar site was serious business. Each Marine commander on Samoa kept one eye on his training, the other on his assigned sector to defend the island against Japanese surprise attack. Island security became more significant in late May amid widespread indicators and rumors of another massive Japanese offensive. Gunnery Sergeant Angus Goss, fresh from his demolition training, teamed with electronics expert Horse Collar Smith to prepare for emergency destruction of U.S. radar facilities on Samoa in the event of a Japanese landing. Smith knew plenty about radar; he showed Goss the critical components; Goss planned the specific explosive package. "That's where I came to know Angus Goss," recalled Smith later, "and in my humble view there was never a finer professional Marine."[22]

Busy as they were, Edson's Raiders could not help but notice—out of the corners of their eyes, mind you—that many of the Samoan women went about their business topless. "These Polynesians are blessed with beautiful bodies," recorded Henry Poppell enthusiastically. Frank Guidone remembered how the Marines would cast hopeful eyes on the village shower whenever a particularly comely Samoan woman would perform her ablutions. They were rarely rewarded; the Polynesian ladies "made skillful use of their lava-lavas, showering very well without exposing very much of their bodies."[23]

Gy. Sgt. Angus Goss, role model for many new Raiders.

Corporal Guidone was a member of Able Company. "Captain Lew Walt was our company commander; First Lieutenant Bill Sperling was the exec; Lieutenants Mullahey, Dupras, and Haake the platoon leaders. Our training consisted of forced marches, reconn patrols, night compass marches, weapons firing, and rubber-boat landings. We trained hard on skimpy rations, and it was only a matter of time before we became lean and hard and knowledgeable in surviving the jungle." On one occasion Lew Walt challenged his NCOs with a special mission, a forced march to the top of a notoriously steep mountain. "Walt took off at a gallop and we followed," recounted Guidone. "It was straight up. Most of us were about to give up but we were determined to keep going as long as Walt was still on his feet." Near the summit Walt suddenly stopped and sat down, gasping hard. "This was the first time I ever saw Captain Walt halted in his tracks," said Guidone, "and it was just in time for us. But then shortly he was on his feet again and away he went to the top."[24]

The Samoan hills were alive with Raiders. "We are off on an overnight hike to Leopards Point which compels us to cross the mountains," recorded Private First Class Poppell in mid-May, adding, "The hike is very tiresome." Training intensified the next week. "We [now] have a schedule of from five in the morn to ten or twelve at night along such lines as: Rubber Boating, Judo, Bayonet Fighting, Stalking, Demolition, First Aid, Mountain Climbing, Communication work..."[25]

Red Mike Edson's insistence on effective communications was one of his distinctive characteristics. He had purposefully assembled a cracker-jack comm platoon, consisting of hard-nosed Lieutenant Bill Stevenson and a covey of bright, innovative youngsters. Taking a page from Edson's book, Stevenson insisted each member be able to operate and repair every piece of comm gear and become equally proficient with every infantry weapon (an investment that would yield great dividends at Guadalcanal).

Unfortunately, the field radio equipment available to the Marines in 1942–43 left much to be desired. In the boondocks, most of it proved bulky, erratic, and inadequately waterproofed. The TBX, the standard long-range radio (15–30 miles max), was perhaps the best of the lot, but it consisted of three large components weighing a total of 120 pounds and required a three-man team of operators/humpers. Corporal Fred Serral led one TBX team. He later recalled how diligently they prepared for combat. "We trained at night," he said, "and we had contests setting up our radio as quickly as possible and contacting a party on a designated frequency. With our equipment on our backs, we would march quietly to a chosen location, set up as fast as we could, and make contact. We repeated this process time and again until we could tear down, march, and set up again almost in our sleep."[26]

Edson demanded weapons proficiency on the part of all hands, from intelligence specialists to cooks and bakers. Private First Class Poppell's diary for mid-June contains a representative entry: "We fire the range with the various weapons. Practice wire cutting and problems under live fire."[27]

Most Raiders were proud of their field marksmanship with the bolt-action Springfield '03, the Browning Automatic Rifle, and the Colt automatic pistol. The venerable Springfield fired slowly, but its well-aimed rounds would have equal impact on an enemy five hundred yards down range. The reliable BAR would become a faithful friend on many a jungle patrol or night defensive line. The pistol? Well, at least it was highly portable.

Proficiency with the Browning air-cooled light machine gun, however, required the discipline that could only come from long practice. The piece was easy enough to lay, charge, and fire, but it took discipline to avoid firing wild fusillades and instead stick with methodical, ammo-saving, four-to-six-round bursts. And it took skilled fingers on the left hand to manipulate the elevating and traversing mechanism while the right hand carefully squeezed the trigger. When Corporal Gerry West abruptly found himself converted from mortar-man/demolitionist to machine gunner just before the Japanese attacked Edson's Ridge, the regular gunners let him stand the first watch of the night. "Just pull the trigger when they come," they cautioned him before they went to sleep. "Don't frig with the 'E and T.' We'll relieve you by the time you fire the second round!" (Which is exactly the way things happened that night.)[28]

One Raider firearm that drew a lot of attention was the exotic Boys .55 caliber bolt-action anti-tank (AT) rifle, a Canadian weapon requested by Edson. It was not a capricious selection. Steadied by its fold-down monopod, the Boys rifle could nail a target at 2,000 yards with an awesome 3,250 feet-per-second muzzle velocity (Carlson's Raiders would use their Boys weapons to destroy two Japanese seaplanes during the Makin Raid). Edson knew the Japanese typically reinforced their naval defense forces with light tanks and figured the weapons might come in handy some day. He didn't like the alternatives. There were then no bazookas available. "Neither the 20mm anti-aircraft/anti-tank gun nor the .50 caliber machine gun meet the requirements...of hand-carried mobility," Edson had written Holland Smith in early February, pointing out that the Boys weapon "has been used successfully by the British in France and Africa." As a result of this endorsement, the commandant authorized the 1st Raider Battalion a basic allowance of twelve Boys AT guns, and these they dutifully lugged from Tulagi to Bairoko. Yet the huge weapon, with its three-foot barrel and thirty-six-pound weight (Edson mistakenly thought it weighed twenty-three pounds), proved inappropriate in the jungle. The troops would rarely fire a round in anger.[29]

Soon the battalion's officers and designated NCOs traded in their Colt automatic pistols for the new M-50 Reising .45 caliber submachine guns. Admittedly an interim weapon until new carbines (or more old Thompsons) could reach the Fleet Marine Force, the Reising had a checkered history in its brief service with the Raiders.

The U.S. Army had rejected the Harrington and Richardson weapon, but the Marines had little choice. The Reising was available in large quan-

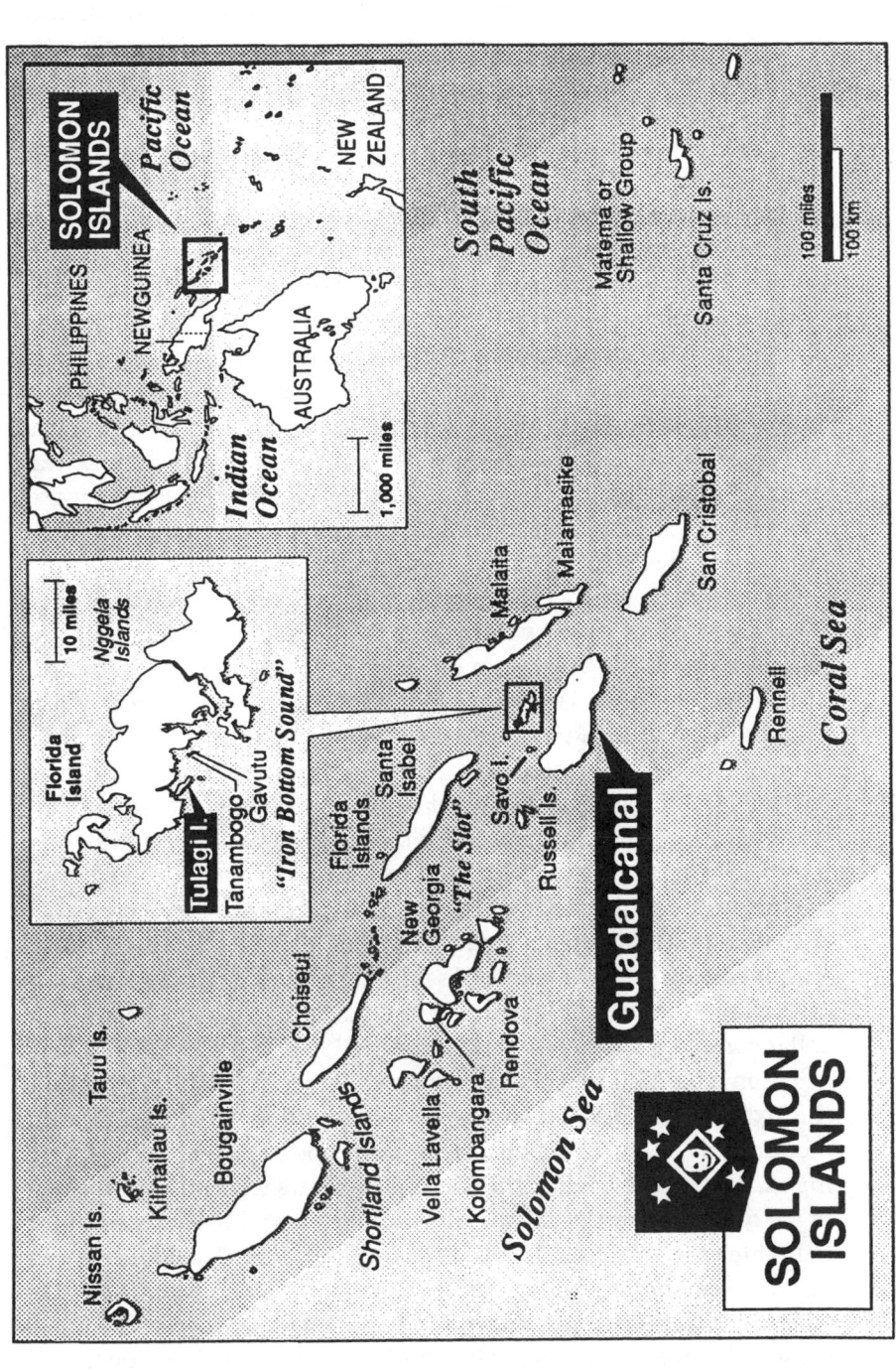

tities, performed promisingly on a stateside proving ground, and seemed an ideal weapon for jungle fighting. It was four pounds lighter than the Thompson, and because it fired from a closed bolt the weapon was uncommonly accurate for a submachine gun. But the Reising could not sustain heavy combat use in the jungle. So tightly designed were the tolerances between its bolt and locking recesses that the weapon would frequently malfunction amid the slightest dirt or debris. Nor could the magazines sustain rough handling. Many troops quickly lost confidence in their Reisings. Jumping Joe Chambers dismissed it as "a poor man's Thompson submachine gun." Sam Griffith called it "an absolute dud." Photographs taken of Raiders after the Battle of The Ridge portray a diminished number of Reisings in evidence. An exhausted Captain John Sweeney is shown with his Reising the day after the battle—and the corpsmen whom Edson had deliberately armed still found the Reising suitably handy—but a survey of post-battle photos of the mortar and machine gun sections reflect few Reisings, more BARs, and several of the rare but reliable M1941 Johnson light machine guns.[30]

Infantry firearms, including the Reising, came with bayonets because the U.S. armed forces knew in advance they would be fighting a foe who placed an almost spiritual valor on close combat with edged weapons.

In early 1941 army Lieutenant John Scofield published a widely-read essay in *The American Rifleman* describing the arms and equipment of the Japanese soldier. Reprinted after Pearl Harbor in a small field manual entitled *How the Japanese Army Fights*, the Scofield report described the emphasis placed by the Japanese on blade fighting. "They consider the bayonet the most essential weapon they carry," observed Scofield, "and are taught to indulge in bayonet sticking whenever they can close with the enemy." The lieutenant also described the antique, two-handed swords carried by descendants of samurai families, feudal blades sharp enough to "slice a handkerchief in mid-air, or part a man's body from collar bone to waist in a single clean slash."[31]

Edson taught his men to expect both the Japanese samurai sword and the sixteen-inch bayonet with its hooked quillon, used in a twisting motion at the moment of impact to disarm opponents for the kill. Knowing what to expect was half the battle, Edson taught them; knowing how to parry the enemy thrust and kill with one's own blade was the other half—plus the intestinal fortitude to finish the job. The Raiders commonly used the M1905 bayonets, even later in the war when they changed to M1 Garands. The old World War I blades were as long as those of the Japanese, and the Raiders kept them well-sharpened.

Edson's Raiders did not use the over-sized Bowie blades—the "Gung Ho knives"—that became the trademark of Carlson's 2d Raider Battalion. For awhile Edson's men carried the special USMC stiletto, a stabbing knife with a seven-inch blade, manufactured by Camilius Cutlery and modeled after the Fairbairn-Sykes design made popular by the British Commandos. The Raiders found the Marine stiletto to be well suited for silent killing but little use for anything else. Later in 1943 they would gratefully welcome the arrival of the ubiquitous Ka-Bar, the all-purpose field combat knife, lethal enough for hand-to-hand fighting, sturdy enough for campcraft jobs—opening rations, cutting tent pegs, even digging an emergency foxhole or latrine. The stiletto was too frail for any of these common tasks.

In time the Raiders came to value their personal edged weapons as dearly as any Japanese warrior. Tastes varied. The handful of Nicaraguan veterans in the ranks of Edson's Raiders preferred jungle machetes, equally effective for fighting or clearing fields of fire or chopping firewood. The Navy corpsmen made good use of their eleven-inch, snub-nosed bolo knives, sturdy tools as handy for self-defense as they were for lopping down saplings to improvise a stretcher.[32]

The Raiders never hesitated to let their officers know how they felt about the weapons and gear they were expected to carry into combat. Edson and Griffith listened. Even something as small and innocuous as the standard first aid packet became the focus of troop suggestions. By the time the Raiders landed on New Georgia, these small kits would be tailored for jungle warfare, including individual applications of both opium and morphine. Griffith for one paid close attention to what is commonly called "the soldier's load." "The whole equipment thing was a compromise from the very start," he stated. "We had to be lightly equipped, lightly armed....[The troops] have got enough to carry, in fact they've got too goddamn much to carry as it is."[33]

Each Raider undergoing training in Samoa and New Caledonia received his own toggle rope, about eight feet of heavy manila, formed with a toggle handle on one end, a loop on the other, and frequently knotted at intervals. The ropes proved very useful in ascending and descending steep grades and broken country. They also helped produce teamwork, the final goal of Edson's "post-graduate training." He knew the Raiders could fight as small units; now he challenged them to fight as a battalion.

The Raiders' realistic training took its toll. During Baker Company's 22 May live-firing exercise, Private Edward A. Chambers, twenty-nine, from Cleveland, was accidentally shot in the abdomen. He died the next day.

Edson wrote a condolence letter to his sister, telling her "your brother gave his life for his country fully as much as though he had died in battle."[34]

A month later, Corporal David R. Toland, twenty-three, also of Baker Company, tumbled down a 150-foot cliff and struck his head. The four-year veteran died the next day, leaving a young widow in Cambridge, Massachusetts. Another dangerous fall happened three weeks later. This time it was Gunnery Sergeant Tony Yelanich, the inspirational veteran of Edson's long-ago Coco River patrols. Yelanich broke his back and would be out of service for a full year. Edson was shaken. "I hate to lose him," he wrote his wife, "for he is one of my standbys."[35]

The Raiders were fortunate not to lose anyone to drowning. Rubber-boat practice occupied a prominent role in the training cycle. Samoa's plunging surf challenged every seaward or shoreward transit. Men and boats frequently took a beating. Gunnery Sergeant Stackpole, the "Admiral of the Condom Navy," naturally took concern over the condition of the latter. On one occasion, recorded in Lieutenant Peacock's diary, Edson came down to the beach to observe the day's boat training. Stackpole stood at the water's edge, arms akimbo, regarding his boats with a baleful eye. One Raider had the temerity to stand upright in his boat. Stackpole began wading out to yell at the miscreant. A Raider in front of Edson remarked, "I bet he's going to walk on the water!" Edson murmured, "a man hasn't done that for 2,000 years, so I doubt he will today." "Buddy," replied the trooper, still unaware he was addressing Edson, "stick around—you ain't never seen Stackpole when he's mad!"[36]

For Lieutenant John Erskine, the undersized Japanese linguist, Samoa represented boot camp, OCS, and Basic School, all in one. Erskine learned fast, but the rigorous training sapped his strength, and he came down with a respiratory ailment. A few days in the hospital restored him to duty but left him a ravenous appetite. He was chowing down wholeheartedly when Edson walked in the mess tent. "My God!" said Red Mike, "You're eating like a tiger!" "Sir," replied the diminutive lieutenant, "we're going into combat soon, and I want to at least rate a flesh wound!" He became "Tiger" Erskine for the rest of his life.[37]

Major Chester R. Allen, a former member of Edson's national rifle team, commanded the Marine barrage balloon squadron on Samoa. The light-fingered Raiders misappropriated some of the balloonists' tents one night. Allen knew his man. He gathered some whiskey, visited Edson, traded him the whiskey for the return of his tents. Allen later remarked, perhaps with grudging admiration, "The Raiders were the only ones that rated any alcohol. They had it in little ponies. It was their grog."[38]

Edson expended all his special services recreation funds on boxing gloves. The battalion held weekly smokers, widely popular with the Raiders. Horse Collar Smith, Lou Longo, and Joe Sciarra were some of the popular fighters. It was Smith's exhausting loss to Longo that earned Edson's crooked grin and admiration. The other boxers called Sciarra "Windmill" because of his wild roundhouse rights. Frank Guidone, who had boxed in amateur matches along the Ohio River as a teenager, won his weight class in the first two smokers. Joe Connolly appointed himself Guidone's manager for the finale against Charlie Company's stalwart, Greenwood, and he insisted his boxer enter the ring smoking a cigar. At the sight, the Able Company partisans hooted in delight, Captain Bailey and Charlie Company booed lustily, and Edson flashed his famous grin. Guidone lost, in a split decision, but it was a hell of a fight. One interested observer was Lieutenant Clay Boyd, the former regional boxing champ. A year later Boyd would pick Guidone and Sciarra for his long-range reconnaissance patrols behind Japanese lines on New Georgia.[39]

So popular were these battalion boxing smokers that the irrepressible Jinx Powers once again tempted fate. Assigned to a guard post the night of the final smoker, Powers decided "to hell with it," snuck off, joined the fun. The officer of the day brought charges against him for abandoning his post, "the United States then being in a state of war." Powers appeared before the battalion commander, knees knocking. Edson ordered ten days confinement on bread and water, saying, not unkindly, "This will make the fight tickets expensive." Powers knew he had been spared a big bullet.[40]

Raider Frank Fitz could claim the most memorable saga of Samoa. One day a native boy got himself painfully snagged in anti-invasion barbed wire and was about to drown in the surf. Fitz rescued the youngster, took him to the navy hospital to have his wounds stitched up, then carried him piggyback to his village. There he learned he'd saved the chief's son. Abruptly he was the village hero. The chief bestowed gifts on him—tapa cloth, a canoe, his delightful sixteen-year-old daughter Teealeetae. Young Fitz did not demur. For an idyllic week he would "escape and evade" from camp to meet Teealeetae in a nearby *fale*, thatched roof and all, provided by her obliging father. Then came the unsympathetic provost marshal. By then it was getting time for all members of Edson's Raiders to go to war. Fitz did so reluctantly.[41]

Red Mike Edson needed every man. He was still short-handed, even with the rear echelon issue settled and Sam Griffith and company underway in June from San Diego, finally bound for Samoa. Edson restlessly prowled other ships temporarily docking in port en route elsewhere in the South Pacific. In this fashion he "liberated" Lieutenant Houston Stiff from the transient 3d Battalion, 8th Marines, even though he had to leapfrog the brigade chief of staff to make it stick. A sweep of another ship by Major Bob Brown produced "Red" Hills, soon to prove himself quite a warrior at Tulagi and Guadalcanal.

While other commanders began to view Edson as the modern equivalent of the nineteenth-century Royal Navy "press gang," Red Mike kept raiding the troopships for more likely candidates. On one ship he found Ben Quintana, who admitted he had wanted to be a Raider since graduating from the San Diego Recruit Depot. Rejected by the 2d Raiders and depressed about the lost opportunity, Quintana shipped out for the Pacific as a faceless member of a replacement draft. Then Leiutenant Colonel Edson came aboard in Samoa asking for seven volunteers for hazardous duty with the 1st Raiders. "I don't recall whether I stepped forward or everybody else stepped backward," said Quintana, "but I was sure this is what I was looking for." In a flash Edson made him a Raider, gave him his distinctive toggle rope, and assigned him to a 60mm mortar section in Easy Company. Quintana was elated. "Then it was all business" he said, "Nothing but night hikes, rubber-boat landings, and mortar drills."[42]

For all of his focus on training and sector security, Edson kept a close eye on intelligence reports of the Japanese offensive in the Central Pacific as it boiled to a crisis during the first week of June 1942. A Japanese victory over the still-crippled U.S. Pacific Fleet appeared likely. In that event, Edson realized, their thinly-held outpost at Samoa would soon be vulnerable to the irresistible Imperial tidal wave.

The aura of subsequent U.S. victories in the Pacific War has diminished the impact of the Battle of Midway, but the surprising defeat of Yamamoto was a stunning triumph at the time. Jumping Joe Chambers remembered how Edson gave him the news: "I'll never forget Eddie coming to us and in one of the few times I ever saw him show emotion, he said, 'It was a clean sweep! They got all the Jap carriers, and we'll be moving up!'"[43]

## A Strategic Crisis

Edson was correct about the change in momentum, but the Raiders' first combat commitment would take another two months. Edson likely chafed at the fact that the first Raiders to see combat were two companies of Carlson's 2d Battalion, hurriedly dispatched by Nimitz to Midway to stiffen the island's defenses in the face of the pending Japanese invasion. Captain John Apergis, the former company commander in Edson's 1st Separate Battalion, led one of the companies to Midway and may have garnered the honor of firing the Raiders' first shot in anger. Under heavy air attack during the onset of the battle, Apergis shared a foxhole with a machine gunner from another command. An Imperial Navy fighter pilot targeted the gunpit for a low-level strafing run. The Marines' machine gun malfunctioned at the worst possible time. Apergis gulped but drew his pistol and blazed away at the onrushing Zero, bravely but futilely. It was a hell of a way to start the war.[44]

Admiral Nimitz continued to think of ways to employ the Raiders he had demanded. In late April he had proposed to Admiral King the use of Raiders against installations "in the Japanese homeland." This was pure fantasy, possibly influenced by the euphoria following the Doolittle Raid that same week. Soon Nimitz would realize from radio intercepts and ship movements how much Doolittle and Halsey had spooked and embarrassed the Japanese high command. The Imperial Navy committed many more ships and aircraft to patrolling the home waters. There was little chance of another stealthy approach to the homeland, even to deliver a small detachment of Raiders. Nimitz was a bold but sensible commander. In late May he proposed to General MacArthur (whose domain, to that point, included the Solomon Islands) that the 1st Marine Raider Battalion attack the new Japanese seaplane base at Tulagi. As Nimitz envisioned the mission, the Raiders could destroy the facility, then be replaced by army occupation troops under MacArthur. But MacArthur replied he had no troops to spare, and Admiral King fretted about the lack of Allied air cover, although he admitted a "disabling or destroying raid" might suffice in lieu of permanent occupation. The Raiders, frustrated by these postponements, would get their crack at Tulagi—but not as a solo act.[45]

On 14 June the advance elements of the 1st Marine Division under Major General Alexander A. Vandegrift arrived in New Zealand. Vandegrift's command was still a work in progress, still rebuilding from the turmoil of spinning off the 1st Raiders and the 7th Marines. Vandegrift looked forward to a six-month grace period to conduct advanced amphibious training before commitment to combat.

Two weeks later, Allied intelligence agents reported startling news. The Japanese had crossed Sealark Channel from Tulagi and were constructing a bomber strip on Guadalcanal.

The news could scarcely have been any worse. A bomber strip on the far southeastern edge of the Japanese perimeter represented a much more serious threat to the Allies than did the seaplanes at Tulagi. Bombers based on Guadalcanal would force a critical eastward "bulge" in the vital sealanes between the United States and New Zealand and Australia. An operational bomber strip on Guadalcanal would also encourage a return of Japanese carrier task forces to the Coral Sea and thus pose a grave threat to New Caledonia, Samoa, and Fiji. To his consternation, Vandegrift learned that his short-handed division must be ready to execute a forcible landing on Guadalcanal and Tulagi in little more than a month.

By all standards of amphibious doctrine, Operation Watchtower, the campaign for Guadalcanal, should never have been executed. The Allied invasion force lacked command of the sea, command of the air, sufficient amphibious ships and landing craft, adequate maps, and most intelligence information on enemy order of battle, capabilities, and intentions. The wondrous undercover system of British and Commonwealth "coastwatchers" would prove invaluable, but the key agent on Guadalcanal, Martin Clemens, had sprained an ankle and was off the air. Essential combat equipment was in such short supply that the troops would quickly dub the campaign "Operation Shoestring." The amphibious force commander, brilliant, arrogant Rear Admiral Kelly Turner, would not be able to meet with Vandegrift and his staff until 24 July, two weeks before the landings. Vandegrift's unity of command was a patchwork quilt—lacking the 7th Marines in Samoa, but reinforced by the assignment of the 2d Marines, the 1st Parachute Battalion, and Merritt Edson's 1st Marine Raider Battalion.

One thing was certain. Several hundred *rikusentai,* the Japanese Special Naval Landing Forces, would be defending Tulagi, making the small island a tough nut to crack. The island's reefs and coral heads would limit any landing to light forces. Vandegrift and his staff earmarked Edson's Raiders to seize Tulagi from the beginning. In time, the 2d Battalion, 5th Marines drew the assignment of following the Raiders ashore at Tulagi, while the Parachute Battalion would assault the twin islands of Gavutu and Tanambogo, and elements of the 2d Marines would seize key outposts in the neighboring Florida Islands, prepared to reinforce anyone who ran into trouble.

Vandegrift and his staff respected the extensive training Edson's battalion had achieved in night landings with rubber boats. They proposed a predawn assault. Kelly Turner refused. His ships would require daylight to navigate the shallow waters and reefs around Tulagi to launch and

An "Able-Peter-Dog" in the South Pacific, the beloved USS *Gregory* (APD-3).

control boats and provide close-in naval gunfire. A morning landing would suffice. The Marines won their argument for landing on the island's south shore, a more difficult approach but the complete opposite of where the Japanese *rikusentai* had landed in early May.[46]

The Tulagi mission pleased Edson. It was hardly a raid, but he had confidence that the Raiders would function well as a conventional battalion under these conditions. It might even be possible to seize the place early enough on D-Day to be able to lend a hand across the channel at Guadalcanal in case the 1st and 5th Marines encountered stiff resistance.

Abruptly, the passage of time, which had been languishing on Samoa, began to accelerate.

## On to Westward

The 1st Marine Raider Battalion finally regained its full organizational strength on 3 July when the transport *Heywood* docked at Tutuila, Samoa, with Sam Griffith's rear echelon, all present or accounted for. There was no time for a reunion. On the 4th of July (one year to the day before a markedly different 1st Raider Battalion would sail for New Georgia), Edson loaded the main body on board the transport. The next day the Raiders took one last fond look at Samoa as the island slowly disappeared beyond *Heywood*'s fantail.

The Raiders arrived in Nouméa, New Caledonia, on 10 July 1942. The French colonial island would be their advance training base for each operation in the Solomons, and here they would eventually spend forty-five weeks in three separate increments. This time, however, they would remain barely twelve days. The Raiders hurriedly established a bare-bones tent camp and launched a final round of company and battalion-level training.

The rapid expansion of the Marine Corps in 1942 led to unexpectedly early promotions for many of the Raiders: Edson to colonel, Griffith to lieutenant colonel, and Walt, Bailey, and Chambers to major. All five officers were abruptly too senior for their assigned billets and thus vulnerable to transfer, but Edson had foreseen the situation and arranged special consideration on the basis of his anticipated dangerous and likely fragmented missions. In addition, two colorful sergeants, James "Red" Sullivan and Astle "Spike" Ryder, became the first of many Raider NCOs to receive direct, meritorious commissions as lieutenants based on Edson's recommendations.[47]

Edson made last minute reassignments. Impressed with the leadership of Jumping Joe Chambers—and still cool to the unproven capabilities of Captain Jake Irwin—Edson reassigned Chambers to command Irwin's newly arrived Dog Company, made Irwin the Battalion Quartermaster, and rewarded Captain George Herring with command of Easy Company's weaponeers.

The Raiders of Dog Company, comfortable with Irwin's laid-back style, were taken aback by the hard-charging Chambers. Jumping Joe quickly challenged his platoon commanders and squad leaders to meet him at the top of the highest nearby peak by noon or lose their jobs. It was hardly fair. Dog Company had lost its physical edge during the long journey by train and ship from Quantico to New Caledonia, while Chambers had developed the legs and lungs of a mountain goat in the highlands of Samoa. But these men had their own Raider pride—damned if they were going to let this smart-mouth new major run them into the ground. All hands scaled the 1,500-foot peak on time, panting heavily but impressing Chambers.

Nor would Lew Walt let his rival gain bragging rights. As Able Company's Private First Class Poppell recorded in his diary, "We climb the mountain behind our camp which the army told us a couple of days ago was impossible to climb."[48]

Lieutenant Colonel Merrill B. Twining, assistant operations officer, 1st Marine Division, visited Edson on New Caledonia fresh from a hair-raising reconn flight in a B-17 over Tulagi and Guadalcanal. Twining expressed concern that the division had no contact with Martin Clemens on Guadalcanal. Edson offered to send in a patrol of Raiders to find the elusive coastwatcher. Twining liked the idea and made arrangements for either a submarine from Townsville, Australia, or a small boat to deliver the patrol by dark of night.

Edson gave this mission to Lieutenant Ed Wheeler of Dog Company. Platoon Sergeant Gene Martin was one of several other Raiders picked to accompany him. The men disappeared for several days to rehearse for their night landing. Twining for his part had no trouble getting approval from General Vandegrift but failed to get the patrol cleared through Vice Admiral Robert L. Ghormley, commanding the South Pacific Area. "Too dangerous," said Ghormley. "Dangerous?" fumed Twining. "This patrol would've been a piece of cake for Edson's men." Martin recalled Edson's words of consolation: "The time tables have been changed. We are ALL going to move out now." Watchtower was underway, and the division would find Clemens forthwith.[49]

Edson and Griffith had done all they could to prepare their Raiders for combat against the Japanese. By every imaginable measure of combat readiness, the 1st Marine Raider Battalion was as well-trained, well-led, physically fit, and highly motivated as any untested battalion in the South Pacific. Edson assembled the outfit after a particularly grueling all-night exercise. "I'm ready to stack you men up alongside any other outfit in the world," he said with obvious pride. "The next time we pull this operation it'll be for keeps."[50]

Shortly, the battalion left the boondocks and returned to Nouméa to board its assault shipping. The men were delighted to find their old standbys, the same APDs with whom they had made so many cold-weather landings along the Atlantic coast. The sailors made them welcome. Edson established his command post on board USS *Little*.

At first the ships steamed east. After several days they joined up with an enormous task force. Private First Class Poppell recorded the thrill: "Ship after ship breaks over the horizon—five, ten, twenty, seventy—God knows how many more!" The amphibious task force branched off for rehearsal landings at Koro, Fiji. Vandegrift would call the rehearsal a "disaster," and Edson would grow morose at the chaos, but the Raiders-

APD team worked well, reflecting their long hours together the preceding fall and winter. Raider Herbert L. Coffin reported all went well at first, the Higgins boats towing strings of rafts as usual, but then the navy boat commander misread the distance to the beach and cast off the towlines way too far at sea. "We had to paddle forever—it was supposed to be a night landing but we didn't reach shore until morning."[51]

Sobered by this ragged experience, the amphibious task force patched up its boats, amended its plans, and swung westward for the long haul across the Coral Sea towards the southern Solomons. Only then did the rank and file learn their destination and mission. The paucity of maps did not help with troop orientation. Sam Griffith's ship was fortunate to have three British colonial officers embarked who knew the lower Solomons intimately. They drew and distributed first-rate maps of Tulagi, then built a three-dimensional, ten-foot-long, sand-table model of the island. The Raiders on other ships were much less fortunate.

Edson gave thought to his communications and announced a series of code names for the key officers should it become necessary to establish quick authenticity. He, of course, was Red Mike. Sam Griffith was easy: Sam Griff. Ken Bailey became Ken Dill, Lew Walt became Silent Lew, Joe Chambers became Joe Pots (for Chamber Pot), and Lieutenant John Sweeney became John Wolf. The simple system would twice prove invaluable: on Tulagi, and again during the second night at Edson's Ridge.[52]

D-Day for Watchtower was set for 7 August 1942, exactly eight months after the Pearl Harbor disaster. The assault landings on Tulagi and Guadalcanal would represent America's first offensive against the Japanese.

The task force entered the Solomon Sea under a providential cloud bank and remained undetected by Japanese patrol aircraft. The Raiders drew ammunition and grenades the night before the landing. Several men, among them Jack F. Tracy of Company A, remember the word being passed not to take any Japanese prisoners.[53]

There was one more touch. Each Raider received a sixteen-inch square of burlap to wear as a cover on his steel helmet during the battle. Some smeared the material with green paint. Others cut strips in the rear and let them dangle below the collar. Those on board USS *Little* tried not to snicker at the sight of Red Mike Edson in his bulky burlap. The troops already dubbed him "Eddy the Mole" because the M1 helmet dwarfed his diminutive head; the burlap heightened the effect. But Colonel Edson was all business now. He knew from experience what most of his men did not. After tomorrow, nothing would ever be the same again....

## Notes

1. Maj. Gen. Holcomb to Maj. Gen. Clayton Vogel, 10 February 1942, 2, Record Group 127, Box 1806, WNRC.
2. Henry C. Poppell, "My Stretch in the Service," unpublished manuscript, 1 April 1942 entry [Poppell Diary].
3. *Ibid.*, 2 April and 3 April 1942 entries.
4. *Ibid.*, 12 April 1942 entry.
5. Tom Bartlett, "Tiger Erskine," *Leatherneck*, April 1984, 40–43. Erskine would retire from active duty in 1946 as a colonel, then continue to serve the country as an intelligence officer.
6. Edson to CMC, "Revisions in T/O and TBA, Marine Raider Battalions," 7 April 1942, Box 3, Serial 127-6587, WNRC.
7. Edson to CG, Amphibious Corps, Pacific Fleet, "Movement of Rear Echelon," 9 April 1942, Edson Papers, Personal Files, Box 4, Library of Congress.
8. Paul H. Silverstone, *U.S. Warships of World War II* (New York: Doubleday, 1968), 335–341; interviews with veterans of the USS *Zeilin* Association and the 2d Marine Division Association during the writing of *Utmost Savagery: The Three Days of Tarawa* during 1993–1995. Most transports were converted to APAs (attack transports) during February 1943 with the addition of Welin boat davits and additional antiaircraft weapons. USS *Zeilin* became APA 3 at that point.
9. Jinx Powers interview with Jon T. Hoffman, 24 August 1991.
10. Poppell Diary, entries for 12–28 April 1942.
11. James E. Blessing to Jon T. Hoffman, February 1992; Peatross, *Bless 'em All*, Chapter 3; Frank Guidone to John Sweeney, 1995. HQMC changed the Raider battalion table of organization on 27 May 1942, replacing the 81mm mortar platoon with a demolitions platoon.
12. "Fighting Men Off to Battle," Washington *Times-Herald*, 24 April 1942. Clipping in author's possession.
13. Commander Transport Division Eleven to Commander Transports Amphibious Force U.S. Atlantic Fleet, "Training Exercises with Embarked Marines during 21–30 April 1942," and CO, 1st Marine Raider Battalion (Rear Echelon) to CG, Amphibious Corps, Atlantic Fleet, "Ship-to-Shore Training in Solomon's Island area during 21-30 April 1942," both documents from Operations and Training File, Box 1, Serial 63A-2535, WNRC. The navy document closed with the recommendation that extensive rehearsals would be required to attain "perfect timing, particularly if stealth and surprise are to be used." Excellent advice. There would never be enough time....
14. Battalion Muster Roll, April 1942: "14–30 April: Maj. Griffith observing 2d Raider Battalion training at San Diego."
15. Griffith Oral Memoir, 1976, MCOHC, MCHC, 79; Holcomb to Edson, "Rear Echelon, 1st Marine Raider Battalion," 20 April 1942, Box 2, Serial 63A-2535, WNRC.

16. RDD Tutuila Samoa to CMC, info CINCPAC 181135, May 1942, Box 1, Serial 127-93-0051, WNRC.

17. Holcomb to King, "Personnel for Samoa," 16 May 1942; King to Holcomb, same subject, 18 May 1942; both documents from Box 45, Serial 65A-5188, WNRC.

18. Poppell Diary, entries 28–29 April 1942.

19. Sterling W. Schaar, "Brief History of the U.S. Marines, The British Commandos," *Dope Sheet,* May 1985, 11, 16; Griffith Oral Memoir, 1976, MCOHC, MCHC, 72.

20. James V. Mallamas interview with Jon T. Hoffman, 1991; Anthony Massar to Jon T. Hoffman, 1992; Jinx Powers interview with Jon T. Hoffman, 24 August 1991.

21. Chambers Oral Memoir, MCOHC, MCHC, 286–88; Dr. Robert Skinner interview with Jon T. Hoffman, 1992; Poppell Diary, 9–12 June 1942.

22. James Smith to author, 9 April 1999.

23. Poppell Diary, 30 April–7 May 1942; Guidone Memoirs, 1992.

24. Guidone Memoirs, 1992.

25. Poppell Diary, 18–25 May 1942.

26. Fred A. Serral to author, 9 April 1999; see also Serral to Pete Pettus, "A TBX Team on the Tasimboko Raid," n.d.

27. Poppell Diary, 13–17 June 1942.

28. Gerald V. West to author, 9 April 1999.

29. Raider Battalion Table of Organization D-175 (and Raider Rifle Company D-169), both dated 12 February 1942, author's possession; Bruce N. Canfield, *U.S. Infantry Weapons of World War II* (Lincoln, RI: Andrew Mobray Publishers, 1994), 210–11, 289 [Canfield, *Infantry Weapons*]; CO, 1st Separate Battalion to CG, Amphibious Force, Atlantic Fleet, "Recommended Organization for a Battalion Embarked on Destroyer Transport," 8 February 1942, 6, Raider Battalion Correspondence File, Archives Section, MCHC. Canfield mistakenly lists the Boys AT rifle's weight as fifty-six pounds on page 289; page 210 shows the correct weight of thirty-six pounds. Canada's Inglis Corporation manufactured the Mark I Boys AT rifles used by the Raiders.

30. Canfield, *Infantry Weapons*, 148–155; Justice M. Chambers Oral Memoir, MCOHC, MCHC, 311; Samuel B. Griffith Oral Memoir, 1976, MCOHC, MCHC, 99.

31. Paul W. Thompson, Harold Doud, and John Scofield, *How the Japanese Army Fights* (Washington, D.C.: Infantry Journal Press, 1942), 35–36.

32. Canfield, *Infantry Weapons*, 15–48. The author is indebted to Lt. Col. James C. Hitz, USMC (Ret.), an arms collector and ordnance scholar, for his contributions here.

33. Samuel B. Griffith Oral Memoir, 1976, MCOHC, MCHC, 99.

34. Casualty Card, Edward A. Chambers, author's possession; Edson to Mrs. Hennessey, 7 June 1942, Box 4, Personal Files, Edson Papers, Library of Congress.

35. Casualty Card, Daniel R. Toland. Edson to Mrs. Edson, 21 July 1942, Box 2, Family Correspondence, Edson Papers, Library of Congress. An earlier letter from Edson to his wife in this file (4 July 1942) mentions the loss of Corporal Toland and said the troops were collecting money to send his widow.

36. Peacock Diary, 11 June 1942.

37. Bartlett, "Tiger Erskine," 41.

38. Maj. Gen. Chester R. Allen Oral Memoir, MCOHC, MCHC, 145.

39. Guidone Memoirs, 1992, and interviews with author, March 1999.

40. Jinx Powers interview with Jon T. Hoffman, 24 August 1991.

41. Frank Fitz to John Sweeney, 16 November 1992; David Robinson, "Marine Raiders," *Marine Corps League,* Spring 1992, 27.

42. Houston Stiff interview with Jon T. Hoffman, 17 September 1991; Guidone Memoirs, 1992; Ben Quintana to Irv Reynolds, 13 August 1991.

43. Chambers Oral Memoir, MCOHC, MCHC, 290.

44. John Apergis letter, 10 June 1991, page V, as forwarded to Thomas Mullahey 25 November 1991 by James Childs.

45. George C. Dyer, *The Amphibians Came to Conquer* (reprint edition, Washington, D.C.: HQMC, 1991), Vol I, 257; Griffith, *The Battle of Guadalcanal* , 25.

46. Claffy Papers, Marine Corps Personal Papers Collection, MCHC.

47. James Sullivan to John Sweeney, 1991.

48. Gene C. Martin interview with Jon T. Hoffman, 1991; Poppell Diary, 15 July 1942.

49. Gene C. Martin to Jon T. Hoffman, 7 June 1991; Merrill B. Twining, *No Bended Knee* (Novato: Presidio Press, 1996), 39–41.

50. Doying, "Red Mike and his Do or Die Men," 15.

51. Poppell Diary, 26 July 1942; Griffith, *Guadalcanal,* 36; Griffith Oral Memoir, MCOHC, MCHC, 81–82; Herbert L. Coffin interview with Jon T. Hoffman, 1991.

52. Houston Stiff interview with Jon T. Hoffman, 17 September 1991.

53. Jack T. Tracy interview with Jon T. Hoffman, 1992.

# 4

## Assault on Tulagi, August 1942

*This is war, boys—nothing like starting it in a graveyard!*

Marine Gunner Cecil H. Clark, 3d Platoon, Baker Company
D-Day, Tulagi, 7 August 1942[1]

PRIVATE ASHLEY RAY LARGE of Able Company, slim, seventeen, a farm boy from Pigeon Forge, Tennessee, listened intently as his platoon commander gave his final briefing the night before D-Day at Tulagi. "By this time tomorrow," the officer said matter-of-factly, "some of you will be dead." Ash Large swallowed hard.[2]

On D-Day morning, Private First Class Vincent H. D. Cassidy of Baker Company, eighteen, a budding poet (and future professor of medieval history) from Manchester, New Hampshire, spider-walked over the side of USS *Colhoun* (APD 2) and into the bobbing Higgins boat alongside. The noise alone was unnerving. Fire support ships nearby blasted Tulagi; planes shrieked overhead, bombing and strafing the island. "Waiting," Cassidy later recorded. "Wondering if my grin looked as sickly as the others in the boat. Knowing it did. To the shore. A crunching noise, over the side and scrambling to land, looking for cover..."[3]

Private First Class Thomas D. ("T. D.") Smith of Dog Company, eighteen, an assistant squad leader, waited tensely in the crowded troop compartment of USS *McKean* (APD 5). Finally came the word to debark. "As we passed across the deck," Smith recorded, "the sailors clapped us on the back and said 'Give 'em hell—see you tonight,' and Morgan, the cook, said 'Chocolate cake tonight!' (we got the word somewhere that this was a six-hour raid). Over the side, fix bayonets, head for shore. Lieutenant Neuffer passed the word to keep down. I remember: how easily a

80

burst of machine gun could kill us all. *Why weren't they firing at us?*"[4]

The American invasion force caught the Japanese flat-footed in the southern Solomons, achieving both strategic and tactical surprise. The local Japanese commander on Tulagi could hardly believe his eyes when dawn revealed Sealark Channel swarming with enemy warships. Then American F4F Wildcats and SBD Dauntless divebombers streaked overhead—unequivocal evidence of a carrier task force in proximity. Numerous transports appeared, anchored, began launching boats laden with troops. This was no raid.

Radio Tulagi broadcast an emergency report to Rabaul at 0705: "Enemy task force...attacking Tulagi, undergoing severe bombings, landing preparations under way; help requested." Minutes later came a final message: "Enemy troop strength is overwhelming. We will defend to the last man."[5]

Both of the latter statements proved factual. Although the several hundred veteran *rikusentai* of the 3d Kure Special Naval Landing Force would sell their lives dearly in the next week, they were spread too thinly among the contested islands to prevent the 1st Marine Division's capture of Tulagi and establishment of a beachhead on Guadalcanal. The success of this unexpected amphibious assault would provide just enough momentum for the Allies to hold onto Guadalcanal—with its strategic prize, the airfield—against all the forces of hell that the Japanese in Rabaul could muster. In many respects, the six-month struggle for Guadalcanal proved to be as significant a turning point in the Pacific War as the Battle of Midway.

The D-Day assaults succeeded despite a complicated, five-phased landing plan, the collective inexperience of the invasion force, and a significant shortage of boats. Kelly Turner's decision to rule out a night landing on Tulagi by the Raiders had the effect of increasing the demand for Higgins boats, because using rubber boats in a daylight assault would have been suicidal. The Raiders assaulted Tulagi in ramp-less, first-model Higgins boats (the ramped LCVPs by Andrew Higgins had yet to arrive). When coral outcroppings grounded the boats several hundred yards offshore, the troops had to execute a clumsy exit over the gunwales into armpit-deep water and wade ashore, the smaller men bobbing along on their tiptoes. But Merritt Edson had chosen the southwest "beach" for its very unlikeliness. Aerial photographs revealed Japanese defenses oriented towards the north coast. The Raiders came in the back door without losing a man.

Breaking out the live ammunition the night before Tulagi.

General Vandegrift deduced from his skimpy intelligence reports that the smaller, hillier, cave-dotted islands of Tulagi and Gavutu-Tanambogo would be harder to take, and he purposefully assigned these missions to his best trained units: Edson's Raiders, the 1st Parachute Battalion, the 2d Battalion, 5th Marines ("2/5"), and elements of the 2d Marines.

At Tulagi, the Raiders led with Baker and Dog companies landing abreast across "Blue Beach" at 0800, followed directly by the other two rifle companies, then the remnants of Easy Company (whose machine-gun platoons were attached to the rifle companies). The leading units climbed the parallel ridge and cut the island in two, then reformed, swung eastward, with all four companies on line. Lieutenant Colonel Harold E. Rosecrans' 2/5 followed the Raiders ashore in trace, initially turned left to secure the island's west end, then reversed direction to reinforce the Raiders later in the fight.

South of Tulagi at Guadalcanal, the 5th and 1st Marines landed against slight opposition; the next day they seized the airstrip. The only D-Day landing to run into trouble occurred at Gavutu, mainly because there were insufficient boats available to land the 1st Parachute Battalion simultaneously with everyone else. The *rikusentai* on Gavutu had plenty of warning to prepare fields of fire from their cave-emplaced machine guns. The parachutists stepped into a buzz saw. Their fight for the twin islands took two full days and proved extremely costly.

On Tulagi all went well until the Raiders reached a phase line that ran from the wharf along the eastern nose of the long ridge. The real battle began here.

The Tulagi defenders were veteran *rikusentai,* too professional to panic at the surprise landing over their one undefended beach, and now very determined to inflict pain on their visitors.

Edson and Griffith had expected a tough fight. Both men had closely observed Imperial Japanese fighting men in combat against the Chinese five years earlier. They were not surprised by the deadly pockets of Nambu machine guns firing from camouflaged log-and-coral fortifications and protected by marksmen tied to treetops in the vicinity (the combination which on a larger scale at Bairoko the next year would stymie the Raiders). Nor were they surprised by the enemy's systematic night attacks, always probing for unit boundaries and automatic weapons positions, and frequently preceded by a "noise campaign" to unnerve or distract the defenders. Lieutenant John ("Black Jack") Salmon of Charlie Company endured his first night in combat against the Japanese with aplomb, largely because Edson had warned his men to expect the "noise campaign" and maintain fire discipline.[6]

Yet there was one dramatic element of the Japanese defense of Tulagi that neither Edson nor Griffith nor anyone else in the Pacific antici-pated. The Japanese defenders on small islands, from Tulagi and Gavutu to Tarawa and Saipan, would fight to the death—or commit suicide—rather than surrender. For the Americans, nothing distinguished the Pacific War from that against the Germans more than this incompre-hensible policy of *gyokusai*—no surrender. The battles for the small islands of Tulagi and Gavutu-Tanambogo may have been relatively small in scale, but to the discerning observer they provided a sobering foretaste of the battles to come across the Central Pacific. In short, it was at Tulagi that the Japanese first demonstrated those attributes that would make the future, larger battles so bloody—disciplined marksmanship, a pro-clivity for night-fighting, an uncanny ability to dig sunken fortifications, and their unearthly commitment to *gyokusai*.[7]

Tulagi was the first of three battles the 1st Marine Raider Battalion would wage against the Japanese Special Naval Landing Forces. Each would be characterized by vicious, point-blank, bloody fighting.

### First Blood

The Japanese offered no main line of resistance at Tulagi, as they would at Bairoko the following year. Instead they manned a scattering of improvised outposts—caves, ditches, small hills, a few buildings—to slow the Raiders' advance until dark when they could launch a counterattack out of the steep ravines. Edson controlled the advance and called in naval gunfire as needed, but the Raiders initially fought more as squads than as a battalion.

The war began for T.D. Smith's squad of Dog Company as soon as they dashed across the exposed bridge over the north-south road cut. "As we cleared the bridge," he said, "we started taking fire from the right and right front. Flanagan in front of me was hit in the neck and rolled down the bank. I stopped momentarily to make him comfortable. He was paralyzed. Adams had gone to throw a couple grenades into the house. As he returned he was hit three times in the back from the same house." Smith's squad sought shelter in a shell hole, dangerously concentrated. Jumping Joe Chambers tumbled into the hole, sized up the situation, pointed forward. "He ordered us to move out 'right now and to hell with the fire.' The rest of the day was a nightmare."[8]

Baker Company's advance was held up when word reached Major Nickerson that the rear guard had captured some Japanese. "Shoot 'em," said Nickerson reflexively, then thought it through and belayed the order. Good thing. The prisoners turned out to be a Japanese family—a terrified mother and several small kids. The Marines, legendary softies around kids, gave away their secretly-stashed chocolate bars to stem the tears. Tiger Erskine arrived, spoke comforting words in Japanese, and led them to a secure place.

Private First Class Herbert L. Coffin, a BAR-man in Baker Company, being too far in the rear of the column to share his chocolate bar with the Japanese children, paused to consume his treat for "lunch." He noticed an unremarkable cave opening in the face of the small cliff that paralleled the trail but gave it little thought since the entire company had just passed by it without incident. Suddenly he saw a faint movement in the shadows, then a helmet, a pointing weapon. Coffin swore, swung his BAR towards the cave, took a split-second to focus on his front sight blade—then felt a searing pain in his shoulder. "A sniper hidden above the cave zapped me," he said. Coffin yelled for help before he hit the ground. "Maurice Pion came back, grabbed the BAR and began firing at the cave." More than a dozen Japanese boiled out of the small opening.

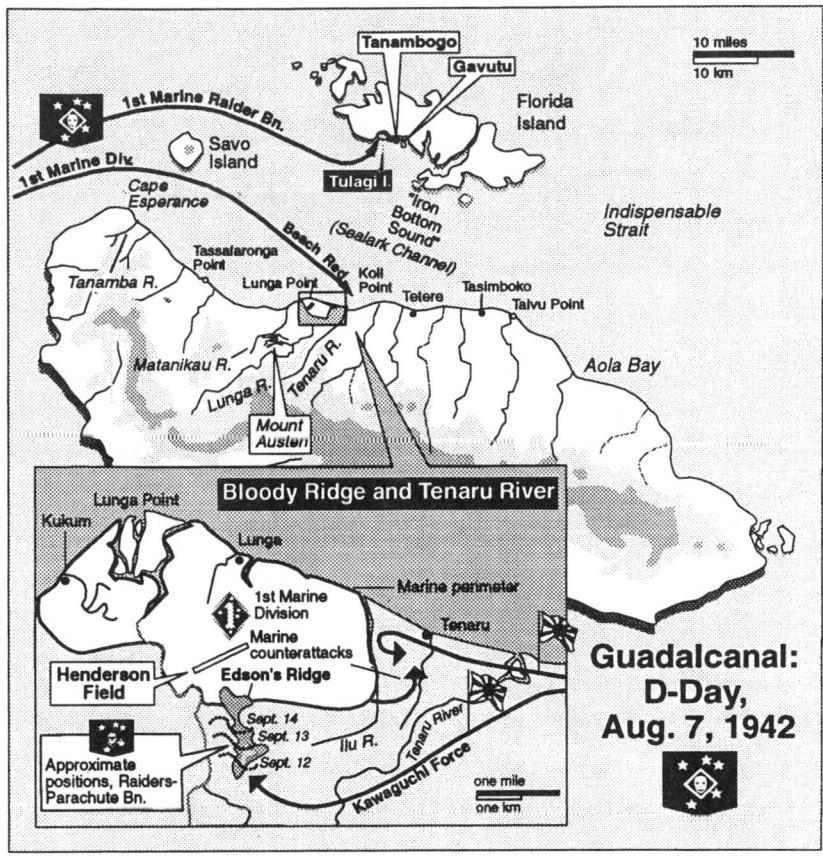

Some dropped in the furious fusillade; others disappeared, only to pop up again from atop the cliff, rifles blazing. Another Marine went down. Heavy firing erupted along a fifty-yard stretch. Lieutenant Rex Crockett's platoon was abruptly cut off from the rest of Baker Company.[9]

It was not a perfect ambush. The *rikusentai* had likely established it in haste when they discovered the Americans were coming at them from an unexpected direction. Private First Class Coffin's detection of the first hidden gunner had triggered it prematurely. Now there was hell to pay.

The ensuing firefight proved so vivid to Private First Class Vince Cassidy that he would shortly express his emotions in award-winning poetry. His first reaction, naturally, was fear; then, immediate action. "Still no sign," he recalled. "Then suddenly shots, shouts, screams....Other shouts, from which we knew that Gilligan was badly hit....the desperate feeling that something had to be done." Cassidy shook off his temporary paralysis, began scaling the cliff, aware of a sniper nearby "and the grateful realization that he wasn't a very good shot." He reached the crest, lobbed two hand grenades, slid down for more, retraced his climb, threw these as well. "I don't believe any of us in the squad had ever thrown live grenades before." The first time proved a charm. The Japanese broke contact, the platoon moved on, but Private John J. Gilligan, nineteen, from East Orange, New Jersey, would die from his wounds on board the troopship *Neville* the following day.[10]

Baker Company's first hour of combat was proving a costly introduction. Just as the first platoon swept through the boat docks on the northeast shore, Japanese fire caught them in the open. A Marine went down, mortally wounded, in the field. The others took cover behind a retaining wall. The Japanese riflemen knew from experience that their opponents would soon cross the wall in an attempt to rescue the wounded man. They took aim and waited.

First Lieutenant Eugene M. ("Tex") Key, a twenty-five-year-old preacher's son from Dallas, had a tough decision to make. Both his company commander, Major Nickerson, and the executive officer, Captain Louis Monville, were nearby, urging him to get his platoon moving forward again, but Key sensed they were facing a shooting gallery. Key ordered BAR-man John A. Van Ness to lead the way over the wall, then changed his mind. "Stay here and cover me," Key told Van Ness and leapt over the wall. One step more and he was down, shot in the chest, fatally. Private Thomas F. Nickel of Lansing, Michigan, tried to follow his lieutenant. An Arisaka rifle cracked, killing Nickel instantly. At this, Navy Lieutenant Junior Grade Samuel S. Miles, twenty-eight, Princeton-educated, a graduate of Johns Hopkins Medical School, and the battalion's junior surgeon, grabbed his black bag and struggled over the wall to attend to Key and Nickel. The Arisaka spoke again, killing Doctor Miles. Three shots, three dead Raiders.

The Raiders were stunned, then enraged. Their sergeants kicked them into action, sent them streaming along both ends of the sea wall, seeking an angle on the shooters. One sharp-eyed Marine spotted a sniper lying prone behind a barrel. Key's platoon riddled both barrel and sniper. A second *rikusentai* tried to dash to cover in a large crack in the opposing cliff. The Raiders' fire caught him just as he was trying to squeeze inside, virtually nailing him to the rock. The company crossed the wall and moved inland, shaken by their abrupt losses—and the Japanese marksmanship.[11]

Tulagi as a battlefield had plenty of thick underbrush and head-high grass, but some of the bloodiest fighting that first afternoon occurred in and around the cleared fields and buildings that marked the territorial offices of the British colonial administration. Crossing the open ground became increasingly hazardous as the afternoon wore on.

Sergeant Frank Guidone, the cigar-smoking boxer from Able Company, led his squad down the ridge and into exposed country. "Half way down the slope we received fire from the low ground ahead," Guidone said. "Two squad members were hit: Leonard Butts and Louie Lovin. Butts died later that night; Lovin was evacuated to a hospital ship where he subsequently died. Jerry Diovisalvo in the adjacent squad was also killed during this charge."

Running hard to avoid the machine gun's searching fire, Guidone suddenly encountered a sheer drop. Tight spot. The Raiders quickly unwrapped their toggle ropes, strung six together, and scampered down the cliff. Guidone reformed his skirmish line, and they drove the Japanese gunners out of a small building, losing Private First Class Albert Belfield to a painful wound that shattered the bone in his upper arm. Guidone applied a sulfa dressing, then wrapped a tight bandage around Belfield's arm and chest as a splint, but the shot-up squad was now cut off from the rest of Able Company.[12]

Guidone's colorful company commander, "Silent Lew" Walt, had an inauspicious beginning to his long combat career. Trotting through scrub brush as he watched the forward elements of Able Company cross the fire-swept golf course, Walt spotted just in time a Japanese sniper aiming at him from forty yards away. "I dropped as fast as I could and his first shot hit the tree four inches above my head." Walt heard the sniper work his bolt and felt a frustrating fear—he couldn't squirm any lower. The second shot hit the tree about two inches below the first, very nearly slicing his burlap helmet cover. But then Platoon Sergeant Clifford H. McGlocklin and new BAR-man Red Hills killed the luckless sniper with converging bursts of fire.[13]

In Dog Company's sector, Jumping Joe Chambers' combat experience with the Raiders would prove short-lived, despite his audacity—or perhaps because of it. Although Edson twice took Chambers to task for minor misjudgements on D-Day, he remained quite pleased with Chambers' upfront leadership. The company kept moving, kept the pressure on the *rikusentai*.

At one point Chambers stepped into a small clearing just as a Japanese appeared across the way. "It was just a question of who was the most

**D-Day morning at Tulagi. The 1st Raiders landed by Higgins boats and did not use their rubber boats. Offshore coral clusters prevented a dry landing.**

scared," said Chambers. "I dove to my left and started firing my [Reising gun] as I went down. Don't know whether I got him or not; I didn't see him again."[14]

The Japanese Special Naval Landing Forces at this point in the war were still configured for offensive, light-infantry tactics. The Kure 3d Special Naval Landing Force lacked the 90mm mortars or the 70mm howitzers and 75mm mountain guns that their more defensive-oriented counterparts would possess the next year at Bairoko and Tarawa, respectively. The Kure *rikusentai* on Tulagi fought principally with Arisaka .25 caliber rifles, hand grenades, Nambu light and medium machine guns, and a curiously effective device they called a "grenade thrower." This weapon was a 50mm, lanyard-fired, trench mortar, light in weight and quick to employ, though not altogether accurate. The Raiders called it a "knee mortar," a dangerous nickname, because placing the curved baseplate against one's thigh during firing would fracture the leg. Most

Raider casualties on Tulagi resulted from gunshot wounds and grenade fragments (and a few edged weapons), but there were a number caused by fragments from a knee-mortar explosive shell.

Jumping Joe Chambers believed a knee-mortar did him in, although there were some who did not agree.

By D-Day afternoon Chambers' Dog Company had secured a piece of high ground from which they could observe Major Ken Bailey's Charlie Company battling for a hilltop off to their right. "I spotted some Japs firing down on Bailey's people," Chambers stated, "So I got my 60mm mortars set up and was calling the fire. I thought that it was a premature burst of one of my own mortars, but all of a sudden there was this great flash of fire right in front of me, oh maybe ten or fifteen feet up in the air. It smashed my left wrist, broke my right wrist and took a hunk out of my right leg." As Chambers pondered over the incident, he changed his opinion, concluding "it was a Jap knee mortar that had spotted us. They had a time fuse on their projectiles and I think that's what got me. But in any event I was got."[15]

Several other Marines fell to the same explosion. One was mortarman James F. Thompson, who later claimed a defective round had exploded just after being fired from the tube. He blamed the premature explosion on the rounds getting soaked during the wade ashore that morning. "We were using World War I ammo, and faulty firing would occur if the ammo got wet," said Thomas. Elton Whisenhunt and Finley Foden disagreed, blaming insufficient overhead clearance. Said Foden, the loader, "We kept arguing with the Major about the angle of the mortar tube. He kept raising the angle. We were under a tree and the round hit a branch."

Whatever the cause—enemy shell, defective round, or "friendly fire"—Jumping Joe Chambers was done. He departed with class, seeing to the evacuation of the other wounded, staying with the company until they secured their objective, rallying his fellow casualties to rise up and resist the Japanese attack on the sickbay that night. Captain Bill Sperling, another class act, took command of Dog Company, but the Raiders would miss Jumping Joe. He personified the Raiders' cocky aggressiveness, and his subsequent Medal of Honor on Iwo Jima would be fairly won. The Navy admired him equally. At 0420 the next morning, the fast transport *McKean,* whose crew had become enchanted by the big, outspoken Raider during the transit from Nouméa to Fiji to Tulagi, sent a worried message to the hospital ship, seeking verification of a report that "Maj. Chambers, Dog Company—wounded both hands?"[16]

South of Chambers's position, Lieutenant Black Jack Salmon established Charlie Company's own 60mm mortars on a spur of the ridge
with a clear view of Major Bailey's attack on knob-like Hill 208. Brisk
enemy fire from a cave in the south face of Hill 208 contested the
Raiders' attempt to bypass the knob along its seaward side.

Salmon watched intently as Bailey deployed the platoons of Lieutenants Clay Boyd and Spike Ryder. Boyd, whom Salmon considered "a
superlative officer," took the lead. With the two platoons formed in a
cautious half-circle around the cave, Boyd and Ryder duck-walked forward to toss in grenades. The *rikusentai* promptly tossed them back. The
lieutenants then popped spoons on a fresh set of grenades, holding them
icily until the last second, before tossing and dodging. Fire continued to
emit from the cave. Boyd and Ryder then dashed up to the mouth, firing long blasts with their Reising guns. "Back to their corner they go,"
said Salmon, "and thanks to some of Red Mike's doctrines, both reloaded
just in time to cut down the Nips that came running out of that hole.
One had a sword and ran like [Bronco] Nagurski. Got real close, too.
About then one of my men, young Paine, got killed—after one hell of a
Jap-fighting performance."[17]

Brave as they were, Boyd and Ryder could not outdo their company
commander. When a built-up emplacement thwarted Charlie Company,
"Ken Dill" Bailey ran forward, leapt on top of the bunker, kicked open
the peep holes and firing ports so other Raiders could stuff grenades
inside, then shot down the survivors with his Reising gun as they fled.
The exchange was not entirely one-sided. A departing *rikusentai* turned
and shot Bailey through the fleshy part of his thigh.

Bailey shook it off, moved forward, signaling Platoon Sergeant Robert
Jernigan and Lieutenant Ryder to join him to plot the next advance.
Black Jack Salmon had rejoined the main body and saw that Bailey and
Jernigan were dangerously exposed. In Jernigan's account, "Major Bailey had gone forward to reconnoiter with me at his heels. I was hit by a
sniper's bullet coming from the top of a coconut palm tree, the bullet no
doubt intended for Bailey who was on my left. It entered my left upper
chest, went through a lung, and exited out the center of my back, near
my spine." Salmon was there. "Bang! and Jernigan went down. There
were only a few trees, and I saw this round hat in one of them and
opened fire, and much to my surprise I got him."[18]

The firing became heavier. Bailey divided his company, ordering Boyd
to reinforce Lieutenant Sullivan, while he and Ryder led a bayonet
charge against the next bunker. Here Bailey's luck ran out. Both he and

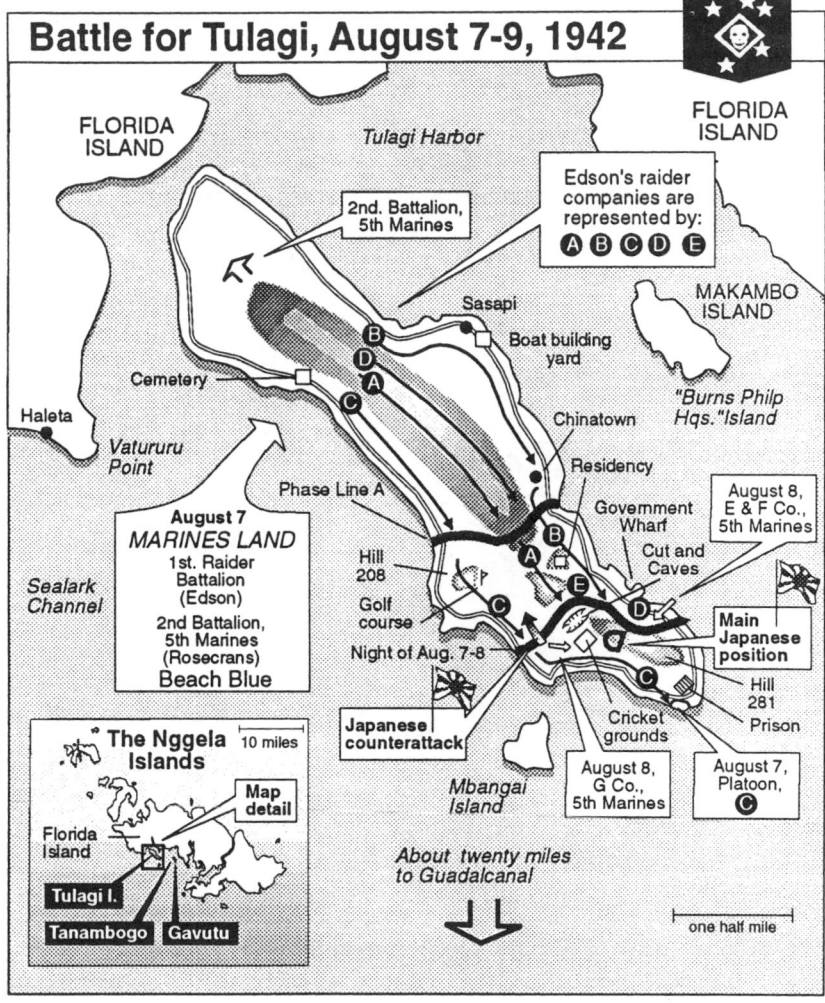

Battle for Tulagi, August 7-9, 1942

Ryder went down hard, along with a number of Ryder's men. Both officers were evacuated, along with Jernigan. Bailey never lost his presence of mind. "You know, Black Jack," he said to Salmon as he was being carried to the aid station, "That Jap Arisaka isn't a bad rifle at all." Captain Robert Thomas, Bailey's exec, took command of Charlie Company, although Edson would eventually ask Sam Griffith to provide direct oversight.[19]

The near-simultaneous loss of such popular company commanders

**"Immediate Action," by Doug Greenbowe, captures the close-quarters fighting on D-Day at Tulagi. Note the burlap helmet cover and Reising submachine gun.**

as Bailey and Chambers stunned the Raiders. Few realized how close they had come to losing Silent Lew Walt at the same time. The Japanese rifleman twice had Walt in his sights, aiming from a prone position forty yards away in broad daylight. A single "click" lower elevation on the rear sight of his Arisaka would have altered the history of several future battles in three Pacific wars.

Red Mike Edson had warned his men about the fighting skills of the Japanese, but he did not totally succeed in erasing a decade of popular propaganda in America that portrayed Japanese soldiers as scrawny, buck-toothed, myopic draftees. Reality was sobering. "Big guys," admitted Ash Large, recalling his opponents from Hiroshima Prefecture in southern Honshu, "and they'd been in a fight before." Word had spread among the Raiders of the virtuoso Japanese marksmen who had pinned down Baker Company behind the seawall. Said Private First Class Hugh Davis, "An amazing discovery. The Nips can shoot! A couple of our dead were shot through the temple."[20]

One particular Japanese sharpshooter proved unerringly accurate during the confused fighting around Hill 208. Platoon Sergeant Alexander J. Luke, a twenty-six-year-old Philadelphian, commanded a light machine-gun platoon from Easy Company in direct support of Major Bailey's company. Luke had been a Marine for eight years—had in fact served in the 4th Marines in Shanghai with Edson during the crisis of 1937. Ash Large described Luke as one of the Raiders' "real artists with a machine gun—you could tell by listening to his controlled bursts." On Tulagi, Luke quickly took over the Browning when the hidden sniper took out the assigned gunner with a well-placed shot. He opened fire but could not spot his man. The sniper fired again, hitting Luke right between the eyes, killing him.[21]

In turn, the Japanese defenders were likely even more astonished with the marksmanship of the Raiders. Red Mike had trained them well. The least Marine was deadly with his '03 Springfield at ranges up to 500 yards, and eastern Tulagi's open ground offered many targets at that range. Some, like Private First Class John C. Holladay of Baker Company, were world-class shooters. Johnny Holladay was thirty, a native of Florence, South Carolina, a free spirit who could make a guitar sing and knew all twenty-seven verses of the ballad "John Henry." He could also shoot the eyes out of an ant with "Ol' Lucifer," his well-oiled Springfield. As recorded by Private First Class John H. Gann, a Baker radio operator, Holladay took aim at a sniper in a distant palm tree and carefully squeezed the trigger. Nothing. "Better shoot him again," suggested First Sergeant Brice Maddox. Holladay demurred: "Top, ol' Lucifer don't lie; he'll fall in a minute." Gann and Maddox then shook their heads in amazement as the sniper's body slid out of the tree.

Holladay's counterpart on the Browning Automatic Rifle was Red Hills in Able Company. A good man with a BAR was an invaluable asset in this kind of fighting, ranging from point-blank ambushes to suppressive fire against caves and bunkers. Hills had already assisted in saving Silent Lew's life. Later he used a pool-shark's trigonometry to bank his automatic fire off an overhead rock and into a stoutly-defended cave.[22]

It had been a long day, and the battalion was running out of gas. Every successful "processing" of a Japanese position that afternoon seemed to be followed by an even tougher nut to crack. Sam Griffith was upbeat about the day's events: "Everything had clicked beautifully." Edson was less sanguine. The battle was far from over, he had lost some invaluable leaders, the Japanese would surely counterattack during the night, and there was no way the battalion would be ready for additional missions in support of General Vandegrift at first light on the 8th.[23]

Communicator Henry Poppell's impressions of Able Company's situation at day's end reinforced Edson's assessment. "We move over to the ridge. Men are being dragged back wounded. It is now five in the afternoon....Our 1st Platoon is in a bad way in an attempt to take out a number of machine guns over the cliff. They have to withdraw. Darkness is now falling." The unit Poppell described as "in a bad way" was Sergeant Frank Guidone's squad, pinned down and isolated for much of the afternoon. At twilight Guidone led his depleted squad out of their trap on the dead run, somehow managing to get the painfully wounded Private First Class Belfield up the toggle ropes to the top of the cliff. Guidone reported to the company exec, Captain Tony Antonelli, then moved his squad into his assigned sector of the line. By then it was dark and Guidone's men were too tired to dig in. They settled down behind their packs and waited.[24]

### Tulagi by Night

"We knew the Japanese were good fighters," recalled Sam Griffith after the battle for Tulagi, "[But] we were taken by surprise by the viciousness and tenacity of these night attacks."[25]

Few Raiders got any sleep that first night. The Japanese launched a half-dozen attacks, ranging from platoon-sized to a handful of stealthy infiltrators. The noise of the parachutists' battle raging on nearby Gavutu and Tanambogo added to the din. On Tulagi, the screams and cries of a Marine dying from a stomach wound haunted the defenders.

Red Mike Edson established his battalion command post in the "The Residency," the fancy former home of the British resident commissioner. His four rifle companies were arrayed roughly on line, north to south, in this order: Dog, Baker, Able, and Charlie. Edson had moved George Herring's Easy Company up from Blue Beach, and the weapons men helped bridge some of the gaps towards the center, an imperfect fit. Rosecrans' 2/5 had moved up somewhat to the rear, westward, of the line. It was a

The Browning .30 caliber light machine gun was a mainstay of the 1st Raiders' battle for Tulagi.

decent night position, largely along the high ground. Each company placed listening posts partially down the slope.

A unit's first night in combat is usually one the survivors would rather forget, but few battalions had more peacetime night training than Edson's Raiders. With few exceptions they maintained superb fire discipline throughout Tulagi's first night. Unfortunately, there was little that training could have done to prepare the men for the rampant "fog of war" confusion that attended the wild counterattacks.

The battalion passwords for the night contained the usual proliferation of the letter "L"—Philippines, Lollipop, Laura Lee—in the reasonable belief that they would be unpronounceable by the Japanese. But the nervous Raiders often failed to allow the system to work. Captain Tony Antonelli of Able Company recalled hearing too many times during the night: "Quick—what's the password?—*BANG!*" Too often, Antonelli said, the individual challenged had no time to respond, regardless of his ability to pronounce "L." Indeed, nervous sentries shot one of Antonelli's platoon commanders, First Lieutenant Arthur R. Gewehr, in the shoulder as he returned from checking his lines after dark.[26]

Red Mike Edson was at risk himself that long night. Never one to sit in his command post, Edson departed often to inspect the lines. Each passage provided high drama. He scared hell out of Ashley Large, serving as an Able Company scout and nervous about his exposed forward position. "How're you doing, lad?" Edson asked calmly. Large could hardly answer, pleased enough to see the Old Man, but extremely glad he had not shot him. So was Baker Company radio operator John Gann, occupying a forward post down the slope from the Residency. This time the challenge worked. Edson identified himself as "Red Mike." Gann was not convinced. "Say something, Red Mike." Edson retorted with a litany of "L's:" "Lucky Strike, Lilly Thistle, Lola's Thighs—is that enough, son?"[27]

Edson had grounds for concern as the tropic darkness settled over smoking Tulagi. Tiger Erskine's interpretation of captured *rikusentai* maps confirmed Edson's suspicion that the bulk of the Japanese force had gone to ground in a large, cave-invested ravine that ran parallel to the Raiders' line. The ravine's wide mouth opened on the south end, closest to Charlie and Able companies. Charlie Company was the most vulnerable. Captain Thomas' first act after taking command from the fallen Bailey was to order Clay Boyd's platoon forward to Tulagi's southeast corner. It was a misguided mission; darkness forced Boyd to remain on the point overnight, depriving Thomas of his most aggressive officer and one fourth his command.

The two most dangerous Japanese counterattacks would boil out of the ravine and strike these two companies—first hitting the boundary between the units, then fully against Able Company. Both assaults were plenty scary—there were few experiences in the Pacific War more unnerving than a Japanese night attack—but the initial onslaught constituted the greatest threat. Here the Japanese cracked the Raiders' line and created local chaos.

Private First Class Henry Poppell manned Able Company's last outpost on the right flank. An enemy hand grenade suddenly landed near his position, the explosion blowing the rifle out of his hands. The night was filled with shouts and explosions and shadowy figures. Poppell fumbled for his grenades, staring into the darkness. There was no more contact with the Charlie Company outpost to his right. A wild outburst of firing erupted to his right rear. "Charlie Company is being attacked at the base of the ridge, and I begin to realize that we are becoming disorganized.....Japs are crawling closer. I withdraw to my left rear about forty yards...and discover that Red Hills has taken over about ten men and formed a skirmish line."[28]

Warrant Officer Albert E. ("Bud") Fisher commanded Easy Com-

pany's 2d Machine-Gun Platoon, which had been firing in direct support of Charlie Company all day. By night his gunners covered too broad
a front and Fisher worried about the gaps. "We were all pretty nervous
as darkness fell," he admitted. After awhile his skin began to crawl. "The
Nips came out of their caves making all sorts of weird noises."

Not very far north along the ridge stood Lieutenant Houston Stiff,
commanding Easy's mortars, and the nominal senior officer among the
three weapons platoons in the area. Stiff was disoriented and anxious.
Easy Company had arrived late. Both Captain Herring and the exec, Lieutenant Myles Fox, had remained at the Residency to be near Edson. Stiff
thought Charlie Company was off to the front and did not realize until
dangerously late that there was no one between his gunners and the
Japanese. At this point Edson called Stiff on the field phone, suggesting
he lead his men in a bayonet charge, a spoiling attack to disrupt the
Japanese now forming downhill for the charge. Although he mumbled
"aye, aye, sir" to Edson, Stiff considered this "a lousy idea from all angles.
For one thing there wasn't a bayonet in the whole crew..." Stiff's dutiful
orders dumbfounded Bud Fisher—"I had never heard of a machine gun
company making a bayonet attack"—but then the Japanese struck and
the issue became moot.

Bud Fisher ran back to his platoon in the midst of a great cacophony
of sound. "The Japs had broken through our right flank and captured one
of my machine guns and had turned it on us," he explained. He grabbed
six men, "each with two grenades and the useless Reising guns," and
eventually recaptured the piece, killing its temporary owners. Farther up
the ridge, Houston Stiff and his men used their hodgepodge of weapons
to drive off another group of infiltrators, although they shot one of their
own in the confusion, a frightened sentry racing back into the perimeter without identifying himself, hit in the stomach with a .45 caliber pistol bullet. The incoherent fighting lapped around the grounds of the Residency and left two members of the intelligence section dead and highly
regarded Lieutenant Myles Fox, twenty-three, mortally wounded.[29]

Baker Company's Private First Class Vince Cassidy, the unlikely hero
of the first day's firefight, assumed a defensive position along the path
leading up the ridge to the Residency. With him on the opposite side of
the path was Private Michael F. Nee, twenty years old, from South
Boston, the company's 130-pound boxing champ in Samoa. The men
heard unmistakable sounds of movement in the brush but could see
nothing. "The battle came suddenly and firing was intense," Cassidy said.
"I heard Mike Nee yell something about moving out and turned toward

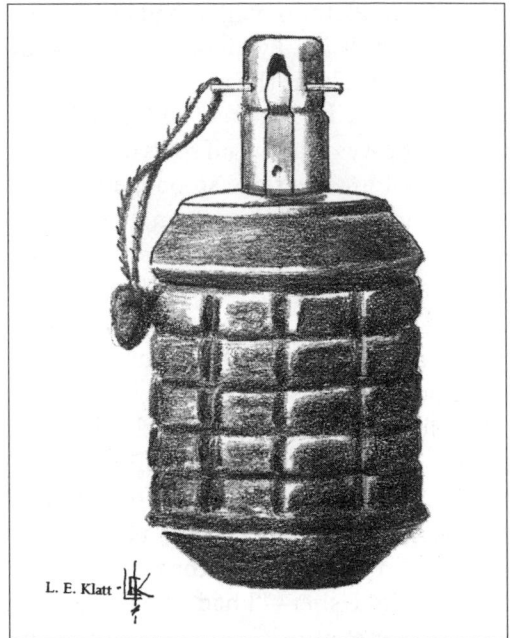

L. E. Klatt

"Lethal Weapon," by Larry E. Klatt. **Many surviving Raiders still carry slivers from the Japanese Type 97 fragmentation grenade.**

him, only to hear him scream as a burst of automatic fire, from what seemed to be right in front of us, cut him down. I fired madly."

Cassidy somehow found a corpsman for his buddy, but Nee, like Lieutenant Fox and several others, would die in the morning. Then Cassidy found himself alone on the forward slope. "Everyone I could see was dead." He eased back towards the crest, saw a familiar form, recognized the sharpshooting Johnnie Holladay and hastily identified himself. Holladay led him to safety.[30]

Further to the left of this action, still within Able Company's sector, Sergeant Frank Guidone's exhausted squad hunkered behind their packs and waited for the night battle to come to them. "We knew there were plenty of Japs in the low ground we had just vacated," said Guidone, "and we were sure they were about to visit us." The squad occupied reverse slope positions. Light from a burning building on the far side of the topographic crest provided a fortuitous advantage; the Japanese were fatally backlit against that illuminated skyline. Guidone and his men quickly learned the first principal of night-fighting: "Fire thy weapon only as a last resort, otherwise the muzzle blast is a dead giveaway; fight the battle with hand grenades." Guidone held a prime position, directly downslope from the silhouetted figures as they topped the ridge. "We lay prone and threw our grenades with a side-armed motion, lobbing them twenty yards with a high arc," he said. Gray dawn revealed the grenadiers' gruesome harvest; nearly two dozen Japanese bodies strewn along the ridge.[31]

At first light Major Lew Walt walked his lines to assess Able Company's condition. "I came across a foxhole occupied by Private First Class Ahrens, a small man of about 140 pounds....He was slumped down in one corner of the foxhole covered with blood from head to foot. In the foxhole with him were two dead Japs, a lieutenant and a sergeant. There were eleven more dead Japs on the ground in front of his position. In his hands he clutched the dead officer's sword."

Ahrens was dying from multiple gunshot and stab wounds. His last whispered words, according to Walt: "The bastards tried to come over me last night—I guess they didn't know I was a Marine." Private First Class Edward H. Ahrens, twenty-two, unmarried, from Dayton, Kentucky, died in Silent Lew's arms.

### Securing the Island

The Japanese infiltrators vanished at daybreak like mythic vampires. Rooting them out of their caves and bunkers would require painstaking work throughout the next several days, and the light-weight Raiders had few tools for the job. Three years later the Marines would tackle Okinawa's caves with "Zippo" flamethrower tanks, bazookas, and 105mm self-propelled "siege guns." The Raiders on Tulagi had neither flame throwers nor bazookas. Their demolition platoon improvised its own Bangalore torpedoes and satchel charges, but each of these crude explosives had to be "delivered" by hand. The platoon led by Captain John Sweeney and Gunnery Sergeant Angus Goss earned their special duty pay in spades. Among several others, Private George A. Johnson, nineteen, from Coatesville, Pennsylvania, died trying to stuff an explosive into a bunker opening. Each position, defended to the last man by the hard-nosed *rikusentai,* had to be reduced by the combination of creative ingenuity and primitive courage. It made for slow going.

Edson effectively employed the fresh troops of the 2d Battalion, 5th Marines throughout the second day, making such encouraging progress that by sunset he radioed Vandegrift that organized resistance on Tulagi had ended; the island was "secure." The troops guffawed at the news, aware that plenty of well-armed *rikusentai* were still holed-up in the ravine, waiting for dark.

As if to underscore their continued resistance, the Japanese counterattacked again the second night, and while these forays lacked the fear and fury of the previous night, they still proved unsettling. By then the Marines were zombies. Most had not slept for three nights (few could sleep on the crowded APDs the night before D-Day).

Platoon Sergeant Gene Martin of Dog Company posted his men in the ditches along both sides of a main path after dark, then dozed off. His sense of smell snapped him awake. "I knew before I opened my eyes that a Jap was near, damned near; for I could smell the unmistakable sweet odor of rice powder—strong! As a Gate Sentry at the American Embassy in Peking I had long been exposed to this smell which hung on every Jap that passed." Martin's eyes flew open, revealing four Japanese troops with a machine gun standing beside him in the trail, seemingly unaware they were surrounded by a platoon of sleeping Marines. For all their later bad rap, the Raiders' Reising guns rarely failed them at Tulagi, and Martin's weapon performed beautifully. He cut down two; the others dove for the far ditch, startled to find it alive with equally startled Raiders, bounced out again and ran for their lives. Something glistened on the path in the moonlight. Martin bent over and picked up a handsome trophy, an antique samurai sword with a burnished bronze guard and a frosted silver ornament in the form of three cherry blossoms on each side of the rayskin handle. It was surely one of the first of these distinctive swords to be captured by a Marine in the war.[32]

The rains came, followed by a period of man-made thunder and lightning. The Japanese fleet from Rabaul had surprised the Allied screening force, and a terrific sea battle raged around Savo Island. The Raiders watched in awe, assuming naively that the Allies were giving the Imperial Navy a good licking. Morning's light revealed the opposite to have been true. The U.S. Navy suffered the worst defeat of its long history at Savo Island, losing three heavy cruisers and an Australian cruiser. This development, combined with the earlier withdrawal of the U.S. carriers, meant Admiral Kelly Turner no longer had any protection for his thin-skinned amphibious ships, and he had to withdraw them from the Solomons well before the 1st Marine Division's critical supplies could be offloaded. Soon the troops would begin to call Guadalcanal "Starvation Island."

At Tulagi, Edson's Raiders fought Japanese Special Landing Forces similar to these troops, shown training with a heavy machine gun in 1942. (Naval Historical Center)

Elimination of the final Japanese caves and bunkers on Tulagi on 10 August devolved into the capable hands of Angus Goss. He proved worthy of the responsibility. In one case, stymied by a cave in a steep cliff, he climbed to the top of the cliff, carefully lowered a time-fused satchel charge at the end of long rope, and swung it into the cave just before detonation. "The best noncom in the Marine Corps was my platoon sergeant, Angus Goss," said John Sweeney. "He was the model 'old-timer' and all Marine."[33]

One particular cave in a small hill just west of the cricket field seemed almost impregnable. Its entrance was ten feet above ground; a stone parapet provided further protection to the defenders. As the fighting elsewhere on Tulagi died down, a crowd gathered on the high ground that formed a natural amphitheater for the drama unfolding below. Horse Collar Smith helped Goss prepare a short-fused "stick" charge behind a nearby shack. Goss then raced for the cave mouth, lobbed the charge squarely in the hole, turned to run for cover. But the Japanese threw the charge back at Goss. The explosion slammed him against the shack, blew off his trousers, and wounded him painfully. Smith pulled him to safety and tried to apply first aid. Goss would have none of it. In a cold rage, he grabbed his Reising gun, shuffled back towards the cave, clambered up to the parapet, and hosed down the astonished occupants, killing them all. Then he collapsed.

Edson nominated Angus Goss for the Medal of Honor. Vandegrift, Ghormley, and Nimitz concurred, but a stateside awards board downgraded it to a Navy Cross the following year. Additionally, the King of England awarded him the British government's Conspicuous Gallantry Medal. The hard-luck Goss would not live to see either medal.[34]

Raider Clifford J. Fitzpatrick credited victory at Tulagi to Goss and Major Ken Bailey. "I never saw any Marines braver or more dedicated. It was inevitable that they were to be killed in action later. They had nothing but scorn both for the enemy and for their own personal safety."[35]

"The people on Tulagi I want to recommend recognition for excellent work," wrote General Vandegrift to Commandant Holcomb four days after D-Day. "It was a mean fight. Edson...[and his] crowd deserve the best."[36]

The Raiders remained on Tulagi another three weeks, rooting out diehard snipers, conducting patrols throughout the nearby Florida Islands, dodging shells from "Reveille Charlie," a Japanese destroyer that pounded the island from close range for three mornings running. Meager rations and unsanitary battlefield conditions caused increasing cases of debilitating sickness, including rampant dysentery. Malaria began to appear. Both Major Walt and Lieutenant Mullahey came down sick, so acutely ill they would miss the Raiders' next critical battles.

Another painful loss occurred on 27 August when Platoon Sergeant Alvin M. Dismukes of Baker Company was killed by an accidental discharge of a fellow Marine's BAR. Dismukes was thirty-seven, a veteran of seventeen years active service, and left a widow in Charleston, West Virginia, and a big hole in the ranks of the company's staff NCOs. The fatal accident provided an unhappy "bookend" to the Raiders' otherwise sterling performance on Tulagi. On D-Day morning, the headquarters intelligence section lost a Marine on USS *Little*, fatally shot by an accidental discharge of a Springfield rifle just as debarkation began.[37]

The 1st Marine Raider Battalion's sweeping victory against a tough and well-fortified foe on Tulagi thus came at a considerable cost. While killing all but three of Tulagi's approximately 350 defenders, the Raiders had sustained thirty-eight killed and fifty-five wounded themselves, a figure representing almost ten percent of the command, mostly in the first twenty-four hours. The ratio of killed to wounded reflected the point-blank nature of most of the fighting, especially at night.[38]

If pleased by the performance of his highly trained battalion in this first crucible, Edson must also have worried about the loss of such proven leaders as Bailey, Chambers, and Walt—three top-notch company commanders—plus veteran NCOs like Goss, Dismukes, and Luke. In fact, an interesting transformation was beginning to unfold within the Raiders. While the battalion still included a number of towering prototypical athletes—Anthony J. "Big Stoop" Palonis comes immediately to mind—the surprise heroics were coming from the feather merchants, the little guys, wiry but tough. Edward Ahrens weighed 140 pounds, Frank Guidone 135, Ashley Large 130, Fred Serral 116. Robert Paine's weight is unknown, but Black Jack Salmon described him as "a little guy who had it where it counted." Paine and Ahrens would be among twelve Raiders slain on Tulagi for whom United States Navy ships would soon be named.

Most of those who survived looked back favorably on Tulagi later in their years. In 1957 Salmon wrote, "I can still smell Tulagi and that moldy barley, and I remember our great friends on the gallant APDs, and those finest ones we left behind."[39]

Vince Cassidy captured the essence of the Raiders' first combat experience in this remarkable poem written shortly after the battle for Tulagi:

Yesterday

*Yesterday? Yes, I remember yesterday.*
  *I was young then, light of heart and gay,*
*a stranger still to fear and sleepless nights,*
    *but that was yesterday.*

*The clang of steel, the pang of pain,*
  *the bitter tang of twice-born hate,*
*I had not known, nor yet been at war.*

*I had not noticed day by day*
  *dear ones' faces fade away*
*and home becomes a dream, a thing remembered—*
  *hoped for—all but lost in memory.*

*But now I've seen more than I'll say.*
  *How old I've grown since yesterday!*[40]

## Notes

1. Cecil H. Clark exhorting his platoon to get off the landing beach, quoted in Hugh C. Davis to Francis "Pete" Pettus, 29 January 1957, 3.
2. Ashley R. Large, interview with author, Horse Shoe, NC, 1 October 1990.
3. Vincent H. D. Cassidy to Pete Pettus, 5 December 1956, 1.
4. Thomas D. Smith to Pete Pettus, 7 December 1957; diary entry 7 August 1942, 2 [T. D. Smith diary].
5. Alexander, *Storm Landings: Epic Amphibious Battles of the Central Pacific* (Annapolis: Naval Institute Press, 1997), 1.
6. Griffith, *The Battle for Guadalcanal*, 46; John B. Salmon to Pete Pettus, 8 January 1957, 3.
7. Haruko Taya Cook and Theodore E. Cook, *Japan at War: An Oral History* (New York: The New Press, 1992), 263–64. The fiercely defended caves of Tulagi and Gavutu presaged similar nightmarish battles on Peleliu, Iwo Jima, and Okinawa.
8. T. D. Smith diary, 7 August 1942, 3.
9. Herbert L. Coffin memoir to Thomas Mullahey, 1991. Hospital corpsman Charles B. Coleman gave Coffin quick and royal treatment: sulfa powder, morphine, "and as an extra treat, a jigger of brandy," said Coffin.
10. Cassidy to Pettus, 5 December 1956, 2–3; Casualty Card, John J. Gilligan, Jr.
11. Casualty Cards, Eugene M. Key, Thomas F. Nickel; Pete Pettus, "Raiders on Tulagi," *Dope Sheet*, 1959; John H. Gann to Pete Pettus, 1 December 1956; Dr. Miles' biographical details from *Dictionary of American Naval Fighting Ships*, Vol VI (Washington, D.C.: Department of the Navy, 1976), 285. Fittingly, the destroyer escort USS *Samuel S. Miles* (DE 183), commissioned in honor of Dr. Miles in late 1943, sank the Japanese fleet submarine *I-177* north of the Palaus on 3 October 1944, during the height of the Marines' battle for Peleliu. See Carl Boyd and Akihiko Yoshida, *The Japanese Submarine Force and World War II* (Annapolis: Naval Institute Press, 1995), 213.
12. Frank Guidone to Thomas Mullahey, 1992; Guidone interview with author, 1999.
13. Lew Walt, "Notes on the First Day and Night at Tulagi," to Pete Pettus, *ca.* 1956.
14. Justice M. Chambers Oral Memoir, MCOHC, MCHC, 311.
15. *Ibid.*, 311–12.
16. James F. Thomas, "Vet Recalls Bitter Fight," *Dope Sheet*, January 1991, 6; Elton Whisenhunt and Finley Foden to James Smith, *Dope Sheet*, March 1997, 23; Message, USS *McKean* to USS *Neville*, 080420 August 1942, author's possession. The explosive blast caused compound fractures in both Chambers' wrists, preventing him thereafter from participating in strength training or leading his 3d Battalion, 25th Marines over the obstacle course, to his per-

sonal embarrassment, according to Dr. Michael F. Keleher, Chambers' battalion surgeon throughout 1944–45 (Keleher interview with author, 20 February 1999).

17. Salmon to Pettus, 8 January 1957, 1–2. Pvt. Robert I. Paine, nineteen, killed in this action, was from Cambridge, Massachusetts.

18. Robert Jernigan to Thomas Mullahey, 1991; Salmon to Pettus, 8 January 1957, 2.

19. Clay Boyd to Thomas Mullahey, 1991; Salmon to Pettus, 8 January 1957, 2.

20. Ashley Large interview with author, 1 October 1990; Hugh Davis to Thomas Mullahey, 1991.

21. Large interview with author, 1 October 1990; Platoon Sergeant Luke Casualty Card, author's possession; citation, commissioning of USS *Alexander J. Luke* (DE 577), 19 February 1944.

22. John Gann to Pete Pettus, 1 December 1956, 4.

23. Samuel B. Griffith Oral memoir, MCOHC, MCHC, 85.

24. Poppell Diary, 7 August 1942; Frank Guidone to Thomas Mullahey, 1992.

25. Griffith Oral Memoir, MCOHC, MCHC, 91.

26. Brig. Gen. John W. Antonelli to Pete Pettus, 25 January 1957, 4.

27. Ashley Large interview with author, 1 October 1990; John Gann to Pete Pettus, 1 December 1956, 4.

28. Poppell Diary, 7 August 1942.

29. Albert E. Fisher to Pete Pettus, undated, *ca.* 1956–57; Houston Stiff to Pete Pettus, 4 December 1956 [note: General Lew Walt's account states that the Japanese captured *two* machine guns plus a walkie-talkie during the initial breakthrough; he also credits "A" Company's Red Hills with recapturing both weapons. Walt may not have been in position to see this action, but it is likely that both Hills and Fisher (and others) took part in the recapture]; Casualty Card, 1st Lt. Myles C. Fox, author's possession.

30. Cassidy to Pettus, 5 December 1956, 3–4.

31. Frank J. Guidone, "The Tulagi Landing," *Dope Sheet*, 1999, 15; Guidone to John Sweeney, 1992.

32. Gene C. Martin to Pete Pettus, 1957, later published as "The Night By the Ditch," *Dope Sheet*, 1957, 3–4; Kenneth L. Smith-Christmas, "Sword Here May be First Taken from Japanese by Marine," *Fortitudine*, Fall, 1995, 17.

33. John Sweeney to Pete Pettus, September 1956, 1.

34. Navy Cross citation, Angus R. Goss, 8 October 1943; James Smith, "Angus R. Goss, A Marine's Marine," undated; Endorsement summary, Goss Medal of Honor nomination, provided by Awards Branch, HQMC 1994; CMC to Angus R. Goss, 19 July 1943 [Goss was killed in New Georgia on the 20th, which was still 19 July in Washington].

35. Clifford J. Fitzpatrick to Pete Pettus, 15 November 1956, 2.

36. Archer Vandegrift to Thomas Holcomb, 11 August 1942, Holcomb Papers, MCHC, 4.

37. Casualty Card, Alvin M. Dismukes, author's possession, plus Raider interviews with author, April 1999.
38. Hoffman, *Legend*, 183.
39. Salmon to Pettus, 8 January 1957, 2–4.
40. "Yesterday," written on Guadalcanal by Vincent Cassidy, from a collection sent by Cassidy to Pete Pettus, 1957. *The Congressional Record* reportedly published this poem shortly after the Guadalcanal campaign.

# 5

## The Tasimboko Raid, August–September 1942

*Came in back door. Overran two field pieces. Enemy withdrawing to Tasimboko, strength unknown. Keep bombers in air...*

Colonel Edson message to CG, 1st Marine Division
0855, 8 September 1942[1]

GUADALCANAL QUICKLY ECLIPSED TULAGI as the center stage for what became an enormous, five-month campaign fought with equal desperation in all three dimensions of air, ground, and sea. The vortex of this titanic struggle remained, first to last, Henderson Field.

Merrill B. Twining described Guadalcanal's contested airstrip as "The Unsinkable Aircraft Carrier." The phrase is apt. The year 1942 was a bleak one for America's six fleet carriers in the Pacific: four sunk, two heavily damaged. *Lexington* (the beloved "Lady Lex") went down at Coral Sea, *Yorktown* at Midway. The violent sea battles fought in the waters surrounding Guadalcanal in the autumn claimed both *Wasp* and *Hornet*. Japanese torpedoes damaged *Saratoga* so badly she had to return to a west coast shipyard for lengthy repairs. And feisty *Enterprise* received major bomb damage in the Battle of the Santa Cruz Islands, northeast of Tulagi. The proliferation of new Japanese airfields, now spreading southward from Rabaul, made the Solomon Sea increasingly dangerous for carriers.

Yet Henderson Field—bombed, shelled, and attacked literally around the clock for much of the campaign—proved indeed unsinkable. The field became known for its code name "Cactus," and the intrepid pilots of all services and several nations proudly called themselves "The Cactus Air Force." Each earned his flight pay. Under primitive conditions, flying patched up aircraft that were patently inferior in range, armament, and maneuverability to the nimble Zeros, the Cactus flight crews somehow bloodied every Japanese advance.

Imperial General Headquarters wasted no time in launching a counter-landing to recapture the field. Two weeks after D-Day the Ichiki Detachment, the assault forces of a highly regarded regiment, came screaming out of the jungles against the 1st Marine Division's lines along Alligator Creek. Colonel Ichiki's defeat and subsequent suicide led IGHQ to order Major General Kawaguchi to lead his brigade to Guadalcanal to oust the invaders.

Guadalcanal was British Captain Martin Clemens' assigned bailiwick, and he supervised a priceless network of coastwatchers and native scouts, including the legendary Sergeant Major Jacob Vouza. It was Vouza whom the Ichiki troops captured, tortured with bayonets, and left for dead. Vouza out-toughed his tormentors, chewed through his bindings, and limped through the jungle in great pain to warn Vandegrift the Japanese were coming. Now they were coming again. As Clemens recorded the situation, "from information available at our disposal on the 1st of September, it was clear that another Jap attack was pending, and the Marines were not the strong force of the 7th of August. We had had a lot of casualties, malaria was beginning to incapacitate units, and...every Marine was needed for the front line."[2]

General Vandegrift critically needed more combat troops to bolster his defense of Henderson Field. After three weeks he concluded that the Japanese had little interest in counter-attacking Tulagi. He decided to transfer his highly-trained Raider and parachute battalions to Guadalcanal.

By now the Raiders had occupied Tulagi for three weeks. Although Edson had become edgy at being left on the sidelines, most Raiders welcomed the opportunity to recover from their slugfest. Admitted one squad leader, "The general feeling was that we had won our battle and it was over for us." Tulagi had been an important baptism by fire for the 1st Raiders, a successful proving ground. Yet their greater destiny lay waiting on Guadalcanal against General Kawaguchi's veterans, first in an incisive surprise raid, then in a protracted pitched battle, toe-to-toe.[3]

### From the Frying Pan to the Fire

The battalion's crossing from Tulagi to Guadalcanal on 30 August had its own tragic aspects, related in the next section. The passage was always dangerous. When not searching for enemy subs or aircraft, most Raiders crowded along the lifelines of their small ships to stare speculatively at

Guadalcanal. The dark island still evokes vivid first impressions. Writer Matthew Stevenson, tracing the path of his father, a Marine company commander who landed there on D-Day, saw Guadalcanal first as "a rocky jungle, whose inhospitable mountaintops were encased in clouds." His father recorded his own memories of 1942: "At first light we stood along the rail and looked out across the calm, violet water. There lay the island, dark and impassively sinister, shrouded in an early morning haze pinpricked by bright orange flashes of shell fire from our ships."[4]

The Raiders established a bivouac in "The Coconut Grove," the stately rows of an abandoned coconut palm plantation. This beat living in the jungle, but the open spaces attracted unwelcome attention. While the Cactus Air Force was doing its best to wrest control of the air over Guadalcanal during daylight from their Japanese counterparts, the nights were a different story. With darkness came the "Tokyo Express," fast Imperial Navy task forces from Rabaul, arriving like clockwork to deliver reinforcements and combat cargo to the Japanese enclaves along the coast. That mission achieved, the ships invariably paused offshore to bombard Henderson Field and its environs.

To further disrupt the sleep of the Marines and the Cactus pilots, the Japanese also dispatched every night a pair of bothersome night stalkers, "Louie the Louse" and "Washing Machine Charlie." Louie's job was to drop parachute flares and mark targets for Charlie in his low-flying floatplane. Charlie's bombs rarely killed Marines, but his tell-tale irregular engine invariably prompted a "Condition Red" and a dash to the nearest "bomb-proof" hole in the swamp. Sleep was always the first casualty.

Henry Poppell's diary entries for the period are indicative. "31 August 1942: A bad night's sleep. Shelling from the Channel by Jap surface ships. Just another night in the fox hole. 2 September 1942: A night of very little sleep. Bombs from planes—shelling from the sea—rain as usual." That was the same night that Japanese shells set fire to a parked SBD. The plane exploded, spreading tongues of fire that detonated an ammo dump filled with 90mm antiaircraft shells, creating a long and lethal pyrotechnic show throughout the night.[5]

The Cactus Air Force did its damnedest to stave off the bombing and shelling. Alert coastwatchers up "The Slot" warned of oncoming strikes from Rabaul. Often these warnings would provide just enough time to scramble a handful of Grumman F4F Wildcats to begin their laborious climb to 30,000 feet to counterattack the raiders. Brave-hearted young fighter pilots somehow kept their wits about them to survive dogfights with

Japanese Zeros; many became the war's earliest aces. Yet combat and operational losses (the invariable accidents resulting from the primitive field and over-stressed pilots and planes) proved staggering. On several occasions Cactus could launch only a half dozen functional fighters.

The fate of Henderson Field hung in the balance for more than three months. Close air support missions for infantry operations became a luxury during this extended emergency. With the Wildcats needed to disrupt the daily air raids from Rabaul, and the SBD divebombers needed to attack Japanese shipping, the Marines on the ground often had to rely on the army's 67th Fighter Squadron, a dozen or so P-400 Bell Airacobras. Unfairly nicknamed "Klunkers," these unusual airplanes (the engine positioned behind and below the pilot, not in the nose) were ineffective in high altitude dogfights, but they carried a great armament payload, and their experienced pilots were as bold as any Marines. Under Captain Dale D. Brannon's inspirational command, the *Jagstaffel* squadron would sparkle in close air support missions and would twice lend a welcome and lethal hand to Edson's Raiders on Guadalcanal.[6]

Captain Brannon may have never realized the V.I.P. nature of his target, but the 67th Fighter Squadron provided a scorching greeting to Major General Kawaguchi at Taivu Point the day after he stepped ashore. Concerning his operations on 1 September, Brannon reported cryptically: "P-400s found the Japanese landing many troops near Tasimboko. Three missions on them with four aircraft per mission. They suffered heavy losses." Kawaguchi believed as many as forty aircraft attacked him that morning, although he claimed only light casualties among his men. "However," he admitted, "my hearing was damaged, and since then I have been having difficulty in speech."[7]

More Japanese came ashore each night—some as waterlogged and bedraggled as shipwreck victims from having been interdicted by the Cactus Air Force—but many others arrived with full unit integrity and crew-served weapons. All this night-time activity began to spook the Marines. When natives reported "Jap-an man on Savo," the division ordered Red Mike Edson to send a combat patrol to Savo Island.

Edson gave this mission to his exec, Sam Griffith, and Able and Baker Companies. The force embarked on two of their friendly high speed transports, the *Gregory* (APD 3) and the *Little* (APD 4), and landed at Panuila the morning of 4 September. Griffith divided the companies. The Raiders circled the island, searching for Japanese in a wide swath from the beach up to the steep slopes of Savo's volcanic cone. The Marines found plenty of evidence of the sea fight on 8–9 August but no Japanese. The Raiders re-embarked, tired and dusty from their circumnavigation of the island. The ships got underway for Guadalcanal late in the afternoon.[8]

Ironically, that night four hundred members of the Kawaguchi Brigade sought refuge on Savo Island. These were some of the survivors of Kawaguchi's ill-advised barge deployment, shot up and scattered by Cactus flyers during the day. While likely cursing their fates, these Imperial soldiers never realized their extreme good fortune. Had they drifted into Savo only a few hours earlier they would have been greeted by several hundred teed-off Raiders, loaded for bear. The Japanese instead arrived unmolested and left the following night to complete their long journey to Guadalcanal.

The fates were working overtime that night of 4 September. Restless, Red Mike Edson had spent the day at the division command post, seeking more raider missions from Colonel Gerald Thomas, Vandegrift's operations officer. Edson reminded Thomas of the temporary availability of four of the same APDs that the Raiders had literally called "home" the past two years. Thomas recalled Red Mike's persistence: "After Edson came over to the island he didn't want to just be an ordinary infantry battalion. He wanted to carry out operations like his Raiders were equipped and trained to do."[9]

The two officers devised a predawn raid on suspected Japanese positions at Cape Esperance on the island's northwest coast for the next morning. Edson intended to keep Able and Baker companies embarked on the two APDs overnight to ensure an early start on the mission. But the ships returned late from Savo, delayed both by a sluggish re-embarkation of tired troops from Panuila and yet another air raid on Henderson Field. Said Edson: "A message went to Griffith directing him to leave all men on board and informing him that I would embark. By the time this message reached Sam, however, the troops from one APD were already halfway to the beach and those from the other were embarked alongside ready to shove off…[We] therefore decided to postpone the Esperance show for 24 hours."[10]

By then darkness had fallen like a black cloak over Iron Bottom Sound. The senior captain of the APDs, ordered to return to the relative security of Tulagi harbor, decided to forego the transit of the island's coral reefs in such inky darkness and opted instead for the two ships to steam in close company in the open waters off the Marine beachhead.

## "Ol' Lady Luck"

Good units make their own good luck. Exceptional commanders also generate good luck simply by their hard work and preparedness. Lady Luck, on the other hand, is famously fickle. The 1st Raiders' collective luck would turn sour after Edson's departure, especially in the fighting along the Matanikau and again at Bairoko. Yet it cannot be denied that their luck was golden during the two-week stretch from their transit from Tulagi to the Battle of the Ridge. Some of the scenarios seemed downright scary. On these occasions the Raiders just missed a colossal disaster by a matter of minutes. Often, their luck was not shared by their friends and neighbors.

The Raiders first lucked out in their transit to Guadalcanal from Tulagi the afternoon of 30 August. One company crossed on the auxiliary cargo ship *Kopara* (AG 50), a flimsy vessel loaded to the gunwales with aviation gasoline, bombs, and fuses. The troops spent an exceedingly nervous two hours in the transit. They missed a major air raid by less than an hour.

The luck of the USS *Colhoun* (APD 2) succumbed to that same air raid. Dog Company of Edson's Raiders had just debarked and straggled ashore when a flight of eighteen Betty bombers appeared overhead at 15,000 feet. Japanese bombing proved unerringly accurate. At least four bombs struck the small ship—one went right down her stack—and *Colhoun* sank almost immediately. Fifty sailors, a third of her complement, went down with her.

The Raiders were thunderstruck. Dog Company's Corporal Maxwell Miller had just hit the beach when he heard the air raid alarm. "Everyone took off for cover in the tree line along the shore," Miller recalled later. "About halfway there I heard the explosions and turned around. *Colhoun* had been hit dead center. Her bow and stern were lifted up in the air, out of the water, and she began sinking rapidly....It was a horrifying sight." Private First Class Ben Quintana held similar impressions: "As I hit the beach I dove behind the first tree I came to, and as I looked back out to sea, all I could see was the bow of the ship settling into the water." The Raiders spent the next eighteen hours helping rescue the oil-soaked survivors.[11]

Losing so many shipmates on *Colhoun* was bad enough, but the greater tragedy occurred six nights later with *Gregory* and *Little*. The two transports, it will be recalled, had offloaded their Raider companies after the Savo Island mission late in the day—Edson's late message to remain on board for the night notwithstanding. Three Japanese destroyers, part of a larger force that had just delivered another contingent of the Kawaguchi Brigade to Taivu Point, paused to bombard Henderson Field enroute back to Rabaul. An overly helpful PBY patrol aircraft pilot sought to illuminate the bombarding ships for Marine shore gunners. His parachute flares, however, suddenly revealed to the Japanese the unexpected presence of the two destroyer transports just offshore. It was no contest. The Japanese cut them to pieces.

Lieutenant Senzou Kabashima, Imperial Japanese Navy, was gunnery officer on the destroyer *Yudachi* that night. Five minutes after beginning its bombardment of the airfield, *Yudachi* sighted the two small ships in the flare's bright light. The three Japanese destroyers closed the range, illuminating the American ships with their spotlights. Kabashima logged the events: "23:02 [0102 local] we sighted enemy at 80 degrees of our left. Opened fire 23:03. Hit it head on. Hit second one too."

*Gregory* and *Little* had not been caught napping. The crews were at General Quarters and promptly returned fire. But their three-inch guns and

Part of the 1st Raiders communications platoon in the "Coconut Grove" bivouac area of Guadalcanal. Edson's insistence on effective combat communications led him to seek these skilled men with special care.

primitive fire control systems proved no match for the Japanese destroyers. Soon both ships were burning fiercely, careening out of control.

The Japanese kept pouring it on, firing nearly 500 rounds in thirty-three minutes. As Lieutenant Kabashima recorded the battle: "23:23 [0123 local]: rushed into [contact] again. Two enemy ships are burning. We approached them. We continued firing towards those burning ships. 23:26: stopped our firing. We retreated by quite slow speed to hide our trace to air sight. This was miraculous success!"[12]

In his exuberance Kabashima neglected to record the fact that the three Japanese ships deliberately steamed through the survivors, running over some with their screws and machine-gunning others. Both U.S. Navy captains died, as did thirty-one others. Boats from the Marine beachhead rescued 238 survivors the next morning, including seventy severely wounded.[13]

News of this disaster devastated the Raiders. They were still grieving over the loss of *Colhoun* and so many of her crew—and now this. Captain John Sweeney of Baker Company described the pall this havoc cast over the Raiders. "We lost many comrades-in-arms among the crews of those three ships....They brought us to Tulagi where they literally cheered us over the side to make that first assault....They were part of us and we hurt for them." Everyone on Guadalcanal grieved. Martin Clemens called the loss "a chief blow." Lieutenant John W. Bernhardt, the boat group commander on USS *McKean* (APD 5), recorded that the loss of the two ships left "our spirits as low that day as they had ever been." *McKean* was now the sole survivor of Transport Division 12, whose APDs had made six round trips between Espiritu Santo or Efate and Guadalcanal during the campaign's first twenty days, "carrying in everything from toilet paper to coast artillery." The ships spent so much time close to shore, Bernhardt explained, that the sailors painted them green with intermittent palm trees (not to mention a few mermaids) as camouflage from prying eyes to seaward. With understandable pride they had called themselves "The Green Dragons."[14]

The Raiders realized with a cold shiver that but for the grace of God they would have shared the same fate as *Gregory* and *Little*. Fatalistic Edson put it down as merely "another example of 'Ol' Lady Luck,'" but he went on to admit that "had the [Cape Esperance raid] plan been carried out the Raider Battalion would have gone down with the destroyers that night, for we would have been in approximately their identical location when the shooting started—steaming towards our planned 0400 debarkation area."[15]

Reports by the surviving sailors that the Japanese ships deliberately tried to kill the men in the water left the Raiders in a cold rage. Initially the Marines had regarded their enemies with a wary antipathy. Subsequent reports of the Japanese slaughter of Lieutenant Colonel Frank Goettge and his patrol on 12 August, their butchery of Sergeant Major Vouza on the 20th, and now their cold-blooded attempts to kill helpless sailors in the water created an abiding hatred. For many this would last a lifetime.

Vengeance against the three Japanese destroyers came in due time. Marine aviators sank *Murakumo* off Cape Esperance the day before the Raiders departed Guadalcanal. Other aviators sank *Hatsuyuki* near Bougainville. The heavy cruiser *Portland* sank Lieutenant Kabashima's *Yudachi* during the bloody "Naval Battle for Guadalcanal" on 13 November.[16]

## General Kawaguchi

In Rabaul, both the Seventeenth Army and the Eighth Fleet expected great things from Major General Kiyotake Kawaguchi. His success in commanding his brigade against British Borneo and Sarawak, followed by his selection to spearhead the invasion of Fiji and Samoa (albeit canceled by the Midway reverse) made him popular among campaign planners. They fully expected him to recapture the airfield, scatter the American Marines into the jungle, and restore the southern Solomons to Imperial domain. So confident were the commanders in Rabaul of Kawaguchi's success they designated ships to converge and planes to land on Guadalcanal as soon as the field commander flashed his victory signal.

Kawaguchi was forty-nine years old in September 1942, a native of Kochi Prefecture in eastern Shikoku, the son of an army lieutenant colonel and the son-in-law of Major General Suekichi Hagino. Kawaguchi's bristling black mustache offset his receding hairline and conveyed a fierce bearing. He was a veteran of twenty-eight years of commissioned service, having received his appointment as a second lieutenant in 1914, three years before Merritt Edson. Eight years later, in 1922, he graduated from the Military Staff College. For the next seventeen years he served as a staff officer, except for one year's duty as an instructor in the Army Heavy Artillery School. Kawaguchi no doubt learned valuable lessons from so many years of staff duty, but his conspicuous lack of a field command during this extended period is a telling deficiency. Yet he sparkled in Borneo while leading his brigade against the 2d Battalion, 15th Punjabi Infantry of the Indian Army. Guadalcanal's clinging jungles, hostile natives, and enraged Raiders would constitute a different challenge.[17]

Kawaguchi's shortcomings had little to do with his intellect or candor. When news of the Americans landing on Guadalcanal reached him through a naval attaché in Palau, he responded gravely. "The battles of the Pacific War had so far been with the military forces of the enemies' colonies. This time the forces (at Guadalcanal) had come from their mother countries. I thought the situation had become serious..."[18]

Kawaguchi's innate stubbornness contributed to the ragged deployment of his reinforced brigade to Guadalcanal. He wanted to deploy by barge—after all, he had launched his attack on Borneo in December with a surprise, five-hundred-mile barge approach across the South China Sea—but the Navy now wanted to take him in by fast destroyers. In truth, both modes of delivery were coming under increasing attack from the Cactus Air Force as they approached the island, even at night. Kawaguchi argued that barges could move at night, pull into sheltered jungle coves during the day. A compromise ensued. At least one battalion would move by barge, the others on the destroyers the Americans dubbed the "Tokyo Express."

Ironically, most of the destroyers got through (at least a thousand troops landed safely from destroyers at Taivu Point the night the *Gregory* and *Little* came to grief). The barges foolishly came down the wrong side (the north side) of The Slot and were unable to complete the crossing to Guadalcanal during darkness. Caught in transit in broad daylight by Cactus pilots, the battalion lost its commander and half its men to the mercilessly strafing planes. Several hundred survivors, as we have seen, took refuge on Savo Island just hours after Griffith's group of Raiders departed empty-handed. These men would make it to Guadalcanal, but not in the place or condition desired by Kawaguchi.[19]

Kawaguchi's orderly mind had difficulty dealing with the chaos of the deployment. He had five infantry battalions, but two were last-minute additions, the rear echelon of the Ichiki Detachment and the advance echelon of the Sendai Division. The commanders hardly knew each other. The barge-borne survivors, Kawaguchi's Second Battalion, were scattered fifty miles away, west of the Matanikau. His headquarters in Rabaul added to the stress by suggesting an earlier attack date, the 12th of September, vice the 13th. Kawaguchi regretted his acquiescence almost immediately.

The former heavy artillery instructor also bemoaned the loss of his bigger guns. His force, he exclaimed, was "just infantry," with but "twelve light guns," which left him no other option but "to attack with our bayonets." He ordered a complex three-prong attack on Henderson Field for

Six junior officers who earned their combat spurs at Tulagi and Guadalcanal. Left to right: kneeling, John Sweeney, John Salmon, Rex Crockett; standing, Robert Neuffer, Edwin Wheeler, Edward Dupras.

the night of the 12th, naively believing he could move his four Taivu Point battalions and their field pieces through the heart of the jungle, from Tetere to the southern approach to the airfield, in less than a week. He would be marching blindly. There were no trails. He would cross—and recross—six major rivers. Moreover, Kawaguchi had a defective compass and no land maps or aerial photographs. "An army fighting without a map is just like a merchant doing business without an abacus," he said wryly. At least, he thought, his main force at Taivu had landed with plenty of supplies and equipment to sustain the jungle expedition.[20]

## A Perfect Raid

Edson's Raiders had learned to keep their leader under careful scrutiny. Knowing his inclination to propose difficult missions for the battalion, the men grew particularly nervous every time he visited the division command post. Then, according to Lieutenant Houston Stiff, a familiar lament would arise: "Oh, Christ! The Old Man's got that so-and-so grin on his face again. Now there'll be hell to pay!" Added Stiff: "And there usually was."[21]

Although nowhere recorded as a fact, it is safe to assume that Red Mike Edson returned to his bivouac on 7 September with just a hint of that enigmatic smile. He had gone to the division command post that morning to propose yet another Raider mission to Colonel Thomas and his assistant, Lieutenant Colonel Merrill Twining. The Cape Esperance raid had been canceled with the loss of the two APDs, but there were at least temporarily two more destroyer transports in the area, plus a pair of California tuna boats that had reached Guadalcanal on 1 September for harbor utility work. Edson figured the Raiders could ride to war on anything that floated.

Thomas and Twining were a step ahead of Edson this particular morning. Martin Clemens' scouts were reporting more Japanese troops in the vicinity of Taivu Point than Cape Esperance. The enemy soldiers seemed to be concentrated near Tasimboko, a deserted village on the coast about eighteen miles east of the Marine perimeter. While several hundred in number, the troops appeared ill-equipped and half starved (as it turned out, the initial scout reports concerned the survivors of the Ichiki Detachment). Could Edson, temporarily reinforced by the shot-up 1st Parachute Battalion, execute a one-day raid to disrupt the build-up and gather combat intelligence?

Edson expressed immediate interest. Amphibious lift would present the biggest problem. The Raiders and parachutists combined numbered 833 officers and men (605 + 208, respectively), virtually a complete battalion. By no means could the two APDs (*McKean* and *Manley*) embark that many Marines for a tactical landing. The tuna boats could help (designated YPs, the Marines swiftly nicknamed them "Yippees."). Still, the destroyers would have to make a turnaround lift to bring in the balance of the composite battalion. The assault elements would be in grave danger in that long interval.

Other nagging details popped up. The shortage of landing boats for this makeshift flotilla meant the first two companies ashore would be truly vulnerable until the boats could return to the ships to bring in the second half of the landing force. The objective was well beyond supporting fires from field artillery, and the guns of the destroyers would be of little help. The Cactus Air Force could provide some fire support— but only after full daylight and only *if* there were no air raids. The whole scheme was damned risky. Could Edson undertake such a mission? Edson grinned.

The Raiders had just moved their base camp from the coconut grove and were busy clearing new fields of fire. The sudden embarkation orders surprised them. "About four we stop our work to check our gear and draw more ammo," said Henry Poppell. "Five, we take the six-mile journey to the seashore to board our APDs for a raid on the Japs....We are told [we] will run into about two thousand Japs poorly armed—ill fed—and war weary. They have one rifle for every ten men we hope." Poppell's "scuttlebutt" was wrong on both enemy intelligence and his assigned shipping. Able Company would ride the Yippees to this war, not the more "luxurious" APDs.[22]

Edson planned for Baker and Charlie Company to land abreast at Taivu Point in two waves of four boats each. These Raiders would stake out and defend the beachhead while the boats returned for Captain Antonelli's Able Company from the Yippees. The destroyers would reload their boats, pause to bombard the coastline, then return to the Kukum landing to embark the Parachutists and the Raiders' Easy Company (typically reduced to Houston Stiff's mortar platoon since the machine gun platoons were attached to the rifle companies) and Dog Company (already reduced to forty-six men by Edson's proclivity to reassign its members as combat replacements for the other three rifle companies). At day's end all hands would shoehorn themselves back aboard the ships for the return to Kukum. Correspondents Richard Tregaskis and Robert C. Miller would accompany the force. So would Sergeant Major Jacob Vouza, still recovering from his wounds but fiercely determined to help guide the Raiders towards his home village of Tasimboko (Clemens quietly asked Sam Griffith to keep Vouza on the ship).

Critical new intelligence from Clemens' scouts arrived just before the raiding force departed the evening of September 7th. The scouts now counted two or three thousand Japanese in the Taivu Point area, a ten-fold increase even if they were in fact "ill-equipped and half-starved." Edson consulted with Sam Griffith and Bob Brown. He was hampered by the temporary absence of his gunslinging intelligence officer Hank Adams, down with malaria. He also missed his three dynamic company commanders, Ken Bailey, Lew Walt, and Jumping Joe Chambers. Despite the reinforcement of the Parachutists, the Raiders were going into this fight thin on the ground in terms of leadership. Tasimboko would have to be a proving ground for several junior officers.

Edson never wavered in the face of the scouting reports. He listened, reflected, then ordered the raid to proceed.

General Vandegrift and Colonel Thomas did not share Edson's confidence. Thomas in particular had misgivings about the whole scheme, even though he had been its principal author. The 1st Marine Division was increasingly hard-pressed to cover the twelve-mile perimeter around Henderson Field. The Tokyo Express delivered more troops to the island each night. Deploying eight hundred highly-trained Marines in a makeshift flotilla on a dubious mission eighteen miles down the coast had the makings of a great disaster. If Edson became trapped the division would have no real means to mount a seaborne rescue force. The next twenty-four hours would be nail-biting time for the commanding general and his operations officer.

"We had the damnedest fleet you've ever seen," recalled Sam Griffith, who rode to war with his small command group on a Yippee. Griffith slept in the captain's bunk, but there was little sleep for the seventy or so other Marines and corpsmen crammed aboard the trawler. "I will always remember that night as the most miserable I ever spent," stated Able Company's T. D. Smith, whose squad had left a hot meal untouched when ordered to Kukum:

> We were hungry, really hungry. The smoking lamp was out but the stack of that YP poured sparks into the air all night. We were extremely crowded...so we huddled in a sitting position and attempted to brace ourselves to cat-nap....It was cold! The rolling vessel made some seasick and as they heaved we were all awash in cold sea water and vomit.[23]

The Raiders' luck prevailed throughout this dangerous night. The unescorted mini-convoy edged down the coast undetected, despite the constant swirl of bright sparks emitted by the laboring diesel engines of both YPs. Further, the Raiders missed a large Japanese task force at Taivu Point by less than twelve hours. Once again they would surprise their enemy.

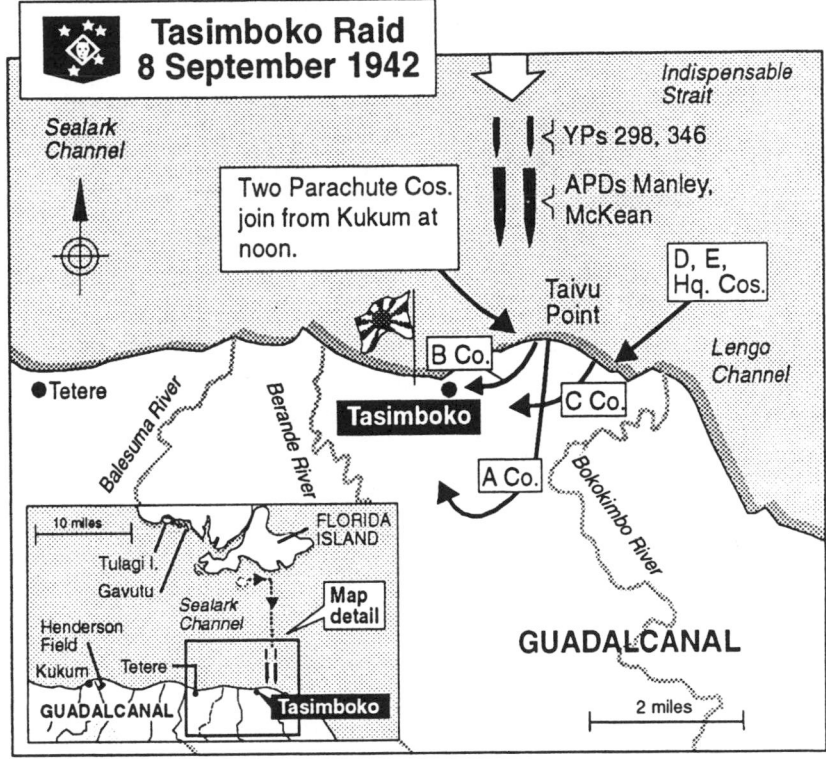

As at Tulagi, the Raiders decided against using their rubber boats for the assault. A stealthy approach was important, but the larger payload of the Higgins boats and the critical demand for a rapid turnaround to bring Able Company ashore were more essential. The ships anchored a thousand yards off Taivu Point at 0430 on 8 September, launched their Higgins boats, and began debarking Baker and Charlie Companies over the side. Navy Lieutenant Bernhardt, tasked to shepherd the eight boats ashore in the lingering darkness, received a compass azimuth from the *McKean*'s bridge and headed shoreward, deliberately maintaining half-throttle to reduce the giveaway noise of the boat engines.

No amphibious forces had more experience in executing night landings than Edson's Raiders and their original APDs, but such complex operations are never easy. An unexpectedly strong littoral current overpowered Bernhardt's reduced speed and forced the assault waves ashore a thousand yards west of Taivu Point. Yet here was more good luck for the Raiders; the new landing site was not only that much closer to their objective, Tasimboko, but they also managed to come ashore virtually in the footprints of the most recent Japanese reinforcements.

"We soon discovered that we were not the first to be there that night," recalled John Sweeney, then a captain commanding Baker Company's 1st Platoon. "Just above the high tide line we came upon several rows of neatly stacked soldiers' marching packs, perhaps several hundred in number. *Where were the owners?*"[24]

Sweeney showed the mysterious line of packs to Red Mike Edson when the second wave landed. Edson put Japanese linguist Tiger Erskine to work. Erskine soon found enough evidence to reveal that the tidily arrayed packs had been stashed by elements of the 2d Field Artillery Regiment of the Sendai Division. But Erskine could provide no clue as to their current whereabouts.

Sergeant Pete Pettus, the intelligence chief, examined the packs and reported each well stocked with new clothes, "leather hiking shoes with cobble nails in the soles," and about five pounds of rice. With growing uneasiness the Raiders went to ground in the trees, waiting for the boats to return with Able and Dog Companies.[25]

The raid had reached its critical point. Edson had barely three hundred Raiders ashore in the rear of what appeared to be a large and very well-equipped Japanese force. Two hundred more Raiders waited impatiently on the ships anchored offshore for the return of the Higgins boats. Getting them boated and ashore would take another forty minutes. The battalion was fragmented and vulnerable.

At this point occurred yet another freakish example of Raiders' luck. A sizable flotilla of warships suddenly appeared on the horizon, barely discernible in the hazy dawn. Consternation broke out among the men still on board the YPs. Captains John Antonelli and Edwin Wheeler quailed at the sight. "Ed and I saw them as Japanese reinforcements," said Antonelli, and "we considered ourselves doomed." So did Henry Poppell: "It looks as if our time is up." Only at the last minute did the ships identify themselves as an American convoy—a troopship and cargo ship, escorted by a cruiser and several destroyers—bound for Guadalcanal. Scary as their appearance was to the embarked Raiders, the coincidence of so many ships on the horizon during an obvious American landing operation truly alarmed the Japanese in the jungle surrounding the beach. To them it looked for all the world like a major invasion was underway against the Taivu Point–Tasimboko area. Many of the men in Kawaguchi's rear guard opted to disappear at this fearful sight. Said

John Antonelli afterwards, "The coincidental arrival of the convoy was a stroke of genius on the part of nobody, except our Good Lord." Sam Griffith agreed, adding some important amplifying details in 1963: "Members of Kawaguchi's excited rear echelon stayed around only long enough to get off a frantic message that a major landing was under way, and abandoning hot breakfasts, rifles, and two antitank guns which could have blown the landing craft out of the water, headed for the boondocks."[26]

United Press staff correspondent Robert C. Miller posted a dispatch about his landing with Able Company in the second echelon that morning. Reflecting the nervousness shared by all hands, he noted: "It took us 20 minutes to make the shore in the landing boats, the longest 20 minutes in my life. I made the mistake of being in the front of the boat and got pushed ashore first—unarmed. Ran like hell for the bush and found four Marines had beaten me to it." An unidentified Baker Company Raider perhaps described the landing more eloquently. "It was like a training exercise back in Samoa," he said. "Everyone—despite being scared shitless—seemed to know what he was expected to do and did so."[27]

Not quite. Too many Raiders milled around, examining the packs, admiring the captured antitank gun, and ignoring their tactical jeopardy. Edson set things straight. To Private First Class James Mallamas, crouched behind a dune, Edson said in his raspy, impersonal voice, "Mallamas, get up on top, you have no field of fire." As Sergeant Tony Massar checked his section at sunrise the Raiders began receiving scattered rifle fire and Edson trotted by hissing, "Get your section off the beach and into the trees." The Raiders settled down to business and began their move against Tasimboko.[28]

Meanwhile, the naval flotilla departed on its two-hour journey back to Kukum to pick up the parachutists and Lieutenant Stiff's mortar people. The APDs paused to shell the Japanese supply base at Tasimboko, an unusual mission for the Green Dragons but executed with particular relish. Exclaimed Lieutenant Bernhardt: "We had a beautiful time blasting hell out of them. We felt we were making up in some measure for the *Little, Gregory,* and the *Colhoun.*" By 0700 Captain Dale Brannon roared overhead with the first of what would become four P-400 strike missions by his squadron against Tasimboko. If Kawaguchi had a "soft underbelly" in his campaign, it was surely his lightly defended supply base. The local Japanese defenders, rocked by this concentrated aerial and seaborne bombardment, became even more convinced that they were the target of a concerted American invasion and edged farther into the jungle.[29]

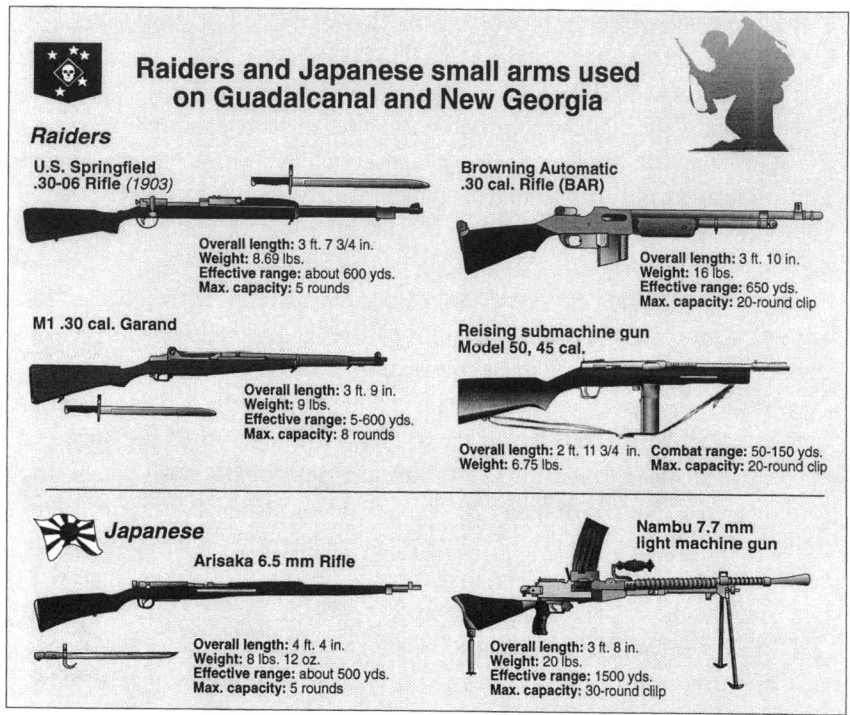

"Raiders and Japanese small arms used on Guadalcanal and New Georgia," by Raider Carl Fox. The battalion did not transition to the new M1 rifles until 1943.

The Raiders began the day less than 4,000 yards from Tasimboko, an abandoned village of eighteen structures situated astride a coastal trail crossing. The approach from the east seemed simple—level ground, occasional clearings in the underbrush, a shallow ford across the Kema River near its mouth—yet getting there would take Edson much of the day. Part of this delay stemmed from his complex tactics, another part from sharp fire received from pockets of enemy resistance, but the main reason appeared to be Edson's extreme caution. He knew he had a bear by the tail. As Edson would later report to Vandegrift, "This is no motley of Japs." Kawaguchi, as it turned out, was near Tetere, perhaps six miles beyond Tasimboko and across two sizable rivers, when the Raiders landed. He had in fact just launched his lead battalion into the interior jungle along the Balesuna River. Edson, unaware of either his opponent's location or intentions, had to be wary of a large-scale counterattack.

Leery but hardly timid, Edson divided his command and launched a two-pronged attack on the village hours before the final third of his composite command would arrive. He ordered Major Lloyd Nickerson's Baker Company to advance along the coastal trail and sent Captain Antonelli's Able Company on a long swing southwest through the jungle to envelop the village from the south. Captain Bob Thomas, who had replaced the wounded Major Ken Bailey in command of Charlie Company, would guard the landing beach until the parachutists could arrive with the second APD lift. Dog Company, one-third its original strength and now commanded by Captain Bill Sperling, would reinforce Thomas's outfit.

Edson, likely estimating that any concerted attack by Kawaguchi would come along the coast trail, chose to advance with Nickerson, accompanied by his runner, Corporal Walter Burak, and operations officer Major Bob Brown. Edson sent Sam Griffith and three native scouts with Antonelli's flanking attack through the jungle.

Corporal Fred Serral's TBX radio team started out with Griffith. The 120-pound, three-component TBX could not reach the division CP from the jungle, so Griffith posted Sergeant Horsecollar Smith on *Manley* to relay both voice and telegraph key messages. Each TBX component weighed about forty pounds. Serral carried the transmitter-receiver; Private First Class David Tabor, the accessory package; and Private First Class Herschel Sterling, the antenna and hand-cranked generator. During this long day Serral's team would assemble and tear down the rig a record thirty-seven times. Erecting and dismantling the twenty-four-foot antenna took too much time. Sterling wound up dragging the beast behind him through the jungle. The Raider communicators surpassed themselves to keep their radios both forward and functional, but overall communications during the raid would alternate between fair and awful, the latter a function of the terrain and the heavy rains which came at midday.[30]

Baker Company's advance soon encountered even more evidence of recent arrivals of large numbers of the enemy: back packs, fully a thousand discarded life preservers, another antitank gun, a pile of freshly opened clam shells. Captain Sweeney gingerly directed his platoon into the thicker woods along the Kema River.

"John Wolf" Sweeney was twenty-three and just coming into his own as a field Marine. Born in Columbus, Ohio, the 1940 Xavier University graduate decided to forego a career in business administration to become a Marine officer. Red Mike Edson was his first battalion commander, and Sweeney learned well at the feet of the master. He led Easy Company's demolition platoon during the assault on Tulagi, but with the death of Lieutenant Eugene Key, Edson transferred Sweeney to Baker Company to take over Key's platoon. Sweeney would participate with distinction in all seven of the Raiders' battles. Edson would place him in command of Baker Company five days after Tasimboko.

Sweeney's platoon contained a microcosm of the Raiders. "Platoon Sergeant Robert Anielski taught me well," Sweeney remembered in a 1956 letter, "and we had terrific squad leaders like Corporals William Carney, Ben Howland, and Johnnie Holladay [and his rifle 'Ol' Lucifer']." Other distinctive characters filled the ranks, including worldly Private First Class Guy Castle, who had volunteered in the 1930s for service as an expatriate in the Lincoln Brigade in the Spanish Civil War, and Private First Class Frank Russell Whittlesey, a Yale student, cerebral and shy, the nephew of Army Major Charles W. Whittlesey who earned the Medal of Honor and great fame in command of the celebrated "Lost Battalion" (308th Infantry) in World War I.[31]

Sweeney's platoon eased across the waist-deep Kema River, astonished to discover an abandoned 75mm gun sitting in a clearing along the western bank. A second abandoned gun loomed ahead—"this was getting weird"—then the lead Marines spotted several Japanese soldiers sprinting towards the weapon. The Raiders' fusillade missed. The soldiers, obviously artillerymen, heaved the handspikes, leveled the muzzle, slammed home a shell. An instant's pause, then a blinding flash and an ear-splitting *crack!*

Few combat experiences are more unnerving than being on the receiving end of point-blank direct fire from an artillery piece. The shell shrieked down the long column of Raiders with a velocity of 1,160 feet per second, making instant believers of many a salty rifleman. Henry Poppell was far in the rear, waiting to accompany Able Company's plunge into the jungle, when the first projectile flared by—"I bounce off the deck like a rubber ball!" Even Red Mike Edson dove for cover, according to Richard Tregaskis, who took note of the shell's "furry whistle" even as he "burrowed deeper into the wet jungle foliage."[32]

The Sendai gunners were good. Each slam of the breech block was followed instantaneously by another blinding blast. Men took hideous hits. Sweeney's promising squad leader, Corporal William D. Carney, a twenty-three-year-old Pennsylvanian, died instantly. One high round hit a tree, clipping off an enormous limb which pinned Private First Class Kenneth Brubaker to the earth, badly injured. Whizzing fragments slashed into Corporal Maurice Pion, leaving his arm hanging in shreds. The Raiders reeled under this pounding.

One young Raider reacted as he had been trained. Private First Class Andrew J. Klejnot hit the deck, snaked his way furiously through the underbrush to a fallen log three dozen yards off to the flank, assumed a good firing position, adjusted the sights on his Springfield, and drilled the near gunner in the head. The other crewmen whirled in consternation. Klejnot worked his bolt, took a deep breath, squeezed off another shot. A second gunner tumbled off his seat; the third member fled. The logjam was broken.

Among Merritt Edson's many legacies was his fervent emphasis on combat marksmanship training. Not long after Guadalcanal Edson stated his principles in a national magazine: "Teach target marksmanship at known ranges first. Then teach the man to estimate his own ranges. Teach him to shoot at indistinct targets, at moving targets....Above all else give him confidence in his own weapon." Private First Class Klejnot had learned these lessons exceedingly well.[33]

The 1st Marine Raider Battalion was blessed with superb corpsmen. Two of these went to work on the casualties. In John Sweeney's words, "Alfred W. Cleveland from South Dartmouth, Massachusetts, and Karl B. Coleman from McAndrews, Kentucky, concentrated on Pion. Using a penknife as a scalpel they amputated his shattered left arm at the shoulder, pinned the skin around the stump, and applied a field dressing." (Pion would live; in fact, many Raiders returning to the States in later years would be surprised and delighted to be greeted by a one-armed dock sentry in San Diego, still proudly wearing Marine green—Sergeant Maurice Pion, USMC.)[34]

The Raiders paused briefly to examine the lethal field piece. Sergeant Pettus properly identified it as a 1908 vintage 75mm gun. It was the Japanese M41 mountain or "regimental" gun, akin to the Marines' 75mm pack howitzer in that the weapon could be disassembled into six pieces for transport by man or beast. Kawaguchi, unfortunately, had no beasts for his jungle trek, and, with an average weight of two hundred pounds per component, very few of the weapons would arrive at The Ridge intact.[35]

The crisis on the west bank of the Kema River resolved, Sam Griffith and John Antonelli led their column cautiously into the jungle. This was a high-risk mission. Able Company would be jungle-bound and frequently out of radio contact for the next seven hours. For the first half of this period Edson would be operating in the vicinity of an unknown superior force with his own battalion splintered into four fragments. The parachutists enroute from Kukum would not arrive until 1130, while

Charlie and Dog Companies guarded the beachhead, Baker Company edged along the coast, and Able Company stumbled through the jungle to the southwest.

Griffith and Antonelli encountered some of the same difficulties that had already begun to bedevil Kawaguchi—poor maps, disorientation, slow progress. The Kema River proved more of an obstacle upstream, narrower but swifter flowing. Crossing tactically took time.

Griffith kept an eye on the native scouts as a hunter watches a good bird dog. He also kept an appraising eye on young Captain Antonelli in his first combat performance as a company commander, subbing for the malaria-ridden Lew Walt. Antonelli was twenty-five, a native of Lawrence, Massachusetts, and a Naval Academy graduate. Yet he was barely eighteen months out of Basic School and now led 150 Raiders in close proximity to a force of experienced Japanese jungle fighters. Griffith was impressed with Antonelli's steadiness and toughness.

Griffith would never admit that the column became lost in the jungle ("only temporarily" he would later say). Private First Class T. D. Smith put the shoe on the other foot: "We knew where WE were—the rest of the battalion was lost." It took hours but the column finally cut the north-south foot trail, turned right, and fell upon Tasimboko from the south, their sudden appearance from that unexpected quarter scaring hell out of the few remaining defenders of the supply dump.[36]

The long lapses when Edson lost communications with Griffith's column surely worried Red Mike. His cool exterior masked his concern, but there is little doubt Edson worried whether he had entered a trap or when Kawaguchi would come roaring back from wherever he had been marching. As the day wore on, Nickerson's Baker Company began to encounter more professional infantry outposts, the same deadly mixture of Nambu machine gunners protected by snipers the Raiders had faced in Tulagi. "Estimate at least 1,000 well-armed, well-equipped troops," Edson reported to Division at 1130. Griffith later disagreed, avowing in 1949 that the resistance came from "several hundred service troops, left to guard Kawaguchi's stores." This may have been true of the scattered troops Griffith encountered around the village, but Edson's opposition was of a decidedly experienced force. Historian Richard Frank, whose ten years of research place him at the forefront of Guadalcanal historians, reports that Kawaguchi dispatched the 10th Company, 124th Infantry to reinforce the service troops and artillerymen around Tasimboko.[37]

Conditions improved after noontime. The parachutists and Houston Stiff's mortar platoon arrived, linked up with Charlie and Dog companies, and moved west along the coast in trace of Edson. Red Mike regained communications with Griffith's column. The rains abated enough to permit a return to action by Dale Brannon's shark-tooth-painted P-400s. This took guts. The fighter strip was abruptly a quagmire. The second Airacobra down the runway crashed and burned. The third pilot radioed Brannon for advice. "Your call," Brannon answered. The pilot closed his canopy and took off. Within minutes the two P-400s were screeching low over Tasimboko.[38]

While Edson's confidence grew, Colonel Thomas still nursed his misgivings as he fretted and paced in the division command post. In his memoir, Thomas recalled that Edson radioed, "I've landed in the rear echelon of a sizable Jap force," then later reported, "If they turn around and come after me I'm in a bad fix." A review of the message traffic recorded in the D-3 Journal for 8 September reveals two different outlooks on the situation. Edson, wary but aggressive, requested air strikes, a supporting landing by another infantry battalion west of Tasimboko, even a couple of gun crews for his captured 75mm regimental guns. Thomas (presumably—he admitted to spending the entire day by the radio) seemed cautious and concerned, denying any reinforcement landings as "impractical." On three occasions, beginning as early as 1056, he ordered Edson to "re-embark your battalion and return to Kukum." Edson ignored him.[39]

Sweeney's platoon still had the point just east of Tasimboko. One well-sited Nambu machine-gun nest held up the advance. Sweeney sent Corporal Ben Howland's squad around the flank while he distracted the gunner with choice insults in Japanese he had learned from Tiger Erskine. Edson dispatched Major Bob Brown forward to assess the delay. Brown crawled up behind Sweeney. "What the hell's going on?" "Watch," Sweeney said, and scurried to a banyan tree. "*Bakuo!*" he hollered, at which the Nambu gunner responded with a prolonged blast that shivered the massive tree. Brown, seeing Howland approaching from behind the enemy, grinned, and elbowed his way back to Edson. Before he arrived he heard the tell-tale rattle of a Browning Automatic Rifle. Two Private First Classes, John Van Ness and Harold Brown, riddled the three distracted Japanese gunners.[40]

Tasimboko at last! The starving Raiders had uncovered a food cache as memorable as that ransacked by Stonewall Jackson's infantry at Manassas Junction in 1862. Tins of crabmeat, big brown bottles of lager beer, cans of sliced beef in soy sauce, fancy Dutch cigarettes—many a dungaree pocket remained suspiciously bulging after the Raiders officially destroyed the well-stocked depot. This took hours, an undeniable highlight for every Raider and parachutist on the scene.

Edson and Griffith, finally reunited, knew they had an opportunity to strike a telling blow against Kawaguchi in but little time. Quickly they restored discipline. Forget the delicacies, they ordered, destroy the rice, the mainstay of the enemy. The Raiders cheerfully slashed open thousands of rice bags, strewing the grain along the ground, then polluting them with both urine and gasoline. They stacked food, clothing, and equipment in the village houses and set them afire. They found a sophisticated long-range radio transmitter, destroyed the generator, and lugged the receiver back to the beachhead. Captain Harry L. Torgerson, of the parachute battalion, reported the discovery and destruction of "ten rubber boats completely equipped with outboard motors." Sam Griffith claimed he "threw 300 anti-tank mines into the sea myself." Sergeant Pettus found three dumps of first aid supplies and convinced enough men to lug the invaluable material back to base. Correspondent Richard Tregaskis had the presence of mind to gather up a bonanza of intelligence documents in an army blanket. Before midnight the division G-2 would know Kawaguchi's order of battle and mission orders.[41]

Edson was exultant. At 1430 he radioed division, "Am destroying Tasimboko and as much property as possible. Will re-embark about 1530 unless you desire we remain here until tomorrow." Five minutes later General Vandegrift, not Jerry Thomas, answered, "Reembark and return to Kukum. Well done." The Raiders and parachutists left the bonfires to return to their beachhead. Chortled correspondent Robert Miller in his dispatch, "Just finished a first class act of arson...it was fun."[42]

At some point an exhausted and highly agitated lieutenant ran into General Kawaguchi's command post near Tetere. Second Lieutenant Osa was Kawaguchi's "intendant," or supply officer, responsible for the Tasimboko depot. First he told the general of the unexpected arrival of the battery of the Sendai Division's field artillery regiment during the night. "After awhile," Osa continued, "battleships and transports came to the same spot. At first we thought they were our own forces, but instead they were enemy forces. The sick and wounded men, too, fought against them, also the field artillery forces just landed...but four of our artillery pieces were captured...and we had to retreat." Kawaguchi's heart sank, yet there was little he could do. The airfield was his objective, not Tasimboko, but now his forces would risk unimaginable hardships without their food reserves and supporting arms.[43]

The raid on Tasimboko had instant repercussions throughout the South Pacific. Rabaul reported to IGHQ that "Kawaguchi was sandwiched" between two forces. Admiral Mikawa dispatched a large force of cruisers and destroyers to bombard the new American enclave west of Taivu Point. IGHQ alerted reinforcements in Batavia and New Guinea to prepare for quick embarkation. Lieutenant Kabashima on board the destroyer *Yudachi* logged the day's events: "Received news of enemy ships near Taivu. They begin landing. We need to destroy them as soon as possible. If we do not, they will increase in power again."[44]

Edson's force re-embarked before dusk, pausing to ruin their captured field pieces by removing the breech blocks and towing the guns into the sea behind straining Higgins boats. The men clambered aboard the ships with their captured Nambus, 81mm mortar shells, and medical supplies—hindered undeniably by the contraband bottles clinking in their skivvies. Again Raider luck prevailed. The entire command—with all their booty—absolutely jammed chockablock into the four craft, slowly beat its way back to Kukum, as vulnerable a target as the angry Japanese would ever desire, while the Tokyo Express led by the cruiser *Sendai* came racing down The Slot at flank speed. Somehow the small force reached Kukum ahead of the Express, offloaded the troops, then scattered. It was not a clean escape. Lieutenant Kabashima reported at midnight, "No enemy at Lunga, we advanced to Tulagi. Sighted two destroyers in harbor. Shot them. One sunk."[45]

It was the tuna boat YP 346, not a destroyer, that took the hit, but thanks to the bravery of its wounded skipper, Joaquin S. Theodore, the burning trawler beached but did not sink. Less than two hours earlier more than a hundred Raiders had jammed her decks.

Two Raiders died in action during the Tasimboko Raid: Sweeney's squad leader Corporal Carney and an Easy Company machine gunner, twenty-year-old Private Seraphine Buddy Smith from Canton, Ohio. Six other Raiders were wounded, the most serious being Corporal Pion. Tasimboko received little external notice. No ships were named for valorous participants; few men received awards for bravery (one notable exception: a Navy Cross for Pharmacists Mate Second Class Karl B. Coleman). It was a short, risky but relatively bloodless action, and it would soon be subsumed by a much more violent battle.[46]

Yet Tasimboko was the perfect spoiling attack, an ideal mission for the Raiders. Kawaguchi had been dealt a crippling blow before the Battle of the Ridge even began. Loss of four-dozen crew-served weapons and much of his reserve ammunition would hamper Kawaguchi's expedition against the airfield. And the loss of so much of his rations and medical supplies would turn his subsequent retreat through the jungle into a trail of horrors.

"That little raid," Sam Griffith would later state, "was one of the really very successful small operations of World War II." Merrill Twining declared that Tasimboko "will stand as a classic example of the brilliant employment of hit and run tactics by a raider." The troops themselves felt good about the outcome. Said Raider Jack F. Tracy later to Frank Guidone, "that was the type raid I had joined the outfit for."[47]

"God favors the bold at heart," General Vandegrift had said of the Raiders at Tulagi. The "Bold-at-Hearts" had been favored again at Tasimboko.

## Notes

1. CO Raider Battalion message to CG, 1st Marine Division, 0855 8 September 1942, D-3 Journal, Guadalcanal File, MCHC [D-3 Journal].
2. Diary entry, Martin Clemens Papers, MCHC, 168.
3. Frank Guidone, "Outline of 1st Raiders History," n.d., 2, author's possession.
4. Matthew Stevenson, "Guadalcanal," *The American Scholar* 59 (Summer 1990), 360. The second quote is by his father, Colonel Nikolai Stevenson, USMC (Ret.).
5. Poppell Diary, entries 31 August 1942 and 2 September 1942, 13; CG, 1st Marine Division, Division Commander's Final Report on Guadalcanal Operation, Phase IV, 252, campaign file, Reference Section, MCHC.
6. Kenneth Munson, *Aircraft of World War II* (Garden City, NJ: Doubleday, 1972), 30. The F-100 was the export version of the P-39. According to Munson, the P-39Q model Airacobra mounted a 37mm cannon and four .50 caliber machine guns; it could also carry a 500-pound bomb. The United States delivered about 5,000 of the later models to the Soviet Union under the Lend Lease program. The author is indebted to former Marine Sloan McCloskey of New Orleans for this reference material.
7. Col. Dale D. Brannon, USAF (Ret.), paper presented in Guadalcanal Symposium, New Mexico State University, 1 November 1991 [Brannon Account]; Maj. Gen. Kawaguchi memoir, translated by Yukihisa Suzuki and transmitted to Brig. Gen. Sam Griffith on 7 June 1962, 13, Griffith Papers, MCHC [Kawaguchi Memoir].
8. Lt. Col. S. B. Griffith to CO, 1st Marine Raider Battalion, "Patrol on Savo Island," 5 September 1942, Raiders File, Reference Section, MCHC.
9. Gen. Gerald Thomas Oral Memoir, MCOHC, MCHC, 352.
10. Edson annotations on draft postwar essay by Houston Stiff, "That So-and-So Grin" [Edson/Stiff Draft Memoir]. Copy provided by Jon T. Hoffman.
11. Maxwell Miller to John Sweeney, 11 March 1994; Ben Quintana to *Dope Sheet*

editor Irv Reynolds, 13 August 1991; Gene Martin to Thomas Mullahey, 22 July 1992.

12. Former Lt. Senzou Kabashima, Imperial Japanese Navy memoir, translated and furnished by Maj. Akio Tani, paper presented during Guadalcanal Symposium, New Mexico State University, 1 November 1991 [Kabashima Memoir].

13. Frank, *Guadalcanal*, 211–212.

14. Colonel John Sweeney Tasimboko Memoir, n.d., 33–34 [Sweeney Tasimboko Memoir]; Diary entry, Martin Clemens Papers, MCHC, 171; John W. Bernhardt and Foster Hailey, "Saga of the Unsung—The Destroyer Transports," *Naval Institute Proceedings* 71 (February 1945), 178–182.

15. Edson/Stiff Draft Memoir.

16. Anthony J. Watts, *Japanese Warships of World War II* (London: Ian Allan, 1971), 371–76. Lt. Kabashima survived the war.

17. Kiyotake Kawaguchi biography from Ikuhiko Hata, *Nippon Rikukaigun Sogo Jitin* (Tokyo: Daigaku Shuppankai, 1991), 45. Additional details from Hayashi and Coox, *Kogun: The Japanese Army in the Pacific War* (Quantico, VA: Marine Corps Association, 1959), 38, 227.

18. Kawaguchi Memoir, 8.

19. *Ibid*, 9–12; Frank, *Guadalcanal*, 212–13; Griffith, *The Battle for Guadalcanal*, 89–103.

20. Kawaguchi Memoir, 12–15.

21. Edson/Stiff Draft Memoir. Colonel Stiff's polite "so-and-so" was a deliberate coverup for the common 1940s expression, "a shit-eating grin," implying someone up to certain mischief or illicit behavior.

22. Poppell Diary, 7 September 1942, 13–14.

23. Griffith Oral memoir, MCOHC, MCHC, 101; T. D. Smith Diary, 7–8 September 1942, 6.

24. Sweeney Tasimboko Memoir, 46.

25. Colonel John Erskine interview with Jon T. Hoffman, 1991. Pete Pettus "Tasimboko Raid," n.d.

26. Brig. Gen. John W. Antonelli, USMC (Ret.) comments on Tasimboko raid published in *The Raider Patch, ca.* 1973, 5; Poppell Diary, 8 September 1942, 14; Griffith, *The Battle for Guadalcanal*, 108. Griffith in a 1949 letter to the Marine Corps Historical Section, HQMC, stated that the "37mm" AT guns captured that morning were actually the new 47mm AT models, a weapon which would cause so much havoc against Marines at Peleliu, Iwo Jima, and Okinawa (15 February 1949).

27. Robert C. Miller, "Diary Tells How Marines Chased 2,000 Japs Into Solomons Jungle," *Washington Times-Herald,* 16 October 1942, Box 35, Edson Papers, Library of Congress; Sweeney Tasimboko Memoir, p. 47.

28. James Mallamas interview with Jon T. Hoffman, 1992; Anthony Massar interview with Jon T. Hoffman, 1992.

29. Bernhardt and Hailey, "Saga of the Unsung," 182; Brannon Account, 1 November 1991.

30. Fred A. Serral, "A TBX Team on the Tasimboko Raid," *Dope Sheet*, 1958, 3–4.

31. John Sweeney to Pete Pettus, *ca.* September 1956, 4; Sweeney Tasimboko Memoir, 48; Sweeney interview with author, 1999.

32. Poppell Diary, 8 September 1942, 14; Richard Tregaskis, "Tasimboko Blow Surprises Japs," *Boston Sunday Advertiser,* n.d., byline date: "Sept 8, 1942 (Delayed)."

33. Merritt A. Edson, "U.S. Rifleman, M-1944," *American Rifleman* 92 (March 1944), 9. Edson went on to say that marksmanship and fieldcraft were the essentials to finding and killing Japanese soldiers.

34. Sweeney Tasimboko Memoir, 49; Sweeney interview with author, 1999.

35. War Department Technical Manual TM-E30-480, *Handbook on Japanese Military Forces*, October 1944–September 1945 [Japanese Handbook], 393–94. Many Raiders believed these weapons to be 77mm guns, but the Imperial Army had no artillery pieces in this caliber. The M41 was lethal enough, despite its age, with a maximum range of 7,000 yards and a muzzle velocity of 1,160 feet per second.

36. Griffith Oral Memoir, MCOHC, MCHC, 102; T. D. Smith Diary, 8 September 1942, 6.

37. Edson to CG, 1st Marine Division, 0811 30 September 1942; D-3 Journal, 8 September 1942, 18; Griffith to Marine Corps Historical Section, HQMC, 15 February 1949, 2; Frank, *Guadalcanal*, 691.

38. Brannon Account; Serral, "A TBX Team."

39. Gen. Gerald Thomas Oral Memoir, MCOHC, MCHC, 353–4; D-3 Journal, 8 September 1942, 18–19.

40. Sweeney Tasimboko Memoir, 50–51. *"Bakuo"* reportedly meant "Fool!"

41. *Ibid*, 51–52; CO, 1st Parachute Battalion, "Report on the Tasimboco [sic] Raid," 8 September 1942, Box 6, Serial 63A 2534, WNRC, 5; Samuel Griffith to Merrill Twining, 19 December 1961, Griffith Papers, MCHC; Pete Pettus "Tasimboko Raid," n.d., 3; Miller, "Diary Tells How Marines Chased 2,000 Japs Into Solomons Jungle."

42. D-3 Journal, 8 September 1942, 19.

43. Kawaguchi Memoir, 14.

44. Griffith, *The Battle for Guadalcanal*, 108; Kabashima Memoir, 8 September 1942.

45. Kabashima Memoir, 8–9 September 1942.

46. 1st Raider Battalion muster roll, September 1942; Casualty Cards for Corporals Carney and Smith.

47. Twining, *No Bended Knee*, 93–94; Griffith Oral Memoir, MCOHC, MCHC, 105; Jack F. Tracy to Frank Guidone, 5 May 1996.

# 6

## Edson's Ridge: The Opening Round, September 1942

*We never felt we'd get out of it. We thought we'd either be paraded in cages in Tokyo or be pulling rickshaws somewhere. It came out our way. By the skin of our teeth.*

Lieutenant Thomas Mullahey, USMC
Able Company, 1st Marine Raider Battalion[1]

THE BATTLE FOR "BLOODY RIDGE" during 12–14 September 1942 represented an absolute zenith for Merritt Edson and the Raider battalion he had formed and trained.

While the campaign for Guadalcanal featured a dozen different crisis points on land, sea, and air, none quite matched the sheer drama of this savage battle. The opposing forces, both as yet undefeated, exchanged mortal blows at close quarters throughout two consecutive nights for possession of a critical terrain feature that dominated Henderson Field and the 1st Marine Division command post.

Personal bravery abounded on both sides. At one point in the darkest hours of the second night's fighting, a hodgepodge group of fewer than three hundred Raiders and parachutists stood back-to-back to defend the last and highest rise of the long ridge. At another juncture, the decimated remnants of one Japanese rifle company penetrated the cordon and spilled down into the command post and onto the lower edge of the fighter strip.

Kawaguchi had unwittingly attacked The Ridge with less than half his force. He frittered away his other units on secondary missions, lost control of his largest battalion, and retained no real reserve. Yet the final outcome might have been decidedly different had he been able to reinforce his stalwart attackers with a single fresh battalion when the issue remained in doubt on either night. In the end, Edson and his composite force and their supporting arms prevailed—convincingly.

## Teamwork

The battleground is deservedly known as "Edson's Ridge" or "Raiders' Ridge." But it would be inappropriate, and bad history as well, to ignore the sizable contribution of several other units. The Cactus Air Force surely contributed by shooting up 70 percent of the barge-borne II/124 in advance. The artillerymen of the 11th Marines probably killed more attacking Japanese than did all the riflemen and machine gunners. The reinforcing 2d Battalion, 5th Marines and elements of the 1st Engineer Battalion faced the enemy and suffered casualties during the battle. And the 1st Marine Parachute Battalion, reduced to three small companies by its losses at Gavutu, earned its share of glory the hard way. While some of the parachutists broke ranks during the second night's pullback—as did some of the Raiders—the balance stood and delivered. Captain Harry Torgerson's dramatic counterattack was one of the battle's turning points. By Sam Griffith's reckoning, the parachutists suffered 128 casualties, the Raiders 135 (other historians count Raider losses as high as 163). As one Raider said after the battle, "I saw an awful lot of parachute boots sticking out from under the ponchos of the dead being brought back down the ridge."[2]

The battle underscored another aspect of teamwork frequently overlooked by historians. Close examination of the casualty lists and the award nominations indicates The Ridge was not just an infantryman's fight. An inordinate number of communicators, medical personnel, and staff specialists fought just as fiercely, fully exposed. This reflects both the desperate nature of the fighting *and* Red Mike Edson's providential insistence that, in the Raiders, every man must be a rifleman.

## The Ridge

Sam Griffith described Edson's Ridge as "a broken, rugged, kunai-covered coral hogback which paralleled the Lunga [River] south of the airfield. Jungle lapped at its south, east, and west slopes; towards the north the ground gave way gently toward battered Henderson Field." Writer Matthew Stevenson, visiting the battleground a half-century later, stood on The Ridge and marveled at its dominance of the airfield below. "If

Cpl. Lee Minier mans his light machine gun in this bivouac snapshot in the Coconut Grove. Easy Company's machine gunners took a heavy toll in both nights on Edson's Ridge. Note the Raider behind Minier with a Johnson light machine gun.

Guadalcanal was Gettysburg in the Pacific," he mused, then "this was Little Round Top."[3]

Red Mike Edson was not the only Marine officer who assessed The Ridge as a likely avenue of approach for Japanese expeditionary forces. When the Tasimboko Raid's captured documents revealed Kawaguchi's intention to forego the coastal road and plunge into the jungled interior, Colonels Jerry Thomas, Merrill Twining, and Pedro del Valle (commanding the 11th Marines) each concluded, with Edson, that The Ridge represented the natural funnel from the south.

The officers knew from the intelligence documents that Henderson Field constituted Kawaguchi's operational objective. They knew from experience and study that the Japanese Army preferred to attack at night in order to maximize surprise and minimize enemy fire power. Attacking at night on Guadalcanal also made sense in view of the Imperial

Navy's command of the sea after sunset. Naval gunfire, properly coordinated, might offset Kawaguchi's shortfalls in heavy artillery. Yet even with veteran troops, any commander would experience extreme difficulty in controlling a reinforced brigade attacking at night through the dense jungle. The Ridge, with its broad swath of treeless kunai grass, represented the best avenue of approach for a concentrated night attack.

Indeed, two great night battles would be fought in this vicinity—Chesty Puller's 1st Battalion, 7th Marines, reinforced by the army's 164th Infantry, would make another desperate stand in the low ground adjoining the ridge against even larger forces the next month.

The 1st Raiders fought their battle for Edson's Ridge under somewhat more critical conditions, before the arrival of the 7th Marines from Samoa, a time of critical shortfalls in ships, aircraft, and manpower, a low point when the theater commander became so pessimistic about the Marines' ability to hold the island that he forwarded secret authority for Vandegrift to surrender. Of all the many dark days of the Guadalcanal campaign, the brief period leading up to the Battle of the Ridge can be described as the darkest. The intensity of Japanese bombing and naval shelling increased by an order of magnitude. Every native or Marine patrol returned with reports of Kawaguchi's veterans inexorably chopping their way through the jungle, moving ever closer.[4]

General Vandegrift lacked sufficient manpower to establish a true perimeter defense. The best he could do was to retain an emergency reserve and establish cordons and outposts along the likely avenues of approach (which included not only The Ridge but also the north-flowing rivers and the entire eight-mile beach stretching from the Tenaru to the Matanikau). Gaps existed everywhere. West of the Lunga, the three outposts of the Pioneer Battalion, the 1st Amphibian Tractor Battalion, and the 3d Battalion, 5th Marines were separated by at least a thousand yards. "None of these positions were complete or well organized," admitted Vandegrift in his report, because "the dense jungle represented a terrific obstacle to be overcome only by weeks of labor at a time when it was all too obvious that only days remained open to us....A penetration was almost a certainty."[5]

Despite repeated warnings by his colonels about The Ridge, Vandegrift persisted in his estimate that Kawaguchi would cut his approach shallow, hitting the 1st Marines' positions along Alligator Creek (as in fact the Kuma Battalion, in one of Kawaguchi's ill-advised diversions, attempted to do). The Ridge remained unguarded until the 10th. Kawaguchi could have walked straight through to the airfield had his hamstrung force moved with more alacrity. Nor did Vandegrift reposition his division reserve, the 2d Battalion, 5th Marines (now commanded by Colonel William Whaling) from west of the Lunga to backstop his Ridge defenders until the 13th. Vandegrift was by no means blind to the threat, but with Kawaguchi's far-flung battalions reported variously along three sides of his perimeter, he had to wait till the last minute to determine where the main attack would materialize.

Kawaguchi was at times as confused as Vandegrift about the location of his units. They were scattered from his rear guard at smoldering Tasimboko to the newest arrivals east of Cape Esperance. The costly barge deployment had splintered his regimental headquarters, under Colonel Akinosuka Oka, and his 2d Battalion, 124th Infantry. The Seventeenth Army had then sent him three reinforcing infantry battalions, the "Kuma" ("Bear") Battalion of the late Colonel Ichiki's 28th Infantry plus two battalions of the "Aoba Detachment," the veteran 4th Infantry from Davao in the Philippines. The 4th Infantry represented the advance elements of the 2d ("Sendai") Division, itself deploying to Guadalcanal from Sumatra. Confusing as it appears (then and now), this was the nominal order of battle for the "Ka Force," as Japanese planners labeled Kawaguchi's brigade:

*Main Force* (with Kawaguchi, approaching The Ridge)
  1st Battalion, 124th Infantry (**I/124**), Major Yukichi **Kokusho**
  3d Battalion, 124th Infantry (**III/124**), Lieutenant Colonel Kusukichi **Watanabe**
  2d Battalion, 4th Infantry (**II/4**), Major Masuro **Tamura**

*"Right Wing"* (initially with Kawaguchi, then independent)
  Kuma Battalion, 28th Infantry (Ichiki 2d echelon), Major Eishi **Mizuno**

*"Left Wing"* (northwest coast, well beyond the Matanikau)
  Headquarters, 124th Infantry, Colonel Akinosuka **Oka**
  2d Battalion, 124th Infantry (**II/124**), Major **Takamatsu** (KIA enroute)
  3d Battalion, 4th Infantry (**III/4**), (arrived too late, too far west)[6]

General Kawaguchi's complicated plan directed Mizuno's Kuma Battalion to penetrate Marine positions along Alligator Creek, Colonel Oka's mongrel group to attack east across the Matanikau, while his own Main Body advanced north along the Lunga, then along the thousand-yard expanse of The Ridge (which the Japanese would call "The Centipede" for the multiple spurs that emanated from both sides like the legs of an insect). Having reluctantly agreed to advance the attack date one

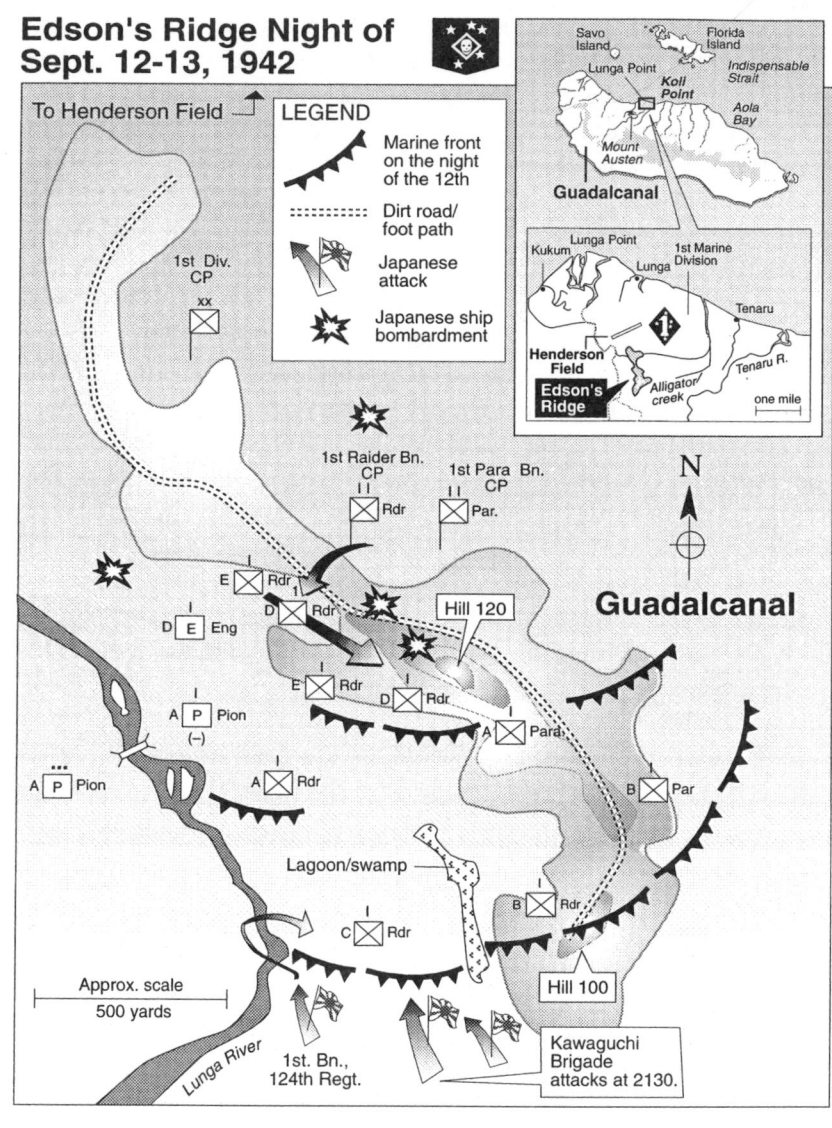

# Edson's Ridge Night of Sept. 12-13, 1942

**LEGEND**

- Marine front on the night of the 12th
- Dirt road/foot path
- Japanese attack
- Japanese ship bombardment

To Henderson Field →

1st Div. CP

**Guadalcanal**

Savo Island
Florida Island
Lunga Point
Koli Point
Indispensable Strait
Aola Bay
Mount Austen
Guadalcanal

Lunga Point
Kukum
Lunga
1st Marine Division
Tenaru
Henderson Field
Edson's Ridge
Alligator creek
Tenaru R.
one mile

1st Raider Bn. CP — Rdr

1st Para Bn. CP — Par.

E — Rdr

D — E Eng

D — Rdr

Hill 120

E — Rdr

D — Rdr

A — Para

A — P Pion (–)

A — P Pion

A — Rdr

B — Par

Lagoon/swamp

B — Rdr

C — Rdr

Hill 100

Approx. scale
500 yards

Lunga River

1st. Bn., 124th Regt.

Kawaguchi Brigade attacks at 2130.

N

full day, Kawaguchi ordered all units to commence their assault at 2000 on the night of 12 September. His few artillery weapons that had survived the zig-zag trek through the jungle ("one mountain gun [probably the Type 41 75mm] and two rapid-fire guns [typically Type 94 37mm guns]"), would open fire at that moment as a signal to attack. Having eschewed a reserve force, Kawaguchi would rely on surprise to gain the tactical advantage.[7]

General Vandegrift finally consented to move Edson's Raiders, with the 1st Parachute Battalion attached, to occupy The Ridge barely two days before Kawaguchi's initial assault. Jerry Thomas convinced the general that the open ground would serve as both a rest site for the exhausted troops and a show of force "just in case" Kawaguchi should attack through the jungle from the south. Edson and Thomas exchanged knowing glances. Both believed the main attack would come that way.

Edson had actually reconnoitered The Ridge a week earlier, before the Tasimboko Raid. He saw that the high ground, running straight towards the airfield, would provide a well-defined line of approach in a night attack. According to Houston Stiff, Edson then turned to Corporal Burak and said: "This is the place. This is where they'll hit."[8]

"We're moving our bivouac up to The Ridge," Edson told his men on the morning of the 10th. "It'll be a rest area for us. We'll get out of the V-ring for the Jap bombers." Perceptive Raiders nearby would have detected the trace of that enigmatic grin. Others would have observed how unobtrusively Edson gathered up what scant fortification material he could find—mainly barbed wire—for the rest area.[9]

The troops could use a legitimate rest. The composite battalion numbered more than eight hundred men as it toiled up the grassy slopes from the airfield, but sickness and exhaustion were beginning to take effect. The troops had not yet recovered from losing two consecutive nights' sleep on the Tasimboko mission. In addition, The Ridge proved to be ungodly hot, as compared to their previous bivouac along the coast.

The Raiders found little rest for the weary on the hogback. Edson ordered foxholes dug and barbed wire staked and strung. Digging proved difficult among the kunai roots and coral outcroppings, compounded by the general absence of engineering tools. The backpack folding entrenching tool had to serve as improvised spade, pick, and sledge hammer. Tiger Erskine, lacking even an e-tool, spent much of the day scraping a hole with his helmet and a borrowed bayonet. By twilight his hole measured ten inches deep. Able Company's Private First Class Henry Neal gave up in frustration. "I announced I wasn't digging any more. Just then Sergeant

Tom Pollard came by, reached down, jerked me about a foot off the deck, said one word—'*DIG!*' I dug."[10]

By the 11th all but the most oblivious Raiders could deduce that something big was heading their way. That morning they saw Colonel del Valle and several officers from the 11th Marines carefully charting every foot of ground along The Ridge and its approaches. Artillery forward observer teams appeared, surveyed the ground, plotted concentrations, began digging in. Behind them, in the low defiles south of the airfield, three batteries of 105mm howitzers moved into supporting positions and erected camouflage nets.

At noon came the daily Japanese air raid, but this time the Betty bombers ignored Henderson Field and dropped their sticks of daisy-cutters and 500-pound bombs directly along The Ridge. The Raiders were terrified. "It wasn't like the 'boom' of a distant bomb," said Private First Class Ben Quintana, "This was 'CRACK!'—like lightning coming right down your spine." Charlie Company BARman Joseph M. Rushton was "hit by the last bomb of the stick, even though I was tucked in the folds of a banyan tree forty yards away. Between the heat of the blast, the concussion and the flying debris I was sure I was a goner." Shrapnel splinters peppered Rushton's backside and upper legs. Two Raiders died and nine were wounded during the raid. "Some goddamned rest area," swore a shaken corporal.[11]

Edson and Griffith had conducted a limited reconnaissance patrol shortly after the Raiders and parachutists arrived on The Ridge. Edson then ordered Captain Antonelli to dispatch a larger combat patrol southward into the jungle on the 11th. Antonelli assigned Platoon Sergeant Joseph S. Buntin to lead the probe and told Gunnery Sergeant Cliff McGlocklin to provide a squad from his platoon. McGlocklin summoned Sergeant Harold C. Floeter and Sergeant Frank Guidone, explained the mission, and flipped a coin. Floeter won the toss and opted to remain in the perimeter. Guidone saddled up his squad to hustle after Buntin.

The Raiders ran into a Japanese patrol not far beyond the southern nose of The Ridge at the same time of the bombing raid. The bombs tumbled down along the axis of The Ridge and continued into the jungle, endangering both patrols. Guidone and Sylvester Niedbalski dove for the base of a huge tree. "The last bomb was close enough to pick Ski and me up and then cover us with jungle debris," said Guidone.

Both patrols broke contact after the bombing, and the Raiders now knew what Edson had known all along—a large enemy force was bearing down on The Ridge. But the shattered bivouac distracted the returning

**60mm Mortar Squad, Guadalcanal. Left to right: kneeling, Bob Addison, Ed Rutkowski; standing, John Burke, Arnold Nadeau, Pat Reath.**

patrol from their stimulating discovery. T. D. Smith recorded: "When we got back we found our area had been blown to bits by [the] bombers. Two men dead, some wounded. Ruined our galley." Guidone was stunned to see Sergeant Floeter sitting upright at the base of a banyan tree. He was dead. Floeter, twenty-five, from Roscommin, Michigan, had won the coin toss and lost his life.[12]

The Raiders spent a nervous night, especially those on listening posts in the jungle. This marked the Raiders' first real experience in a tropical rain forest; many grew jumpy at the rasping, screaming sounds of hidden jungle denizens that pierced the night. Japanese warships shelled The Ridge. Few men were able to sleep, but no Imperial foot soldiers materialized out of the darkness this night.

Not far away, Admiral Kelly Turner arrived on the island for an overnight emergency planning session with General Vandegrift. The ominous signs of a relentless new Japanese offensive sobered both commanders, but neither shared the pessimism of Admiral Ghormley. Turner promised to deliver the 7th Marines soon, ending a long feud with Vandegrift over the deployment of the last significant Marine infantry rein-

forcements available. Meanwhile, twenty-five miles west, Colonel Hiroshi Matsumoto, operations chief and point man for General Hyakutake's Seventeenth Army, stepped ashore. The Japanese were beginning to take seriously the recapture of Guadalcanal.

## The First Night

The morning of the 12th brought the unexpected and most welcome return of Major Ken Bailey from the hospital in New Caledonia. Bailey and Lieutenant "Spike" Ryder had simply walked out—a flagrant case of unauthorized absence—and hitched a series of rides to get back to Guadalcanal. The two wounded officers, seeking ways to make themselves useful during the long recuperative process, had volunteered to speak to groups of the army's Guadalcanal-bound 164th Infantry about Japanese weapons and tactics.[13]

Bailey was exuberant but still pale and weak. Edson decided to keep him on a tether as an operational assistant—some would describe him as a "roving linebacker"—instead of returning him to full duty as Charlie Company's commander. The decision proved expensive for C Company but inspirational for the battalion. Ken Dill Bailey, bearing the invisible angel of death on his broad shoulders, had barely two more weeks to give to his country and his Corps.

Bailey further endeared himself to the Raiders by bringing with him hundreds of sacks of mail, the first "Mail Call" the battalion had enjoyed since the campaign began. It was a touch of grace. Many men due to die in the next two nights' fighting received at least one final connection with home and family. T. D. Smith's diary for that date simply reads: "First Mail!" Popeye Poppell received a hundred letters. "Our first mail in three months!" he recorded. "My most prized possession...was a tooth brush. I had gone five and a half weeks without brushing my teeth...within five minutes I had an offer of $50 for my brush, but no sale!" Private First Class Henry Neal, having vigorously dug his fox hole in compliance with Sergeant Pollard's cryptic dictate, received a bag of popcorn from his sister, huddled deep in his hole to pop the kernels then and there "in my ol' steel helmet—delicious!!"[14]

Kawaguchi was coming. He had endured four days of interior Guadalcanal's "Green Hell," suffered the attrition of scores of men and weapons, and experienced long periods of disorientation and lack of communications with his far-flung components. Now at last his three battalions were homing in on the narrow neck between the Tenaru and the Lunga Rivers.

He still hoped to launch a surprise attack the night of the 12th.

The Imperial "Sea Eagles," the Rabaul-based Betty bombers, reappeared overhead around noon on the 12th for a second pounding of The Ridge. The Raiders had deeper holes by now, but the concussion and blast of the heavy bombs caused more casualties, including New Jersey-born Harold W. Smith, the former captain of the Millburn High School football team, wounded and evacuated. Able Company's Private First Class John H. Carson "felt a burning sensation on the back of my leg." Reaching back fearfully, he discovered "a bomb fragment the size of a silver dollar. It had cut through the shelter half, hit the edge of my canteen cup, bounced out the bottom, then came to rest on my leg. Didn't even break the skin."[15]

This may have been the point when Edson assembled his staff and commanders for a motivational pep talk. As recalled by Tiger Erskine, Edson simply looked each man in the face and remarked "in his low, gruff voice, that we had to hold The Ridge." Should we fail, Edson said, "It'll be us, not the Japs, roaming the jungles and eating raw coconuts."[16]

With increasing intelligence of Kawaguchi's approach, Edson disposed his combined force along a ragged 1,800-yard horseshoe with its rounded center conforming to the grassy, south-facing nose of The Ridge.

The terrain was deceiving. The jungle lapped close to the sides of The Ridge, too close to permit much of a reaction to a sudden assault. The Marines would have to establish vulnerable combat outposts in the jungle on both flanks. The Ridge would then serve as a rallying point, a place to make one last stand, if needed.

The Ridge had two modest "crests" at opposite ends separated by a long curving saddle: Hill 120, just above the northern descent to the airfield, and Hill 100, the forward (southern) nose. A broad footpath bisected the topographical spine of The Ridge and continued south into the jungle, the route taken earlier by the Buntin Patrol. West of The Ridge, and parallel to it, the Lunga makes a distinct bow, bending eastward opposite Hill 100 and bending back to the west opposite Hill 120, thus narrowing the maneuver room available in that corridor to less than nine hundred yards. A swampy lagoon running parallel both to the river and The Ridge provided a dangerous avenue of approach into the position.

John B. Sweeney's recollections are crucial to understanding the battle. With Baker Company, he had a grandstand seat to observe the first night's fighting, then endured the battle of his life throughout the second night. According to Sweeney, "Edson initially established his command post in the jungle north of Hill 120 and just off the dirt road [although he would fight both battles from the hilltop, his "forward CP"]. The aid station was nearby. The depleted D Company, now with a strength of about twenty-five men, was across the road to the east."

George Herring's Easy Company, as usual stripped of its deployed machine-gun platoons, dug positions near Dog Company. At Edson's order, Herring disbanded his demolitions platoon (Angus Goss was still recovering from his Tulagi wounds, and the platoon's special talents would not be required in this defensive struggle). By this means, mortarman/explosives expert Gerry West suddenly found himself a novice machine gunner attached to Baker. On the western flank of The Ridge, John Antonelli's Able Company backed up Charlie and protected a long stretch of the Lunga in the jungle.

Sweeney described the exposed southern and southwestern segments: "Captain Thomas's C Company was sent forward to occupy the right front sector between the Lunga and a swampy lagoon at the edge of the jungle on the east. Major Nickerson's B Company held the southernmost tip of the grassy ridge around Hill 100 from the lagoon to B Company of the parachute battalion on the left." Two other parachute companies defended positions in echelon east of The Ridge. Neither flank had direct physical or visual contact with other friendly units. Only jungle filled the gaps.[17]

Defending The Ridge with such thin lines against Kawaguchi's approaching multitudes would require the utmost in combat leadership. Yet the Raiders lacked an alarming number of their best standard-bearers. Lew Walt and Hank Adams remained hospitalized with malaria. Bailey was back, but the battalion lost another field grade officer the same day. Baker Company's Major Lloyd Nickerson, hampered by severe stomach cramps since Tasimboko, relinquished command to his exec, Captain Louis Monville, and turned himself in for treatment, joining ninety other stricken Raiders. Malaria attacks weakened Baker Company's Captain Ed Wheeler and Platoon Sergeant Hugh Davis. Meanwhile, Charlie Company lost Lieutenant Clay Boyd, the former boxer and polo champion, injured during a local patrol. Jungle branches snared his Reising submachine gun, poked the trigger, and fired a round into his foot. It was a freak accident, but no one looked askance at such a proven fighter. Still, Boyd would miss his company's most desperate fight. His troops would sorely miss him.[18]

With eight hundred yards of jungle to cover, Charlie Company had all three platoons on line in separate outposts. Easy Company machine-gun squads bolstered each platoon. The dense jungle prevented the deploy-

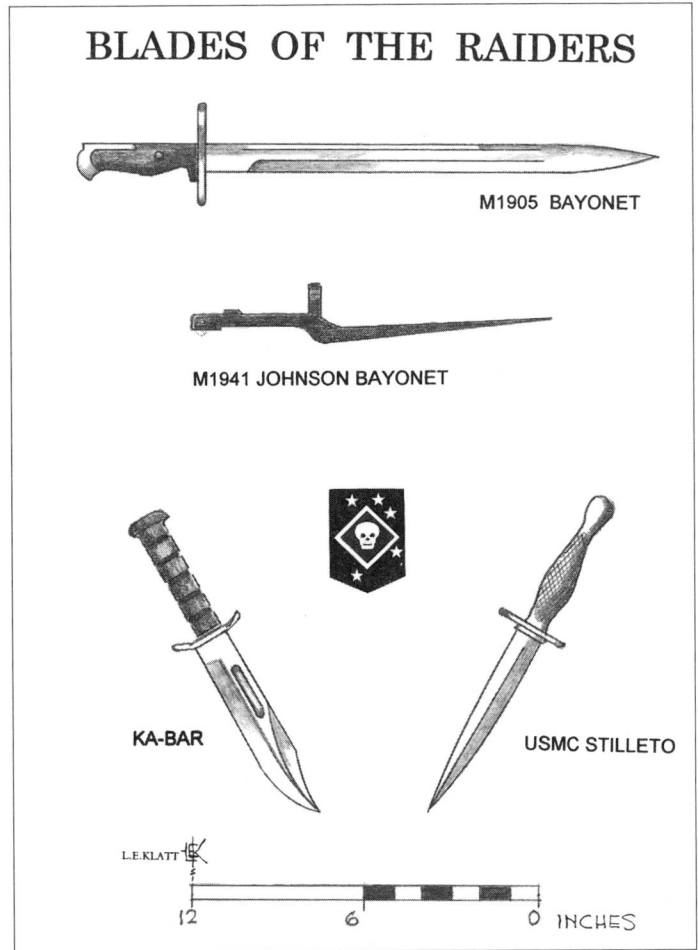

# BLADES OF THE RAIDERS

M1905 BAYONET

M1941 JOHNSON BAYONET

KA-BAR

USMC STILLETO

L.E.KLATT

12        6        0  INCHES

"Blades of the Raiders," by Larry Klatt. Most 1st Raiders welcomed the arrival of the multi-purpose Ka-Bar in 1943. It was sturdier, more useful in fieldcraft, and just as lethal in close combat as the stiletto.

ment of concertina wire; at best the Marines stretched single-strand barbed wire from tree to tree. Some gunners cleared artful fields of fire; others cleared firing lanes so broad the Japanese mistook them for native trails. Strands of black comm wire connected field telephones at some outposts to Captain Thomas's command post slightly uphill.

The administrative route to Charlie Company's line of outposts was a faint trail that wound through Baker Company's wire, down the southwest nose and into the jungle. Crossing the lagoon meant careful balancing along a slippery fallen log. Corporal Robert Youngdeer, the sure-footed hand-to-hand combat instructor from Cherokee, North Carolina, slipped off and tumbled into the muck, losing his e-tool. Youngdeer wondered darkly what it would be like recrossing the same log under heavy fire.[19]

BARman Joe Rushton, he with the bomb shrapnel in his hindquarters, crossed the same log with Charlie Company's second platoon, noticing the same potential bottleneck. "As the long afternoon was drawing to a close it became apparent to even the dim-witted that we were in for big trouble," Rushton later recalled. "If our positions became untenable we were then to withdraw back across the log, or that not being possible to fight our way out as best we could....We were expendable."

The battalion cooks made a special effort to issue hot rations to all hands that evening, even including the Raiders along the exposed line of outposts in the jungle. "Vienna sausage, string beans, and hot coffee," said Rushton, "WOW!" Rushton was also glad to have a visit from Private Paul Ratcliffe, his buddy from their teenage years in Philadelphia. But Ratcliffe had an apathetic look that Rushton would later recognize as a fatal premonition. They shared one last smoke, shook hands, and parted. Neither Rushton nor anyone else would ever see Ratcliffe again.

Later, Captain Thomas stopped by, checked Rushton's firing lanes, wished him good shooting. Darkness was nigh.[20]

Several dozen yards to Rushton's right, a thirty-man machine-gun section from Easy Company settled in along the river slightly to the rear of C Company's exposed right flank. Private First Class John W. Mielke served as an ammunition carrier, armed like all other riflemen in this battle with the Springfield '03 bolt-action rifle. "I had just turned nineteen in July," said Mielke, "and was proud to be a Marine and very proud to be a Raider." Mielke was the fifth man in a five-man gun crew. Jack McGovern was the gunner, assisted by Andrew Radich. The trio of Joseph Kaminowski, Mielke, and a new man nicknamed "Bear—from California" [certainly this was Leslie V. Frink, eighteen, from Seattle, one of the very few westerners in the ranks of the Raiders, who joined the battalion in July] humped the linked belts of .30 caliber ammo. "We crossed the lagoon on a fallen tree...which appeared to be our only exit other than...along the river. This was very dense jungle, a heavy growth of banyan trees....It was getting too dark to see, and we settled down for the night."[21]

Several hundred yards north of Mielke's position along the Lunga, Able Company riflemen settled uneasily into their own foxholes. T. D. Smith recalled how Platoon Sergeant Joe Buntin "came down the line just before dark. I asked him how we would get out of here if we had to. He said, 'Stay where you are. The word is nobody moves, just die in your holes.'"[22]

Merritt Edson convened his company commanders just before dark. He revealed his plans to execute a major spoiling attack against the oncoming Japanese the next morning, hoping to catch them in their labored approach, still in column formation, unsuspecting. It simply was not in Edson's ice-water blood to sit and wait for an opponent to come hammer him.

But time had run out. Kawaguchi may have been losing overall control of the assault, but the two battalions of his own 124th infantry were advancing through the jungle at virtually a dead run, striving to meet the attack schedule.

At the same time, two miles north of Edson's CP, the 5,000-ton Imperial Navy cruiser *Sendai* steamed into Ironbottom Sound, reduced speed, took a careful navigational fix, elevated her seven 5.5-inch guns, and, at 2130, opened fire. The *Sendai* and her three escorting destroyers bombarded The Ridge at leisure for well over an hour. Five high-explosive shells struck the Raider battalion CP; only one exploded. There were no casualties. Yet the experience was onerous to the Raiders cringing in their holes. "The shelling that night from Jap ships in the Straits was terrific," recorded T. D. Smith.[23]

The night became weirder when *Sendai* began illuminating the ridge with her searchlight every few minutes. "It was so bright," said one platoon commander, "that I knew the ship's skipper could see me moving on the ridge. I felt naked." Baker Company's Irv Reynolds accompanied Corporal Gerry West on a risky patrol south of The Ridge that evening. The onset of the shelling unnerved the men. "Suddenly," said Reynolds, "I heard a noise like a runaway freight train and at the same time saw a bright blue light illuminating the hills to our front." The patrol halted, crouched down, totally mystified. It took minutes to deduce that the crashing noise had been a dud naval shell skidding through the jungle, that the light came from the same warship.[24]

Reynolds and West were fortunate to escape the abundance of "overs," the naval shells that missed the modest peak of the ridge and exploded much farther south. There was another danger in the jungle that night. Had the patrol drifted a mere three hundred yards more to the west they would have been overrun by Lieutenant Colonel Watanabe's III/124 streaming purposefully north through the rain forest.

The advance of Kawaguchi's main force is often represented by a single broad arrow on a map, but a better representation would be a dozen squiggly darts. The assault, deadly as it proved to be, was ragged and haphazard. *Sendai's* searchlight no doubt provided a welcome beacon to the soldiers struggling through the jungle and may have helped orient about half of Kawaguchi's force. The long noisy bombardment also masked the approach of the initial assault troops until many were near—or within—the Marine lines.

Yet this would prove to be more a night of missed opportunities than great tactical glory for the Ka Force. Major Tamura's crack Sendai battalion evidently failed to find its attack positions in time to contribute materially to the assault. Major Kokusho's I/124 came closest to meeting its time and place responsibilities, but the men became entangled with Watanabe's uncontrolled surge, forcing Kokusho west of the Lunga. Historian Richard Frank, after long research through translations of the many unit reports and diaries contained in the *Senshi Sosho* volumes, artfully summarized Kawaguchi's attack the first night: "The battalions...lost their sense of direction, almost entirely missed the ridge, and instead drifted into the low, waterlogged swath of jungle between the ridge and the Lunga. Units became lost; lost units became scattered; scattered units became intermingled. Control slipped away from Kawaguchi and his battalion commanders."[25]

Until his leading elements hit the Marine lines on Edson's right flank, Kawaguchi evidently believed the airfield's southern sector was still undefended. "I was confident and rejoiced over the prospect of the success of our attack," he said after the war, "But due to the devilish jungle, the forces of the brigade were scattered all over and was completely beyond control. In my whole life, I have never felt so disappointed and helpless."[26]

Kawaguchi may have bewailed his loss of control, but those few assault units that struck Charlie Company Raiders that first night were extremely professional. Whether led by gifted junior officers or savvy veteran NCOs, the Japanese approached stealthily, sought out unit boundaries and automatic weapons, and fought with a brutal lethality that reflected their prowess in the jungles of Borneo. They sliced into Charlie Company with surgical skill.

The Japanese attacked along both sides of the lagoon, scattering Lieutenant Black Jack Salmon's platoon and driving a major wedge between Charlie and Baker Companies at the southwest foot of The Ridge. They also infiltrated across the Lunga and overran several Charlie Company positions along the river side of the lagoon.

Corporal Bob Youngdeer served as a scout/rifleman in Sergeant Frank Boone's Easy Company machine-gun squad (with Private First Class

Maj. Gen. Kawaguchi, Imperial Japanese Army (front row, center).

Mielke) occupying a strongpoint along the river on Charlie Company's right flank. "When the enemy shelling stopped," he recalled, "I distinctly heard splashing in the river, the sound of many people wading and coming in our direction." Youngdeer never saw a soul. The splashing stopped, he heard Japanese voices, a bolt being released, then a sudden burst of fire. The Raiders, expecting a probe, withheld their weapons and responded with hand grenades. Youngdeer threw his grenades, straining to see through the darkness. A pause, then an abrupt outbreak of shouts, firing, and movement. In an instant the Japanese had surged past Youngdeer's outpost, moving up the high ground. The Marines were surrounded.[27]

John Mielke had heard the same approaching voices. "Warren Morse was the machine gunner on the far right flank," said Mielke. Morse had industriously cleared a broad firing lane for his weapon. "The Japanese thought they had found a trail, and they followed it virtually to the muzzle of [Morse's] gun. He began firing incessantly. There were cries of pain." When Morse's gun fell silent, Mielke threw his grenades, all he had. More confusion ensued, then movement, then local silence. Near Mielke, Private First Class Edward Proffitt, a C Company rifleman, clutched a grenade with its pin pulled, ready to toss. Now, surrounded but no longer directly threatened, the Marines sought to conceal their presence. Proffitt squeezed the armed grenade until his hand cramped. Mielke took it from him, gingerly, and secured the spoon with a string. The men kneeled uneasily, waiting for the enemy to return.[28]

Captain George Herring, under Edson's tutelage, had trained his Easy Company machine-gun platoons well. The platoon attached to C Company featured first-rate NCO leaders like Platoon Sergeants Lawrence Harrison and Lawrence "Pappy" Holdren (who had fought with the Marine brigade in Belleau Wood in 1918), plus hard-nosed squad leaders like sergeants Neil Champoux and Frank Boone. Champoux's squad, slightly upstream from the position defended by Boone, Youngdeer, Mielke, and Proffitt, took a more direct hit. The Japanese killed the squad leader and scattered his men. Champoux, twenty-one, was a three-year veteran from Canandaigua, New York.[29]

A fusillade of Japanese grenades rendered the Champoux fighting holes untenable. Private First Class Charles Everett from Meadville, Mississippi, knew it was time to vacate. "We withdrew with them hot after us," he said. "We tried to carry the gun but that was impossible so we left it and took off." Everett became separated from the other survivors. In the black jungle he stumbled across a Japanese machine-gun crew, grenaded them, but was hit in the return fire. "My left hand was hit, it sailed away like I'd thrown it...they fired another burst and hit both my legs pretty bad." Everett collapsed, then dragged himself deeper into the brush. He would endure a hellish night.[30]

A separate group of Japanese hit Lieutenant Salmon's platoon with savage suddenness at the onset of the firing. Minutes later Captain Sweeney was astonished to see his friend leading a handful of survivors through the Baker Company wire on Hill 100. Salmon was as promising a troop leader as any the Raiders would develop, but Sweeney found him this night to be "visibly shaken, in bad shape, and deeply concerned about several of his men who had been cut off during the withdrawal." Baker Company bent back its right flank sharply to contain the penetration.[31]

Charlie Company's ordeal continued. A large column of Japanese struck the right flank of the 2d platoon, arrayed in a long line in the company center, adjacent to the lagoon. Two sections of the company's own machine guns protected both flanks. Private First Class Martin "Jeeper" Heitz, still recovering from his Tasimboko wound four days earlier, commanded the gun crew on the right. Nearby was the fighting hole of BAR-man Joe Rushton, who heard voices in the dark as soon as the naval shelling ceased. "Jeeper Heitz's machine-gun crew opened up on them with one hell of a blast which set them screaming and moaning," recounted Rushton. "Then they started coming in all directions—shouting and yelling—and overran Jeeper's gun." Shortly, said Rushton, "word came to move out and go back across the log. This was very difficult because of the extreme darkness and heavy vegetation....We had to carefully find the comm wire and follow it along on our hands and knees."

Just as Rushton had feared, the log bridge had become a bottleneck. The Japanese had the slippery crossing flanked. Stymied and confused, Rushton's squad went to ground. They could hear a large band of the enemy working their way towards them, pausing to hack other survivors to death with swords or machetes. Rushton lay on his stomach in the darkness, cradling his BAR but frozen "in sheer terror." A Japanese soldier stepped on Rushton's calf, stepped back, prodded him with his two-toed shoe, called a superior. Rushton heard the unmistakable swish of a sword being drawn from its scabbard. Desperately he sprang to his knees, fumbling with his BAR. The nearest Japanese was faster, blazing away with his shoulder-slung light machine gun, flattening Rushton with 6.5mm bullets in his arm and leg. Rushton—stunned, deafened, and enraged—rolled once, then emptied his BAR at the circle of enemy troops—"eighteen frigging rounds." In the melee a Raider grenade further injured everyone in the circle, friend and foe alike.

The nightmare got worse. "At this point," said Rushton, "people were crawling in all directions, mainly away from the log crossing. It wasn't long before they were overrun by the swarming attackers of the main charge. It was horrible and frightening hearing our small group of overrun Raiders screaming as the bastards bayoneted and hacked them with their Samurai swords." Rushton discovered his assistant BARman, Private First Class Kenneth E. Ritter, sprawled nearby, badly shot in the back by the same spray of pointblank automatic fire that had wounded Rushton. "He was in great pain and shock and asked me not to leave him." Rushton's long night was just beginning.[32]

The Japanese captured one or two Raiders alive, interrogated them, then tortured them brutally with their blades. The screams of their dying comrades that night haunted the Marines crouched in their holes along The Ridge, waiting for the storm to break against their sector. "The sound of someone being worked over out there in the darkness remains with me until this day," said Robert Youngdeer fifty-two years later. "The whole battalion could hear their screams," said Edward Proffitt. Farther north, three hundred to five hundred yards away in Able Company, T. D. Smith reported: "All night we could hear a Marine evidently being tortured out front."

Popeye Poppell recorded: "We can hear our buddies in the swamps along the line towards the river. It seems as if a few have been overcome and they must be being tortured by the Japs." A sense of outrage and helplessness swept The Ridge.[33]

Charlie Company was shattered. Many of the men "exfiltrated" in good order back towards Hill 120 where Edson, Brown, and Bailey calmly reorganized them into a fighting reserve. But many others were surrounded and cut down. Platoon Sergeant Stanley Kops, thirty-two, from Hollywood, died. Sergeant Tony "Big Stoop" Palonis, another of Easy Company's intrepid machine gunners, fell wounded. The jungle swarmed with Japanese.

Dodging the random groups of Japanese troops preoccupied Private First Class Joe Rushton throughout the night. He crawled laboriously and painfully, pulling Ken Ritter with his right arm, dragging his BAR with his wounded left. The Japanese were noisy. He could hear them jabbering in their strange, choppy language as they searched the jungle for their own wounded and any surviving Raiders. He knew they were watching the few trails and even the ubiquitous comm wire leading back to The Ridge. It took Rushton hours to drag Ritter through the swampy northern terminus of the lagoon, hoping to emerge at the midpoint of The Ridge.

Three Japanese soldiers jumped the pair of wounded men in the swamp. One bayoneted Ritter in the leg. Rushton shot him, but then his BAR jammed from being wrenched through the muck. In the struggle Rushton somehow reversed the heavy weapon and clubbed his second assailant in the face. The third man disappeared, but now Rushton was weaponless and Ritter was in dire condition. He became delirious, calling for his mother. Rushton wrapped his hand over his friend's mouth.

Ritter was twenty years old, a volunteer from Moatsville, West Virginia. Sometime in the predawn hours of 13 September he died from his wounds. Rushton placed his body under a large fern near the edge of the swamp and crawled uphill alone, racked with pain and faint from loss of blood. At daybreak he heard the welcome "crack!" of a Springfield '03 from the high ground. He called for help. A corpsman came down the slope warily, Reising gun muzzle first—*"God, what a blessed sight!"* Then Corporal Ersel T. Patrick, a fellow survivor from C Company's second platoon, scrambled down to lift Rushton into his arms and carry him uphill to safety.[34]

West of Rushton's drama, along the river, Private First Class Mielke and the survivors of Sergeant Boone's machine-gun squad still manned their outpost. Mielke took advantage of a lull in the fighting to ask "Pappy" Holdren whether Belleau Wood or the Argonne Forest had been any worse than this wild night. Holdren shook his head ruefully.

"Vertical Butt-stroke," by Doug Greenbowe typifies the desperate, close combat around Edson's Ridge during 12–14 September 1942.

"No," he told Mielke, "This is the worst situation I've ever been in."[35]

Daylight came reluctantly to the dark jungle. Corporal Robert Youngdeer, the squad scout, and Pappy Holdren eased into the underbrush to search for survivors. The trampled vegetation was littered with dead bodies and abandoned packs. There were faint sounds of movement.

Private First Class Charles Everett had crawled considerably north of the log bridge spanning the lagoon before he was shot. Actually he was not too far from Boone's outpost, but he was closer—dangerously close— to the Japanese machine-gun crew. "I couldn't move my legs, I was bleeding awful, and my shoes were filled with blood," he said, "So I put on a tourniquet and tried to call for help."[36]

Holdren and Youngdeer dragged a dying Marine out of the brush and back to Boone's perimeter. Youngdeer then made a wider search, accompanied this time by Private First Class John D. Simonich. The two heard a faint voice, "Anyone from C Company out there?" They found a badly wounded Charlie Everett (although his identity would not be known to them for another forty years). "He was shot through the legs and could not walk," said Youngdeer. Other Raiders came up to help. Youngdeer told someone to grab a blanket from one of the nearby abandoned packs to use as a sled to drag the casualty to safety. Then a burst of fire shredded the underbrush and the Marines hit the deck. The Japanese were very close.

John Mielke and "Bear" Frink heard the shots ring out and left their foxhole to race over to help. Frink got ahead of Mielke and disappeared in the jungle. Mielke heard sudden shouts, then a scream. Frink evidently emerged from the brush directly into the Japanese machine-gun nest. Startled riflemen bayoneted him in the chest.[37]

A Japanese sniper in a tree near the machine gun had a clear field of fire on the men around the wounded Everett. He shot Simonich in the leg. Baffled and angry, Youngdeer raised his Springfield and stood up to take on the shooter. The unseen sniper shot Youngdeer in the face. The .25 caliber bullet struck him beneath his left nostril and exited under his right ear. He fell heavily, blacked out, then rolled to shelter. "My teeth were shattered, my tongue was creased, I could not speak distinctly," he recalled. And he was pinned down.

Mielke fared better. He avoided the route taken by Frink and managed to find a fallen tree overlooking the Japanese machine-gun squad from the flank. "Their attention was in the direction of the shooting," he said, "and I had a clear shot at the machine gunner and another man nearest me." He fired one deliberate shot, jerked the bolt, fired a hasty second shot, then dropped below the log. There was a burst of fire his way, then the Japanese continued firing at the Raiders clustered around Youngdeer, Simonich, and Everett. When Mielke peeked back over the log he saw his shots had hit home. He fired again, dropped instantly, withstood another rattle of fire, waited for the enemy to resume fire in the other direction, then repeated the process. In this fashion Mielke fired every round in his belt, accounted for at least six of the Japanese, and surely saved the wounded Marines from death.

Pharmacist's Mate Second Class Wilbur V. Molloy bandaged Youngdeer the best he could and led him out of the line of fire. Pappy Holdren took care of several other wounded men, and Platoon Sergeant Harrison rounded up Mielke and the other survivors to fight their way back to The Ridge—lugging their machine guns and dragging on a poncho the badly wounded Raider first found by Youngdeer (probably Private Francis L. Roberts of Indianapolis). It was all they could do. Everett was still too exposed to be rescued—a sad fact which depressed Youngdeer for four decades—nor could they evacuate Bear Frink's body. The Japanese still commanded this battlefield.

Roberts died just as the small band reached a reinforcing patrol, but Youngdeer made it to the field hospital. As he lay in surgery, having bits of teeth and bone extracted from his mouth, he was visited by his brother Jesse, one of the parachutists on The Ridge. The brothers clasped hands— both still in imminent danger.

Charlie Everett knew he had been abandoned and understood why, but his spirits sagged. At one point he considered shooting himself—anything to keep the Japanese from capturing him alive. By a small miracle, a Raider patrol eventually found him, barely alive, and carried him out on a blanket.[38]

Some Raiders would never leave that disputed jungle along the Lunga.

## A Final Accounting

The first night's battle for The Ridge had a surreal nature. Most of Kawaguchi's converging columns missed the objective altogether. Many of the Raiders and parachutists never fired a shot. The opening battle was restricted to a narrow corridor along the river between Charlie Company Raiders and several companies of the 124th Infantry, likely an intermingled force mainly from Lieutenant Colonel Watanabe's battalion with some from Major Kokusho's battalion. The senior officer on either side was at best a captain. The fiercest fighting occurred in two violent outbursts: the initial assaults before midnight, then again at daybreak.

The opening round may have been localized and small in scale, but the close-quarters combat was intensively violent. Charlie Company and its attached machine-gun platoon from Easy Company suffered more than fifty casualties, fully half of them fatal. The Japanese likely lost twice that number, principally among those who attacked in column across the river and up the fire lanes cleared by the machine-gun crews.

The experience alarmed Edson's battalion. For the first time a Japanese force had driven Raiders from prepared positions, forcing them to abandon weapons and their dead and wounded. It rankled. And it could have been worse.

The outcome of this epic battle may have been markedly different had Major General Kawaguchi not lost control of his force from the onset of the first night's assault. But the brigade commander had no clue of the successful penetration attained by his rifle companies; nor did he retain a reserve force with which to exploit the breakthrough. His loss of control reduced him to teeth-gnashing impotence.

For his part, Red Mike Edson was concerned but not discouraged. There is no evidence he ever regretted retaining Major Bailey at his side rather than reinstating him among Charlie Company's forward lines. The company had given ground grudgingly and inflicted stinging casualties among the assaulting Japanese. The remainder of Edson's force— Raiders and parachutists—had maintained superb fire discipline throughout a very fearful night. The surviving Japanese had gained no useful intelligence to report about the main defenses along The Ridge.

Understandably, many Charlie Company Raiders remain distressed about the fate of their members left on the battlefield. Postwar newsletters and private correspondence often referred to "the seven MIAs" (Missing-in-Action). Actually, the battalion reported *eleven* Raiders missing in this action, plus a twelfth classified as killed in action—"body not recovered."

Coming out of a major victory with a dozen bodies unaccounted for is serious business. American MIAs of any twentieth-century war continue to stir deep emotions. Final accountability for these Raiders bears an updated examination. Primary reference sources are the battalion's muster roll for September 1942 (especially the "Addendum"), the surviving 5x8 "Casualty Cards" which record minimal data about the battalion's fatalities, testimonials from eye witnesses, and (to an extent) the initial burial records for the 1st Marine Division cemetery on Guadalcanal. While authoritative, the composite information is skimpy. Additional research is encouraged.

There are no "missing" Raiders in the sense of the persistent rumor of American POWs still being held long after the Vietnam War. The Japanese took no prisoners in this battle. They hacked wounded Raiders to death and evidently tortured to death those few they captured alive. The problem facing the Raiders after the battle therefore became one of finding and identifying the twelve missing bodies.

Positive identification of the remains was difficult, grisly work. Slash wounds typically cause much more bleeding than punctures; the features of the dead would have been blackened by dried blood. The tropical rain forest would have accelerated decomposition. Also, bodies could readily have been blown up by subsequent high explosives—Charlie Company's battleground the first night became ground zero for countless artillery barrages throughout the second night's clash. And the Japanese executioners may have looted their victim's belongings, including dogtags. Finally, those conducting the search were hardly forensic scientists or graves registration specialists. They were Marines, looking for slain fellow Marines, but in a dense jungle still infested with vengeful snipers and Japanese patrols on the same mission for their own missing and dead.

That being said, however, it is safe to conclude that each of the missing Raiders was eventually found and buried where he fell. Even in advance stages of decomposition, an American corpse could always be distinguished from a Japanese by his distinctive boondockers, as opposed to the traditional wrap-around leggings of the Imperial Army troops. In two cases, related subsequently, Raider officers led combat patrols into the jungle searching for their own missing and succeeded in finding, identifying, and burying their lost sheep. Other missing Marines were likely found and buried by elements of the 2d Battalion, 5th Marines, who first reinforced, then relieved Edson's composite force, becoming the inheritors of the contested battlefield and with it, the dubious distinction of burying the dead from both sides. By the time the 2/5 burial parties reached the jungled outguard posts west of The Ridge, the American bodies they found would likely have been nearly impossible to identify (for the reasons cited above), and a simple interment on the spot would likely have occurred. Most of them likely remain in their jungle graves, but at the very least they received a Marine burial. Perhaps only fellow Marines can appreciate the comfort in that fact.

These Raiders were declared Missing in Action (MIA) in the initial battalion Muster Roll report for September 1942:

PFC Salvatore A. Cracco, twenty-five, Spring City, PA, C Company
Pvt. Leslie R. Frink, eighteen, Seattle, E Company
Pvt. Malcolm J. Hogan, no record, C Company (USMCR)
PFC Francis C. Potter, twenty-one, Plymouth, NH, C Company
Plt. Sgt. John J. Quigley, twenty-six, Brooklyn, C Company
Pvt. Paul P. Ratcliffe, twenty, Philadelphia, C Company
PFC Kenneth E. Ritter, twenty, Moatsville, WV, E Company
PFC Charles W. Roberts, twenty-one, Saltville, VA, C Company
  (USMCR)
Pvt. Francis L. Roberts, twenty, Indianapolis, C Company
Pvt. John C. Rock, nineteen, Saginaw, MI, C Company
1st Sgt. Jerome J. Stark, twenty-seven, Dunlo, PA, C Company

In addition, Private John M. Langdon, twenty, C Company, from Boston, was reported Killed in Action (KIA) although his body was not recovered.

The "Addendum" to the same Muster Roll reclassifies Frink, both Roberts, and Ritter from MIA to KIA, and this must be related to subsequent testimony from witnesses to their deaths (as related in these chapters, testimony could well have originated from Rushton for Ritter; Mielke, Lawrence, or Holdren for Frink; Mielke, Antonelli, Lawrence, or Proffitt for F.I. Roberts; and Proffitt for C.W. Roberts). Six months later, the battalion administrative chief inserted another Addendum to the September 1942 Muster Roll to reflect a 26 March 1943 letter from the Bureau of Medicine and Surgery which directed the reclassification of Quigley and Rock to KIA, based evidently on forensic examination, as their casualty cards indicate "remains buried in Guadalcanal cemetery." Langdon's classification as KIA from the start may have resulted from an immediate testimonial of his death (James Mallamas stated in 1993 he saw Langdon machine gunned to death and fall into the lagoon, as one possibility). With the passage of a full year, in accordance with Public Law #490 and in the absence of any new evidence, the secretary of the navy directed the redesignation to KIA status for Cracco, Potter, Ratcliffe, and Stark.

Private Hogan's casualty card is missing from the stack, but a subsequent statement by Lieutenant Salmon, his platoon commander, attests that four or five days after the battle he led a patrol back to the site, searching for three of his missing Marines. By then the bodies were beyond their means of identification. "We found three badly decomposed bodies in the near vicinity of Hogan's position, and although we were positive that the bodies were those of Marines, positive personal identification was impossible." Such a statement likely led to Hogan's reclassification from MIA to KIA, but there is, unfortunately, no confirmation available.

In his book on the Guadalcanal campaign, Sam Griffith wrote that "the bodies of seven missing Raiders were never found." Whether he had access to the same muster rolls and casualty cards is problematic. To the best of my knowledge, the following eight bodies may have been buried but were never positively identified: Cracco, Frink, Hogan, Langdon, Potter, Ratcliffe, C. W. Roberts, and Ritter. I have insufficient evidence to reach a judgment on Private Langdon. In today's parlance, these Marines would be assigned the more specific category of "MIAPD"—Missing-in-Action Presumed Dead—but they clearly deserve more than an acronym. May the souls of these special Raiders rest in eternal peace....[39]

Defiance at Dawn
(written after Bloody Ridge by Private First Class Vincent H. D. Cassidy)

*Another day!*
  *And here I am,*
*alive and well.*
  *Yes, I might say*
*I'm feeling swell,*
  *in spite of Japs,*
*in spite of hell.*

*Does it grieve you, Death,*
  *that I defy you,*
*that I refuse to be taken by you?*

*Be aforehand warned*
  *and plan it well,*
*if you intend my doom to spell,*
  *for I intend to fight....* [40]

# Notes

1. Thomas Mullahey quoted in an undated postwar military news magazine (possibly *Leatherneck*), clipping in author's collection.
2. Griffith, *The Battle for Guadalcanal*, 121; Hoffman, *Legend*, 206.
3. Griffith, *The Battle for Guadalcanal*, 110; Stevenson, "Guadalcanal," *The American Scholar*, 367.
4. See Merrill B. Twining, "Head for the Hills," *Marine Corps Gazette*, August 1987, 46–55.
5. Division Commander's Final Report on Guadalcanal Operation, Phase IV [20 August–18 September 1942], Reference Section, MCHC, 7.
6. Frank, *Guadalcanal*, 219, 225, 63; Kawaguchi Memoir, 11–12.
7. Kawaguchi Memoir, 17–19; *Handbook on Japanese Military Forces*, 387–88, 393–94.
8. Edson/Stiff Draft Memoir.
9. *Ibid.*
10. Col. John Erskine, "The Battle of Bloody Ridge: A Memoire," 29 July 1992, 4; Corporal Henry Neal to Thomas Mullahey, n.d.
11. Quintana letter, 2; Joseph M. Rushton to James Smith, n.d., 1 [Rushton Account]; Griffith, *The Battle for Guadalcanal*, 113. The Japanese bombed the ridge on both the 11th and 12th; survivors frequently mix the two events in their memories. The same confusion applies to the combat patrols launched from The Ridge on those dates.

12. Frank Guidone to John Sweeney, 2 April 1994; Thomas Pollard to Jon Hoffman, September 1991; T. D. Smith diary, 11–12 September 1942; Casualty Card, Sgt. Harold C. Floeter. His date of death indicates the 12th vice the 11th, which either reflects the hasty accounting done during the battle or the above mentioned confusion over the air raids and preliminary patrols.

13. Bailey and Ryder's motivational talks to the 164th Infantry are described in John E. Stannard, *The Battle of Coffin Corner,* according to Jon Hoffman, 19 October 1998.

14. T. D. Smith Diary, 11 September 1942. Poppell Diary, 12 September 1942, 18 [note: The discrepancy in the dates is further reflection of the confusion about these preliminary events. Most records indicate Bailey rejoined the battalion on the morning of the 12th. He may have hitched a ride on the final leg of his return with Admiral Turner's plane on the PM of the 11th. Captain Bob Thomas, it appears, retained command of Charlie Company throughout the battle]; Neal to Mullahey, 1992.

15. Casualty Card, Harold Smith; John H. Carson to Frank Guidone, 26 July 1991, 2.

16. Col. John Erskine, "The Battle of Bloody Ridge: A Memoire," 29 July 1992, 5.

17. Sweeney Ridge Memoir, 10 January 1995, 60; Gerry West to author, 9 April 1999.

18. Author interviews with John Sweeney and Frank Guidone, 1999.

19. Author interview with Robert Youngdeer, 9 April 1999.

20. Rushton Account, 1–3. Ratcliffe would become "missing in action, body not recovered" before daybreak.

21. John Mielke to Irv Reynolds, n.d., 1–2 [Mielke Account].

22. T. D. Smith Diary, 12 September 1942, 7.

23. *Ibid.* CO, 1st Marine Raider Battalion, "Report of Operations, 12–14 September 1942," Raider Files, Reference Section, MCHC, 1. The official report states the enemy naval bombardment occurred between 2208 and 2320. Richard Frank (*Guadalcanal*, 231) places the commencement at 2130, quite likely in view of the scheduled 2200 attack. Corporal Robert Youngdeer's memoir (13 February 1994) states 2130 as the start.

24. Sweeney Ridge Memoir, 70; Irv Reynolds to John Sweeney, 17 May 1988, 1.

25. Frank, *Guadalcanal*, 231–32. *Senshi Sosho* is the valuable 104-volume "Japanese War History" that, regrettably, has yet to be translated into English.

26. Kawaguchi Memoir, 21.

27. Robert S. Youngdeer Memoir, 13 February 1994, 2.

28. Mielke Account, 2; Edward S. Proffitt to James Smith, n.d., 2 (page one is missing) [Proffitt Account].

29. Casualty Cards for Frank Boone and Neil Champoux.

30. Charles Everett Memoir, forwarded by his widow, Hilda Everett, to John Sweeney, 2 February 1994, 12–13 [Everett Memoir].

31. Sweeney Ridge Memoir, 72.

32. Rushton Account, 3–6.

33. Youngdeer Memoir, 2; Proffitt Account, 3; T. D. Smith Diary, 12 September 1942, 7; Poppell Diary, 12 September 1942, 16.

34. Rushton Account, 6–9 [Rushton's ordeal did not end upon being rescued by Corp. Patrick. Japanese snipers opened fire on the stretcher team carrying him down The Ridge to the airstrip, spilling him on the trail and requiring a furious crawl to the nearest defilade]; Kenneth E. Ritter Casualty Card.

35. Mielke Account, 3.

36. Everett Memoir, 13.

37. Battalion Muster Roll, September 1942, Sheet 12, Leslie V. Frink.

38. Youngdeer Memoir, 3–4; Youngdeer interview with author, 9 April 1999 and 24 June 1999; Everett Memoir, 13–14; Mielke Account, 2–3 [Mielke received the Navy Cross from Admiral "Bull" Halsey for this action]; Proffitt Account, 2. According to Proffitt, the badly wounded Marine the squad dragged out on a poncho was Pvt. Francis L. Roberts. Roberts' Casualty Card indicates he was "buried along the Lunga." The Battalion Muster Roll for September, sheet 12, indicates "buried in field approximately 300 yards from Pioneer Bridge on eastern branch of Lunga River."

39. Information on the twelve Raiders classified initially as Missing in Action (or "KIA-Body not Recovered" in one case) is based on the author's research during June and July 1999 using the battalion muster roll report for September 1942 as amended as late as March 1943, the casualty cards for each fatality (Pvt. Malcolm Hogan's card is missing), and some of the 1st Marine Division cemetery rolls on Guadalcanal. Special thanks for significant assistance to Mr. Robert V. Aquilina, Reference Section, MCHC, and Col. John Sweeney. Sweeney's search for his own missing man is described in the next chapter. Griffith, *The Battle for Guadalcanal*, 116; James Mallamas interview with Bob O'Neil, 16 February 1993, although I cannot account for the fact that Mallamas was in B Company and Langdon in C Company; Statement of John P. Salmon re: finding Pvt .Hogan and others, n.d., copy provided by John Sweeney.

40. "Defiance at Dawn," by Vincent Cassidy, copy provided by the poet to Pete Pettus, Edson's Raiders Association, *ca.* 1956. A longer version of this poem appeared in *Saturday Evening Post*, 31 July 1943.

# 7

## Edson's Ridge: The Climax, 13–14 September 1942

*You're all Marines—come up on this ridge and fight!*

attributed to Merritt Edson by Merrill Twining
during the night of 13–14 September,
but probably yelled by Major Ken Bailey[1]

DAYBREAK ON THE 13TH found the Marines on The Ridge in a precarious position. The jungles around the grassy hogback teemed with Kawaguchi's veteran infantry. While one battalion had been shredded in the previous night's piecemeal attacks, the fresh battalions of majors Kokusho and Tamura were now in position to launch a concerted assault after dark. The Ka Force may have lost most of its modest artillery to the jungle, but the infantry battalions possessed plenty of mortars, Nambu machine guns, and the damnable "knee mortars" to hammer the objective in advance.

Yet the outlook of the two commanders seemed reversed. General Kawaguchi had a heavy heart that morning, not Colonel Edson. Kawaguchi still regarded the opening night's engagement to have been "a tragedy....a miserable failure." His attack orders for the night of the 13th were hardly inspirational. "On the morning of the 13th to the officers of each battalion I sent the order," he recalled, "'The Brigade will again execute a night attack tonight. The duty of each battalion is same as before.'"[2]

Edson by contrast was matter-of-fact and almost cheerful when he convened his officers that same morning. "They'll be back," he said, "But maybe not as many of them." He thought about that for a moment, then shrugged. "Or maybe more. I want all positions improved, all wire lines

164

paralleled, a hot meal for the men. Today, dig, wire up tight, get some sleep. We'll all need it." He looked in the faces of each of his company commanders. "The Nip will be back. I want to surprise him."[3]

Executing Edson's planned surprises would exclude any sleep. Edson wanted to keep Kawaguchi off balance, learn his strength and dispositions, and recover the large salient in the Raiders' perimeter seized by the Japanese during the night. The salient was critical. Baker Company's position would be untenable if the Japanese held it after dark. Edson ordered John Antonelli to lead Able Company and the understrength Dog Company in a combination counterattack and combat patrol through the swampy ground between The Ridge and the Lunga. If the Japanese were too strongly entrenched, Edson planned a late afternoon pull-back of his lines.

Edson also dispatched the parachutists on a reconn patrol southeast in their sector and ordered Platoon Sergeant Pete Pettus to lead his intelligence section in a probe southwest, cutting through the edge of C Company's former positions.

Each of these small unit operations proved difficult to execute. One problem was the day's extreme heat. As Baker's Irv Reynolds recalled, "We spent much of the next day pinned down in the tall grass, and it was boiling hot with no wind stirring. The sun looked like a red ball, directly overhead." Able Company's Jack Tracy thought the extreme heat of 13 September was "particularly unbearable on the tree-less ridge."[4]

The unrelenting sun evidently forced Captain Louis Monville, Baker Company's newly designated commander, to became incoherent with heat stroke. Edson ordered him evacuated and directed Captain John Sweeney to take command. Sweeney welcomed the command but not the circumstances. He was the third CO in twenty-four hours. He was also, First Sergeant Brice Maddox advised him, the last remaining officer in the company. Two veteran platoon commanders had just been evacuated: Marine Gunner Cecil Clark with malaria, and Captain Rex Crockett with malaria and gastroenteritis. Sweeney was abruptly the point company in the expected attack of several thousand Japanese. He had 115 men and three brand new platoon commanders.[5]

High noon provided one unexpected break. The Rabaul-based "Sea Eagles" returned to Guadalcanal on schedule, two-dozen Betty bombers and their escorts, but since the Seventeenth Army had no clue of Kawaguchi's current location, they ordered the bomber pilots to avoid striking The Ridge. The bombers instead raided the suspected American beachhead at Tasimboko, reflecting the continued belief held in Rabaul and Tokyo that Edson's one-day raid on the 8th had in effect been the opening of a major second front by the Americans. From the jungles Martin Clemens' native scouts watched in grim satisfaction as Kawaguchi's rear guard troops at Tasimboko desperately waved Japanese flags amid the death and destruction being rained down upon them.

Hyperactive Pete Pettus launched his patrol ahead of the larger probes to follow. He led a small force of four other members of the battalion intelligence section, with Sergeant Horse Collar Smith as the radioman. The patrol slid down the southwestern slope of The Ridge into the jungle, crossed the vulnerable log bridge over the lagoon with great uneasiness, then moved cautiously through the fighting holes abandoned the night before by Charlie Company's 2d platoon. Here Joe Rushton's and Ken Ritter's deadly ordeal had begun. Smith felt his skin crawl. Pettus, whose energy was only surpassed by a deep reservoir of personal bravery, signaled the patrol forward. Private First Class Dan Heslin tapped Smith on the shoulder, murmuring, "That sonofabitch isn't going to be happy until he makes contact!"

Pettus soon stepped into a buzzsaw of automatic weapons fire. The men took quick cover. Trained by Edson to identify the type weapon by its signature sound characteristics, the men exchanged puzzled glances. Said Smith, "the machine-gun fire sounded more like an American .30 caliber than the distinctive sound of the Nambu." Pettus feared they had encountered a lost outpost of their own men. He yelled out the day's challenge, then the previous night's codeword. More fire. The Japanese, it turns out, had captured six Marine machine guns in the first battle. At least two Brownings under new ownership now peppered the banyan trees and kunai grass just above the heads of the flattened Raiders.

Pettus signaled an abrupt withdrawal. The intel section, well-trained by Pettus, arose as one and dashed back up the trail. Horse Collar Smith missed the signal and remained pinned down, a painfully lonesome sensation. Through the intermittent machine-gun fire he could hear sounds of the Japanese approaching through the brush. He fixed his bayonet, laid out his two grenades, took a very deep breath. A sudden burst of firing behind him announced the hell-for-leather return of Pettus and Tom Driscoll. This time Smith beat his rescuers back down the trail, the air around them snapping with .30 caliber bees.

Pettus led the patrol at high port back to The Ridge. John Antonelli and Bill Sperling appeared at the head of their companies, alarmed to encounter Marines running pell-mell out of the jungle. Pettus told them what lay ahead. The Japanese still occupied the swampy bottom-land in force.[6]

Antonelli had a difficult assignment. He entered the jungle slowly, wary of both a Japanese ambush and the possibility of Charlie Company survivors. Ghostly figures emerging through the morning mist proved to be Platoon Sergeant Harrison's shot-up machine-gun section, eleven exhausted Raiders, half-dragging Corporal Bob Youngdeer and laboriously carrying Private Francis Roberts up the incline in a bloody poncho. John Mielke, struggling to bear one corner of Roberts' poncho, wondered if he was still alive. Roberts' eyes flickered open. "Don't worry," said Mielke with perhaps more conviction than he felt, "We're going to get you out." Able Company's Popeye Pettus watched the small band approach in awe. They had clearly endured a hell of a night, he thought. "Almost every man was wounded at least twice. One fellow [surely Francis Roberts] told our corpsman he was fine when we picked him off the ground, but then he died in Marsh's hands [Pharmacist's Mate First Class Wilbur L. Marsh, USN] a few seconds later."[7] Antonelli had little time to dwell with Harrison's survivors. He assigned a crew to bury Roberts along the Lunga, peeled off a squad to escort the wounded back to the aid station, then hurried his force into the jungle. The Japanese, fully aroused by the Pettus probe, hunkered over their weapons.

The day's second firefight proved equally inconclusive. The Raiders closed within grenade range, but their advance ground to a halt. Antonelli and Sperling soon realized they would need more than a reinforced company to retake the salient. After an hour's sporadic firing, Antonelli ordered a withdrawal. He had suffered one fatality, Private First Class Donald J. Coffey, twenty-three, from Lansing, Michigan. "Coffey's death was a terrible loss to me," said BARman C. F. "Beaver" Wilson, who fired his automatic rifle with its "worn-out bore" at the enemy machine-gun nest, the bullets twisting and tumbling "to whom it may concern."[8]

T. D. Smith's laconic account summed up the day, "Patrolled up the river a short ways and were hit from the sides and front. The Japs had broken through by the river and the evidence of battle was all around. Returned down river firing and moving."[9]

The Marines evened the odds a little, catching a few Japanese as they dashed through a clearing across the river. Lowell Dunn, a Dog Company rifleman, suddenly had his first live target, and he opened fire. "Now I knew what they meant when the old salts talked about the Springfield kicking like a mule at both ends." The rifle's painful recoil was exceeded by the bullet's knockdown velocity on impact, said Dunn, pleased with his reflex marksmanship against a moving target.[10]

Sergeant Frank Guidone's squad, pinned down in the trampled vegetation west of the lagoon, became the last to pull back. As his men withdrew by a series of small rushes, Guidone heard a feeble voice quaver the word *"Marine!"* The men froze, aiming their rifles at a patch of underbrush, fearing a Japanese trick. Guidone and another man crawled forward cautiously. "He was a Raider," said Guidone, "a member of C Company, lying there all night. He was wounded in both lower legs and had strapped his legs together with his web belt as a tourniquet." Vicious fire snapped overhead. Guidone began dragging the casualty out, an act made difficult by the man's husky build and cries of pain, each of which prompted another burst of fire. Other Raiders crawled up to help. It seemed to take an eternity, but Guidone's squad got their man to safety and medical care. Unlike Francis Roberts, this Charlie Company survivor would live. Fourteen hours after the Japanese attack, and six hours after Corporal Youngdeer's costly attempt to rescue him, Private First Class Charlie Everett's long ordeal had ended.[11]

Antonelli's report confirmed for Edson what Pettus had earlier told him. The Japanese had taken a significant bite out of his forward right flank. They had the numbers and firepower not only to hold the salient but, come night, to hit Baker Company's exposed right flank. Edson discussed a pull-back of his lines with his three field grade officers, Sam Griffith, Bob Brown, and Ken Bailey. He talked to Jerry Thomas and Merrill Twining on the field phone about reinforcements and reserves. Then he announced his decision.

In Houston Stiff's postwar interview, Edson described his late afternoon redeployment in these terms. "To avoid an exposed right flank, we withdrew our forward elements to the battalion reserve line of the 12th. This actually extended our lines at least five hundred yards, a gap partially filled by Company C [actually Company D], 1st Division Engineers. Ordered this realignment about 1500 on the 13th when it became definitely apparent we could not regain the position held the night before."[12]

Merrill Twining visited the Raiders at mid-afternoon and was appalled. "Edson seemed terribly fatigued," said Twining, and the glassy-eyed, stumbling men he commanded looked totally exhausted. Alarmed, Twining recommended that Colonel William J. Whaling's 2d Battalion, 5th Marines move at once to reinforce the Raiders. It was too late. Japanese carrier-based air raids prevented Whaling from crossing the long axis of Henderson Field until dark. At best, Whaling and his company commanders reconnoitered the approaches to The Ridge to facilitate a night reinforcement. Twining and Thomas also expedited the reinforcement by an engineer company.[13]

Edson replaced Charlie Company with Able Company in the low ground along the Lunga and put Charlie and Dog in immediate reserve, just behind his forward CP. He shortened Sweeney's forward position but extended his flank further west into the jungle. A significant gap still existed between Baker and Able. Here he plugged the engineers.

Captain William A. Stiles' Dog Company of the 1st Engineer Battalion, 115 men strong, advanced up The Ridge as provisional riflemen. Major Ken Bailey met the engineers at the Raiders CP. Bailey wore tennis shoes, Stiles noted, unaware that the major was still AWOL from a distant hospital. Yet Stiles found Bailey to be all business as he "personally placed my bunch in the defensive position where we spent the night under orders *not* to move or fall back under *any* conditions."[14]

Sam Griffith admired Edson's handiwork. This contraction and tightening of the lines, he said, "greatly improved fields of fire for automatic weapons and imposed upon the attacker a trip of about one hundred yards from the jungle's edge before he could physically contact the battle position. In traversing this open space he could be brought under killing grazing fire." Maintaining that hundred-yard standoff distance in the jungle, however, would prove nightmarish for scores of Raiders and parachutists.[15]

Edson placed Griffith on his right flank, coordinating the defensive efforts of Antonelli's Able Company and Stiles' engineers, put Bailey to work improving the fighting positions of Charlie, Dog, and Easy Companies, and went forward with Bob Brown to take a final look at John Sweeney's lines, the anticipated eye of the storm.

Edson had moved Baker Company and two companies of parachutists several hundred yards to the rear, perhaps half the distance along the curved saddle towards the battalion CP on Hill 120. Sweeney's new disposition left him with two platoons down the slope in the canopied forest (one on the high ground looking over the swampy end of the lagoon), and a third defending a main western spur of the grassy ridge. By fate, Baker Company of the Raiders tied in with Baker Company of the parachutists in the center, a coincidence that would cause heightened confusion during the night.

Edson, accompanied by Corporal Walter Burak, made one final reconnaissance of the immediate front late in the day, emerging from the brush in the middle of the Baker second platoon position, scaring hell out of Corporal Joseph Sweeda, the squad leader. "It was Edson and Burak, of all people!" Sweeda exclaimed in relief. But Sweeda was jumpy. Darkness was coming; the men would never complete their

"Japanese Type 92 (1932) 7.7mm Heavy Machine Gun," by Larry Klatt. The 1st Raiders rarely saw this dangerous weapon in the open, but when the Japanese tried to deploy such guns forward in the offensive their crews became sitting ducks. The gun and its tripod and carrying handles weighed more than 125 pounds, a cumbersome load in the jungle.

holes in time. The advanced position was weak, he thought. "There was too much space between each man, with poor contact." BARman Irv Reynolds, newly assigned to Sweeda's squad, recalled "we were spread out about ten yards apart." Another newcomer to Baker Company (from Easy), machine-gun squad leader Theodore M. Eleston, was disoriented and anxious as night fell. Elleston described his hole sat "at the bottom of the hill. We were so badly spread out I couldn't see the next Marine." Several hundred yards farther north along the Lunga, an Able Company squad leader had similar qualms. Sergeant Jack Tracy thought the minimum distance between his foxholes was ten yards; some were farther apart. Tracy had seen the overrun C Company positions during the morning's combat patrol. Now he worried whether his eight men could defend half a football field against a concentrated attack.[16]

Edson and Burak returned to the CP through Sweeney's position on the spur. Red Mike surveyed the jungle one last time with his field glasses, looked at Sweeney appraisingly, then said in his husky, matter-of-fact voice, "John, this is it. We are the only ones between the Japs and the airfield. You must hold this position."[17]

Edson worried about his communications, usually one of his tactical strong points. Tonight, many of his walkie-talkies were inoperative and the few field telephone lines were very vulnerable. He would have to rely heavily on Burak's strong legs, he thought. There was one encouraging sign. Both forward observer teams from the 11th Marines had working radios. Edson's link to the artillery would prove to be the most critical communications network of the battle.

## The Second Night

Sharp-eyed Major Tamura spotted Edson's late-afternoon redeployment. The Sendai battalion commander cautiously moved his rifle companies forward through the jungle to a more advantageous jump-off position. On the west, Major Kokusho's I/124 stirred for its attack along the lagoon. But General Kawaguchi's control, never strong in this battle, began to unravel again. Kawaguchi expected Lieutenant Colonel Watanabe to lead the charge against the Marines' left flank. He had no clue that Watanabe, nearly crippled by old wounds and the protracted approach march, would spend this critical night hobbling through the jungle, searching fruitlessly for his brigade commander. He would be adrift throughout the night while his leaderless battalion made disjointed and piecemeal attacks.

Seven Japanese destroyers opened fire on The Ridge at 2100, but the battle in the jungle commenced almost immediately after dark. Major Kokusho's platoons filtered forward stealthily, guiding on the parallel lagoon, looking for the boundary between Sweeney's company and Stiles' engineers, searching for ways to encircle the outposts.

Those Raiders who survived being posted in such a thin line in the jungle later questioned Edson's tactics, but it is difficult in retrospect to devise a suitable alternative. Edson's mission was to defend Henderson Field at all costs. He made the hard-nosed decision to risk a portion of his command as outguards to detect and disrupt the Japanese advance. In this regard, Red Mike established the line of outposts as Civil War generals employed skirmishers. Their duties were remarkably similar: to provide the main body early warning, then force the approaching enemy into a premature deployment, thus slowing his advance. Modern Marines might call this a "speed bump" mission. As costly and traumatic as the experience proved to be for the outguards, there exists plenty of evidence that their exposed position disrupted Major Kokusho's advance significantly.

As Edson predicted, the Japanese hit Baker Company first. This time the "V-ring" centered on John Sweeney's former platoon, the 1st, now led by Gunnery Sergeant Robert J. Anielski, and arrayed in a rambling line in the jungle along the southwest corner, just above the lagoon. Private Russ Whittlesey, barely eight months removed from being a Yale student, occupied one of the hasty foxholes in this line. He was all eyes and ears, his ever-present book of poetry now stashed in his pack. Each man was on full alert. In a hole near Whittlesey crouched Private First Class Edward Shepherd of Welch, West Virginia, whose 1943 letter left one of the earliest descriptions of the battle on record. "All was quiet except for the movement of small animals," he wrote. "Then we could hear the Japs cautiously advancing. They reached the far edge of the lagoon. The word was passed to hold our fire until they started crossing."[18]

Farther north, in Gunnery Sergeant Clinton F. Haines' 2d Platoon, Corporal Joe Sweeda cocked his head, straining to distinguish between natural jungle sounds and an increasing level of "unnatural" noises. "It seemed like only minutes when darkness fell and the jungle seemed to come alive in front of us," Sweeda said. "We could hear jabbering, then movement in the brush."[19]

BARman James Mallamas and Sergeant John "Squeaky" Morrell occupied a fighting hole at the outer limit of Haines' outpost. The platoon's mission, as understood by Mallamas, was to detect the Japanese advance, call in preregistered artillery fire, then fight their way back to The Ridge. "I heard a twig snap, then another, and more," he recalled shortly after the war. "We were quiet, hardly breathing. The Japs were crawling directly towards us."[20]

Major Kokusho's Borneo veterans crawled forward through the brush on a wide front. They would strike at several points, but the first thrust hit Anielski's platoon. The epicenter may have been the defensive positions along the east bank of the lagoon manned by Ed Shepard and Russ Whittlesey. Shepard could hear the Japanese crossing the lagoon directly towards him. He threw a grenade. It splashed loudly in the water but failed to detonate. "Then," he said, "all hell broke loose, the jungle was lit up like a stage, battles cries broke out from both sides." As Shepard raised his rifle he was cut down by a blinding blast at pointblank range

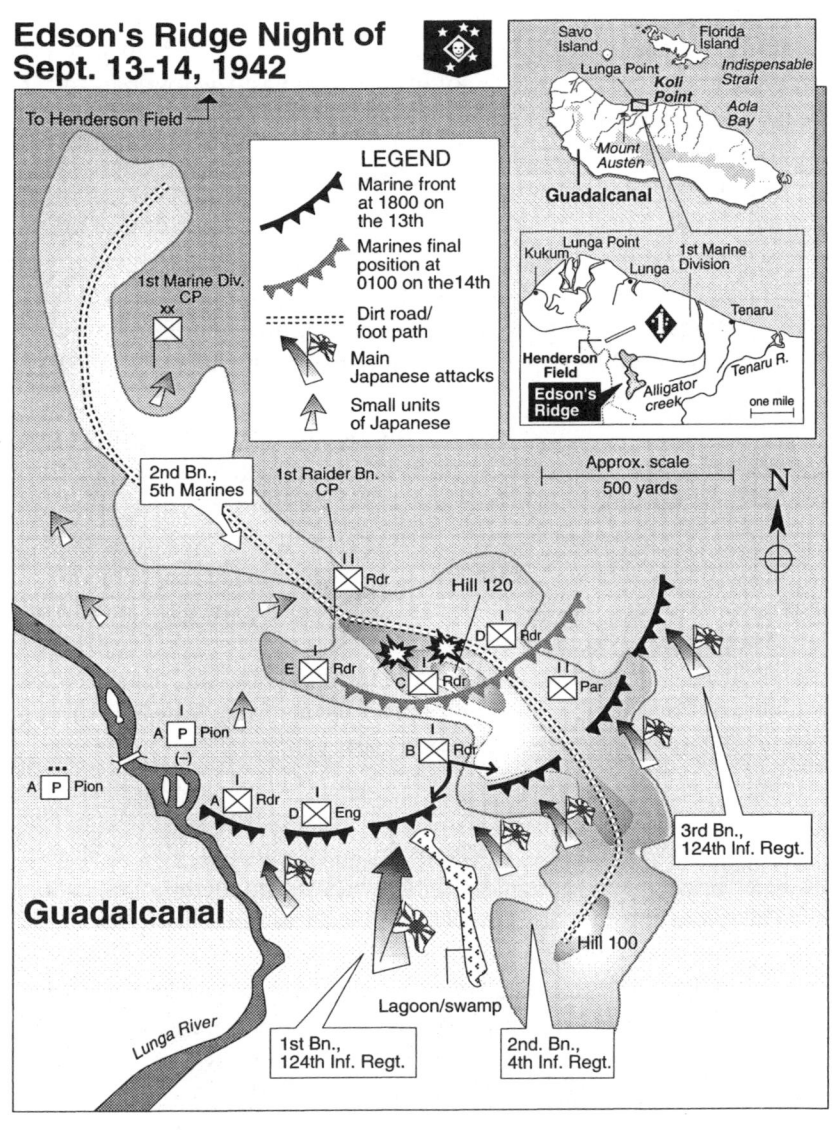

# Edson's Ridge Night of Sept. 13-14, 1942

**LEGEND**

- Marine front at 1800 on the 13th
- Marines final position at 0100 on the 14th
- Dirt road/ foot path
- Main Japanese attacks
- Small units of Japanese

To Henderson Field

1st Marine Div. CP
xx

2nd Bn., 5th Marines

1st Raider Bn. CP

Rdr

Hill 120

D | Rdr

E | Rdr

C | Rdr

| Par

A | P | Pion
(−)

A | P | Pion

B | Rdr

A | Rdr

D | Eng

**Guadalcanal**

3rd Bn., 124th Inf. Regt.

Hill 100

Lagoon/swamp

Lunga River

1st Bn., 124th Inf. Regt.

2nd. Bn., 4th Inf. Regt.

Approx. scale
500 yards

N

**Inset map (top right):**

Savo Island

Florida Island

Lunga Point

Koli Point

Indispensable Strait

Aola Bay

Mount Austen

**Guadalcanal**

Lunga Point

Kukum

Lunga

1st Marine Division

Henderson Field

Tenaru

Edson's Ridge

Alligator creek

Tenaru R.

one mile

(likely by the same kind of shoulder-slung Nambu light machine gun that Rushton and Ritter had faced the night before). Hit by bullets in his chest, left arm, and right shoulder, Shepard cried out to Whitt, his arms so numb he could not stop his rifle from sliding down the bank into the lagoon. Camouflaged Japanese soldiers rushed past the foxholes in the flickering light. Whittlesey grabbed Shepard, pulled him into the shadows, and looked for the trail back to The Ridge.[21]

"Hell broke out all around us," said Jim Mallamas. He and Squeaky Morrell threw their grenades, then scrambled back towards The Ridge. They were not quick enough. Japanese infiltrators had cut them off; in fact, the brush was filled with running, stumbling, swearing men of both sides. Mallamas and Morrell went to ground, now acutely aware that they were in a double jeopardy, caught between the Japanese riflemen and their own incoming artillery.[22]

Corporal Sweeda's concerns about his squad's exposed position proved well-founded. Japanese soldiers crawled close enough to shower the thin line of fighting holes with grenades. "All hell broke loose," said Irv Reynolds. "The Japs were crashing through the brush throwing grenades in front of them. They got the last two or three men at the end of our line." Fragments wounded BARman Robert G. Schneider in the neck and shoulders. Sweeda quickly concluded his outpost was now useless. The line had leaked "like a sieve, and we were already short of grenades." He ordered a pullback to The Ridge, a dicey maneuver with so many heavily armed enemy soldiers running through the underbrush.[23]

Japanese infiltrators overwhelmed Corporal Gene Eleston's machine-gun crew. In the subsequent melee, Eleston collided with an enemy soldier and killed him with his knife. "We just bumped into each other," Eleston recalled. "It was black as pitch. But I knew he was my enemy and he knew I was his. From the direction he was coming, there weren't any Marines." Knife fighting does not come naturally to most men, but Eleston was struggling for his life. "We grappled. He was smaller, but stocky. He was strong. He was brave—they all were brave." Eleston's stiletto prevailed but the memory haunted him—"one of my nightmares; he comes without a face."[24]

Eleston's machine-gun squad lost Sergeant Wallace Bergstrand, shot in the chest at close range. Bergstrand, twenty-four, from Wausau, Wisconsin, had been delighted the previous day to receive a package of fine cigars from his sister Ellen, according to Richard MacNeilly, who helped bring his body out.[25]

Sweeda's squad froze at the sounds of a good-sized force crashing through the bush along their flank. Then came a unmistakable American voice close at hand: "Where in hell is that goddamned trail?" It was Corporal Alfred Camlin's squad. Sweeda managed to get both squads out of the bush and back to The Ridge in time to help Captain Sweeney defend his hotly contested final position.[26]

Haines' platoon thereby escaped the initial Japanese onslaught with reasonable tactical integrity. But the Japanese had hit and scattered Anielski's platoon as if someone with a cudgel had smashed a Mexican *piñata*. That corner of the jungle was alive with groups of Japanese trying to stage for a dash up The Ridge, interspersed with individual Raiders striving to break clear to safety.

Russ Whittlesey struggled to assist badly wounded Ed Shepard up the trail. Japanese voices erupted in the dark, just uphill, heading back their way. With but a second to react, Whittlesey shoved Shepard into the underbrush off the trail to the left, then dove for cover on the opposite side. Shepard landed painfully, bit his tongue, and froze. He heard Whittlesey struggling, tangled in the heavy vines. There the Japanese caught him. "I heard a rush, voices, a commotion," said Shepard, followed by a burst of fire and a scream. Shepard inched away, keenly aware that Whittlesey had saved his life, most likely at the cost of his own.

Shepard was terrified. For the next hour he crawled back towards The Ridge, his odyssey made even more frightening by the onset of the artillery fire missions (although "going over much too high," he judged). Corpsman Karl B. Coleman—he who had so nimbly amputated Corporal Pion's arm at Tasimboko—found Shepard, dressed his wounds, and assisted him to the aid station, resolutely being run by Doctor Ed McLarney and Doctor Bob Skinner.[27]

The initial salvos from the 11th Marines may have been "too high" from Shepard's viewpoint, but they landed in the jungle dangerously near where Jim Mallamas and Squeaky Morrell lay hiding. Cut off by a swelling number of Japanese, Mallamas heard the familiar deep booming of a 105mm battery and figured his end had come. The third round exploded almost on top of the men. The blast threw them end over end into the air. Then, groggy and nearly deaf, bleeding from the nose and ears, the pair scrambled to escape from the killing zone. In the darkness the two men became separated. Morrell made it to the Raiders' lines; Mallamas spent hours evading columns of Japanese, hiding in wild boar dens, until he reached the Engineers' outpost.[28]

Private First Class James G. Hall, already wounded, suffered a similar concussion from the artillery explosions. Five weeks earlier he had exposed himself to sweeping Japanese machine-gun fire to pull Lieutenant Eugene Key's body to safety behind the Tulagi seawall. Now, stunned by the shell blast, he retained sufficient presence of mind to play dead when a Japanese patrol poked at his body and stripped him of his rifle and cartridge belt.[29]

At considerable cost, Baker Company's "speed bumps" had fulfilled their mission, alerting the battalion and channeling the Japanese into prepared killing zones. Captain Stiles' engineers, adjacent to Gunnery Sergeant Haines' platoon, received a glancing blow as Major Kokusho's I/124 paused to suffocate the Baker Company outposts. Stiles' diary entry for Sunday, 13 September concluded cryptically: "Lots of grenades, MG fire and artillery. Three wounded on left end. Terrible night." The engineers may have been profligate with their ammo, but they stood their ground throughout the night and plugged that critical gap.[30]

Farther north and closer to the river, Able Company spent an equally scary night. Small bands of Japanese lapped against Able Company's lines from time to time, but Captain Antonelli's men were more concerned with the sounds of fighting to their left rear where a battle royal seemed to be building around the battalion command post. Scout Ashley Large fired his rifle at close targets in the dark, "too busy to be scared." Poppell's diary reflected his extreme concern. "The dirty work is now on," he recorded. "We notice that the center of our [battalion] lines are breaking. Small Jap units may be heard within our lines." Poppell's field phone lines had all been cut, and his ears were ringing from the nonstop firing by the nearby 11th Marines. Diarist T. D. Smith recorded, "The shells, grenades, and machine-gun fire made a rifleman feel pretty impotent. I kept eyes peeled to the front and threw an occasional grenade."[31]

This was one night when the Marine rifle became more useful as a bayonet mount than a firearm. While the howitzers of the 11th Marines would do the most damage, the close confrontations would be determined by hand grenades and machine guns. Grenades, the infantryman's "pocket artillery," quickly became more precious than gold. Sensing this, Edson at first turned and yelled back down the hill to his S-4, Captain Jake Irwin—"*more grenades, more machine-gun belts!*" Irwin and his men broke out and distributed all they had in the battalion supply point. It was not enough.[32]

A handful of men—the battle's unsung heroes—took it upon themselves to find and deliver more grenades and machine-gun ammo to the Raiders and parachutists now hotly defending The Ridge. Their number included the members of Edson's immediate command post—Major Ken Bailey, Corporal Walter Burak, Field Sergeant Major James Childs, and

Platoon Sergeant Pete Pettus, Edson's chief scout. Others appeared. Captain Clarence R. Schwenke, Twining's assistant operations officer, volunteered to leave the division command post to lend Edson a hand. He rounded up a few good Marines, loaded a truck with cases of grenades and boxes of linked machine-gun bullets, and drove forward. When Japanese fire halted the truck well shy of Hill 120, Schwenke and Edson's staff risked their lives to deliver the vital ordnance material by hand. "Grenades were used by the case—it was a hell of a battle!" exclaimed Pete Pettus.[33]

Other Raiders helped distribute cases of grenades. Captain Houston Stiff did so until he got lost and nearly cut off by the surging Japanese. He was wounded twice in this protracted battle. One of Stiff's mortarmen, Sergeant Erland Coombs, retrieved two cases of grenades from the stalled truck and hauled them through heavy fire to the desperate parachutists. Before long, backlit by flares and explosions, Coombs became too obvious a target. He saw two grenades tumbling towards him, spitting sparks. The dual blasts blew him into a small tree, knocking him senseless. "When I came to, there was Sergeant Noah James, asking if I was hurt." Coombs could not move his legs. James dragged him laboriously back over the spur and into the small declivity that only partially hid the battalion aid station. Coombs never forgot the reaction of the first corpsman who saw him: "Holy cow, lookit all the holes in this guy!"[34]

By now the corpsmen had little time for small talk. Gravely wounded Raiders and parachutists flooded the small tent—some shot, others stabbed, most shredded or burned by grenade fragments or mortar shells. Sam Griffith later described the facility as "a primitive dressing station where two navy doctors [McLarney and Skinner] and their men, flashlight beams shielded by ponchos, applied tourniquets, gave transfusions, cleaned wounds." The station was no more than thirty feet behind the spot where Edson stood exposed on the military crest of Hill 120, directing the battle which was increasingly surging towards him.[35]

The fighting in the jungle on both nights had been savage and costly, but the battle would be won or lost on the grassy slopes of The Ridge itself. Defending the most exposed portion of the horseshoe were the two adjacent Baker Companies: Raiders on the right (southwest), Captain William J. McKennan's parachutists on the left. Sweeney's understrength company was now smaller, no more than sixty men, principally his 3d Platoon, augmented by a few depleted squads that had safely returned from the overrun outposts.

The Japanese destroyers fired down the long axis of The Ridge for more

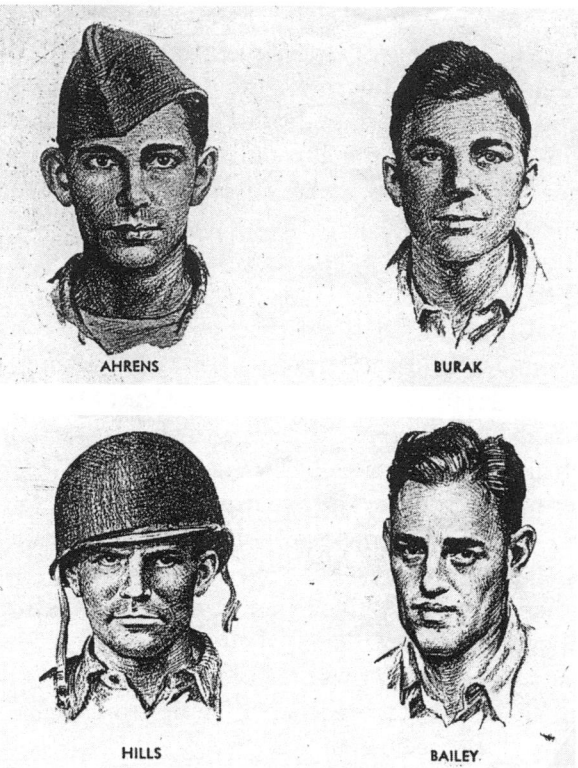

AHRENS · BURAK · HILLS · BAILEY

Four early heroes among the 1st Raiders: PFC Edward Ahrens (KIA, Navy Cross, Tulagi), Cpl. Walter Burak (KIA, Matanikau; Navy Cross, The Ridge), Clifford "Red" Hills (Navy Cross, Tulagi), and Kenneth Bailey (KIA, Matanikau; Medal of Honor, The Ridge).

than a half-hour. The hideous shriek of five-inch shells ripping the air just over their hunkered-down heads was intensely nerve-wracking to the Marines, but most of the rounds were "overs," missing the low ridge and slamming into the jungle just beyond.

The Japanese assault troops crouching at the edge of the jungle commenced their version of psychological warfare against The Ridge defenders—chanting, slapping their rifle stocks, throwing fire-crackers. But the Raiders and parachutists had experienced these mind games the previous month at Tulagi. John Sweeney hustled along the 3d Platoon's firing line, steadying his men, reminding them of what they had learned from fighting the *rikusentai:* "Don't shoot at noises or shadows."[36]

The Japanese kicked off their assault with a bright magnesium flare. Major Kokusho drew his sword and led his battalion out of the shadows, the riflemen screaming *"Banzai!"* and "Death to Roosevelt!" The burning flare backlit the Raiders, but they were squatting in their shallow fighting holes, heads bent forward along rifle stocks or sighting down machine-gun barrels. The Japanese attacked into the artificial light, running uphill through the thick grass, bunching up against the barbed wire—a virtual shooting gallery for the Marines. Disciplined cross-fire scissored Kokusho's front ranks. Grenades exploded in the crowded back ranks. On they came, lapping up towards the line of foxholes. Raiders on the crest of the spur picked their onrushing targets carefully, shooting the first man, bayoneting the second. The wave broke, receded back down the bloody slope. Yet the casualties were not entirely one-sided. Japanese mortar fire never stopped, and hidden Nambu machine gunners raked the slopes from a distance.

The Raiders barely had time to draw a deep breath before a fresh assault came boiling out of the jungle. By now the Raiders and parachutists were under attack along their entire front. Major Tamura, commanding the Sendai Battalion and mindful of the punishing his staged troops were receiving from the Marines' artillery, decided not to wait for Kawaguchi's orders and advanced his II/4 against the southern and southeastern sector of The Ridge. The Borneo veterans of Major Kokusho's battalion, incensed at their first repulse in the war, renewed their attack with a fury.

This time the Japanese used either smudge pots or smoke grenades in conjunction with the magnesium signal flare to mask their frenzied dash through the cross-fire. The sudden smoke combined with the acrid smell of burning magnesium, and the Japanese screams of *"Tsu-geki!"* ["Charge!"] curdled the blood of the Marine defenders—*a goddamned gas attack??* The war was still new. Nobody really knew whether or when the Japanese would resort to poison gas in battle—yet every Marine on The Ridge had long ago abandoned his bulky gas mask. Some troops panicked. Sweeney and First Sergeant Maddox and the Parachutist McKennan manhandled their men back to their holes. The Japanese might have swept the position had Kawaguchi been poised to commit an immediate reserve force.

General Kawaguchi had compounded his control problems the first night by establishing a haphazard brigade command post in the middle of the Lunga River, then taking shelter in dense vegetation along the bank. This night he found a more centralized, accessible site, moving his CP to the edge of the jungle just south of Hill 100 at the southern terminus of The Ridge. Unwittingly, however, he had just moved into the impact zone for both the Imperial Navy's long-range shelling and part of the 11th Marines' relentless howitzer fire. Although Kawaguchi would later state that the vivid tracer fire erupting along The Ridge reminded him of a festive fireworks display, it is likely he spent little time admiring the view and instead sought shelter behind the fattest banyan tree he could find. This was no reflection on his bravery. No one stands erect very long during a firestorm of five-inch and 105mm high explosive shells.

Kawaguchi intended his night assaults on the 13th and 14th to atone for the previous night's disappointments. Assaulting The Ridge with his three battalions would be the linchpin of his grand, three-pronged advance, with the Kuma Battalion striking the thin Marine lines along Alligator Creek to the east, and Colonel Oka with the remnants of II/124 attacking across the Matanikau from the west.

But both flank attacks, late to develop and ragged in execution, failed. The 3d Battalion, 1st Marines repulsed the Kuma Battalion and killed Major Mizuno in two nights of tense fighting. Colonel Oka failed to cross the Matanikau until sunrise the next day, yet he surprised the 3d Battalion, 5th Marines with an unexpected daylight attack against their jungle outpost. This battle, too, was a near run thing, but Oka eventually lost both control and momentum and had to withdraw.

Meanwhile, Kawaguchi's initial reports from The Ridge were all bad: "This battalion commander killed. That battalion completely annihilated. Whereabouts of [the other] battalion commander not known." He was baffled by the disappearance of Lieutenant Colonel Watanabe and saddened by the death of Major Kokusho, who, as Kawaguchi reconstructed events, "took the lead with drawn sword in his hand, fought like a demon in fury, killed several enemy soldiers, [and] occupied an important enemy position."[37]

Had Kawaguchi been closer to the fighting he might have been less discouraged. While true that Kokusho's battalion, bloodied early by the unexpected Baker Company outposts and demoralized by the major's death, was reduced to modest threats against the Raiders' entire right flank, the other two battalions were poised to sweep The Ridge. Evidently some subaltern in the leaderless III/124 took the initiative to launch several tactical units against the parachutists. Major Tamura's 5th and 7th Companies were locked in mortal combat against the diminishing number of Marines defending the rounded nose of the horseshoe.

Edson ordered the curtain of artillery fire to be drawn closer—dangerously closer—to his front lines. Sweeney's frail walkie-talkie still worked—although a smooth-talking, English-speaking Japanese disrupted the frequency at one point, evidently using a radio captured from Charlie Company the previous night. Like the biblical good shepherd, however, Edson knew his subordinates' voices. Sweeney then gave the radio to First Sergeant Maddox who maintained a stoic dialogue with Corporal Thomas Watson, the 11th Marines' forward observer at Edson's side (whom Edson would recommend for a battlefield commission the next day). Watson was an invaluable forward observer; so was Staff Sergeant Robert Delanoy elsewhere along The Ridge. Several hundred Raiders and parachutists would owe their very lives to this pair of artillerymen, and to the sweating gun crews of the 11th Marines who fired a regimental record 2,800 rounds that night. "The artillery fired continuously," said Pete Pettus appreciatively.[38]

Other Marines manning the scattered strongpoints around the division's perimeter watched the distant battle in awe. Seen from afar, The Ridge appeared to pulsate with yellow-orange explosions. Machine-gun tracer rounds split the night; ricochets spun away in bright tangents. Waves of gunfire and frenzied shouts would reach a dramatic crescendo, slowly fade, then build up again. The steady "boom" of the 11th Marines' howitzers echoed incessantly, each followed by its corresponding "*crump*" on impact. Pressure waves from the ceaseless explosions rocked the palms.

The Japanese had never faced artillery fire like this. Some of Kawaguchi's remnants would marvel at the Marines' "automatic artillery." Surviving officers of the Tamura Battalion (II/4) suspected the Marines had somehow positioned "sound detectors and automatic communication devices" along their approach path. Yet seismic intrusion devices lay two decades in the future. "Artillery Hell" for the Japanese the night of 13 September 1942 resulted not from high technology but from Merritt Edson's terrain analysis, Pedro del Valle's careful registration, the proficiency of the howitzer crews—and the dangerously fragile radio link between First Sergeant Maddox at the point of attack to Corporal Watkins at Edson's side, thence via phone line to the Raiders' switchboard and down the slope to the 11th Marines Fire Direction Center.[39]

Edson needed more men. While Bailey rounded up stragglers, Edson ordered Captain Bill Stevenson, the communications officer, to dispatch a provisional rifle squad of radio operators to John Sweeney. Stevenson, who had earlier volunteered to lead out a patrol, took over the vital switchboard and ordered Sergeant James "Horse Collar" Smith to assemble the "riflemen." Smith nodded at the men around him—Corporals Morris Snyder and Hubert Milanowski, and Privates William Carey and Willis Neeley—and led the way south along the contested crest. Privates Herman Arnold and David Taber moved out separately.

John Sweeney's exposed position was now *"in extremis."* His eyes widened at the sight of Horse Collar Smith and the shadows following behind. "Deploy your company over here," Sweeney indicated. Smith waved him off: "We're not a company—just seven men." "Oh, shit!" said Sweeney. He inserted the makeshift squad into the gap between his 3d Platoon and the parachutists, virtually the apex of the "V-ring."

Smith's communicators fought with Sweeney's little band throughout the night. "The battle," reflected Smith, "would be moments of incredible activity as the Japs attacked our position and we responded with hand grenades and our weapons when they reached the top of the ridge, followed by unreal lulls in activity while the Japs regrouped." Hand grenades were in high demand. "Burak and Childs made repeated runs to the rear to obtain more grenades and we expended them on the charging Japs until our arms were weary."

Six of the seven communicators became casualties. Snyder and Milanowski were wounded. Then "Carey got shot," said Smith, "and a Japanese grenade, fuse fizzing, landed right on me. I rolled twice before it exploded. I caught two large chunks of the grenade in my shoulder; many other chunks found a home in my butt, knee, and ankle....I bled like a pig." Other Marines dragged Smith to the aid station. There he encountered Dave Taber, badly wounded, who told Smith that Ikey Arnold had been shot in the neck and died in Taber's arms. Smith wept. He considered Herman "Ikey" Arnold, twenty, from Baltimore, to be "one of the world's few good guys."[40]

Edson saw that his center could not hold. Needing to send an unmistakable message to Sweeney, Red Mike dispatched Corporal Burak to the most exposed edge of the forward command post. "JOHN WOLF!" Burak bellowed, using Sweeney's code name. "THIS IS BURAK—DO YOU HEAR ME?"

Sweeney, startled, yelled back an affirmative. Burak continued: "RED MIKE SAYS IT'S OKAY TO WITHDRAW!"[41]

Easier said than done for Sweeney's besieged defenders. The Japanese were at their throats, casualties abounded, and the spur was rocked by a cacophony of fire and explosions.

Sweeney did the best he could. He called in a final ring of artillery fire "super close," ordered First Sergeant Maddox to go back and establish an assembly point near Edson's position on Hill 120, tried to extract his survivors by alternate rushes. But a night withdrawal under heavy fire and direct attack is almost impossible to execute in orderly fashion. Disorder soon prevailed. This became the night's worst hour for the parachutists, but plenty of Raiders joined them in scrambling pell-mell to the rear. Confusion raged as the two Baker Companies intermingled in the dark.

Sweeney, Maddox, and McKennan struggled to re-establish a new line, but Edson and Bailey were the giants in this crisis. Bailey was big enough to collar retreating Marines and shake some sense into them. "It was hard to stop the stampede," admitted Pete Pettus, but Bailey "waved his pistol menacingly and the men stopped and went back." Edson applied stinging sarcasm to his wayward Raiders: "The only difference between you and the Japs is they've got more guts! Get back!"[42]

When Edson could not find the parachute battalion commander he grabbed fiery Captain Harry L. Torgerson and ordered him to organize a counter-attack against the threatened left flank. Torgerson achieved the seemingly impossible. He assembled enough parachutists to form two composite companies—painfully slow work amid the darkness, noise, confusion, and renewed Japanese attacks—then personally led them forward in an inspirational assault, driving what must have been a good-sized element of Watanabe's men from their dangerous foothold along the entire left of The Ridge. "This counterattack was carried out successfully," wrote Edson in a commendation letter six days after the battle. The attack cost the two improvised parachutist companies 40 percent casualties, Edson noted, but in the process they completely stopped "a flanking movement initiated by the enemy which if carried to completion would have resulted in the loss of the battalion reserve line."[43]

The parachutists reclaimed the salient and held the steep position like bulldogs. The night seemed endless. As Captain McKennan recounted in a 1943 *Saturday Evening Post* essay: "The [Japanese] attack was almost constant, like a rain that subsides for a moment and then pours the harder....When one wave was mowed down—and I mean mowed down—another followed it into death....Some of the Jap rushes were now carrying them into our positions and there was ugly hand-to-hand fighting."[44]

At the height of this hand-to-hand fighting, parachutist Jesse Youngdeer went down, badly wounded by a Japanese bayonet (and again by an *American* blade in the wild brawl). He had just returned that evening from seeing to the evacuation of his brother, the Raiders' Corporal Bob Youngdeer, shot in the face by the tree-borne sniper at daybreak along the lagoon. Jesse Youngdeer would survive his impaling. In fact the two brothers would recover from surgery in the same ward of the hospital ship *Solace* off Espiritu Santo, each astonished to discover the other.[45]

Captain McKennan in his essay paid national tribute to Ken Dill Bailey, calling him "one of the finest Marine Corps officers in the Solomons—or anywhere else." Private Ed Shepard, his nightmarish crawl from the lagoon finally ended, now lay in his stretcher outside the bustling aid station, awaiting farther evacuation to the airfield and watching Major Bailey manhandling replacements into the lines just forward of the command post. "Bailey was one of the most courageous men I ever knew," said Shepard. "He walked the crest of that Ridge, directing and encouraging every Marine as if it was a training exercise." Tiger Erskine likened Bailey's actions "to those of a linebacker." At the climax of the battle Bailey came by Erskine's position, looking for more volunteers to carry grenades forward. Their eyes locked. Erskine hesitated. He was one of only three surviving Japanese language officers on Guadalcanal. Bailey, recalled Erskine, "did not press me. I rationalized holding back [but] have felt survival guilt ever since." [He need not have—Tiger Erskine's translational skills represented an irreplaceable asset for the Raiders].[46]

BARman John P. Ingalls of Charlie Company, whose depleted unit's reserve mission abruptly changed to front-line defense, scrambled up the slope looking for ammo, found some, then got "appropriated" by Bailey to guard himself and Edson as another Japanese attack spilled towards them. Ingalls lay at their feet, firing away, numbly aware that both men were standing erect behind him, calmly talking on their field phones.[47]

Both officers presented attractive upright targets as the attacking Japanese closed the range. One Imperial marksman took aim at Bailey and "rang his chimes," putting a .25 caliber bullet through his helmet, just above his skull. A second rifleman clipped Bailey's cheek with another near miss. Blood smears made Bailey's intense expression appear the more fierce.

Bullets nicked Edson's clothing and equipment, too, but Red Mike was in his element. He coldly watched the Japanese advance, then called in the artillery fire ever closer, overriding the safety concerns of the fire direction center. He put down the receiver and strode away. Seconds later a mortar round exploded on the spot he had just vacated, destroying the phone. Many thought he lived a charmed life. Irving Reynolds, glad to be back on The Ridge after his stint in the jungle outpost, crawled up the slope, pushing a case of grenades ahead of him, when he spotted "some idiot standing straight up with hands on hips; I suspected that was Edson." Field Sergeant Major Jim Childs believed Edson did not care whether he lived or died. "He simply stood there, the other men in the CP all flat on the ground except Bailey, who imitated Edson. Their lack of fear helped the others overcome their own fear."[48]

The mortar round that blew up Edson's just-vacated field phone was one of several dozen shells that saturated Hill 120 prior to a renewed series of enemy attacks. Edson realized his situation had become critical. The Japanese had thrust a large wedge in his right flank, essentially cutting off Griffith's two large units (the companies of Antonelli and Stiles) from The Ridge itself. Torgerson was still rallying his parachutists to root out the threat along the eastern slopes. And the mortar fire had just cut his telephone wires to the Division CP.

This was quite likely the time, about 0400, when Houston Stiff saw Edson and Bailey face the airfield and in unison "yell at the top of their voices, BILL WHALING! BILL WHALING!" Stiff, mystified, watched them repeat this at ten minute intervals, only later realizing they were calling for the commander of the 2d Battalion, 5th Marines to move up to their support.[49]

Edson sent Corporal Burak to the division CP at a dead run to report the line failure and urge the 11th Marines to maintain the last called concentrations. His message delivered, Burak took the initiative to find a couple of reels of comm wire, enlisted a brave-hearted helper, and methodically restrung a new phone line through a gauntlet of fire all the way back up the slope to the Raider switchboard, then unspooled another fifty feet to connect with Edson's exposed CP. His crucial communications link restored, Edson phoned Colonel Jerry Thomas at the division command center. Thomas recalled Edson's husky, unemotional voice saying "I've been hit hard and I need more men." Edson further warned that the Japanese had commenced sneaking a number of infiltrators past the Marines' acutely "refused" flanks. "Unless you do something for yourselves the Japs will come through you like shit through a tin horn." First things first, Thomas thought. He radioed Colonel Bill Whaling, a man by this time extremely curious about just who in hell had been yelling his name that bizarre night. Thomas told Whaling to reinforce Edson immediately.[50]

Whaling had taken command of 2/5 just two days earlier when Lieutenant Colonel Rosecrans and his executive officer were wounded during a Japanese air raid. He was a veteran fighter, but this was no night for a battalion-level Pickett's Charge up the backside of Edson's desperate defenses. He ordered his three rifle company commanders to advance independently, guiding on the paths they had reconnoitered the previous afternoon.

By now the Japanese had advanced close enough to interdict 2/5's approach up the reverse slope of Edson's knoll with machine guns and mortars. Heavy fire pinned down George Company to the left of the knoll, inflicting thirty casualties. Captain Harry J. Connor halted his Easy Company and snaked forward to find Edson. Connor said Red Mike told him to "move my company into the center of his position." Connor's company paid a price moving up—five killed, nine wounded—but the stiffening effect of so many veteran riflemen in the three companies helped Edson cling to Hill 120, the last dominant terrain overlooking Henderson Field.[51]

Whaling's reinforcements arrived literally in the nick of time. To that point Edson's men had resembled the Texan defenders of the Alamo, grossly outnumbered, back-to-back, nearly out of ammo. Edson and Bailey could count fewer than three hundred men defending Hill 120, the intermingled remnants of Raiders' B, C, D, and E Companies, plus two small companies of parachutists. Bailey, Burak, Childs, and Pettus somehow kept the cases of hand grenades coming, but the Japanese had plenty of their own to lob into the closely-packed defenders.

Private First Class Ben Quintana lost a grenade duel with a Japanese rifleman in Easy Company's line. "As I was coiled up waiting for a chance to lob my grenade," he said, "one of the Jap grenades landed at my feet. I crossed my arms over my face and rolled up as tight as I could, but the grenade blew me clean off the ridge." Quintana retained consciousness and crawled back up the slope on his elbows, badly wounded. "I could hear the blood gurgling out of my body, and I begged for someone to stop the bleeding. Now I know why they called it Bloody Ridge." A Marine applied a tourniquet to his legs, others dragged him back to the aid station, where, Quintana recalled, "they cut off what was left of my clothes, salted me down with sulfa powder and shot me full of morphine." The surgeon saved Quintana's life and his shattered legs but could not save his right eye.[52]

Still lacking any communications with the battalion or division, Able Company sweated out the wild night in dread. "About 0430," recorded Popeye Poppell, "we hear mortars open up on the ridge which sound like enemy origin. It is our sincere belief that all is lost, and our only chance of escape will be to sneak through to the coast for a naval pick up."[53]

By 0430, however, Kawaguchi's infantry attacks were running out of steam. The 11th Marines' howitzers never stopped shooting them down in their assembly areas. Similarly, Edson's machine-gun crews still maintained their disciplined short bursts that littered the slopes with a ghastly human harvest. The remaining threats to the Raiders—significant ones at that—came from those Japanese who now occupied positions either past or virtually within the lines. The first group imperiled 2/5's approach, the airfield, and the Raiders' headquarters company. The second group of Japanese, infesting the Marines' lines like wood ticks on a dog's back, had hauled several heavy machine guns well forward. If the attackers' firing had become sporadic with the approach of dawn, their overall tenacity and lethality had increased.

An intriguing yet unauthenticated story serves to illustrate the efforts some Japanese may have gone to win this night-long battle. Captain Torgerson's after-action report states that during the height of the battle the enemy hauled a 75mm field piece to the crest of Hill 100 at the southern end of The Ridge. Torgerson said his men examined the weapon after the battle and were baffled to find it surrounded by 30–40 cast-off live rounds—and no empty shells. Further examination of the live rounds, said Torgerson, revealed a faint dent in each primer, indicative of a short firing pin. Such a weapon would surely have been a Type 41 "mountain gun" of the kind captured by the Raiders near Tasimboko, a piece disassembled, lugged painstakingly through the jungle, then hastily reassembled under fire (hence the malfunctioning firing pin?) on or near Hill 100.[54]

The absence of any corroborating reports from either the Raiders or General Kawaguchi may fatally undermine the authenticity of this report, but Torgerson was not otherwise given to exaggeration. The implications are provocative. Did some of Kawaguchi's artillerymen really succeed in humping their two-hundred-pound components in the long trek through the jungle from Tetere to The Ridge? Did they actually survive the torrent of artillery and machine-gun fire to reassemble the piece and lug it to the northern nose of Hill 100? Did they in fact take level aim at Edson's crowded knoll, a can't-miss target of opportunity only seven hundred yards away—only to experience thirty or more consecutive misfires? We may never know the truth, but if Torgerson was correct we should whistle again at Edson's fabled luck—and wish for that dauntless, frustrated gun crew a well-deserved corner somewhere in Valhalla.

Some of Major Tamura's enterprising platoons infiltrated the trees along both flanks. Some remained as snipers; others continued downhill towards the division CP and the fighter strip. Edson's warning proved true. Three Japanese screamed through Vandegrift's command post, impaling one Marine with a sword. They died in their tracks, one drilled through the head by a single shot from Sergeant Major Sheffield Banta's unerring pistol.

## Dawn's Early Light

Gray dawn rewarded the riflemen on both sides with their first clear targets at any distance. If anything the ghastly battlefield became deadlier. A Japanese sniper shot a Marine defending the nose of one of "The Centipede's" several "legs." As the Raider writhed in agony, Hospital Apprentice First Class Robert L. Smith dashed along the exposed spur to his aid. The heartless sniper killed Smith just as he bent over the casualty.

Farther south along The Ridge, Baker Company squadleader Corporal Joe Sweeda greeted the morning with relief. He had survived both his exposed outpost near the lagoon and the subsequent defense of Hill 120 intact. Then, to his dismay, a Japanese soldier in the edge of the adjacent jungle angled a 50mm knee-mortar round his way—a perfect shot. "I was hit with shrapnel in my right thigh and torso, and I lost my rifle," Sweeda said. Sergeant Tony Massar tried to patch his wounds but could not stem the bleeding. Sweeda "crawled like a wounded dog" to the aid station. There Major Bob Brown, Edson's exhausted operations officer (and Sweeda's former company commander at Quantico), inquired solicitously about his welfare. Sweeda had lost a lot of blood, and the corpsmen worried about his condition. Early daylight made it possible to bring up a reconnaissance truck from the airfield to evacuate the most critically wounded. As stretcher bearers loaded Sweeda in the truck's bed, he saw Major Brown approaching, white in the face, clutching a shattered hand. A nearby Japanese had surprised Brown with a grenade. Brown desperately tied to throw it back, but the grenade exploded as it left his hand. "I saw Major Brown being led to the ambulance with one finger dangling from his hand," observed Irv Reynolds.[55]

The corpsmen overloaded the three-quarter-ton truck with wounded Marines. They placed Brown in the cab next to the driver, loaded Sergeant Frank Boone (the Easy Company machine-gun squad leader who had spent the first night surrounded near the lagoon and was now gravely wounded) in a stretcher next to Sweeda, and packed the wounded communicators Horse Collar Smith and Dave Taber on the front fend-

Fallen Japanese soldiers of the Kawaguchi Brigade lay along the crest of Edson's Ridge at daybreak on 14 September 1942. (Marine Corps Historical Center)

ers. The driver took off, anxious to clear the danger zone but considerate of his frail passengers and the bumpy trail.

A sickening tragedy unfolded. A Japanese Nambu machine gunner hidden in the trees to the immediate west raked the makeshift ambulance with fire. The driver slumped over the steering wheel; the vehicle drifted to a stop, still being stitched with bullets. Sweeda lay helpless in his stretcher, terrified, as "bullets hit the [truck] bed, [making] paint chips fly around." A hundred Raiders opened up on the Nambu gunner, silencing him for eternity, but the damage was done. Rescuers ran to the stricken vehicle to find three dead, the survivors traumatized. The dead included Major Bob Brown, thirty-five, who left a widow and nine-year-old son in Merion, Pennsylvania, and Sergeant Frank Boone, twenty-two, of Bloomburg, Pennsylvania. Bloody Ridge continued to soak up the blood of the Raiders.[56]

The ambulance massacre demonstrated that daybreak had rendered the headquarters Raiders more vulnerable than the front-line defenders of The Ridge. Most of Captain Jake Irwin's supply troops had spent the night distributing grenades and ammunition and assisting the wounded. Their number included the intrepid Gunnery Sergeant Gerald Stackpole, the old-timer who had served with Edson in Nicaragua and now fiercely bore the title of "The Admiral" of the Raiders' rubber boat fleet. After the firing died down at dawn, a Japanese armed with a knee mortar (possibly the same one who had just nailed Corporal Sweeda) made life miserable for the Raiders around the supply tent. As related in 1963 by intel specialist Private First Class Alfred A. Haas, "someone said 'Let's get that damned sonofabitch.'" Seven Raiders grabbed their weapons and scrambled up to the top of the spur. There we stood, said Haas, "like a bunch of fools, silhouetted on the crest."

Shots rang out. Three men pitched down the slope, the rest dove for cover—"except The Admiral," said Haas. "He went to help the nearest casualty, while the rest of us looked for the snipers or tried to find the guts to help Stack." A single Arisaka rifle spoke, drilling Stackpole through the chest, killing him.

Gerald Burton Stackpole died at age forty. He was from Dixon, Illinois, and had attained sixteen years service, including an early stint in the U.S. Navy. Said Haas of his personal hero: "Stack may not have been a recruiting-poster Marine and he may have been an old man by the standards of the day. Most certainly he was a combat Marine...in the truest sense of the words."[57]

The losses of his long-time friends Brown and Stackpole stung Merritt Edson personally, but he knew the infiltrators would be rooted out in time. He worried more about the hundreds of armed Japanese still trying to overrun his knoll from the jungle's edge. Earlier, just before dawn, Edson sent Major Bailey and Sergeant Major Childs down to Henderson Field to beg for a close air support mission at daybreak. Army Captain John A. Thompson of the 67th Fighter Squadron got the assignment. He reported to "The Pagoda" for an urgent briefing from a Marine officer he took to be a first lieutenant, "a company commander...holding a helmet with a bullet hole in it, with blood on his head and the side of his face." It was boyish Ken Bailey, who drew Thompson a crude map of the current positions along the battlefield.

Captain Thompson led his flight of three shark-faced P-400s aloft before sunup, climbed to a thousand feet, then wheeled and dove at high speed for The Ridge. "I saw the Marines on the ridge as I came in over the trees," he said, "and below the ridge in a clearing were hundreds of enemy troops crowded together, caught by surprise." Thompson depressed the nose of his fighter to align his targets, then cut a wide

**"After the Ridge," by Raider Houston Stiff, twice wounded in that battle.**

swath through the troops with his six wing-mounted .30 caliber machine guns. His wingmen roared over The Ridge in quick succession, blazing away. The P-400 pilots' first firing run was a turkey shoot—then the Japanese made them pay. A fusillade of small arms fire greeted their next pass. Thompson and one of his wingmen took identical hits in their coolant radiators and had to execute emergency deadstick landings. Japanese marksmen hit the third plane as well, but the pilot made repeated passes until he ran out of ammunition. The Marines could not have asked for a more timely or effective air attack.[58]

General Kawaguchi knew he had been defeated. With American aircraft scorching the grassy highlands in broad daylight, Kawaguchi had no other choice but to call in his scattered forces and begin a torturous retreat through the jungle to the Japanese enclave along the coast west of the Matanikau. The general later stated his losses to be forty-one officers and 1,092 enlisted killed or wounded, somewhat less than 20 percent of his 6,700-man command. The real casualty level was most assuredly much higher. The Ka Force suffered a virtual hemorrhage of losses from the moment its ships and barges entered the Solomon Sea. The 2d Battalion, 5th Marines, inheritors of the battlefield surrounding The Ridge, buried the slain Japanese, said to surpass six hundred. And Kawaguchi would lose many of his gravely wounded soldiers on his forthcoming trek through the jungle. Concluded historian Richard Frank, "the true Japanese losses may well have exceeded eight hundred killed or missing." Despite its preponderance of assault troops at the main point of attack (at least a five-to-one advantage the second night), the Ka Force had shattered itself against the Marine Raiders and parachutists defending "The Centipede." "For various reasons the night attack failed," said Kawaguchi after the war, admitting the obvious: "I as the commander of the whole force should take responsibility."[59]

General Kawaguchi's bright star faded rapidly. General Hyakutake summoned him to Rabaul to explain his disastrous campaign. Within a month IGHQ assigned him a staff job at a district army headquarters; in another six months he entered a prolonged unassigned status. Only late in the war, as Japan prepared to defend its home islands against the anticipated invasion, did IGHQ restore Kawaguchi to active duty as commander of the Tsushima Fortress. It would be years before Kawaguchi learned that he had been confounded at Tasimboko and The Ridge by Merritt Edson and his Raiders.[60]

Yet the Raiders hardly looked like mighty conquerors when they straggled down from The Ridge after being relieved by 2/5 at midmorning on 14 September. They were burnt out—frazzled, hollow-eyed, feverish, and dehydrated. Their casualties are difficult to validate. Totals range from 166 casualties reported in the September Muster Roll to 135 cited by Sam Griffith (who regrettably did not document his source). The most accurate estimate comes from Edson's definitive biographer, Jon Hoffman, who reported that thirty-four Raiders died and 129 were wounded (total 163) during the period 11–14 September, which includes the early air raids by the "Sea Eagles." The total easily represented one-fourth of the command. The parachutists lost a proportionally greater percentage. One Raider, not otherwise listed as a casualty, broke under the extreme psychological pressures of the night battles and had to be evacuated for "shell shock." It would be safe to say that each of the survivors who came down from that smoking ridge suffered from the initial symptoms of what would soon be identified as "battle fatigue." The ordeal had been that horrific.[61]

General Vandegrift nominated Colonel Edson and Major Bailey for the Medal of Honor. Edson's citation took note of his "cool leadership and personal courage." Bailey's described his "great personal valor while exposed to constant and merciless enemy fire and his indomitable fighting spirit."

In a protracted battle during which virtually every man in the battalion surpassed himself with heroism, commanders had difficulty commending one act of valor over another. As at Tasimboko, none of the twenty-four navy ships named after Edson's Raiders or alumni included men who had distinguished themselves during the Battle of The Ridge (with the obvious exception of the USS *Edson*). Likewise, the number of Navy Crosses awarded seems disproportionate to the countless acts of individual bravery that highlighted the battle. Awards of the nation's second highest medal went to Corporal Walter Burak and Captain John Sweeney, to machine-gun Platoon Sergeants Lawrence Harrison and Lawrence Holdren, to cool-headed rifleman John Mielke, and to intelligence chief/patrol leader "Pete" Pettus, among others. Major Robert Brown received a posthumous Navy Cross, as did radioman-turned-rifleman Herman "Ikey" Arnold. Three headquarters officers who performed their basic duties under extremely hazardous conditions in the final "V-ring" on Edson's knoll—communicator William Stevenson and surgeons Edward McLarney and Robert Skinner—also received the award. Intrepid corpsman Karl Coleman earned his second Navy Cross in a week; other corpsmen, including Delbert Eilers and young Thaddeus Parker, received their first.[62]

As in most battles, few individual riflemen garnered the official recognition they deserved. Yet in this case each man who survived the battle came away with a certain sacrosanct glory for fighting on that grisly hogback with Edson and Bailey, a dramatic encounter that immediately became one of the great legends of the Marine Corps. The battle would acquire several nicknames—"Raiders' Ridge," "Bloody Ridge," "The Ridge"—but the name that endures most today is simply "Edson's Ridge."

Two days after the battle Captain John Sweeney led a heavily armed patrol south along Baker Company's former outpost line, searching for his missing man, Private First Class Russ Whittlesey. The Baker Raiders discovered his body tangled in the thick brush to the right of the trail. Sweeney and his men buried him there, leaving one dogtag in the grave, retaining the second. Sweeney scribbled down the location for posterity: "1,000 yards south of the airfield, just forward of the front lines at Lunga Ridge." Frank Russell Whittlesey, twenty-one, the former Yale student and budding poet with the distinguished uncle, had not let his family down. Or his fellow Raiders. "Rest in peace, Marine," said Sweeney, in tears, then vectored his patrol out of the still-dangerous, shell-splintered rain forest.[63]

## Notes

1. Merrill Twining, who was in the division CP, attests that Edson stood "at the highest point of The Ridge bellowing into the night, 'Raiders, parachutists, engineers, artillerymen, I don't give a damn who you are. You're all Marines. Come on up this ridge and fight!'" Twining, *No Bended Knee*, 100. Yet there is no evidence that Edson ever left his forward CP on the southern nose of Hill 120, nor was it in his character to "bellow" in battle, no matter how great the pressure. Major Ken Bailey, however, had both the temperament and the lungs; in his several passages along the ridge rallying and resupplying the troops he was in a position during the peak of the battle to holler such imprecations down the ravine towards the division CP.
2. Kawaguchi Memoir, 22.
3. Merritt Edson, quoted by Sam Griffith, *The Battle for Guadalcanal*, 116.
4. Irv Reynolds to John Sweeney, 17 May 1988, 1; Jack Tracy interview with Jon Hoffman, 1991.
5. Sweeney Ridge Memoir, 79.
6. Pete Pettus journal, "Combat Intelligence, Practical Experience," n.d., 5–7; James Smith Memoir, "September Patrol," author's possession.
7. Mielke Memoir, 3; Poppell Diary, 13 September 1942, 16–17.
8. Donald J. Coffey Casualty Card; Frank Guidone interview, 1999; C. F. "Beaver" Wilson to James Smith, 7 June 1992.
9. T. D. Smith Diary, 13 September 1942, 7.
10. Lowell Dunn interview with author, 9 April 1999.
11. Frank Guidone, "A Timely Rescue," n.d., 1; Everett Account, 14.
12. Edson/Stiff Draft, "That So-and-So Grin," annotated by Edson.
13. Twining, *No Bended Knee*, 98–100.
14. William A. Stiles to John Sweeney, 16 December 1993, 2 (emphases in original).
15. Griffith, *The Battle for Guadalcanal*, 117.
16. Joseph Sweeda to John Sweeney, 26 July 1989 [Sweeda Account]; Irv Reynolds to John Sweeney, 17 May 1988; Elleston interview with Associated Press in "Quantico Battalion Reunites," *Richmond Times Dispatch*, 16 February 1992 [Eleston Interview]; Jack Tracy interview with Jon Hoffman, 1991.

17. Sweeney Ridge Memoir, 84.
18. PFC Edgar Shepherd to CO, 1st Marine Raider Battalion, 18 September 1943, Box 24, Edson Papers, Library of Congress [Shepherd '43 Letter].
19. Sweeda Account.
20. James Mallamas Memoir, n.d., as provided by Gloria Mallamas, as augmented [somewhat] by taped interview with Robert O'Neil, 16 February 1993 [Mallamas Memoir].
21. Shepard '43 Letter. Shepard to Edson's Raiders Association, 17 October 1989 [Shepard '89 Letter].
22. Mallamas Memoir.
23. Sweeda Account; Reynolds Account.
24. Eleston Interview.
25. Sergeant Wallace Bergstrand Casualty Card; Richard MacNeilly to Edson's Raiders Association, n.d. MacNeilly was one of six members of Edson's Raiders from Oneida, NY. The others included Joseph Arnold, Theodore Benstead, Thomas Newcomb, David Taber (WIA, The Ridge), and James Zophy (KIA, Second Matanikau).
26. Reynolds Account; Sweeda Account.
27. Shepard '89 Letter.
28. Mallamas memoir.
29. James G. Hall to Major Lloyd Nickerson, 22 March 1944, Box 5, Personal Files, Edson Papers, Library of Congress.
30. Stiles to John Sweeney, 16 December 1993, including his diary extract for 13 September 1942.
31. Ashley Large interview with author, 1 October 1990; Poppell Diary, 13 September 1942, 17; T. D. Smith Diary, 13 September 1942, 7.
32. Ira J. Irvin interview with Jon Hoffman, 1991.
33. James Childs Memoir; Pettus Account, 8; Clarence R. Schwenke to Jon Hoffman, November 1991.
34. Erland Coombs to James Childs, *ca.* June 1995.
35. Griffith, *The Battle for Guadalcanal,* 119.
36. Sweeney Ridge Memoir, 86.
37. Kawaguchi Memoir, 22–24. There is no evidence among the many casualties described in the primary sources to support Kawaguchi's claim that his major killed several Americans with his sword the night of the 13th and 14th.
38. Sweeney Ridge Memoir, 91; Gerald West interview with author, 12 November 1998; Robert Addison's contribution about Staff Sergeant Delanoy appeared in the December 1992 *Dope Sheet,* 2; Pettus Account, 8. The number of artillery rounds fired in support of the second night's battle for The Ridge is subject to interpretation. Annex E to the 1st Marine Division "Final Report on Guadalcanal Operation" Phase IV indicates 105 batteries fired 1,992 rounds at ranges from 1,600–2,000 yards, while the 75mm pack howitzers fired 878 rounds. A good percentage of the latter were likely fired in support

of the embattled 3d Battalion, 1st Marines in repulsing the attack of the Kuma Battalion the same night.

39. "Translation of Japanese Circular Taken on Guadalcanal entitled: 'Combat Impressions from the Tamura Battalion (Isamu 1339), October 15, 1942,' translation date 6 January 1943, possibly a 1st Marine Division D-2 document, author's possession.

40. James Smith to author, "Evening of 13 Sep 1942, Guadalcanal," 16 October 1998; Herman Arnold Casualty Card.

41. Sweeney Ridge Memoir, 93. Edson assigned Sweeney the code name "John Wolf" the night before Tulagi, the same time he characterized "Silent Lew Walt" and "Sam Griff" and "Ken Dill" Bailey, among others.

42. Pettus journal, "Combat Intelligence, Practical Experience," 8; Frank, *Guadalcanal*, 240.

43. CO, 1st Marine Raider Battalion to CG, 1st Marine Division, "First Parachute Battalion, commendation of," 18 September 1942, copy in author's possession.

44. William J. McKennan, "The Battle of Bloody Hill," *Saturday Evening Post*, 20 February 1943, 16–17, 80, 82. McKennan commanded Baker Company, 1st Parachute Battalion.

45. Robert Youngdeer interview with author, 9 April 1999. Robert the Raider had not a penny to his name on board *Solace*, but his parachutist brother had retained a salve tube stuffed with a five dollar bill—more than enough for ice cream for two. In the late 1980s, Robert Youngdeer would become the Principal Chief of the Eastern Band of the Cherokee Indians, nine thousand strong.

46. McKennan, "The Battle of Bloody Hill," 82; Sheppard '89 Letter, 2; John Erskine, "The Battle of Bloody Ridge: A Memoire," 29 July 1992, 9.

47. John P. Ingalls, Jr., interview with Jon Hoffman, 1991.

48. Reynolds Account, 2; James Childs interview with Jon Hoffman, 1991.

49. Houston Stiff to Thomas Mullahey, 5 October 1992.

50. Gerald Thomas Oral Memoir, MCOHC, MCHC, 364; Sweeney Ridge Memoir, 94.

51. Maj. Harry J. Connor [CO, E/2/5 at The Ridge] to Historical Division, HQMC, 14 February 1949, Box 2, Serial 14051, WNRC.

52. Ben A. Quintana to Edson's Raiders Association, 13 August 1991, 2. Quintana survived this experience and became a pharmacist in Meridian, Mississippi.

53. Poppell Diary, 13 September 1942, 17.

54. Capt. Harry L. Torgerson, "Report on Operations, 1st Parachute Battalion, Solomons Islands Offensive, Defense of Lunga Ridge, 13–14 September 1942," 8, author's possession. The author is aware of no other reports that corroborate the capture of an abandoned Japanese 75mm cannon on Hill 100 at the conclusion of the battle.

55. Sweeda Account, 8–10; Reynolds Account, 2.

56. James Smith to author, "Evening of 13 September 1942, Guadalcanal," 16 October 1998; Sweeda Account, 10; Robert Youngdeer interview with author 22 June 1999; Casualty Cards for Maj. Robert Brown and Sgt. Frank Boone.

57. Alfred A. Haas, "Lest We Forget: Gy. Sgt. Gerald B. Stackpole," *The Dope Sheet*, November 1963, 2; Gerald B. Stackpole Casualty Card.

58. John A. Thompson to James Childs, 10 February 1994; Dale Brannon to James Childs, 27 December 1993. The story of the P-400s at Bloody Ridge is described by Robert L. Ferguson, *Guadalcanal—The Island of Fire: Reflections of the 347th Fighter Group*, 104–06. Thompson's wingmen in this air strike were Lts. Bryan W. Brown and B. E. Davis. The Marines nominated Thompson for the Navy Cross; General Vandegrift personally handed him a bottle of rye whiskey in gratitude before nightfall.

59. Kawaguchi Memoir, 26–27.

60. Hayashi and Coox, *Kogun*, 38, 227.

61. 1st Raider Battalion Muster Roll for September 1942; Griffith, *The Battle for Guadalcanal*, 121; Hoffman, *Legend*, 205–206; Frank, *Guadalcanal*, 245.

62. Medal of Honor citations for Merritt Edson and Kenneth Bailey. The author is indebted to Jerry Beau of the Marine Raiders Association for his painstaking compilation of rosters and awards for each of the Raider battalions, including their faithful corpsmen. Beau provided John Sweeney with the awards list for Edson's Raiders on 30 December 1994. The Navy Cross citation for "Pete" Pettus specifies his courageous actions in both the Tasimboko Raid and The Ridge. The list of men receiving the Navy Cross in this paragraph is representative only—there were quite a few others, as well.

63. John Sweeney interview with author, 15 February 1999; Frank Russell Whittlesey Casualty Card. The final chapter has a happier ending to this story.

# 8

## Fighting along the Matanikau, September–October 1942

*These Raiders are really rugged. Less than a week after taking 30 percent casualties on The Ridge they are back on the job—at the colonel's own request. I saw them marching across the airfield last evening, on their way to take up positions to the west. I felt my throat tighten as they filed past, but saw no gloom in those faces. What an outfit.*

Herbert A. Merillat, Guadalcanal, 19 September 1942[1]

THE BATTLE OF EDSON'S RIDGE saved Henderson Field for another day, but the struggle for Guadalcanal raged on. General Vandegrift would soon need the services of every unit, even his shot-up, sickly, and decimated 1st Raiders. He could not afford to allow the survivors of Edson's Ridge the fundamental "luxury" of the things they craved the most—a bath, a hot meal, a safe place to tend to one's dysentery, a decent night's sleep, maybe a few weeks in deep reserve. New emergencies developed like tropical thunderstorms.

When the firing died down the morning after Bloody Ridge, Private Ernest J. Gyenese, one of Easy Company's invaluable machine gunners, sprawled in the shade and lit a cigarette from a package "liberated" at Tasimboko. Red Mike Edson came by, sat down beside Gyenese, bummed a smoke. "You know," he said, "Now I know I have a real fighting outfit." Gyenese, utterly spent, could only stare and nod.[2]

Rumors of an imminent withdrawal from the island swept the battalion, especially when the 1st Marine Parachute Battalion received orders to prepare for evacuation. The parachutists had paid dearly for their fights on Gavutu and The Ridge—a battle casualty rate of over 55 percent. The Raiders had sustained higher casualties, but they began the

198

campaign with twice as many men. Nonetheless, many watched with envy as the parachutists packed their gear for embarkation.[3]

Edson, aware of the long faces among his men, spoke to each company. He dispelled the rumors but not the gloom. "He told us it was going to be a bloody road to Japan and forget about going home," said Sergeant Frank Guidone. Jinx Powers heard him say, "The 1st Raiders will lead the victory parade in Tokyo." Others recall the words, "If I had it my way, this battalion will eat Thanksgiving dinner on Bougainville." The Raiders stared out to sea, unhappy with these words. Powers believed the troops around him grew pessimistic at the prospect of more hard campaigning and heavy casualties. Some, according to Powers, began to call Edson "Mad Merritt the Morgue Master."[4]

Lew Walt returned, briefly, from his long bout in the field hospital with a persistent infection. He, too, provided a needed dose of realism to the Raiders. "We were sitting at the mouth of the Lunga looking at the smoke spirals curling up from down past Point Cruz," recorded T. D. Smith, "when Major Walt came along." Smith asked him what caused the smoke beyond the Matanikau. "Those are Japanese cooking fires," replied Walt, adding calmly, "I suppose we'll have to go down there after them soon."[5]

On 18 September the 7th Marines landed, a well-trained regiment, chomping at the bit for action following a half year on the sidelines in Samoa. Their battalion commanders included such legendary Banana War heroes as Lewis "Chesty" Puller and Herman "Hard Head" Hanneken, and their ranks abounded with hand-picked veterans. The beach became a study in contrasts—the boisterous, well-fed 7th Marines striding ashore, staring curiously at the ragged, emaciated parachutists, anxiously awaiting their turn to board the same shipping and sail away. Nearby assembled an even more forlorn group—162 wounded Marines awaiting evacuation with the parachutists, including Raiders Houston Stiff, Bob Youngdeer, and Ed Shepard.

The arrival of the 7th Marines gave General Vandegrift the option of extending his protection of Henderson Field. Now he could risk disrupting the Japanese assembly areas along and across the Matanikau River.

The Raiders were ill-prepared for an offensive campaign. Sickness, compounded by exhaustion and malnutrition, began to reduce their remaining numbers at an alarming rate. Field Sergeant Major Jim Childs described many troops suffering from a combination of malaria, dengue fever, and dysentery: "a horrendous mix of symptoms—everyone had a fever, many men experienced pain in their bones and joints." Gastroen-teritis and virulent fungus infections prevailed. And malaria had become the single most debilitating disease: the division's five hundred cases in August spiked to 1,724 in September and 2,630 in October.[6]

The general malaise that gripped the Raiders following their battle on The Ridge lasted almost a week. Fresh outbreaks of disease and careless handling of weapons further diminished the ranks of effectives. Sickness forced the evacuation from the island of Baker Company's colorful Cor-poral Johnny Holladay, the sharp-shooting ballad singer from the piney piedmont of South Carolina. Two other Raiders, accidentally shot, required evacuation.[7]

Edson and Griffith knew that a return to meaningful action would help shake the malaise, and they welcomed division orders to conduct a two-battalion patrol south along the Lunga with Chesty Puller's 1st Battalion, 7th Marines. The Raiders would take the left (east) bank, 1/7 the right. Edson saddled his men up at dusk on the 19th, moving them across the runway to reach their predawn jump-off position.

The new mission lifted the Raiders' spirits. The aviators, the division command post personnel, and a handful of journalists admired their purposeful advance. "Near dusk," recorded Popeye Poppell, "the Raiders move across Henderson Field like a huge snake. The many workers on the field watch us as we pass by. We have many friends here." Indeed they had. Colonel Jerry Thomas, shortly to become Vandegrift's chief of staff (Merrill Twining would replace him as operations officer), described the Raiders at this point as "the best band of cut-throats you could find any-where in the world." Combat correspondent John Hersey wrote admir-ingly of "Edson's Raiders, a gang of bush-fighting specialists."[8]

Herbert L. Merillat—journalist, historian, Marine—best captured the spirit of the Raiders on this occasion in an account published in 1944 (which differs from his subsequent version used in the chapter epi-graph): "Their numbers had been cut in half," wrote Merillat, watching the Raiders that evening. "They now looked more like a company than a battalion. Their faces were tired, too, but at the same time they had a look of self-assurance and determination, and of refusal to leave the fighting to others, even though they had suffered so heavily in their gal-lant stand on the Ridge."[9]

The patrol found plenty of evidence of Kawaguchi's calamitous retreat and a few residual snipers but saw no signs of a fresh buildup from the south. Coming back in the dusk the Raiders drew nervous fire from the green troops of 2/7 and 3/7, now guarding The Ridge. Edson and Griffith quickly squelched any attempts to return the favor, and the battalion filed back into the perimeter.

The outburst of firing along the Lunga had alarmed the airmen and headquarters personnel along the southern perimeter, and they peered cautiously at the long column approaching out of the jungle. "It's the RAIDERS!" exclaimed one man, and a cheer of relief went up among the others. Private First Class John Mielke recalled how the airmen and rear echelon troops formed a passageway for the returning Raiders, gratefully stuffing packs of cigarettes and candy bars in their dungaree jackets as they passed. "They seemed genuinely glad it had been us Raiders out there in the hills protecting them," Mielke said.[10]

John Hersey took the opportunity to interview Merritt Edson about what he had learned in two months leading his battalion against the Japanese. "I certainly have learned respect for the Japs," responded Edson quietly. "What they have done is to take Indian warfare and apply it to the twentieth century. They use all the Indian tricks to demoralize their enemy. They're good, all right, but..." at which Edson paused and fixed Hersey with his baleful blue eyes, "I think we're better."[11]

Edson's time with the Raiders had expired. He was a colonel filling a lieutenant colonel's billet, a proven combat leader (recent nominations: a Navy Cross for Tulagi, the Medal of Honor for The Ridge) attached to a division with a crying need for dynamic regimental commanders. Vandegrift ordered him to turn over the Raiders to Lieutenant Colonel Sam Griffith and take command of the 5th Marines effective 21 September, the day after the Lunga Patrol. Edson had commanded the battalion, and its immediate predecessors, the past fifteen months.

Edson was there one day, gone the next. Instead of ceremonial farewells, he simply published a Battalion Order expressing his pleasure and honor at commanding such an admirable body of men. Reserved and distant as he often was, there is no doubt Edson keenly felt regret at the passage.[12]

The troops viewed the transition with mixed emotions. Many of them were too ill to dwell on the implications, said Field Sergeant Major Jim Childs, "and those who did think about it felt confident that with Sam Griffith and Ken Bailey they would still be in competent hands." Diarist T. D. Smith recorded more interest in the fact that there was still no sign of the U.S. Army. Irvin Reynolds, on the other hand, recalled a "bittersweet reaction" to Edson's orders. "We cussed him for trying to get us all killed," he admitted, and in that context added, "I was glad to see him go, yet we knew we were losing a great leader." Later, Reynolds would

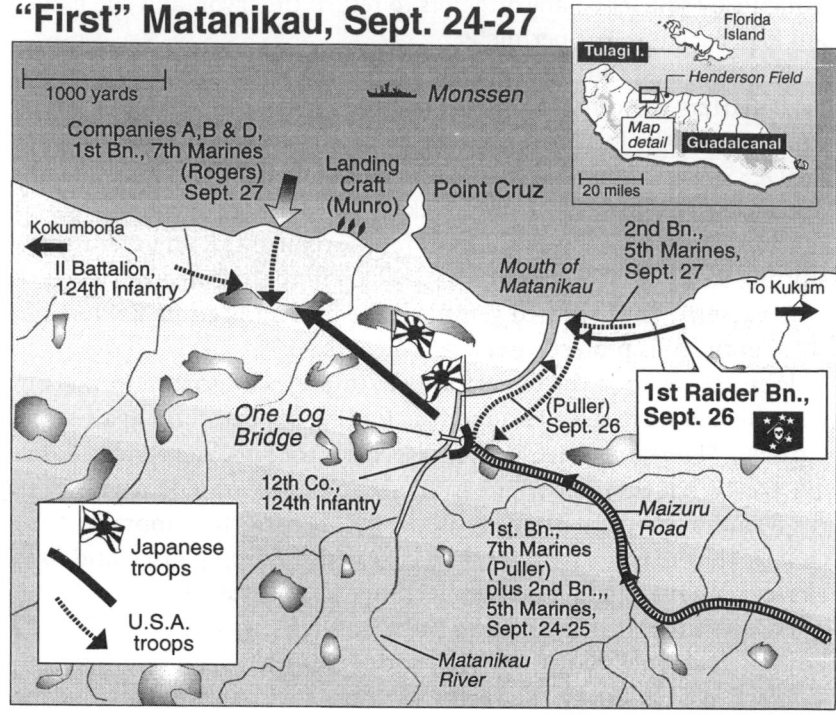

"First" Matanikau, Sept. 24-27

Florida Island
Tulagi I.
Henderson Field
Map detail — Guadalcanal
20 miles

1000 yards
Monssen

Companies A,B & D, 1st Bn., 7th Marines (Rogers) Sept. 27
Landing Craft (Munro)
Point Cruz

Kokumbona
II Battalion, 124th Infantry

Mouth of Matanikau
2nd Bn., 5th Marines, Sept. 27
To Kukum

One Log Bridge
(Puller) Sept. 26
1st Raider Bn., Sept. 26

12th Co., 124th Infantry
Maizuru Road

Japanese troops
U.S.A. troops

1st. Bn., 7th Marines (Puller) plus 2nd Bn.,, 5th Marines, Sept. 24-25

Matanikau River

observe that Edson was "cursed the most when he called us up to the Matanikau, but, deep down, we were bursting with pride that he thought so much of us to help bail him out."[13]

Edson did not leave empty-handed. Within the next two days he "raided" the Raiders with reassignment orders for Major Lew Walt, Captain Hank Adams, and Corporal Walt Burak. Sam Griffith's first official act as new commanding officer of the 1st Marine Raider Battalion was to howl in protest, especially at the loss of Walt, so recently returned from his hospitalization. Edson prevailed. Lew Walt may have been the newest major in the division but Edson considered him well qualified for greater responsibilities—first as regimental operations officer, then, quickly, as commanding officer of the 3d Battalion, 5th Marines.[14]

Sam Griffith's six months as heir apparent to Red Mike Edson had ended. Having served throughout as a loyal and effective "bridesmaid," he now assumed command with joy. He was thirty-six, a veteran of thirteen years commissioned service, physically fit, a thoroughbred. Griffith would actually command the battalion twice, his combined span longer than any of the other four commanders, but his first stint would not last a single week.

## "First" Matanikau

Sam Griffith was by no means the only tactical commander on either side whose bright hopes became shattered along the steep ridges and sinister waters of the Matanikau River valley during the autumn of 1942. Here the antagonists fought at least four major battles—wild, violent fighting both by night and by day in an area that Herbert Merillat described as "the bloodiest battlefield of the Guadalcanal campaign." The Raiders fought in two of these engagements along the river, first while attacking on 27 September in the broken country upstream, then while on the defensive on 8–9 October near the contested sandbar at its mouth. The Raiders, it should be noted, define their two battles as "First and Second Matanikau" and to hell with the historians who insist that the Raiders' fights were actually Matanikau II and III (the author, no dummy, opts to use the Raiders' definition herein).[15]

"First Matanikau" became an unqualified disaster for the Leathernecks, a costly setback that Griffin called "the most ill-conceived and ill-conducted, the only really inept operation that the Marines conducted on Guadalcanal."[16]

The Matanikau is one of the more significant of Guadalcanal's dozen rivers that flow northward from the mountains into Sealark Channel. The river is both more turbulent and less densely-vegetated than the Lunga, five miles east. Sheer coral ridges, steep banks, and intermittent grassy highlands mark the Matanikau's lower passage. Roughly 2,000 yards upstream from the sea the river's northwest fork joins the larger southwest fork, the juncture producing a roiling watercourse too swift and deep to be safely forded by bodies of troops or heavy equipment. The Matanikau therefore posed to Japanese and American planners alike a major obstacle to offensive plans or a welcome barrier for the defense. In either case, control of the fords and bridges meant control of the campaign.

Japanese engineers concluded that the alluvial sandbar at the mouth represented the best means of deploying their tanks and heavy artillery pieces east of the river, but they also constructed a crude, single-log, foot bridge (thereafter "Jap Bridge" or "Nippon Bridge" to the Raiders) across the Matanikau about two hundred yards north (downstream) of the juncture of the two forks. Faint trails existed along both banks of the river, although the one to be used by the Raiders along the east bank from the mouth required the passage of an unnamed fork entering from the east where it drained the foothills leading to Mount Austen. Heavy rains complicated this passage.

Today the city of Honiara, capital of the Solomon Islands and home to 30,000 occupants, straddles the river. But in 1942 the Matanikau was wild and menacing, its broken ridges ideal for ambushes, each towering tree a potential nest for yet another sniper.

General Kawaguchi had led his starving survivors out of the jungle west of the Matanikau. In late September, not yet recalled to Rabaul, he endeavored to assemble the disparate parts of several regiments—starving remnants on one hand, fresh reinforcements on the other—into an offensive force. The Japanese still considered Henderson Field as the linchpin of the campaign. The Seventeenth Army planned to deliver 150mm guns to Guadalcanal in early October, including the Type 96 (1936) howitzer, which could fire a 79-pound high explosive shell 13,000 yards. The stand-off range was crucial. Firing from east of Kokumbona the weapon could reach the edge of Henderson Field, but if advanced to the far side of the Matanikau the howitzer could punish the entire perimeter including the ships offloading at Lunga Point. In neither case could the lighter 105mm howitzers of the 11th Marines provide effective counterbattery fire.[17]

Kawaguchi would be out of the picture by the time the 1st Raiders fought along the Matanikau, but their principal opponents in the river engagements would come from a familiar regiment, the 4th Infantry, the Aoba Force, arriving in increments from the Philippines. The Raiders had experienced a hell of a fight with Major Tamura's II/4 throughout the second night of The Ridge. They would fight their "1st Matanikau" against the 12th Company of III/4, which landed near Cape Esperance on 11 September, and "Second Matanikau" against the 3d Company of I/4, which came ashore the night of 15 September near Kamimbo with the regimental command group.[18]

In general terms, the concept of "First Matanikau" envisioned a wide western sweep by Puller's 1/7 along the headwaters of the Matanikau to flush out any residual Japanese still lurking in the area. The 1st Raider Battalion would then advance in column along the coast road, cross the Matanikau at the sandbar, then proceed to the crossroads village of Kokumbona to establish a patrol base.[19]

The plan, in hindsight, was lunacy. Kokumbona was 6,500 yards beyond the Matanikau, truly in the heart of "Indian Country." Puller's

Approaching the Matanikau. These men marching at sling arms are not likely Raiders, but the setting is appropriate. By late September 1942 on Guadalcanal, all trails led west to the "River of Death."

fresh battalion may have been at full strength, but the Raiders barely mustered two hundred men for the operation. The Japanese easily had 4,000 troops in this sector, a good half of them defending the Matanikau in strength. Sam Griffith in a 1945 letter blamed "faulty intelligence of Japanese strength and dispositions" for the disaster. "No orders would ever have been given for a battalion to go up to Kokumbona and patrol from there," he wrote, "had there been any realization that there were several thousand Japs between the Matanikau and [the village]."[20]

Puller ran into trouble on the first day, sustained a fair number of casualties, and had to send two entire companies back as stretcher bearers. Vandegrift committed the 5th Marines to the fray, placing Edson in command of the task force with Puller as the exec.

Meanwhile Griffith dutifully led his small battalion westward across the Lunga the afternoon of the 26th. Two hours later the battalion heard firing ahead along the Matanikau. Investigation revealed 2/5 and elements of Puller's 1/7 stymied from crossing the river by heavy Japanese resistance. The Raiders went into a defensive bivouac while Edson and Puller conferred by radio with Vandegrift, Thomas, and Twining six miles away at the division command post. The all-star cast agreed on a complex double envelopment to be launched the morning of the 27th. The Raiders would advance south (upstream) along the east bank of the Matanikau, cross the river at the Nippon Bridge, then attack north along the west bank. As they neared the coast 2/5 would attack west across the sandbar and two companies of 1/7 would land by amphibious craft near Point Cruz to cut off the retreating enemy.[21]

Heavy rains the night of the 26th did little to improve the Raiders' gloomy outlook at the complicated choreography expected of them on the morrow. Yet by 0700 they were underway for the river. Griffith and Major Ken Bailey, serving as combination XO and operations officer, watched the thin ranks stride past. Company D had been drawn down to the nub to provide replacements for the other rifle companies, each now commanded by young captains—Tony Antonelli, A Company, Ed Wheeler (senior to John Sweeney by a day), B Company, and Bob Thomas, C Company, the advance guard. Other junior leaders were emerging. That week Griffith awarded meritorious promotions to the rank of platoon sergeant to three hard-charging young men who had performed with conspicuous bravery at Tulagi: former corporals Philip Oldham and Joseph Sciarra and former Private First Class Clifford "Red" Hills, Able Company's gifted BARman.[22]

The column of Raiders moved slowly upstream, advancing no more than five hundred yards per hour, leery of an ambush. Intermittent mortar fire confirmed the suspicion that the Japanese on the opposite bank had them under observation. Back at Edson's improvised command post, Chesty Puller grew impatient. He had led a similar-sized force downstream along the identical track with little difficulty the previous afternoon. But Puller had missed the Aoba Force's 12th Company by a matter of minutes. More than a hundred well-armed members of the 4th Infantry had crossed the log bridge to interdict the east bank trail shortly after 1/7 passed. Other soldiers established firing positions for mortars and heavy machine guns in the ravines and crevasses along the west bank.

"Trouble began just before noon," wrote Griffith in his battle history of Guadalcanal, "when the Raiders, strung out along the narrow track hedged by ridges on the left and the river on the right, approached the 'Jap Bridge.'" The exact location remains unclear. Pete Pettus, writing in 1958, placed the outbreak of "trouble" at "the forks of the Matanikau," but the point platoon commander distinctly remembered the action breaking out along a creek entering the river, surely the unnamed east tributary of the Matanikau, about two hundred yards downstream from the single-log bridge.[23]

Able Company led the column, with Lieutenant Richard E. "Red" Sullivan's 3d Platoon acting as the point. Sullivan, whose meritorious commissioning from the ranks became official on D-Day at Tulagi, had lived up to the potential Edson and Griffith had seen in him. He was becoming one of the best infantry platoon commanders in the battalion.

Behind the point platoon, but still well forward for a battalion executive officer, came Major Ken Bailey, in fine fettle. He had regained more of his stamina and had shrugged off the flesh wound to his face sustained during the second night at The Ridge. As was his frequent custom on a march, Bailey offered to carry a BAR or machine gun for any Raider having difficulty maintaining the pace. This was no act—the man genuinely cared for his troops. Three days earlier, correspondent Richard Tregaskis asked Bailey about the men in the ranks. Bailey replied that he held the enlisted Raiders in such high esteem "that when it comes to a job that's pretty rugged, you'd rather go yourself than send them." From anyone else these words may have sounded phony, but Bailey was remarkably unselfish. No one would forget his thoughtfulness in delivering five weeks of lost mail to the battalion just before their biggest battle.[24]

Sniper fire stopped Lieutenant Sullivan's cautious advance just as his point squad reached the eastern tributary of the Matanikau. "Across the creek was a more or less open field," said Sullivan, "and a ridge beyond the field angling towards the river." Major Bailey came forward to assess the holdup, accompanied by his runner and a radio operator. Sullivan joined the small circle, probably standing along the trail at the top of the bank before it dropped down to cross the creek. The men scanned the steep ridge beyond.

Sullivan suddenly spotted troops running in the open. Just as he turned to point them out to Bailey, Sullivan recounted: "A machine gun opened up. We all hit the deck, Ken went down in front of me, his head on his hands, and he was propped up on one knee. The machine gun was going like mad. I hollered for him to get down—when he didn't I grabbed his ankle and pulled it from under him. He was dead."

The machine-gun fire killed Bailey instantly. "Never knew what hit him," said Sullivan. "Hit right between the eyes, and no one else in that circle was touched." Sullivan was bereft. "He was my idol," he said, and "having seen him in action so much and then [for him to] go out with his hands in his pockets, so to speak, hurt." Sullivan then expressed a widely-felt epitaph: "No finer Marine ever lived or died for his country." Bailey died three weeks shy of his thirty-second birthday.[25]

Bailey's sudden death stunned the Raiders, but the Japanese ambush left them no time to mourn. Now enemy mortars opened up on the head of the column. The men scrambled for cover, searching the broken terrain for an artfully hidden enemy. In Griffith's subsequent analysis, the well-concealed Japanese "put a stopper in the jungle bottleneck, which measured about twenty yards from river to ridge."[26]

Griffith came to the forefront, shocked to find Bailey dead—he had lost both a good friend and a highly competent assistant, the last of his field grade officers. He was also appalled to find the river valley swarming with well-armed Japanese soldiers. By no means could he force a crossing of the single-log bridge against such interlocking fire.

With growing uneasiness Griffith attempted a turning movement farther upstream. Leaving Able Company to engage the ambushing force, Griffith led two companies in a cross-country bypass. Griffith later said he "sought room to maneuver, and led the remainder of the battalion up a precipitous jungle-covered spine....The slow and exhausting [deployment] of a battalion in Indian file was not completed until mid-afternoon and was discerned by Japanese on an adjacent ridge." In a later reflection Griffith boiled his maneuver down to the nub, "there wasn't a damned thing we could do except try to outflank them, which we did, and that didn't work." Griffith's flanking column came under heavy machine-gun and mortar attack; snipers raked the ridge crest. Nor could Able Company make any headway in its engagement along the tributary. "Mortars are now falling heavily," recorded Popeye Poppell, still grieving the death of Bailey. "The Raiders were stalled," Griffith flatly admitted.[27]

Raider T. D. Smith had been transferred to C Company after Edson's Ridge. His diary for the 27th reflected the doleful litany of events:

> We moved up the river to attempt a crossing at another ford. The column was hit and Charlie Company sent to flank to the left. We moved up from the river and pushed on. Suddenly we came under machine-gun fire from the front. The ford was well guarded. The mortars were set up. Word came up that Major Bailey had been killed in the initial contact on the river. Three men in a row were hit by sniper fire attempting to observe for the mortars on the crest of a hill. Sam Griff was mad.[28]

In frustration Sam Griffith strode forward along the open ridge to assess the enemy resistance first hand. A Japanese sniper promptly shot him through the shoulder. Other Raiders scuttled out to drag him out of the line of fire. He was in pain, lucky to be alive. Griffith would gut it out—retaining command as long as he physically could do so—but the Raiders had been thwarted at every turn.

The situation grew worse. Griffith's situation reports to Edson came through either garbled or misleading. Edson chose to believe that his former command had fought their way across the bridge and were now advancing seaward along the west bank of the Matanikau, tardy but back on track. He therefore ordered 2/5 to attack the Japanese fortified positions across from the sandbar and gave Puller's XO the green light to land two companies of 1/7 amphibiously near Point Cruz. The first evolution led to a bloody repulse. The Japanese defending the sandbar, absent any threat to their right flank from the supposedly approaching Raiders, stopped 2/5 in its tracks. Puller's rump battalion had a worse go of it. The Japanese coalesced around the Marines once they advanced into the jungle, killed Major Otho Rogers, the XO, and chopped up the two companies. Puller was both profane and heroic in extracting his embattled men under very heavy fire, or the disaster would have been worse.

The afternoon shadows were lengthening along the Matanikau before Edson realized how bad the situation had become. His Raiders had not crossed the river after all. The Japanese had foiled all three of his attacks and inflicted two hundred casualties on his Marines. Edson had in fact just suffered the only defeat in his operational life—the "abortive Second Matanikau" he later characterized it to Houston Stiff. By 1600 he ordered all forces to disengage and regroup.[29]

Merrill Twining admitted his share of the blame. "What began as a sound and sensible reconnaissance operation," he wrote in 1996, "ended as an improvised, complex, jury-rigged attack for which we had no plan and had made no preparations." In contrast to Twining's gloom, the Japanese in Rabaul celebrated their repulse of the Americans. As recorded in the diary of the chief of staff of the Seventeenth Army, the action along the Matanikau represented "the first good news to come from Guadalcanal."[30]

The melancholy duty of evacuating Major Bailey's body back to the aid station fell to two headquarters NCOs, Sergeant Horse Collar Smith and Corporal Tom Driscoll. "It was quite a shock to both of us to see a man we thought impregnable so very, very dead," said Smith in 1956. The two Raiders carried Bailey back down the riverside trail in a poncho. The trip was nightmarish. "He was a lot of man and it was quite a load to haul; the poncho kept slipping out of our hands and we kept tripping over roots." Horse Collar Smith, still grieving over the death of his friend Ikey Arnold at The Ridge two weeks earlier, experienced an almost overwhelming sense of sadness.

Smith and Driscoll eventually delivered Bailey's body to Doctor Bob Skinner at the battalion aid station. There Smith noticed Private First Class Julian K. Dobson, eighteen, a C Company Raider from Leominster, Massachusetts, lying on the ground with a serious groin wound. "He was in extreme pain, and his face was almost gray," recalled Smith, marveling that Dobson never displayed his fear or agony, "a rare exhibition of guts and courage." Dobson died of his wounds the next day.[31]

Sam Griffith remained on his feet long enough to lead the battered battalion back to its bivouac, a feat of iron-willed stewardship that resulted in the subsequent award of the Navy Cross. Yet his wound was serious—"the bullet nicked the brachial plexus, so I didn't have the use of my arm at all," he said—and he would be out of action for months.[32]

Overall, the Raiders reported light losses in comparison to the other two battalions—two killed, twelve wounded. Most of the recorded wounded seemed to be headquarters troops, including Platoon Sergeant Francis Marasciullo, Sergeant Alexander Sapowicz, Private First Class Paul Didier, and Private Thomas J. Lavin. But the "abortive First Matanikau"—to apply the Raiders' numbering system to Edson's curse—had cost the battalion plenty: the popular and heroic Ken Bailey, the irreplaceable leadership of Sam Griffith, a resolute young rifleman in Julian Dobson, and the Raiders' own sense of invincibility. Even the irrepressible Pete Pettus grew discouraged. "That was a bad day," he said.[33]

## Running on Empty

Captain Ira "Jake" Irwin became the third commander of the 1st Marine Raider Battalion the evening of 27 September 1942. Irwin gave the impression of being an unlikely successor to Edson and Griffith. He was thirty-three, a reservist (and proud of it), pudgy in appearance but jovial and unpretentious in temperament. Fire-breathing combat leadership was not his forte, but he was a competent, caring commander. He had been a manager with Boston Edison Company since graduating from high school and a Marine reservist since 1928, working his way up to greater responsibilities in both professions before the war, and he would return to continued success in both after V-J Day. He knew how to manage resources and look after his people. Now "his people" included several hundred sickly and saddened Raiders, and Jake Irwin would do his best to care for them throughout the ensuing four months.[34]

Captain Bob Thomas, who had replaced the wounded Ken Bailey as Charlie Company commander on Tulagi, now replaced him again as battalion executive officer. Lieutenant Bud "Black Jack" Salmon took command of Charlie Company. Captain Tony Antonelli succumbed to malaria; Captain Robert Neuffer replaced him in command of Able Company. The ranks grew thinner. Field Sergeant Major Jim Childs recalled that the battalion received only two replacements throughout the Tulagi-Guadalcanal campaign. The spreading outbreak of disabling diseases among the survivors alarmed Childs, who described the troops as "sickly, bedraggled, and miserable."[35]

The deteriorating condition of the Raiders came to the attention of the division commander. General Vandegrift wrote Admiral Kelly Turner in early October, expressing regret that "Major Bailey of the Raiders was killed and that Lieutenant Colonel Griffith...was wounded in the shoulder." Vandegrift said he had discussed the situation with Edson and concluded that "with the losses sustained in both officers and men of this battalion, and the strenuous work they have done, that they should be returned to Nouméa...for rebuilding." While both senior officers agreed in principle on withdrawing the Raiders from combat, the actual execution would be forced to wait another two weeks. There existed only one way off the 'Canal—hitch a ride on empty troop transports immediately after a reinforcement delivery. These proved risky and infrequent. Meanwhile, the Raiders would continue to fulfill a critical role in the extended defense of Henderson Field.[36]

The campaign entered a new and more dangerous stage. Admiral Chester Nimitz left his headquarters at Pearl Harbor and flew to Guadalcanal for a first-hand assessment. It was a high-risk flight, both coming and going, but the timing could not have been better. Vandegrift, who never received a visit from Admiral Ghormley, the intermediate theater commander, was damned glad to see the commander in chief of the Pacific Fleet. Nimitz cheerfully withstood the rain, mud, and miasma of Starvation Island. He got a tour of Edson's Ridge from Edson himself, visited the sick and wounded Marines (including many Raiders) in the division's crude field hospital, and held heart-to-heart talks with Vandegrift and his commanders.

The next morning, in between rain showers and air raids, Nimitz conducted an awards ceremony, presenting the Navy Cross to several Raiders for their heroics on Tulagi, including Merritt Edson, Corporal Elmer Hacker, B Company, Platoon Sergeant Clifford "Red" Hills, A Company, and Private First Class Wilfred Hunt, HQ Company.[37]

Nimitz left as the 1st Marine Division struggled to gain operational intelligence about enemy dispositions. Fortunately, the Raiders still had available a competent and field-savvy intelligence section despite the prevalence of debilitating sickness in the battalion. The intel crew may have missed the FBI bravura and blazing pistols of the recently-departed Captain Hank Adams, but Platoon Sergeant Pete Pettus provided plenty of hard-nosed professionalism in his own right. In early October the division intelligence officer selected Pettus to lead a four-day reconnaissance patrol to evaluate a native report of increased Japanese activity in the Aola region, thirty miles east of Henderson Field. Pettus took three of his own men—Corporals Tom Driscoll and Bob Laverty and Private First Class Al Haas (who had retrieved "Admiral" Stackpole's body that last morning of The Ridge)—plus two division scouts and two native guides.

The party traveled down the coast by Higgins boat, well past the earlier raid site at Tasimboko, into virgin territory. Pettus led his patrol ashore at Aola during the night, linking up with Mr. Eroni, the senior native coastwatcher, an enterprising man who five days earlier had rescued and returned downed Leatherneck aviator ace Captain Marion Carl. Eroni reinforced the Pettus patrol with his own scouts, and the composite force skillfully tracked, pin-pointed, and shadowed two company-sized Japanese units in the area. Safely extracted, Pettus provided such detailed information that the 1st Marine Division risked committing a battalion-sized raid into the Aola area.

Earlier in the campaign this would have been a natural mission for the Raiders; now they lacked the punch for an independent, long-range operation. Vandegrift instead deployed the 1st Battalion, 2d Marines from Tulagi to Aola by "Yippee" tuna trawlers and Higgins boats during 9–11 October to surprise the Japanese forces at Gurabusu and Koilotumaria. The raid force suffered bad luck enroute when a Higgins boat sank at night, drowning eighteen men, but the battalion struck successfully, killing thirty-five Japanese, scattering the survivors, and torching their base camps. The Raiders' contribution to these effective strikes had been significant—first-rate amphibious reconnaissance and intelligence analysis, a campaign rarity. The Raiders would soon suffer the consequences of yet another critical intelligence shortfall in their return engagement along the Matanikau.[38]

## The Do-or-Die Men

The Japanese Seventeenth Army was about to commit the works. Tanks and heavy artillery would accompany the Sendai Division; another division was underway. The 1st Marine Division, aware of a renewed build-up of Japanese forces west of the Matanikau but in the dark as to their extent and intention, planned an ambitious five-battalion limited offensive beyond the river. Repeating some of the ingredients of the previous engagement, two battalions would hold and threaten the lower Matanikau while the other three would force a passage of the Nippon Bridge and swing north in a wide arc towards the coast, driving the enemy into the sea. This became the Third Battle of the Matanikau ("Second Matanikau" to the Raiders), and it began with a collision on the 7th of October.

The Japanese stole a march on the Marines, crossing the river in company-sized strength at both the sandbar and the single-log bridge. The 3d Company, 1st Battalion, 4th Infantry, commanded by a First Lieutenant Ito, took advantage of its uncontested crossing via the sand bar to establish a formidable bridgehead slightly upstream from the mouth. Working like ants throughout the afternoon and night of the 6th, Ito's two-hundred-man force dug a semi-circle of camouflaged fighting holes in the swampy jungle along four hundred yards of the Matanikau's east bank. Given the urgent mission of protecting the sandbar crossing to permit the passage of tanks and tractor-drawn heavy artillery, Lieutenant Ito carefully positioned a dozen machine guns around the semi-circle and registered mortars along the avenues of approach.[39]

By the time the 3d Battalion, 5th Marines advanced towards the river at 1000 on 7 October, the swamp was a death trap of interlocking fire that stretched four hundred yards along the river and bulged eastward five hundred yards towards the Lunga. The Marines were appalled to find such a well-fortified force east of the Matanikau. The battalion spent the day battering against the swamp stronghold, calling in air and artillery support, even blasting the jungle point-blank with 75mm half-tracks from the regimental weapons company. Upstream, by comparison, the Marines had forced a passage across the Nippon Bridge and were poised to sweep north, but the Japanese bridgehead along the lower east bank remained a major obstacle.

At this point Raider legend has General Vandegrift ordering "Send for my 'Do-or-Die Men.'" He did not. The call for the Raiders came from Red Mike Edson, seeking initially a reinforced company as his regimental reserve.

Maj. Ken Bailey, intrepid and fearless, killed as the 1st Raiders under Lt. Col. Sam Griffith attempted to cross the upper Matanikau on 27 September 1942.

Technically, he had no business doing so. This was a division operation, not a regimental affair like the previous attempt to force the Matanikau. The Raiders, explained Merrill Twining many years later, were earmarked for evacuation and comprised the *division* reserve. "He had no right to move them...surreptitiously and against orders," Twining fumed.

Edson viewed this as a minor technicality. He had lost confidence in the capability of the commanding officer of 3/5, and would in fact replace him directly with Lew Walt, but in the meantime Edson needed to stiffen his thwarted advance with a proven outfit. For this he would use the Raiders, albeit in company-sized increments. During mid-afternoon of the 7th Edson told Jake Irwin to send up Able Company reinforced with an Easy Company machine-gun section to serve as regimental reserve for the 5th Marines.[40]

This was the unexpected call-up that generated the grumbling against Edson described earlier by Irvin Reynolds and others. Yet most Raiders secretly felt proud to get the call. Sickness and losses had not diminished their esprit. Corporal Joe Murphy would never forget the "walking wounded" who voluntarily left their beds in the field hospital to shuffle along for one more piece of the action. Diarist T. D. Smith proudly noted the alleged report from a prisoner captured by the 5th Marines that the Japanese had placed "a bounty on the men with rags on their helmets," adding, "that was us." By this time, of course, the Raiders' rags appeared mostly on their backs or loins, but they could still smell a fight, still field a lethal force. Irwin told Charlie Company to be prepared to reinforce A Company and placed the remainder of the battalion on alert. The Raiders distributed ammo, oiled their weapons, listened thoughtfully to the distant gunfire along the Matanikau.[41]

As Captain Bob Neuffer led his reinforced Able Company west towards the river, some of his men believed they could see U.S. Navy ships on the horizon. This report naturally spawned rumors of their imminent departure from Starvation Island.

Within the company 60mm mortar platoon, Corporal Joe Connolly entertained his crewmates with a running fantasy of what the next dawn might bring—landing craft lined up along the beach to ferry the triumphant Raiders out to their waiting transports—full-sized transports this time, not their trusty but tiny APDs, new transports large enough to provide each Raider with a hot shower, steak and potatoes, ice cream and apple pie, first-run movies, and clean sheets on a soft mattress. No more mosquitoes or Washing Machine Charlie or nightly shelling by the Tokyo Express.

Connolly captured the men's imaginations as he always did, going back to the days of cold beer and pig's feet at the Quantico Privates Club. He had been the one with the temerity to ask Edson "which sonofabitch thought up this stupid hike?" and got away with it. Connolly was thirty-three, easily twelve years older than most other enlisted Raiders, and he had seen much of life, including seven years' prior service in both the navy and the Marines. At one point he served as a cook aboard a battleship. Short and stocky, he could bitch with profane eloquence, but he also served as an unofficial father figure to a wide circle of young Raiders. He usually carried the baseplate, the heaviest component of the mortar, and if you looked like you were struggling, he would carry your component as well. His long soliloquy this afternoon about the luxury transports awaiting on the morrow distracted the Marines' thoughts from the crescendo of fire building ominously in the direction of their march.[42]

Able Company spent a miserable night in the rain near the 5th

Marines' command post. By 0500 the morning of the eighth they were on their way westward, abruptly committed as front line troops, no longer in reserve. Charlie Company, as expected, received the call from Edson to advance towards the Matanikau to take Able Company's reserve mission. Irwin shaped the balance of the battalion into march formation.

Able Company's advance to the front along the coast road led them past the firing position of the 81mm mortars of the 2d Battalion, 5th Marines. There legendary Lou Diamond, the nonpareil mortarman, squinted at the column of Raiders approaching through the mist, spat, and swore: "Damn! Here come the Raiders—no wonder it's raining. We'll get no sleep tonight!" The Raiders cussed him fondly in return. Diamond's unerring 81mm mortars had provided awesome fire support to the Raiders on Tulagi's third day.[43]

Able Company at first tried to advance the final five hundred yards to the river on line with Love Company, 3/5, but that configuration ran the infantry company directly into the teeth of the Japanese salient, with the same dire consequences as the day before. Sergeant Frank Guidone's rifle squad comprised Able Company's left flank and overlapped the northern sector of the enclave. They drew fire and hit the deck. One of Guidone's sharp-eyed riflemen spotted an enemy machine-gun barrel protruding over a banyan root, covered by a poncho. Guidone motioned his troops to maneuver for a clear shot. BARman Sylvester Niedbalski snaked to the side and cut loose, shredding the poncho and the root. The machine-gun barrel spun skyward. Guidone and Private First Class Bob Hunt scurried forward. Just as they reached the spot the whole jungle came alive with small arms fire. A Raider spun to earth clutching his bleeding hand. Guidone carefully extricated all his men from the trap. The swamp was too deadly for a squad-level frontal attack.[44]

At this point the chain of command became muddled. Both Edson and Walt were well forward, close to the river, not far from the northeast shoulder of the Japanese salient. Captain Neuffer still commanded Able Company; Captain Jake Irwin was five miles back, with the balance of the battalion, still along the Lunga. Walt would later assume command of Able Company, and there are indications he in effect took command of the the entire Raider battalion for the balance of the fight.

In the meantime, someone (Edson? Walt?) ordered Neuffer to slide A Company north along the river to occupy an L-shaped line that would cover the beach, the mouth of the river, and the sand-bar crossing. The 5th Marines had evidently learned of the Japanese plans to advance with tanks and heavy artillery. There also existed a threat of a Japanese land-

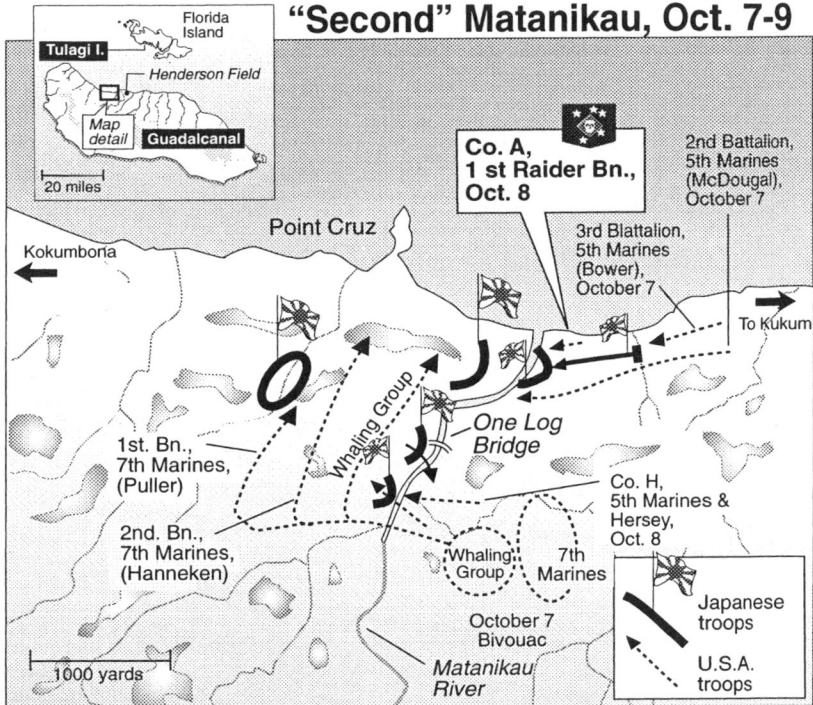

"Second" Matanikau, Oct. 7-9

Florida Island
Tulagi I.
Henderson Field
Map detail | Guadalcanal
20 miles

Point Cruz
Kokumbona

Co. A, 1 st Raider Bn., Oct. 8

2nd Battalion, 5th Marines (McDougal), October 7

3rd Blattalion, 5th Marines (Bower), October 7

To Kukum

One Log Bridge

1st. Bn., 7th Marines, (Puller)

Whaling Group

2nd. Bn., 7th Marines, (Hanneken)

Co. H, 5th Marines & Hersey, Oct. 8

Whaling Group | 7th Marines

Japanese troops

October 7 Bivouac

1000 yards

Matanikau River

U.S.A. troops

ing along the beach. Neuffer's mission became one of defending the crossing and the coast against major Japanese attacks—but his orders evidently included no guidance on containing the well-armed force still occupying the enemy bridgehead to his left rear. The 3d Battalion, 5th Marines, most Raiders assumed, would guard the enclave, tying in with Neuffer's left flank. This link failed to materialize.

Neuffer, understandably concerned about his sudden responsibility as the division's point defense against significant armored or amphibious attacks, devoted the balance of the afternoon preparing for those eventualities. The Able Company Raiders constructed a double-apron barbed wire fence along the broad base of the triangular-shaped sandspit—a good piece of work—and coordinated with the crews of two 37mm anti-tank guns and a disabled but still "shootable" 75mm halftrack provided by the 5th Marines.

As the defensive positions materialized, the company's "sea leg" was longer than its leg along the river. Platoon Sergeant Joe Buntin's 3d Platoon defended the right flank along a line running between the sea and the shore road. The heavy weapons came next, dug into slewable positions to defend both to seaward and westward up the coast against approaching tanks. Gunnery Sergeant Cliff McGlocklin's 1st Platoon continued the line along the beach until it began the curve inland at the river mouth. Lieutenant Red Sullivan's 2d Platoon covered the crucial barbed wire obstacles and extended upstream no more than two hundred yards. Neuffer had no real reserve, only Sergeant Woodrow Thompson's small 60mm mortar section, positioned where their mortars could not clear the jungle canopy and whose only other weapons were pistols.

Confusion reigned beyond Sullivan's left flank. Although the battalion's action report described a solid link at dusk with Baker Company echeloned to the left rear of A Company and tied in with C Company in turn tied in with K/3/5, there is no evidence of a tie-in between the Raiders and 3/5 after mid-afternoon on the eighth. And although both Charlie and Baker Company Raiders moved into that general sector sometime during the afternoon, there is no evidence of a master defense plan coordinating all elements.

Everyone's left flank, it seems, was up in the air. This is difficult to understand. Few Marines were more proficient in tying together defensive positions than Red Mike Edson and Lew Walt (Silent Lew would work miracles in this regard at Cape Gloucester and Peleliu), but one of them dropped the ball here. The two officers dispatched a couple of minor probes. Walt sent Sergeant Frank Guidone and Private First Class Warren Beavers into no-man's-land to throw grenades towards a spot where loud Japanese voices seemed to be concentrated. Later Walt directed Sergeant Tom Pollard to lead a patrol to "recon the heavy bamboo area along the river." Pollard found entrenched machine-gun positions and "a lot of noise and movement" in underbrush so thick the Raiders could not turn around, having to "crawl out backwards on our stomachs." In the main, it seemed Edson and Walt had concentrated on the perceived greater Japanese threat from the sea or across the sandbar—at the expense of worrying about the threat from Able Company's exposed left flank.[45]

Sergeant Guidone encountered Corporal Joe Connolly as he returned to McGlocklin's lines following his grenade mission for Lew Walt. "He asked me how I was doing and cautioned me to be careful," recalled Guidone in 1956, remarking that the exchange represented "one of the few times I had seen a serious Joe Connolly." Guidone shivered.[46]

The onset of nautical twilight along the river brought Japanese mortars into play. Shells exploded within A Company's positions, wounding

Lieutenant Sullivan twice as he crawled back to confer with Captain Neuffer. Sullivan refused Neuffer's order to be evacuated and demanded assistance for his wide open left flank. Neuffer had little to give, but he did offer up his mortar section for use as "listening posts" in the gap. Darkness descended as Sullivan led Corporal Connolly and several other mortarmen back towards the 2d Platoon's line.

"Dusk was rapidly approaching," said Private First Class John Carson, one of Connolly's mortarmen, "and we saw what appeared to be fog rising from the Matanikau—most unusual because we had never seen this before." It was a grim omen. "Turns out it wasn't fog, it was smoke, from the smoke canisters the Japs always seemed to have."[47]

Lieutenant Ito chose this moment to emerge from his swamp fortifications and fight his way back across the river. Using the smoke canister to mask the breakout, he led about 150 survivors of his 3d Company through the gap along A Company's left flank, missing John Carson and Sammie Mitchell by no more than ten yards but colliding immediately with the remainder of the Raiders' unsuspecting mortar section being led towards their posts by Red Sullivan.

Sullivan heard a noise, sounded a challenge in the gloom, then his worst fears came true:

> The Japs broke out of the jungle almost on top of us...I screamed to the platoon we were being attacked from the rear. As I turned around and started firing my Reising gun, Joe Connolly was cut down right by my side with a sword or a bushknife before he even had a chance to get his pistol out of the holster. As the rest of the [headquarters men] were falling I started backing up trying to get to my foxhole in order to direct my platoon. I emptied two magazines and was reaching for a third when I was shot through the left shoulder.[48]

The next few moments were drenched in incredible violence. The Raiders were proficient hand-to-hand fighters—knew how to stab under a ribcage or rip out a windpipe—but the Japanese had the surprise and the numbers. The mortarmen and other headquarters troops went down almost to a man. The surging Japanese then swept through Sullivan's position, hacking and bayoneting the men in their foxholes. Sullivan, weaponless and bleeding, staggered into a hole being defended by Sergeant Donald Wolf and another NCO. They pulled him in and the three men used their knives to intercept and cut down the swirling Japanese in the dark.[49]

The screams and general uproar created by the Japanese breakout to their left rear badly frightened Gunnery Sergeant Cliff McGlocklin and his 1st Platoon. He turned his men to face the threat, but now he had the barbed wire to his back and the sea to his left rear, and he hesitated to open fire because the darkness swarmed with running figures—where were Sullivan's men? Finally, to hell with it, McGlocklin bellowed "Raiders, stay in your holes!" and cut loose. Apparently one of the 37mm guns also cut loose, causing many members of Able Company, in Jack Tracy's words, to "blanko our skivvies." It seemed to help. Given this fire support, surviving members of Sullivan's platoon like Andy Anderscavage, Bill Dodamead, Mike Fedorak, and Red Hills resisted heroically. Sammie Mitchell and John Carson fought their way clear, the former identifying himself to all Marines along the entire expanse of the Matanikau by shouting, "I'M SAMMIE MITCHELL AND I'M COMING OUT!" But Sullivan's group had no such luck. The three men bolted from their hole when their ammo ran out. Only Sullivan survived.[50]

For all their care in silently pinpointing the hole in the Marines' line, the Japanese somehow failed to notice the Raiders building the barbed wire fence along the sandspit. Dozens of Japanese ran right into it at full speed, becoming hopelessly tangled. The Raiders could see them silhouetted against the white sand background and relentlessly shot them dead.

Captain Neuffer believed he had lost the entire company. He placed a desperate call for reinforcements to Edson on the field phone. Edson's calm reaction provided a steadying effect: "Neuffer, you will hold your position." Edson ordered Lew Walt to take command of the company, restore the lines, and keep the men vigilant against the greater threats expected from up the coast or from the sea. Walt reached Neuffer's position after 2100. "How he ever found us in the black of night I'll never know," recalled Neuffer. The firing and screaming had died down, and "all you could hear were the moans and death rattles of many badly hurt men." Walt put Neuffer and McGlocklin to work restoring the defensive line while he carefully walked the perimeter to reassure and remotivate the shaken survivors.[51]

At dawn, Walt sent Neuffer and McGlocklin with Sergeant Frank Guidone's squad to sweep the left flank sector. The discovery of so many friends, dead and butchered, unnerved Guidone. With the exception of John Carson and the badly wounded George Simmons, the entire company mortar section had been slain. The dead mortarmen included Sergeant Woodrow R. Thompson, twenty-three, from Bellepointe, West Virginia; Corporal Joseph E. Connolly, thirty-three, from Astoria, New York; Corporal Neldon T. French, twenty-four, from Campden, Tennessee; Private

"Close Range," by Doug Greenbowe. Jungle fighting placed a premium on rapid and reliable fire. The Reising submachine guns could deliver both—but only if weapon and magazines were kept scrupulously clean, not an easy task in the jungle.

First Class Donald B. Steinaker, twenty, who left a widow, Hazel, in Syracuse, New York; Private First Class Dennis F. Thomas, twenty-two, from Barnstable, Massachusetts; Private First Class James A. Zophy, twenty-five, from Sherrill, New York, and Private Edward L. Smith, twenty, from Rome, New York. French and Smith had been wounded previously during the Battle of Edson's Ridge. Thompson, Connolly, French, and Steinaker would be honored subsequently by having new Navy ships named after them. So would three other Raiders killed in this savage fighting: Sergeant Donald W. Wolf, twenty-three, who left a widow, Barbara, in Hart, Michigan; Private First Class George Heyliger (no card available); and Private William T. Hanna, twenty-one, of Brooklyn. In all, the battalion reported twelve killed and twenty-two wounded, virtually all of them within that wild, thirty-minute melee when the Japanese burst out of the swamp. The Raiders counted fifty-nine dead enemy soldiers within A Company's lines or caught in the barbed wire.[52]

Correspondent John Hersey spotted the Japanese bodies on the sand spit through a telescope from upriver. Later, he made his way to the site and walked through the corpses littering the Raiders left flank position of the previous night. "Apparently Edson had had trouble getting rid of the company on his side of the river," Hersey reported, and consequently he "called on the men who do or die in the worst jams in Guadal, the Raiders." The Japanese, Hersey continued, "mounted a terrifying attack....but in the close-in knife work which followed, the Marines evidently got the best of it, to judge by the number of Jap bodies in the holes."[53]

General Vandegrift inspected the battlefield with Edson. As he stared at the intermingled bodies, often locked in death after desperate hand-to-hand scuffling, the general asked, "Who did this work?" "My Raiders, sir," said Edson hoarsely. Vandegrift corrected him: "They're *my* Raiders now."[54]

The final Raider to die on Guadalcanal was no longer carried on the rolls but remained very much in the hearts of the survivors. On 9 October, the day after A Company's desperate fight along the Matanikau, Merritt Edson dispatched his runner, Corporal Walter Burak, to find an errant battalion commander. Hustling along a hazardous trail near the river, Burak was killed instantly by a burst of Nambu machine-gun fire. He was twenty-two, from Greensburg, Pennsylvania. Even the flinty Edson cried at this news. So did a number of Raiders, already bereft at the loss of the enlisted father figure, Joe Connolly. The Raiders had long respected Burak's uncommon spirituality and fidelity. "Walter Burak was clearly the best of all of us," said Fred Serral. Four years later, on Armistice Day 1946, Edson eulogized the young man at his grave site in Greensburg: "His service was faithful to the end—to me, to you, and to his country—always in keeping with the highest traditions of the United States Marine Corps."[55]

## So We're Saying Goodbye to Them All...

The ambitious operation the Raiders called "Second Matanikau" continued with considerable success. The Marines drove the Japanese well back from the Matanikau, killing nearly seven hundred of them in sharp fighting, while suffering fewer than two hundred of their own casualties. Loss of their bridgeheads on the east bank of the Matanikau proved galling to the Japanese and derailed their mid-October offensive. Indeed, when the Japanese finally dispatched their column of tanks across the sandbar at the river's mouth, Vandegrift had a Marine battalion locked and loaded at the Raiders' old battleground. High explosive 75mm fire from Marine halftracks destroyed the entire column (some of the hulks remain there to this day, visible each low tide).

The Raiders were glad to have been in a winning battle, but most of them remained in shock at the price they had to pay for their limited participation. The loss of fully one third of a reinforced company trying to achieve an unexpected, multi-faceted defensive mission was hard to swallow. The men also grieved over the tragic loss of corporals Burak and Connolly. They were numb, exhausted, played out.

Sam Griffith had been evacuated from the island two weeks before the Raiders finally left, but he remembered how they looked when they first tried to cross the Matanikau. "The battalion was in sad shape," he declared. By that time "everybody in that outfit had either dysentery, malaria, or trench mouth." Griffith said the battalion was "really wrecked" by exceeding the psychological, emotional, and physical limitations which all human beings have, even Raiders.[56]

Guadalcanal seemed increasingly alien to the Raiders. When October brought no relief from the sweltering heat and menacing environment, the thoughts of many men turned to autumn in the United States. Easy Company's Private First Class Lee Minier, homesick and recovering from wounds received when the Japanese attacked his machine-gun crew in the first night's battle of The Ridge, wrote his family in upstate New York: "Just thinking this morning that I would like to be up in the Adirondacks right now. The people in Prospect should consider themselves lucky to live in such a beautiful spot."[57]

A terrific sea battle occurred the night of 11–12 October off Cape Esperance. The costly victory enabled the Navy to deliver the first Army ground troops to Guadalcanal. On 13 October, transports landed the 164th Infantry, a National Guard outfit full of big, strapping fellows from the north central states who would make a name for themselves in the fighting ahead.

The ships that brought in Army troops represented the Raiders' deliverance from Guadalcanal. All day long on the thirteenth the Raiders anxiously watched the offloading and waited for the green light to board the transports *Zeilin* and *McCawley* (named after the seventh and eighth commandants of the Marine Corps, respectively).

The Raiders had landed on Tulagi more than nine hundred strong. A total of 555 men would board these two transports (aggregating officers and enlisted, Marines and navy). In sixty-seven days of nigh-continuous combat the Raiders had suffered ninety-four killed and two hundred wounded. While "Body Counts" at Guadalcanal lacked the command interest of the Vietnam War, the Raiders were nevertheless credited with killing more than 1,100 Japanese soldiers and naval infantry in their five battles.[58]

More significantly, their swift and hard-nosed seizure of Tulagi had provided Imperial General Headquarters with the first unwelcome indicator that American ground troops could fight with convincing effectiveness. Moreover, the combination of the Tasimboko Raid and the victory at Edson's Ridge influenced the Seventeenth Army to cancel its ambitious plans for the overland seizure of Port Moresby, New Guinea, causing them to switch many of those troops to Guadalcanal. Even at the end, with the battalion a mere shadow of its peak prowess, the Raiders had helped hammer the Japanese back across the Matanikau for good.

They had left their mark. Now they wanted out.

The Raiders departed on Friday the Thirteenth. Despite the superstitious date, the Raiders' famous luck—absent perhaps along the Matanikau—returned in spades. Two Japanese air raids scared the hell out of the Raiders (one occurred as Merritt Edson came down to the beach to say goodbye). As the Raiders finally boarded their transports the ships went to General Quarters. The Japanese had finally gotten their 150mm howitzers within range. "Pistol Pete" was shelling the perimeter and the anchorage. The ships scrambled to get under way. The Raiders left the island about four hours before two Japanese battleships steamed down The Slot and delivered the heaviest shelling any American troops would experience in the entire twentieth century. Raiders' luck prevailed through the bitter end.

## Notes

1. Herbert A. Merillat, *Guadalcanal Remembered* (New York: Dodd & Mead, 1984), 150.
2. Ernest Gyenese to John Sweeney, n.d.
3. Griffith, *The Battle for Guadalcanal,* 121–22.
4. Frank Guidone and Jinx Powers interviews with Jon Hoffman, 1991; T. D. Smith Diary, 17–18 September 1942, 8; Hoffman, *Legend,* 211.
5. T. D. Smith Diary, 17–18 September 1942, 8.

6. James Childs interview with Jon Hoffman, 1991; Griffith, *The Battle for Guadalcanal,* 133; Frank, *Guadalcanal,* 259–60.

7. Battalion Muster Roll, September 1942. Mess Sgt. Richard Ballentine, E Company, and PFC John Hunt, HQ Company, are listed as "wounded by accidental discharge."

8. Poppell Diary, 19 September 1942, 19;Thomas quote from his Oral History, cited in Hoffman, *Legend,* 210; John Hersey, *Into the Valley: A Skirmish of the Marines* (New York: Alfred A. Knopf, 1943), 37.

9. Herbert L. Merillat, *The Island* (Boston: Houghton Mifflin, 1944), 116.

10. John Mielke to author, 9 April 1999.

11. Hersey, *Into the Valley,* 11.

12. Battalion Order Number 1, 21 September 1942, contained Edson's salutary farewell.

13. James Childs interview with Jon Hoffman, 1991; T. D. Smith Diary, 21 September 1942, 8; Irvin Reynolds to James Smith, n.d.

14. Battalion Muster Roll reflects Walt's and Adams' transfer on 22 September and Burak's on the 23d. Edson also "borrowed" Lt. James Blessing for a week to teach the 5th Marines what he had learned about the use of land mines, booby traps, and Bangalore Torpedoes (source: Blessing interview with Jon Hoffman, 1991).

15. Merillat, *The Island,* 116. And worth repeating for the record: the author's use of "First and Second Matanikau" refers to the sequence of the Raiders' two battles, notwithstanding the fact that they were technically "Matanikau II and III" in the history of the Guadalcanal campaign.

16. Samuel B. Griffith Oral Memoir, MCOHC, MCHC, 113. There is a certain irony in the fact that an engagement which became an embarrassing defeat for the Marines was planned and executed by five of the most legendary of all Leathernecks—Vandegrift, Thomas, Twining, Edson, and Puller—who between them would one day accumulate seventeen general officer's stars. This operation was hardly their finest effort.

17. *Handbook on Japanese Military Forces,* 406.

18. Griffith, *Battle for Guadalcanal,* 126; Frank, *Guadalcanal,* 251, 272, 287. Col. Nomasu Nakaguma commanded the 4th Infantry.

19. The best analysis of this operation is Jon T. Hoffman, "The Legacy and Lessons of the 2d Matanikau" [by which he means the Raiders' "First" Matanikau], *Marine Corps Gazette,* January 1993, 82–85.

20. Griffith to "Dear Cliff," [Historical Division, HQMC], 6 October 1945, 1st Raider Battalion File, Box 4, Serial 63A-2534, WNRC. In his 1963 book on Guadalcanal, Griffith stated the operation was planned and conducted "in total ignorance of the terrain and of the enemy situation" [135]. Coastwatcher Martin Clemens's usually reliable scouts were of little help because the villages of Kokumbona and Matanikau had been deserted for so many months.

21. CO, 1st Marine Raider Battalion to CG, 1st Marine Division, "Report of Operations of this Battalion from 1330, 26 September to 1930, 27 September 1942," 3 October 1942 [Raiders' Report of Operations, 26–27 September 1942], Reference Section, MCHC. Edson strengthened the Raiders for this flanking movement with the addition of Charlie Company, 1/7.

22. Muster Roll, September 1942.

23. Griffith, *The Battle for Guadalcanal*, 135; Pettus, "Second Battle of the Matanikau," *Dope Sheet*, 1958; Richard E. Sullivan to Lowell V. Bulger, Marine Raider Association, 30 January 1979 [Sullivan Account].

24. Tregaskis, *Guadalcanal Diary*, 251. Bailey's generosity along the march was exemplified by John Carson to Frank Guidone, 26 July 1991: "Moving from the coconut grove towards the Ridge, hot as hell, carrying a bag of 60mm mortar shells, and who should appear but Major Bailey. 'Tired, son? Let me help you with your load,' and took the bag off my shoulder."

25. Sullivan Account, 2. Sullivan states in this 1979 account that he was still in Charlie Company, but he had in fact been transferred to Able Company, which by all other accounts provided the "Advance Guard" for the morning of 27 September. The order of march was A, C, C/1/7, HQ+E, and B Company as the rear guard (Raiders' Report of Operations, 26–27 September 1942, paragraph 5). In any event, Sullivan was undeniably a close and credible witness to Bailey's death, and his testimony in both 1956 and 1979 is invaluable.

26. Griffith, *The Battle for Guadalcanal*, 135.

27. *Ibid.*, 136 [Charlie Raiders and Charlie/1/7 executed the flanking attack]; Griffith Oral memoir, MCOHC, MCHC, 118; Poppell Diary, 27 September 1942, 20.

28. T. D. Smith Diary, 27 September 1942, 9.

29. Hoffman, *Legend*, 218–219.

30. Twining, *No Bended Knee*, 112; Maj. Gen. Akisaburo Futami quoted in Frank, *Guadalcanal*, 274.

31. James Smith to Pete Pettus, n.d., 2; James Smith to author, 13 July 1999; Julian K. Dobson Casualty Card. In a 25 October 1956 letter to Pete Pettus, Clifford J. Fitzpatrick, a member of Corporal Ben Howland's Baker Company rifle squad at First Matanikau, recalls carrying Bailey's body back to the beach on a stretcher. Given Baker Company's position as the rear guard of the battalion, and thus arrayed along the northern end of the column, closest to the aid station, it is quite likely that Howland's squad got tagged to relay Bailey's body from the aid station (hence the stretcher) to the beach, vice from the vicinity of the Nippon Bridge all the way back as Fitzpatrick avers. Fitzpatrick's description of Edson's grief at the news of Bailey's death is compelling.

32. Griffith Oral Memoir, MCOHC, MCHC, 119.

33. Raiders' Report of Operations, 26–27 September 1942; Battalion Muster Roll, September 1942 (which in fact lists only these four Marines as WIAs in the First Matanikau battle); Pete Pettus, *The Dope Sheet,* December 1971, 4.

34. A well-written biographical profile of Ira J. Irwin can be found in Allen G. Mainard, "The Special Breed," *Leatherneck 38* (August 1955), 32–33. Irwin retired from the USMCR in 1955 at the rank of colonel.

35. James Childs interview with Jon Hoffman, 1991; See also Hoffman, *Legend,* 221.

36. Vandegrift to Turner, n.d., text provided author by Jon T. Hoffman. Vandegrift continued the topic by suggesting that, once the 1st Raider Battalion was withdrawn, "I urgently request that the 2d Raider Battalion be sent in to replace them as we will need all the strength we can for this next push."

37. September Muster Roll. There were likely other Raiders who received awards from Admiral Nimitz that day.

38. Francis C. Pettus, "A Four Day Patrol," *Marine Corps Gazette,* June 1944, 26–30; Frank, *Guadalcanal,* 291.

39. Frank, *Guadalcanal,* 282–83; Griffith, *The Battle for Guadalcanal,* 142–43; Hoffman, *Legend,* 222–23.

40. Merrill Twining Oral Memoir, MCOHC, MCHC, 206; CO, 1st Marine Raider Battalion to CG, 1st Marine Division, "Report of operations of this battalion against the enemy from 1530, 7 October to 1900, 9 October 1942," 11 October 1942 [Raiders' Report of Operations, 7–9 October 1942], 1.

41. Joseph Murphy Memoir, n.d., author's possession; T. D. Smith Diary, 3 October 1942, 9.

42. Biographical details on Cpl. Joseph E. Connolly from Frank Guidone to Pete Pettus, "My Memory of Joe Connolly," 28 September 1956; Pete Pettus, "Second Battle of the Matanikau," *The Dope Sheet,* August 1958, 4; and Joseph E. Connolly Casualty Card.

43. Pettus, "Second Matanikau," 5.

44. Frank Guidone, "Along the Matanikau River," *The Dope Sheet,* 1995, 6.

45. Thomas Pollard to Frank Guidone, n.d.

46. Guidone, "My Memory of Joe Connolly," 3. "That was the last time I saw Joe alive."

47. John H. Carson to Frank Guidone, 26 July 1991, 2.

48. Richard E. Sullivan to Pete Pettus, 30 November 1956, 1 [Sullivan Account].

49. *Ibid.,* 2.

50. Clifford McGlocklin to Pete Pettus, 27 June 1956, 2; Jack Tracy to Frank Guidone, 5 May 1996; Sullivan Account, 2; Pettus, "Second Battle of the Matanikau," 7–8.

51. Robert Neuffer report (only last page available), n.d.; Lew Walt to Pete Pettus, 1956.

52. Casualty Cards for the named individuals (PFC George Heyliger's is missing); Raiders' Report of Operations, 7–9 October 1942, 1–3.

53. Hersey, *Into the Valley,* 130–31.

54. Vandegrift quoted in Pettus, "Second Battle of the Matanikau," 8.

55. Hoffman, *Legend,* 225; Walter Burak Casualty Card; John H. Gann, Jr., to Jon Hoffman, 1 November 1991; Fred Serral to author, 5 December 1998; Brig. Gen. Merritt A. Edson remarks, Armistice Day, Greensburg, Pennsylvania, 11 November 1946, copy in author's possession. Burak had been transferred to the 5th Marines with Edson in late September.

56. Samuel Griffith, Oral Memoir, MCOHC, MCHC, 122.

57. PFC Lee Minier to family, 11 October 1942; Lee N. Minier, *Raider,* unpublished manuscript, 1989, 152. Minier was wounded on 12 September 1942 according to the September Muster Roll.

58. Battalion arrival strength and casualties from Peatross, *Bless 'em All,* 119; Departure strength figures compiled by James Childs and John Sweeney, 22 September 1994.

# 9

## Under the Southern Cross, October 1942–July 1943

*The camp of the 1st Marine Raider Battalion in the Saint Louis area is hereby named CAMP BAILEY in honor of Major Kenneth D. Bailey, USMC, who lost his life in the service of his country while engaged in action against the enemy at Guadalcanal, British Solomon Islands[1]*

Lieutenant Colonel Samuel B. Griffith,
USMC, Commanding Officer
January 1943, New Caledonia

THE 1ST MARINE RAIDER BATTALION returned to New Caledonia as a ragged shadow of the force that had departed there eleven weeks earlier.

Sickness swept through rank and file with a vengeance. Two hundred and sixty-seven men who boarded the ships to depart Guadalcanal on 13 October had active cases of malaria. Many more carried latent strains of the disease like ticking time bombs due to erupt after they arrived in New Caledonia. T. D. Smith's account was typical: "When we got ashore I was sick. When we arrived at Camp I was ordered along with many others for Doc McLarney's shock treatment. We had malaria." Sam Griffith's later assessment proved accurate: "I don't suppose there were more than 150 officers and men in that battalion that were really fit for duty by mid-October."[2]

Some would never shake the chills and fever of the disease as long as they remained in the South Pacific. Veterans Hugh Davis and Elton Whisenhunt suffered from malaria so acutely six months after the battalion left Guadalcanal that both had to be evacuated back to the States for treatment and reassignment. Captain Edward Dupras became a company commander one month, then a "jungle fever" evacuee the next. Doctor McLarney had to be evacuated with an amoebic abscess of his liver.[3]

229

Others envied them the chance to go home. Fred A. Serral expressed his homesickness in a poem he wrote his girlfriend while battling malaria in MOB Hospital #5 in Nouméa:

*Now we turn into sickbay nearly every day,*
  *And try to get a survey nearly any old way.*
*Doctors always give use the same ole news:*
  *"Nothing wrong, son, just got the STATESIDE BLUES."*[4]

Yet the Raiders had too much pride—too much inherent "positive buoyancy"—to stay down long. New Caledonia's comparative cleanliness, coolness, and non-hostile environment worked wonders. So did the reunion with so many mates previously evacuated as sick or wounded—and with the long-suffering Rear Echelon under Captain Foster LaHue and Sergeant Major "Parson" Clark, whose necessary but noncombatant role in the Guadalcanal campaign had proven invaluable (Frosty LaHue would get his chance at glory as a member of the 4th Raider Battalion in New Georgia; he would retire in 1974 as a highly-decorated lieutenant general).

The landmark of this recovery period was the battalion's long-anticipated, extended liberty in Wellington, New Zealand, throughout the Christmas and New Year's holiday of 1942–1943. The battalion sailed there and back aboard the "Wacky Mac," the USS *McCawley,* flagship of Rear Admiral Kelly Turner. Like many other flag officers—then and now—nervous about entering an exotic liberty port with a full contingent of combat-weary and hot-blooded Marines, Turner worried about being embarrassed by "incidents." "When I remember what grand fighters all of you are," said Turner in a special message to the embarked Raiders, "I also realize that I will have to stand responsible for all your misdeeds and explain them to my boss. I hope all of you have a grand time—but please remember to maintain the grand name you have established."[5]

The Raiders paid Turner little heed. They celebrated their well-earned liberty in their own ways, some sedate, others wild and woolly. The "Battle of Wellington," a massive street fight with some of the New Zealand troops, added a number of black eyes and cracked skulls to the morning Binnacle List but failed to get Turner in hot water. Most of the Raiders simply fell in love with the place and its friendly people. "We gaze in awe at the beauty that confronts us," wrote Popeye Poppell as the ship entered Wellington. Poppell went to the Majestic Cabana his first night ashore. There, spellbound, "we watch the dancing and admire the girls until the place closes. Then we eat our first ice cream since being overseas."[6]

In a ceremony at St. Louis Mission, New Caledonia, on 16 January 1943 Admiral "Bull" Halsey awarded the Silver Star Medal to (left to right) PFC David Taber, Sgt. James Smith, Cpl. Morris Snyder, and PFC Hubert Milanowski.

So genuine was the hospitality of the people of Wellington that the Raiders who survived the war would speak fondly of that city throughout the next half century. And for those young men who would not survive either the forthcoming Dragon's Peninsula or the reconquest of Guam, this brief haven of grace and normalcy in between campaigns provided a final but felicitous touch of home.

The Wellington interlude rejuvenated the Raiders. Newly promoted Corporal Lee Minier wrote home extolling his "first real vacation since enlisting." Minier took pleasure in simple values: "Ate dinner off of a table, saw movies, went to dances and had a rip-roaring time." Now, he said, "I'm feeling fine and raring to go." Minier joined an irreverent octet of harmonizers soon known as "The Singing Eight Balls," whose profane and funny songs about troop life in the South Pacific entertained the battalion and were recorded for posterity on a phonograph record still maintained at the Library of Congress.[7]

The Raiders would remain in New Caledonia for thirty weeks, by far the longest time they would spend in any one location as a Raider Battalion. Here they would slowly heal, reorganize, rearm, and recover. The new 1st Marine Raider Battalion that returned to combat the following July would be distinctly different from the original version—fewer superstars, mainly a tried and tested core of veteran junior officers and NCOs leading an enthusiastic group of newcomers.

The extent of the changes-in-progress became evident as early as the Thanksgiving dinner the month after the unit returned to New Caledonia. Of the seven senior officers (CO, XO, five company commanders) who had sat at the head table in Quantico just a year earlier, only Captain Jake Irwin remained. Merritt Edson, Major Doyle (XO), and Captain Meyerhoff (A Company) had transferred out; Ken Bailey, Bob Brown, and Henry Cain were dead.

## Other Raiders

The year 1942 encompassed both the birth and the true heyday of the Marine Raider Battalions. In that year the 1st Battalion achieved fame for its seizure of Tulagi and defense of Edson's Ridge, while the 2d Raider Battalion under command of Lieutenant Colonel Evans Carlson defended Midway, executed a dramatic raid on Makin, and conducted an extended, month-long combat patrol behind enemy lines in the jungles of Guadalcanal. Meanwhile, on 20 September, the Marine Corps established the 3d Raider Battalion in Samoa under Lieutenant Colonel Harry B. Liversedge, and on 23 October in Camp Pendleton, the 4th Raider Battalion under Lieutenant Colonel James Roosevelt, formerly Carlson's executive officer.

The 1st Raider Battalion provided cadres to each of the other three battalions. Marine Gunner Anthony Yelanich, the veteran of Merritt Edson's Coco River Patrol in Nicaragua, recovered from his broken back in Samoa in time to join the 3d Raiders. Major Bob Thomas, the battalion executive officer after Bailey's death, and Captain Bob Neuffer, the A Company commander at Second Matanikau, transferred to the 4th Battalion. Gunnery Sergeant Banks W. Staley went to the 2d Battalion and was wounded at Bougainville. Several members of Edson's Raiders wound up serving in three of the four battalions, including Corporal Michael T. Weletok and Private First Class George Novaska (1st, 2d, and 3d Battalions), and Corporal Herbert C. Helpingstine and Private First Class Paul D. Curtin (1st, 2d, and 4th Battalions). Helpingstine died at Guam; Curtin at Okinawa.

In 1943, the 3d Raider Battalion helped seize the Russell Islands to launch Operation Toenails in the Central Solomons. Both the 1st and 4th Raider Battalions served in the 1st Marine Raider Regiment for the New Georgia campaign, the 4th landing initially on Vangunu Island, then rejoining the regiment for the assault on Bairoko. Late in the year the 2d and 3d Raider Battalions served in the 2d Provisional Raider Regiment for the protracted invasion of Bougainville.[8]

The stealthy strike by Carlson's 2d Raider Battalion against Makin on 17–18 August 1942 remains the purest example of a raid executed by the Allies during the Pacific War. Carlson led two companies of his Raiders ashore on Butaritari Island, Makin Atoll, British Gilbert Islands, by rubber boats from a pair of troop transport submarines, USS *Argonaut* (APS 1) and USS *Nautilus* (APS 2). The 2d Raiders completely surprised the Japanese garrison, slew most of them, even "decommissioned" a pair of late-arriving Imperial Navy floatplanes with well-aimed fire from their .55-caliber Boys antitank rifles.

Overall, the raid was valiant but costly. High surf hindered Carlson's evacuation by rubber boat; some men drowned. Nine other Raiders were inadvertently left behind, captured, and beheaded by the Japanese. The negative factors fail to diminish the extreme heroism of the 2d Raiders nor the undeniable psychological benefits their raid achieved.

The Makin Raid for the American people was nearly as great a shot in the national arm as Jimmy Doolittle's bombing of Tokyo the previous May. The raid also stunned and embarrassed the Japanese high command. Vice Admiral Matome Ugaki, chief of staff of the Combined Fleet under the legendary Admiral Isoroku Yamamoto, recorded his reaction to the Makin strike in his diary: "The enemy tried to destroy the island, preceding us in attempting a submarine-borne landing." To Ugaki, the raiders intended to "destroy our eyes at Makin....They will make surprise attacks on other islands in this way, and we must never relax."[9]

Three former members of Edson's Raiders gave their lives in the Makin Raid: Sergeant Robert V. Allard, twenty-two, from Woodside, Long Island, New York; Corporal James W. Beecher, twenty-three, from Baxley, Georgia; and Sergeant Dallas H. Cook, twenty-one, from Red Jacket, West Virginia. All three were originally classified as Missing in Action, then, a year and a day later, reclassified as Killed in Action by the Secretary of the Navy under Public Law #490 (similar to the MIA cases in Charlie and Easy Companies, 1st Raider Battalion, during the first night's battle for Edson's Ridge). The families of both Allard and Cook received their sons' posthumous Navy Crosses.

During refresher training in New Caledonia in April 1943, Marine Gunner Angus Goss (left) examines TNT charges with the NCOs in his Demolition Platoon. Left to right, Platoon Sgt. Nicholas McIver and Sgt. Gerald West.

The Makin raid validated the concept of launching and recovering raids from troop transport submarines, but the 1st Raider Battalion never had the opportunity for such a mission, despite subsequent lobbying by Sam Griffith. All three of the battalion's combat landings—Tulagi, Tasimboko, Rice Anchorage—were launched from APDs (and "Yippees" at Tasimboko). Part of this reflected the origins of the 1st and 2d Raider Battalions. Edson's outfit, born and bred on the East Coast, took great advantage of what became virtually its own APD transport division. Carlson's outfit spent several months in Oahu, home base of the transport subs, *Argonaut* and *Nautilus,* and became proficient in stealthy landings in that setting. Yet Makin represented the sole use of transport submarines by organized Raider units, and in retrospect one has to wonder why Chester Nimitz or Bull Halsey did not use the combination more frequently during the early years.

Both submarines (plus their sister ship, USS *Narwhal*) could readily transport a company of Raiders, along with their light assault weapons and inflatable rubber boats. *Nautilus* landed the 7th Infantry Division's scouts under extremely difficult and risky conditions the night before D-Day at Attu in the Aleutians. She would later deliver the 1st Marine Force Reconnaissance Company under Captain James L. Jones to seize the atoll of Apamama in the Gilberts during Operation Galvanic. Huge *Argonaut,* 381 feet long and displacing 4,080 tons submerged, was the largest submarine in the U.S. Navy. Although built in 1927 as a minelayer, the navy converted *Argonaut* to transport duty immediately after Pearl Harbor. In January 1943, with both the 1st and 2d Marine Raider Battalions undergoing their lengthy recovery from Guadalcanal, and neither the 3d nor 4th Battalion yet ready for combat, the Pacific Fleet assigned *Argonaut* to a conventional attack mission. On 10 January, somewhere between Rabaul and Lae, she attacked a Japanese convoy, torpedoed one destroyer, but succumbed to depth charges. She sank with all hands. The 2d Raiders in particular grieved her loss.[10]

Vivid dispatches about the raiders posted by combat correspondents like Richard Tregaskis caught the national interest in the dark days and even prompted a series of fanciful Hollywood movies. Yet even at the peak of their public appeal in late 1942, the Raiders' days were numbered. An exchange of correspondence in September and October between the highest levels of the U.S. Navy and Marine Corps revealed a lingering belief among senior Marines that elite units were costly and redundant.

The exchange began 1 September when Chester Nimitz radioed Ernest King about prospects for additional Marine Raider units in the Pacific. Writing shortly after the Tulagi and Makin operations, Nimitz observed that "present battalions have proved their effectiveness," and concluded that "more of these special type organizations are desirable for employment." King bucked the issue to Commandant Thomas Holcomb for comment. Holcomb replied the next day that he objected to additional Raider units on three grounds: he needed every man simply to field three full Marine divisions; he believed "hand-picked" units deprived other organizations of natural leaders; and—the crux of his objection—he did not consider hit-and-run raids to be "sufficiently profitable to justify the organization of special units." On the other hand, Holcomb acknowledged that Nimitz was closer to the field than he was in Washington and therefore agreed to the formation of the 3d Raider Battalion in Samoa.[11]

Admiral Turner meanwhile muddied the waters of the debate with a letter to Admiral Ghormley on the employment of Raider Battalions in the South Pacific. Turner thought they were effective units but inadequate for the tasks at hand. He stated that both the 1st Raider Battalion and the 1st Parachute Battalion had "suffered such severe losses" on

Tulagi and Gavutu that they were out of action when Turner needed them for subsequent raiding operations. He wanted more units. He also announced he had directed the commanding officer of the 2d Marines to form a provisional raider battalion within his regiment. The Leathernecks who saw this letter noticed immediately that Turner had ignored General Vandegrift while blatantly meddling in one of his tactical components—a case of bald-faced piracy.

Admiral Ghormley passed this hot potato up the line to Nimitz. The CINCPAC comment, doubtlessly drafted by Nimitz's senior Marine, Colonel Omar T. Pfeiffer, took a quick shot at Turner for "extemporized organization of Marine forces," then inserted a phrase that would be increasingly heard in senior Marine debates on the fate of the Raider Battalions throughout 1943: "The basic training of all Marine Corps infantry units is essentially the same as that of the Raider Battalions and, therefore, all Marine Corps infantry battalions are potentially raider units." General Holcomb reinforced this harbinger in his endorsement to Admiral King, stating, "The regular Marine infantry battalion can, with proper training, carry out the missions normally assigned a raider battalion," and adding this parenthetical caveat: "(In fact, the 1st Raider Battalion was used on a normal infantry mission at Tulagi.)" In the Commandant's outspoken view, Kelly Turner should keep his damned hands out of standard Marine organizations and, should he need more raiders, coordinate with Archer Vandegrift to train one or more regular infantry outfits for the mission.[12]

There the issue remained and festered. Creation of the 3d and 4th Raider Battalions in the fall of 1942 helped keep Kelly Turner's "damned hands" out of the regular infantry outfits and provided sufficient Raiders to meet anticipated requirements for the reduction of Rabaul scheduled for the coming year. In the meantime, unnoticed by the Raiders' supporters and detractors alike, an event occurred in the United States that would soon seal the fate of the Raiders as much as any doctrinal debate. On New Year's Eve 1942, the navy commissioned the USS *Essex* (CV 9), the first of a new class of large, fast, fleet carriers. The eventual arrival of the first significant force of *Essex*-class carriers in the Central Pacific in the second half of 1943—along with new fast battleships, the F-6F Hellcat fighters, and uniquely designed amphibious ships—would render all special units obsolete. No matter how brave and bold the Raiders, the Pacific War would be revolutionized. The days of desperate hit-and-run raids would become history.

Before that landmark day arrived, however, each of the Raider Battalions would face one final, bloody campaign.

## Griffith's Raiders

Lieutenant Colonel Samuel B. Griffith took command of the 1st Marine Raider Battalion from Captain Jake Irwin on 14 January 1943, shortly after the unit returned from its memorable interlude in Wellington. Fully recovered from his shoulder wound, Griffith assumed leadership of the Raiders with a mixture of grim determination and unbridled joy. He would make the utmost of the next eight months.

The Raiders knew they were in good hands. John "Tiger" Erskine described his new battalion commander as "extremely well-read, articulate, and suave." Yet despite Griffith's intellect and education, Erskine found him "not in the least snobbish. He could communicate at all levels from buck private to general. He was physically fit for the field and he knew his craft."

Captain Edwin Wheeler considered Griffith an unforgettable character, "a rare breed of cat." Wheeler believed Griffith "had the stuff of greatness in him—a mix of raw courage, high intellectual ability, intense curiosity, an uncommon facility for communication...a sense of humor that never quit and a flair for spreading optimism. Too, he was tough as a boot."

Wheeler and Erskine had served with Griffith since before Tulagi. One of the newcomers at Camp Bailey, Second Lieutenant Frank Kemp, joined the battalion just before Griffith assumed command. He knew of Griffith's reputation—Nicaragua, China, the Commando School in England and Scotland, Tulagi, and the Matanikau—but he was awed by his professionalism. "I'll never forget the thoroughness of his preparation," said Kemp, "from fire teams up to battalion exercises and work on the APDs that we went through for New Georgia." Kemp remembers visiting Griffith's tent on occasions when the battalion commander was writing directly to Kelly Turner or Chester Nimitz proposing missions for his Raiders, "including one scheme for us to land from submarines in the Philippines and fight as guerrillas."[13]

Later in the spring Major Charles L. Banks came over from the 4th Raider Battalion to serve as Griffith's executive officer. He was twenty-eight, a New Jersey native, and a graduate of Virginia Military Institute, where he played football and wrestled. His father-in-law, Major General E. P. Moses, USMC, commanded the recruit depot at Parris Island. Banks began his career as an artillery officer, attended the Army Field Artillery School in Fort Sill, ran the aerial observation school at Quantico, and served half a year on Holland Smith's staff. The Dragon's Peninsula would provide a gruesome crucible for his first combat experience, but Banks would prove steady and unflappable. In the end, he would be the final commander of Edson's Raiders (and seven years later in Korea would receive the Navy Cross in command of the 1st Service Battalion in the Chosin Reservoir Campaign).[14]

Griffith assigned Major George Herring as Operations and Training Officer and Captain John Sweeney as Intelligence Officer. Proven young captains commanded the rifle companies: Tom Mullahey, "A"; Ed Wheeler, "B"; Black Jack Salmon, "C"; and Clay Boyd, "D". Griffith regarded each of his captains highly, but he especially admired Clay Boyd, whom he later described as "an inspirational leader...men would have gone anywhere with Clay."[15]

Company "E" was no more, a casualty of a Table of Organization revision in late 1942. The machine-gun platoons of the old weapons company went to the rifle companies on a permanent basis. Griffith re-established the demolitions platoon within headquarters company, a natural slot for Angus Goss, back with the Raiders after months of recovery from his Tulagi wounds.

Changes abounded. In addition to Goss and Boyd, other sick or wounded Raiders returned to full duty, including Johnnie Holladay, Joe Sweeda, and John Simonich. At the same time several colorful characters departed, including James "Horse Collar" Smith, whose injured right knee (from a spirited free-for-all during one of Edson's night maneuvers back in Quantico) deteriorated to the point of crippling him; the human dynamo, Pete Pettus; steadfast Captain Jake Irwin; diarist T. D. Smith; Japanese linguist "Tiger" Erskine; and two invaluable platoon commanders, Gunnery Sergeant Cliff McGlocklin and Gunnery Sergeant Joe Buntin. Captain Tony Antonelli's promotion warrant to major arrived accompanied by orders to Camp Pendleton to take command of the new Raider Training Battalion.

Griffith took pains to replace the loss of his combat leaders with men from the ranks who had demonstrated both courage and savvy under fire at Tulagi and Guadalcanal. To season the ranks of young, new lieutenants Griffith recommended battlefield commissions for Tom Pollard, Joe Cuetara, Tom Driscoll, Bob Laverty, Lee Minier, and Phil Oldham, among others. For those old-time senior NCOs who would not be caught dead wearing lieutenant's bars, Griffith nominated to the exalted rank of Marine Gunner the likes of Angus Goss, Clint Haines, John Kennedy, George McKain, and Joe Cafarella. Griffith promoted Frank Guidone and Tony "Big Stoop" Palonis to platoon sergeant (Guidone would

"The Singing Eight Balls" in New Caledonia in 1943. Left to right: George Ward, Rufus Rogers (partially hidden), Bill Vollack, Ed Dunn, Jinx Powers, Joe Kennedy, Eugene "Rebel" Fullerton, and Lee Minier.

receive a battlefield commission to lieutenant in the midst of the Dragon's Peninsula ordeal).

Several hard-nosed squad and section leaders received promotions to sergeant, including Erland Coombs, Johnnie Holladay, Fred Serral, John Simonich, Joe Sweeda, Jack Tracy, and Ben Howland, who had begun his working career in 1940 as a volunteer with the old Civilian Conservation Corps. Harold Smith, Ashley Large, John Carson, Sylvester Niedbalski, and the poetic Vince Cassidy, among others, advanced to corporal. Said Lee Minier of John Simonich, he is "a big bruiser....the toughest man I've ever seen, shot full of holes and still here." The "new look" 1st Raiders would return to the war with great strength in each leadership position, from squad leaders to the battalion commander.[16]

The Navy Department took this occasion to reassign the remaining battalion surgeon, Doctor Robert W. Skinner III, back to Camp Lejeune. The gruff Skinner had startled and amused a generation of sick Raiders with his standard reaction to their complaints, "Yeah, I've had that." At the last, Skinner forever endeared himself to Sam Griffith in New Caledonia by designing a Rube Goldberg–looking but deadly efficient rat trap, using an empty beer can, fencing wire, and the recoil spring from a Reising gun. Griffith slipped a parting bottle of scotch into Skinner's nefarious trap in gratitude.[17]

Good fortune brought two excellent replacement surgeons to the 1st Raider Battalion, Stuart C. Knox and James F. Regan. Doctor Knox, thirty-eight, with an undergraduate degree from Yale, had given up a lucrative medical practice in Los Angeles to volunteer for the navy. When he went home to tell his wife Rozella the news that he had been assigned to the Marines and would soon be shipping out for the South Pacific, she broke into tears, crying, "Oh, Stuart, what did you do to deserve *that?*" John Sweeney recalled Dr. Knox's enthusiastic arrival in early 1943, all smiles, ready for anything, but woefully unprepared in fieldcraft. Doctor Regan brought the same mixture of enthusiasm, compassion, and inexperience. The forthcoming New Georgia campaign would provide both physicians a daunting introduction to life in the Fleet Marine Force—especially the jungle trail from Rice Anchorage to Enogai and the staggering array of casualties and illnesses they would have to treat under unimaginably primitive conditions.[18]

The personnel pipelines to provide replacements for the Raider Battalions were operating full-bore, thanks to the Commandant's reluctant agreement to honor the requests of Kelly Turner and Chester Nimitz for top priority. "We'd send in a truck [to Nouméa] a couple of times a week and bring out 30–40 new candidates," recalled Sam Griffith. "We had a board...we screened everybody." Colorful newcomers accepted into the Raiders in New Caledonia included Lieutenant Fred Kemp, Private First Class Carl Fox, and Private First Class John F. Lartz. Kemp, another Yale graduate, had volunteered for the Raiders on arriving in New Caledonia, passed a screening interview by Jake Irwin, Frosty LaHue, and Parson Clarke, and earned assignment as a platoon commander in Dog Company. Kemp would excel in his profession. By the third week in July he would command Dog Company in the greatest fight of its life, approaching within three hundred yards of the final Japanese defenses at Bairoko.[19]

Carl Fox declined the opportunity to apply for the 1st Raiders in Quantico back in early 1942 and had since regretted his choice. Arriving in New Caledonia as a member of a dispirited replacement battalion, Fox quickly volunteered for reassignment to the nearby Raiders. Griffith's board liked what they saw, made him one of their own, and put him in Corporal Vince Cassidy's squad, in the platoon of another newcomer, Lieutenant Bill Christie, in Baker Company. Fox would earn his spurs in New Georgia, then, as a graphic artist later in life, would design the official maps of the Raiders' campaigns.[20]

The Marines formally trained Jack Lartz as a military photographer, then assigned him to the Raiders. Reporting aboard, however, Lartz discovered the battalion did not even rate a camera. Major Banks gave him the option of requesting reassignment, but Lartz liked what he had already seen of the spirit of the Raiders and decided to forego his military specialty. Banks made him a scout in HQ Company.[21]

In a top-level change that delighted the Raiders, Admiral William "Bull" Halsey replaced Admiral Ghormley as Commander South Pacific Force. None of the Raiders ever saw Ghormley, but they often saw and always admired the pugnacious Halsey. During January 1943, Halsey made the rounds, inspecting units, presenting awards, slapping men on their backs. He awarded the Silver Star Medal to four Raiders recuperating at St. Louis Mission, the radiomen who had fought as riflemen on The Ridge: Sergeant "Horse Collar" Smith, Corporal Morris Snyder, and Private First Classes Hubert Milanowski and David Taber. Smith said none of the four knew the Silver Star was actually a medal. "We thought we were getting tiny silver stars to put on our campaign ribbon," he said. Halsey took time to chat with each recipient, encouraging them to "get more of the 'yellow bastards.'"[22]

Sam Griffith had made it his first official duty as battalion commander to rename Camp St. Louis as Camp Bailey, commemorating Major Ken Bailey. Here Admiral Halsey officiated at a battalion ceremony and presented the Navy Cross to several Raiders, including riflemen Corporal John Mielke and Private First Class Robert Schneider, and communicators Sergeant Roy M. Gay and Captain William Stevenson for their heroics during the Battle of Edson's Ridge. Halsey closed the ceremony by pinning a Navy Cross to Sam Griffith's expansive chest for his steadfastness while wounded at "First" Matanikau.[23]

President Franklin Delano Roosevelt in a White House ceremony on 24 March 1943 presented the posthumous award of the Medal of Honor to Major Ken Bailey's widow, Elizabeth. The president singled out Bailey's "extraordinary courage and heroic conduct" in defending The Ridge during 12–13 September 1942. The citation ended, as posthumous ones always do, with the words "he gallantly gave up his life in the service of his country." At the same time a letter to the editor at *Time* magazine appeared in praise of Bailey. Army Staff Sergeant Vasco Walters was one of the members of the 164th Infantry whom Bailey voluntarily trained while recuperating from his first wounds in New Caledonia. Walters

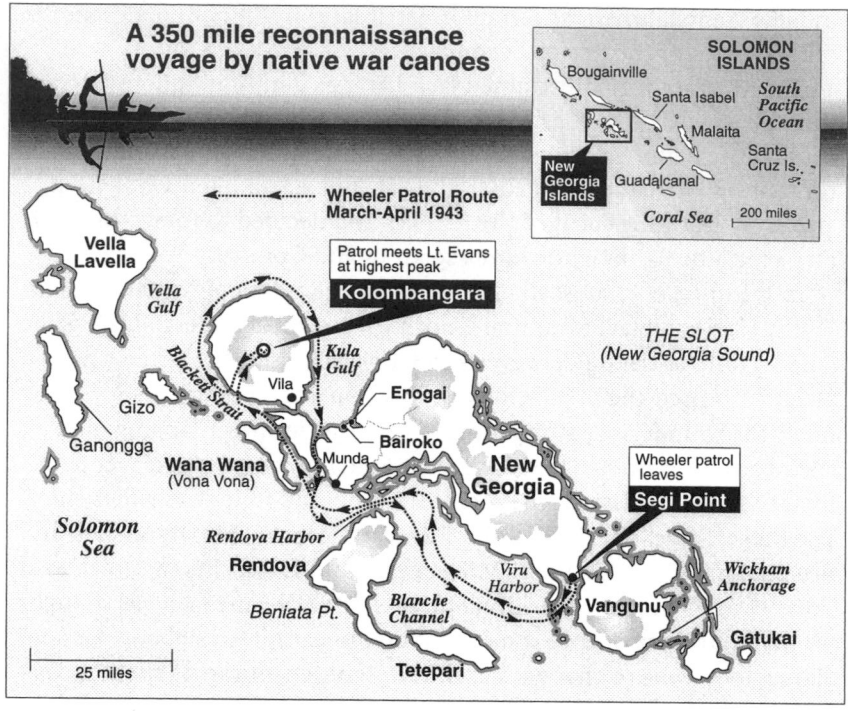

described Bailey as "a tall, well-built, blue-eyed man, the perfect picture of a fighting Marine." Walters and his soldiers expressed shock to learn of Bailey's death just before the 164th arrived on Guadalcanal. "As long as America continues to produce men like him," said Walters, "we'll lose very few battles and never a war." Here was testimony more valid than the citation itself.[24]

Sam Griffith lamented the loss of Ken Bailey so early in their relationship as CO and XO. He surely could have used Bailey's energy and charisma in reorganizing and remotivating the battalion for their next campaign. Now Griffith was truly The Old Man, surrounded by eager youngsters.

Sam Griffith was not the "inventor" of what would become the Marine Corps fire team, but he had long desired to increase the rifle squad's fire power and reduce the ungainly ten-man span of control faced by the existing squad leader. He had been interested in Evans Carlson's use of three-man "combat groups" since his visit to the 2d Battalion's training camp in early 1942. Shortly after taking command of the 1st Raiders Griffith flew from New Caledonia to revisit Carlson and determine how his small units had fared in combat. Impressed, Griffith returned to Camp Bailey and created his own version of subordinate maneuver elements within the rifle squad. He called them "fire groups," and they became legitimate forerunners to the fire team.

Griffith established three three-man teams in each squad, built around a BARman, a rifleman doubling as assistant BARman, and the fire team leader, armed with a rifle (replaced by the M1 carbine just before the New Georgia campaign). "The only change we made [to Carlson's concept] was to replace the Thompson or Reising with a rifle, so we had two rifles and a BAR per team," Griffith said. Rather than assign additional men to the pre-scribed ten-man squad for the traditional roles of assistant squad leader, scout, or grenadier, Griffith simply doubled the duties of certain incumbents. "The third fire team leader became the assistant squadleader," explained Richard W. Ackerman of Charlie Company.[25]

Griffith's concept worked extremely well in New Georgia's chaotic jungle-fighting, and although the Marine Corps would adopt *four*-man fire teams (still built around a BARman) in 1944, the decision to do so would reflect the success of the Raider Battalions in these experimental configurations. Meanwhile, many a Private First Class or buck private gained his first real leadership experience in life as a fire team leader, and both they and the Corps would benefit enormously.

The Raiders by this time had exchanged their beloved bolt-action Springfield '03s, the Marines' weapon of choice since the First World War, for the new Garand .30 caliber semi-automatic M1 rifles. Yet the Springfields did not disappear altogether. A manufacturing glitch rendered the M1's grenade launcher inoperable. Each rifle squad therefore armed one Marine with the Springfield, with its functional grenade launcher, as the designated rifle grenadier. Scoped Springfields remained in favor as sniper rifles.

Technology also rendered obsolete the Raiders' trademark burlap helmet cover. The Marines in 1943 adopted camouflaged utilities and a matching cloth camouflaged helmet cover. The Raiders and parachutists received the first shipments of these distinctive field uniforms and wore them with an arrogance that grated on the regular units (whose supply would begin just before Bougainville and Tarawa). The new "cammies" were uncomfortably hot and took forever to dry, but the tight-fitting camouflaged cover certainly beat the ragged, itchy burlap square.

Griffith intensified field training as the spring of '43 wore on. The old salts recognized the same characteristics in Griffith's training programs as they had experienced under Red Mike Edson: plenty of forced marches with full equipment, frequent night operations, and field firing of all weapons. The men also spent many days and nights in New Caledonia's surf, either experimenting with the new LCI landing craft or employing their standard tools of the amphibious trade, rubber boats and APD destroyer transports.

Marine Gunner Angus Goss put his new demolition platoon through its paces with ferocious rigor. Staff Sergeant Gerry West rejoined the platoon from his Baker Company sojourn, but Goss and West had their hands full teaching demolitions to a largely new crew. Goss illustrated his field instructions on Bangalore torpedoes and satchel charges with practical anecdotes about taking out the caves on Tulagi. West emphasized the need for the demolitionists to be equally proficient in small arms, describing his abrupt assignment as a patrol leader on The Ridge.

No Raider took his responsibilities more seriously than Angus Goss, the consummate professional, but his luck remained distressfully bad even during this "noncombat" interval in New Caledonia. On one occasion, as a tentmate cleaned his .45 service automatic pistol (always a hazardous operation), the weapon accidentally fired, wounding Goss

Kolombangara Patrol: Capt. Ed Wheeler is seated in the middle of the native war canoe.

painfully in the thigh. Later his green troops stuffed a training bunker with too much dynamite. A blast-blown rock struck Goss in the head. His helmet saved his life, but the blow exacerbated the chronic headaches he suffered from too-frequent exposure to noxious fumes from the explosives.[26]

Before leaving Tulagi in late August 1942 Merritt Edson had nominated Goss for the Medal of Honor for his extraordinary performance under fire. Nine months passed with no response. Sam Griffith wrote an impatient query up the chain. Definitive answers proved elusive—and disappointing. Despite positive endorsements from General Vandegrift and Admiral Nimitz, the Board of Awards in Washington voted in April to downgrade the nomination to the Navy Cross. Navy Secretary Frank Knox approved the board's action in May but for some reason did not sign the citation until October. Similarly, the British government's Conspicuous Gallantry Medal did not get forwarded out of Washington until 19 July. Goss would not see either award.[27]

## War Clouds in the Central Solomons

The Japanese had evacuated Guadalcanal in January, but heavily fortified Rabaul still lay unassailable at the northwest end of The Slot, protected by intermediate bastions at Kavieng, Bougainville, and the Shortlands. In December Allied pilots brought alarming news. The Japanese were building new airfields at Munda Point on New Georgia and near the mouth of the Vila River in southern Kolombangara. Once operational, these air strips would extend the range and double the time-on-station of Japanese Zeros deployed to escort Rabaul-based bombers. This would make life miserable on Guadalcanal and jeopardize any approach to Bougainville. The shoe would be on the other foot, however, if the United States could wrest Munda airfield from the Japanese. This would greatly enhance the campaign for Bougainville and place at great risk Rabaul itself.

Although the Joint Chiefs of Staff had planned the New Georgia assault on Munda since January 1943, "Operation Toenails" became a protracted and badly bungled campaign ("all balled up," Griffith called it). No amphibiously trained Marine divisions were available. Thirty thousand army troops would be required to seize New Georgia, plus the 9th Marine Defense Battalion and the newly formed 1st Marine Raider Regiment.

The Raider Regiment came into being on the Ides of March. Colonel

Harry B. Liversedge, who had led his 3d Raider Battalion ashore at
Pavuvu in the Russells the previous month, took command. "Harry the
Horse" was forty-eight years old, nearly as rugged and imposing in
appearance as he had been as a first lieutenant when he won the Bronze
Medal in shot put at the 1920 Olympics. During his twenty-six-year
career to date he had played service football, coached boxing teams, and
served overseas in France, Haiti, and China, and at sea on board the battleship *California*. Through no fault of his own he found himself a
colonel with no real combat experience—arriving a few weeks late for the
heavy fighting in France, an aide-de-camp in Haiti, no service in
Nicaragua, the bloodless landing at Pavuvu. His forthcoming experiences in New Georgia and Iwo Jima would convincingly adjust that
imbalance.[28]

New Georgia would prove more frustrating for Liversedge than commanding the 28th Marines at Iwo. Admiral Kelly Turner, far up the chain
of command and still obsessed with "playing soldier-sailor of the
Solomons" (in Merrill Twining's unblinking assessment), kept changing both the mission and the troop list for Liversedge's light regiment.
Harry the Horse would wind up commanding two Marine and two Army
battalions, the 1st and 4th Marine Raider Battalions, and the 3d Battalion, 145th Infantry and the 3d Battalion, 148th Infantry. Turmoil
plagued these assignments. Turner took away the 4th Raiders for a last-
minute mission and only reluctantly reassigned them just before the
assault on Bairoko, and the two Army battalions, well-trained but green
National Guard outfits from the 37th Division, joined Liversedge's regiment only days before embarkation.[29]

The hodgepodge regiment seemed destined at first to fulfill a reserve role,
then, given the designation of "The Northern Landing Group," assumed
the mission of landing at some site to be designated on New Georgia's long
coastline, then bushwhacking through the jungle to cut the main Japanese resupply line from Bairoko to Munda. Hence, the regiment could not
afford any field artillery attachments and only minimal logistical sustain-
ment—truly bare-bones medical, ammo, and ration supplies. The soldiers
had a few 81mm mortars, the Raiders just their 60s. Under the best of circumstances, Turner would be sending a light-weight, hit-and-run force
into interior New Georgia for multiple and sometimes conflicting missions against a force of unknown size and proficiency. Never did the
Raiders have a greater need for accurate combat intelligence.

The coastwatchers on New Georgia and Kolombangara represented
one key to intelligence gathering. At Liversedge's direction, Sam Griffith

Native meeting site on Japanese-occupied Kolombangara. Left to right: Sgt. George Lewis, native guide, interpreter, Lt. Philip Oldham (KIA, Enogai).

dispatched Captains Ed Wheeler and Clay Boyd on a series of hair-raising patrols to link with the coastwatchers and determine the lay of the land on the two islands.

Captain Wheeler, twenty-five, from Port Chester, New York, had quit NYU Law School to enlist in the Marines two years earlier. In later wars he would command the 2d Amphibian Tractor Battalion in Korea and the 3d Marines in Vietnam, in both cases utilizing the leadership skills he developed under great stress at Kolombangara and New Georgia in 1943.[30]

Wheeler picked newly commissioned Second Lieutenant Phil Oldham and Sergeant George B. Lewis to accompany him on an ambitious reconnaissance of little-known and far-distant Kolombangara. The party left New Caledonia on 22 March, flew to Guadalcanal for briefings, then rode a PBY Catalina flying boat to Segi Point, New Georgia. Native scouts in canoes met the aircraft as soon as it touched down; the three Marines debarked swiftly, and were paddled ashore and hustled into the jungle to meet Lieutenant Donald Kennedy, Royal Australian Navy, the

chief British official for New Georgia's observation and resistance under-
world. Kennedy provided a pair of native war canoes, crewed by strapping Solomon Islanders, for Wheeler's long voyage to Kolombangara.

An incredible 350-mile journey ensued. Traveling only at night, nav-
igating by the stars, dodging Japanese barge traffic that crisscrossed the
Kula Gulf from Vila to Bairoko, and covering up to fifty nautical miles
each night, the natives safely delivered the Marines to the island's west
coast. "Their hearing was miraculous and their bravery unyielding," said
Lewis admiringly. Wheeler made contact with Lieutenant Evans, the
Kolombangara coastwatcher, and from him learned three crucial points:
the Japanese had several thousand combat troops on the small moun-
tainous island; the enemy ran armored barge convoys from Vila to
Bairoko Harbor on New Georgia several nights a week; and Japanese
engineers had stopped or slowed construction on the potential airfield
near the river mouth due to unstable soil. Wheeler, Oldham, and Lewis
brought this report back via war canoe, Wheeler adding his first-hand
professional assessment that the island's few beaches and steep topog-
raphy would make an opposed landing prohibitively costly. The news
would lead Bull Halsey to bypass Kolombangara altogether. Absent a
decent airfield the place was not worth the cost.[31]

Sam Griffith assigned Captain Clay Boyd to reconnoiter New Georgia. He did so twice in the spring and early summer of 1943, and by the
time he was through he could claim he knew that forbidding island as
well as he did his native New Mexico. "There's something fascinating
about fighting in the bush," Boyd said. "It's like playing cops and robbers
when you were a kid." Boyd was a tough kid to begin with. His Dad had
been a Marine in World War I—taught boxing and and bayonet fighting
in Mare Island, went to France with an antiaircraft searchlight crew.
Young Clay became a proficient boxer himself, as well as a football and
polo player. During his four-year enlistment in the late 1930s he served
on the battleship *Pennsylvania* in First Lieutenant Ken Bailey's platoon.
Bailey encouraged him to apply for a commission, recommended him
highly to Merritt Edson, then asked for his assignment to Charlie Company. Boyd learned much about combat leadership from Ken Bailey.

Boyd picked Marine Gunner Charles E. James, a Nicaragua veteran,
plus veteran jungle fighters Frank Guidone and Robert Laverty to accompany him into New Georgia for the first patrol. The party flew in by PBY
on 22 February, linked up with native guides and disappeared for four
weeks. They scouted and mapped much of New Georgia and Rendova by
foot and canoe, awed by "weird forests of giant banyans where the under-

Lt. Frank Guidone, one of a number of gifted young NCOs who rose through the ranks of the 1st Raiders to receive meritorious field commissions.

growth was as thick as the beard on a man's face." One night Boyd and Guidone climbed a tree to watch Halsey's ships bombard Munda Field. It was a spectacular show, said Guidone, with aircraft and ammo dumps exploding and burning. "We could hear the explosions and watch the trails of the shells as they made their way to the target. I was really proud of the U.S. Navy that night."[32]

After a month exploring the trails, beaches, and rivers of New Georgia, Boyd successfully led his patrol to a designated rendezvous point to be airlifted to safety by PBY. Their report represented a windfall of intelligence and operational information for all three services planning the combined assault on Rendova (first) and Munda.

With Kelly Turner still struggling to develop a meaningful mission for the Raiders, Griffith ordered Boyd back to New Georgia for a second patrol in early June. Platoon Sergeant Guidone returned with Boyd, along with Gunnery Sergeants Joe Sciarra and Harry "Swede" Erickson, both wounded at Edson's Ridge. This time things went less smoothly. The Japanese knew something was up and patrolled the beaches and rivers aggressively. Boyd's group made a dangerous crossing of Viru Harbor in two war canoes during a full moon, then cut diagonally across the uncharted northwest head of the island to the Pundakona River below Rice Anchorage. Here the senior coastwatcher was Flight Lieutenant J. A. Corrigan, Royal Australian Air Force, superintendent of an intrepid bunch of Solomon Islanders ("Corry's Boys"). Together, they scouted the Japanese *rikusentai* base at Enogai Inlet, providing a potentially invaluable piece of intelligence about a quartet of 140mm coast defense guns (which the Task Force 31 planners chose to ignore). Over time malaria weakened Boyd and severely disabled Sciarra, but Boyd somehow traversed the island again to assess the landing potential in Roviana Lagoon on the opposite coast.

Guidone and Erickson spent the last week of June and the first few days of July with Corrigan preparing a suitable landing and assembly site on the west bank of the Pundakona River and supervising a crew of strong-armed natives clearing trails south-southeast to the Giza Giza River. Boyd had ordered three parallel trails cut, and progress was slow. "The jungle was thick to very thick," recalled Frank Guidone, and "at least twenty to thirty natives worked for a week with machetes or very large bolos." The trails would prove invaluable on the first leg of the regiment's march, but Corrigan ran out of time. The Raiders would have to bushwhack their way through the increasingly swampy ground between the Giza Giza and Tamakau Rivers, thence the more open but broken ridge country towards Triri on the upper Enogai Inlet.

Corrigan, Guidone, Erickson, and the scouts returned to the Pundakona to figure some way to mark the river mouth for the night landing. It was a thin reed. The Imperial Japanese Navy still dominated the Kula Gulf, and the amphibious task force would be terribly exposed. So would the Raider Regiment, struggling shoreward in Higgins boats and rubber rafts, seeking the river mouth against an ink black, overgrown, and inhospitable coastline.[33]

## Back to the Canal

Most Raiders sensed by May they were destined next for New Georgia. They were as ready as they had been for Tulagi. Griffith was confident. "By this time the battalion was in really good shape," he said.[34]

On 7 June the battalion departed from Nouméa on the transport *President Hayes* and returned to Guadalcanal for final staging. The Raiders found their old battleground changed. The main island now featured seven airstrips and a broad network of roads and bridges; Tulagi had become a major naval base.

The Raiders established a temporary camp near Tetere, the coastal plantation where General Kawaguchi had launched his fateful left hook into the jungle to attack Edson's Ridge. For awhile they shared the place with the 4th Raider Battalion, a first-rate outfit now commanded by Lieutenant Colonel Michael Currin, who had taken command in May when James Roosevelt yielded to jungle sickness. The 4th Raiders deployed first, temporarily detached from the 1st Raider Regiment to facilitate the main army assault. One group landed at Wickham Anchorage, Vangunu Island, on 30 June, the other at Viru Harbor, New Georgia, the following day. Harry the Horse Liversedge would not see the 4th Battalion again until it rejoined his regiment at Enogai on 18 July, somewhat the worse for wear from protracted fighting and patrolling in the south.

The 1st Raider Battalion had time for one last-minute preparation. Sam Griffith and his intelligence officer John Sweeney knew from Wheeler's report that the Japanese were using armored barges in the Kula Gulf. As lightly armed as the Raiders were, it would behoove them to know whether their .55 caliber Boys antitank rifles could penetrate the armor plating. One such barge had washed up on the beach near their old raid site at Tasimboko. Sweeney sent Corporal Ira Gilliland, section leader of the AT guns, with three other men in a rubber boat eastward to Tasimboko to inspect the derelict.

Gilliland found Barge #609 to be forty-five-feet long from stem to stern, diesel powered, equipped with a winch-operated, eight-foot-wide bow ramp, and protected by armor plate averaging three-sixteenths of an inch thick. These were the craft that had ferried one of Kawaguchi's battalions from the Shortlands to Guadalcanal the previous August. The Japanese on Kolombangara now armed such barges with 37mm cannon and heavy machine guns to protect their nighttime passage across the Kula Gulf to Bairoko against raiding U.S. Navy PT boats (including PT-109, commanded by Lieutenant John Fitzgerald Kennedy, USNR).

This was valuable information, but Gilliland took the time to tend to one case of personal unfinished business. After an hour's intense searching, his crew found and marked the remains of Private First Class Seraphine Buddy Smith, killed and lost at Tasimboko on 8 September 1942. Graves registration troops would recover Smith's body for burial in the division cemetery. One more missing Raider had come home.[35]

## Notes

1. Battalion Order, 20 January 1943, signed by Lt. Col. Samuel B. Griffith, commanding.
2. T. D. Smith Diary, 18 October 1942, 11; Griffith Oral Memoir, MCOHC, MCHC, 123.
3. Elton Whisenhunt to Thomas Mullahey, 18 July 1992; Hugh C. Davis biographic sketch from *The Dope Sheet,* May 1992, 3; Cdr. Robert W. Skinner III to John Sweeney, 11 July 1991.
4. Fred A. Serral poem, January 1943, copy provided author, 24 January 1999.
5. COMAMPHFORSOPAC message to 1st Marine Raider Battalion, 24 November 1942, copy in author's possession.
6. Poppell Diary, November–December 1942, 27–28. The inclusive dates of the Wellington liberty vary significantly from account to account and even within the semi-official chronologies. Adm. Turner's "warning message" of 24 November and Lt. Col. Griffith's assumption of command on 14 January 1943 back in New Caledonia (as well as Cpl. Minier's 12 January 1943 letter) provide reasonable evidence of start and return dates.
7. Lee Minier to home, 12 January 1943, in Minier, "Raider," 153; "The Singing Eight Balls," *The Dope Sheet,* October 1987, 1, 12. The Eight Balls recorded on 9 May 1943 in New Caledonia, and the phonograph record is maintained at the Library of Congress under the title "Songs of the 1st Marine Raider Battalion." Although surely more than eight Raiders sang with the group from time to time, the men who made the tape are introduced thereon as Bill Vollack, Rufus Rogers, Lee Minier, George Ward, Joseph "Red" Kennedy, Tom "Jinx" Powers, Ed Dunn, and Eugene "Rebel" Fullerton. In the late 1950s folksinger Oscar Brand published a phonograph album of military drinking songs which included the cleaned-up versions of "Bless 'em All" and "Let's Remember Pua Pua." The originals, however, are priceless, a time capsule.
8. For more information on the history of the other Marine Raider battalions and regiments, see Jon T. Hoffman, *From Makin to Bougainville: Marine Raiders in the Pacific War* (Washington, D.C.: HQMC, 1995); Peatross, *Bless 'em All;* Charles L. Updegraph, Jr., *U.S. Marine Corps Special Units of World War II* (Washington, D.C.: HQMC, 1977); or Martin J. Sexton, *The Marine Raiders' Historical Handbook* (Richmond: The American Historical Foundation, 1983). A visit to the Raiders' Museum in Richmond, Virginia, is also highly recommended.
9. Donald M. Goldstein and Katherine V. Dillon, *Fading Victory: The Diary of Admiral Matome Ugaki, 1941–45* (Pittsburgh: The University of Pittsburgh Press, 1991), 185.
10. Theodore Roscoe, *United States Submarine Operations in World War II* (Annapolis: Naval Institute Press, 1949), 13, 193; special thanks to Capt. William T. Alexander, USNR (Ret.), a submariner; Silverstone, *U.S. Warships of World War II,* 186.

11. CINCPAC 01030 9 September 1942 to COMINCH, "Additional Marine Raider Battalions"; Holcomb memo to Admiral King, same subject, 2 September 1942. Both documents from Box 1806, Record Group 127, WNRC.

12. Commander Amphibious Force, South Pacific to Commander South Pacific Force, "Employment of the Raider Battalions in the Amphibious Force, South Pacific," 29 August 1942; with 1st Endorsement by Commander South Pacific Force, 6 September 1942, 2d Endorsement by CINCPACFLT, 24 September 1942, and special endorsement by the Commandant of the Marine Corps, 3 October 1942, all from Box 1806, RG 127, WNRC.

13. Recollections of Lt. Col. Griffith by John "Tiger" Erskine, Edwin Wheeler, and Frank Kemp appeared in *The Dope Sheet,* November 1983, 2,8, and January 1984, 5.

14. Tech. Sgt. Frank J. McDevitt (a combat correspondent from 1st Marine Amphibious Corps attached for the New Georgia campaign), news release, 26 June 1943, Reference Section, MCHC; official biography, Brig. Gen. Charles L. Banks, USMC (Ret), Reference Section, MCHC.

15. Command billets as reflected in September 1943 Muster Roll; Griffith assessment of Clay Boyd from Griffith to Frank Kemp, quoted *The Dope Sheet,* November 1983, 2.

16. Lee N. Minier to home, 15 April 1943, in Minier, "Raider," 160.

17. Dr. Skinner to John Sweeney, 11 July 1991.

18. John Sweeney, "In Memoriam: Stuart C. Knox," *The Dope Sheet,* September 1985.

19. Griffith Oral Memoir, MCOHC, MCHC, 128; Frank A. Kemp to Jon Hoffman, 24 October 1994.

20. Carl Fox to author, 22 February 1999.

21. John F. Lartz, Jr., interview with author, 3 March 1999. Lartz would excel in the capacity, and, with a borrowed reflex camera, contribute the few good photographs to emerge from the drippy gloom of the Dragon's Peninsula.

22. James Smith to author, 9 February 1999.

23. Battalion Order 20 January 1943 renaming Camp St. Louis in honor of Maj. Kenneth Bailey; Navy Cross citations for individuals named; "Titusville Marine Receiving Navy Cross on Pacific Island," *The Titusville* (Pennsylvania) *Herald,* 24 March 1943, which republished a photograph from an undated issue of *Life* magazine of Admiral Halsey pinning the award to then-Capt. William D. Stevenson, copy provided by Mr. Robert Aquilina, Reference Section, MCHC.

24. Bailey biographical release, September 1949; S. Sgt. Vasco Walters, "A Fighting Marine," Letters Section, *Time,* n.d., both provided courtesy Mr. Robert Aquilina, Reference Section, MCHC.

25. The Marine fire team had many fathers. For a basic summary, see Lee M. Holmes, "Birth of the Fire Team," *Marine Corps Gazette,* November 1952, 16–23, as well as the letters to the editor the article incurred, including Owen

T. Stebbins and John J. Dolan, February 1953, 1, and especially Col. Samuel B. Griffith, "Fire Teams—Big Picture," March 1953, 1; Robert Ackerman to John Sweeney, 29 June 1992.

26. James Smith, "Angus R. Goss, A Marines' Marine," unpublished manuscript, n.d.

27. Package of correspondence on Medal of Honor nominations for Angus Goss and PFC Edward Ahrens from CO, 1st Marine Raider Battalion on 26 August 1942, 6 May 1943, and 7 September 1943, with endorsements thereunto; Secretary of the Navy Navy Cross citation, Angus R. Goss, 8 October 1943; review chain card, Goss Medal of Honor nomination, all contained in RG 127, Box 820, WNRC. A review board at Halsey's COMSOPAC headquarters in March 1943 downgraded Ahrens' Medal of Honor nomination to the posthumous Navy Cross. Ahrens was the small rifleman in A Company whose stabbed and slashed body Lew Walt found surrounded by three dead Japanese the morning after the counterattack at Tulagi.

28. Griffith Oral Memoir, MCOHC, MCHC, 131; Liversedge Biography, Reference Section, MCHC. "Harry the Horse" would receive two Navy Crosses in the Pacific War: one for the Dragon's Peninsula in 1943, the other for Iwo Jima, 1945. He died as a brigadier general on active duty in 1951.

29. Twining, *No Bended Knee,* 185.

30. Maj. Gen. Edwin B. Wheeler biographical summary, Reference Section, MCHC. Wheeler also commanded the 1st Battalion, 5th Marines in Korea, The Basic School, and the 2d Marine Division. He retired in 1972 and died in 1985.

31. George B. Lewis, "A 350-Mile Reconnaissance by Native War Canoes," *The Raider Patch,* May 1993.

32. Clay Boyd biographical information provided by Mr. Robert Aquilina, Reference Section, MCHC; Frank X. Tolbert, "Advance Man," *Leatherneck,* March 1945; Frank Guidone, "New Georgia Reconnaissance Patrol," *The Dope Sheet,* January 1981, 5, 8; Guidone to author, 15 February 1999.

33. Tolbert, "Advance Man"; Guidone to author, 15 February 1999; Guidone to Samuel B. Griffith, 30 June 1944, Box 11, File 1, Griffith Papers, MCHC.

34. Griffith Oral Memoir, MCOHC, MCHC, 128.

35. Ira C. Gilliland, "Barge Recon," in R.G. Rosenquist, Martin J. Sexton, Robert A. Buerlein, eds., *Our Kind of War* (Richmond: The American Historical Foundation, 1990), 86. Gilliland reported finding both of the battalion's fatalities at Tasimboko, Seraphine Smith and William Carney. Yet Smith was the only case at Tasimboko reported as MIA by the September Muster Roll, later reclassified as KIA in the addendum per a death certificate being filed, presumably the result of Gilliland's discovery. The essential point here is that Gilliland's commendable efforts ended the mystery of the last MIAs at Tasimboko. Rest in peace.

# 10

## The Dragon's Peninsula, New Georgia, July–August 1943

*There comes a time in every combat unit's experience when it no longer brags about the extent of its losses.*

General Merrill B. Twining, USMC (Ret.)[1]

THE DRAGON'S PENINSULA is a rugged patchwork of coral ridges, intervening swamps, and alternating rain forest and thick jungle along the northwestern coast of New Georgia. The area forms a trapezoid between Enogai Inlet and its two rivers on one side and Bairoko Harbor and its inland river on the other. The trapezoid's top, which features the irregular coastline and Leland Lagoon, and the two sides measure roughly 3,000 yards each. The bottom, which approximates the native scout trail, measures about 6,000 yards across. Within this small, overgrown area—barely more than four square miles—the 1st Marine Raider Battalion would fight its final two battles, one a shining victory, the other a galling defeat.

"This piece of jungle real estate could not have been more appropriately named," wrote Sam Griffith shortly after the campaign, "for it required no particular effort of the imagination to conjure up from the dim recesses of its rain forest and the muck of its interminable swamps the shapes of the creatures the natives believed made the place their home." The natives who voluntarily scouted for Flight Lieutenant Corrigan—"Corry's Boys"—despised the jungle nearly as much as the Raiders, for, as Griffith learned, "they were not bush people but canoe people whose homes before the coming of the Japanese had been along the shores of coral-encrusted lagoons." Corry's Boys, Griffith noted, helped carry in the Raiders' scant supplies, then, at the end, helped pack

255

out the sick and the wounded "through swamps calf deep, up slopes to the tops of razor-backed ridges." Liversedge spoke more emphatically about the scouts' assistance, telling Oscar Peatross at the end of the campaign, "if it wasn't for the natives and the coastwatchers we wouldn't have got off New Georgia alive!"[2]

The Raiders fought for the Dragon's Peninsula because Admiral Kelly Turner believed this to be the best employment of their talents. Turner's main effort to seize Munda Airfield would never succeed as long as the Japanese could resupply and reinforce the defending garrison through the uncontested "back door," the long route that led from Rabaul to Kolombangara by destroyers, thence by barge to Bairoko and down the jungle trail to the besieged airstrip. Employing the Raider Regiment to cut this lifeline, seize Bairoko and its outguard, Enogai, seemed logical. What worried Turner was how to insert the regiment into the Dragon's Peninsula to begin with—and how to maintain control and logistic support.

Control of the seas around the Central Solomons was still up for grabs. This meant Turner's amphibious force had to hasten every landing—"get the hell in, get the hell out"—before the inevitable Japanese air and naval counterattacks came speeding down "The Slot."

Turner first thought to land the Raider regiment across the coral-infested Roviana Lagoon northeast of Munda Point, expecting them then to march through the jungle to attack Bairoko and Enogai from the south. Captain Clay Boyd reconnoitered the "beach" and the inland terrain, deemed them prohibitive, and came back to Guadalcanal to tell Turner so in person. Rice Anchorage, Boyd reported, was a better landing place and closer to the objectives, despite the rugged terrain inland. By using natives to cut trails in advance, Boyd thought the landing force could seize Enogai within three days.

Turner agreed to land the regiment at Rice, but he insisted on a night landing. The Kula Gulf, much closer to Rabaul than Roviana Lagoon and also subject to coast defense guns near Bairoko and on Kolombangara, was no place for thin-skinned amphibious ships in daylight.

Turner was still asking a lot of the 1st Raider Regiment with its three light battalions, one highly experienced, the other two eager but green. Assumptions about enemy order of battle and weaponry at Enogai and Bairoko proved severely optimistic. Communications would be difficult as well. If the regiment stepped in a bear-trap, or sustained an inordinate amount of casualties, Liversedge would have to rely on radio systems of questionable quality to ask for help. Turner promised to provide a high-powered, long-range navy radio for the expedition. Liversedge acquiesced.

# First Raiders in New Georgia

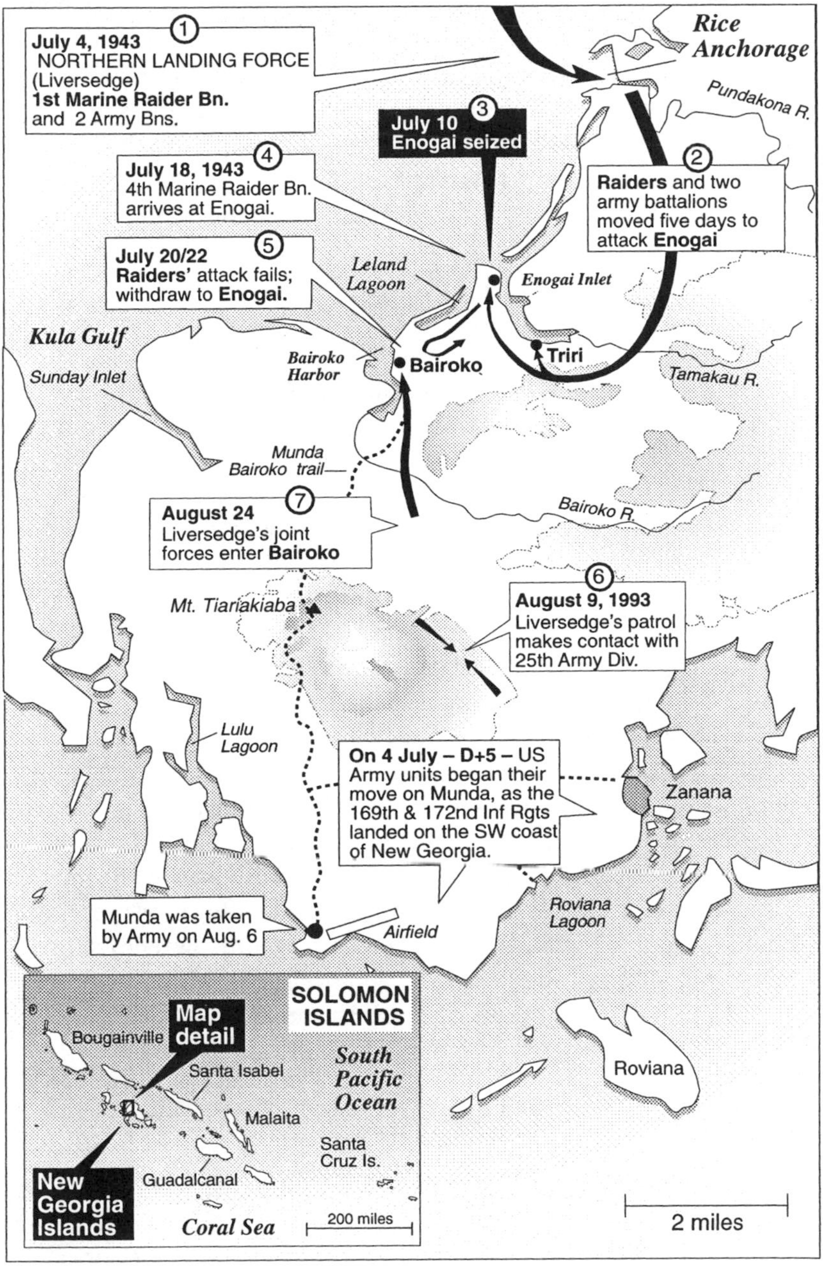

**① July 4, 1943**
NORTHERN LANDING FORCE
(Liversedge)
**1st Marine Raider Bn.**
and 2 Army Bns.

*Rice Anchorage*

*Pundakona R.*

**③ July 10**
**Enogai seized**

**② Raiders** and two army battalions moved five days to attack **Enogai**

**④ July 18, 1943**
4th Marine Raider Bn. arrives at Enogai.

**⑤ July 20/22**
**Raiders'** attack fails; withdraw to **Enogai.**

*Leland Lagoon*

*Enogai Inlet*

*Kula Gulf*

*Sunday Inlet*

*Bairoko Harbor*

● **Bairoko**

**Triri**

*Tamakau R.*

**⑦ August 24**
Liversedge's joint forces enter **Bairoko**

*Munda Bairoko trail*

*Bairoko R.*

*Mt. Tiariakiaba*

**⑥ August 9, 1993**
Liversedge's patrol makes contact with 25th Army Div.

*Lulu Lagoon*

**On 4 July – D+5 – US** Army units began their move on Munda, as the 169th & 172nd Inf Rgts landed on the SW coast of New Georgia.

*Zanana*

*Roviana Lagoon*

Munda was taken by Army on Aug. 6

*Airfield*

## SOLOMON ISLANDS

**Map detail**

Bougainville

Santa Isabel

Malaita

*South Pacific Ocean*

**New Georgia Islands**

Guadalcanal

*Coral Sea*

Santa Cruz Is.

Roviana

200 miles

2 miles

Merritt Edson, with his much greater experience in jungle expeditions, probably would have demanded guaranteed delivery plus backup systems.

Liversedge and Griffith proved themselves to be strong commanders, but the Raiders sorely missed Red Mike Edson's unique skills on this mission. The night landing would be dangerous. Dispatching 2,200 men in small craft towards an indistinct river mouth on a moonless night had the makings of a disaster. And there was one other detail about the Northern Landing Group's assumptions that likely would have caught Edson's careful eye. All of Clay Boyd's reconnaissance work—including his time/distance calculations—had been performed during June. Now it was July, the onset of the rainy season in New Georgia. Based on Boyd's report and his preliminary trail-clearing, Liversedge assumed he could seize Enogai in three days, and he would launch his advance with exactly that many days' rations. But July's heavy rains would convert the knee-deep rivers into torrents and transform the unremarkable swamps on either side of the Tamakau into some of the worst terrain any Marine ever tried to negotiate.

Lacking Edson's Coco River perspective, Liversedge would have to learn his own lessons. Meanwhile, he issued mission orders to his battalion commanders. The 3d Battalion, 148th Infantry under Lieutenant Colonel Delbert "Dutch" Schultz would execute the Bairoko-Munda trail roadblock while the 3d Battalion, 145th Infantry under Lieutenant Colonel George Freer would provide the reserve force and protect the landing site at Rice Anchorage. Sam Griffith's 1st Raiders would tackle the main objectives: land at Rice, "advance southeast, seize and destroy enemy positions at Enogai Inlet, Dragons Peninsula, and Bairoko Harbor, and establish an all around defense" against a counterlanding.

In the Raider Battalion operation order Griffith warned his men to look for natives in canoes in the vicinity of the landing beach serving as guides ("do not fire at any of these"). Captain John Sweeney's intelligence annex directed the Raiders to remove the unit's name from all clothing and equipment prior to embarkation, adding as a thoughtful concession, "The Battalion insignia (the skull) may be worn."[3]

## Off the Deep End

Operation Toenails got off to a ragged start at Rendova Island at the end of June. The army troops landed successfully against scattered opposition, but Admiral Turner lost his flagship, the transport *McCawley*—the Raiders' long-time friend—to a combination of Japanese aerial torpedoes

Raider patrol fords a river in the Dragon's Peninsula of western New Georgia. Note the Boys anti-tank rifle carried by the Marine at left.

and friendly fire. The advance on Munda airfield progressed by fits and starts. New Georgia's brooding jungles exacted a cruel toll on the green troops of the 43d Infantry Division. A thousand men had to be evacuated with "war neuroses" during the first three weeks of the assault.[4]

The 1st Marine Raider Battalion embarked from Guadalcanal on board three APDs and a conventional destroyer on the Fourth of July, Independence Day, 1943. As soon as Liversedge reported his Northern Landing Group fully loaded, the ships took off with their cruiser and destroyer escorts at twenty-three knots towards New Georgia. Tropical darkness fell abruptly. The usual good-natured ribbing between the Raiders and the sailors seemed subdued. The task force would be very much in harm's way once it rounded Blackett Strait and entered the Kula Gulf.

The desire of both antagonists to reinforce their forces engaged in the struggle for Munda Point made the Kula Gulf particularly dangerous. Violent meeting engagements occurred on three nights during 5–13 July. The first of these erupted as the Northern Landing Group sped into the Gulf.

Rear Admiral Walden L. Ainsworth's bombardment group of three light cruisers and nine destroyers did not "go gentle" into the Gulf. The gunships blazed away as soon as they entered Blackett Strait, first at the Japanese shore batteries near Vila on the coast of Kolombangara, then at the barge harbor at Bairoko. The uproar worried Captain Clay Boyd and Gunnery Sergeant Frank Guidone and their crew of native scouts waiting to mark the mouth of the Pundakona River. It was a spooky night anyway, dark as hell, with rain squalls billowing overhead and the Japanese 140mm coast defense guns at Enogai blasting away at the sudden naval activity taking place offshore. Then a enemy floatplane swooped over and dropped a string of flares.

At no other time during its many months of combat was the entire 1st Raider Battalion so critically exposed and vulnerable. The flares illuminated the cluster of small transports, each crammed with members of the Northern Landing Group and slowed to bare steerageway as their captains searched for the elusive anchorage. The Enogai guns zeroed in (those Clay Boyd had reported and staff officers pooh-poohed). Across the Gulf a task force of four Japanese destroyers saw the American ships and began to withdraw, pausing to gauge the distance for their Long Lance torpedoes, with their eleven-mile range and thousand-pound warheads.

Closer aboard, the coastal submarine *RO-108* discovered the cluster of ships, aimed at center of mass, and fired a conventional torpedo. The overloaded destroyer transports averted a catastrophic explosion by the narrowest of margins. The torpedo missed the transports and struck the escorting destroyer *Strong* about 0049. Barely a half hour later she sank "like a punctured beer can," taking forty-seven sailors down with her.[5]

The Raiders wasted no time in debarking. Their months of practicing night landings from small transports now paid off. The men manned the rails, their shoulders hunched against the 140mm shells shrieking overhead, then, at the signal, swarmed over the gunwales and into their rubber boats like teams of water spiders. "We scrambled into our rubber boat and paddle to the Higgins boat and grab a towline," said Sergeant Jack Tracy. "We are being towed to our release point."[6]

The Japanese gun crews at Enogai would never again have such lucrative targets within range. They fired steadily throughout the night but consistently overshot. The small armada of transports sustained only a single hit—a shell struck the mast of one APD—and no casualties. Yet the very act of being shelled during their ship-to-shore movement proved disconcerting to the stealth-loving Raiders. "Shells are landing all around us, and we can see the shore batteries from Bairoko [actually Enogai] are trying to hit our troops in the landing at Rice Anchorage," recorded Popeye Poppell.[7]

Captain Boyd's advance team of Guidone, Corrigan, and Erickson signaled with flashlights for several hours to mark both sides of the seventy-yard mouth of the Pundakona River. Worried whether the coxswains could detect their faint signals, Boyd put some men with flashlights off-shore in native canoes to extend the range. Boyd also worried intensely whether the sandbar offshore from the river mouth would prove too shallow for both the Higgins boats and the rubber rafts. The Raiders in the first wave of landing craft also worried as they approached the dark shore. "All eyes were straining for the lights," said Tracy. "For awhile we had only one light, finally the second gave us our objective. Foliage appeared; the navy coxswain gave the word to drop the [tow] lines. We began paddling..."[8]

All amphibious landings are chaotic. Night landings are doubly so. To this mix of confusion and disorientation, one must add for the New Georgia landing the absence of a beach—the boats straggled several hundred yards up the Pundakona to a series of rough-cut clearings in the mangrove thickets—plus the distracting interference of high explosive 140mm shells impacting in the neighborhood and the torrential rainfall. By unfortunate coincidence, the advent of New Georgia's rainy season coincided with H-Hour that night.

Guidone, Erickson, and the other members of the beacon team swiftly displaced to the landing sites along the west bank to help the men ashore. "Some of the troops debarked from boats with all their gear into water up to their necks," recalled Frank Guidone. "They had to be grabbed and pulled up to the beach. It was a nightmare for an hour and a half." Sergeant Poppell's rubber boat sank halfway to the coast, "but we are picked up by a Higgins and we reach shore amidst the swamp, jungles, rain and pitch black darkness." Corrigan's native scouts showed the Marines how to mark the backs of their packs with phosphorescent bark to maintain contact in the near total blackness. "Someone placed fox-fire bark on the pack," said Sergeant Tracy. "We were in waist-deep water, slipping, falling, keeping an eye on the luminous bark."[9]

Rice Anchorage was Carl Fox's first combat landing. The BARman kept one eye on his veteran squad leader, Vince Cassidy, the other on the nearly indiscernible shoreline. "We could hear shells going over our heads," said Fox, agitated to realize "the element of surprise had been lost." The landing was a traffic jam of boats trying to get in and back out, men shouting and milling about. "The rain was heavy and the mud severe. We were in complete darkness, but by using a twig that shone at night you could see and follow the fellow in front of you in the pitch darkness."[10]

Officers of the 1st Raider Battalion assemble on the site of one of the four Japanese coast defense guns captured in the battle for Enogai on 10 July 1943. Maj. Charles "Gus" Banks, battalion executive officer, stands in the center in a white t-shirt; to his immediate left is Lt. Col. Sam Griffith, commanding.

Surprisingly, in view of the darkness, torrential rain, and intermittent enemy shelling, the Northern Landing Group's landing at Rice Anchorage was the most successful American night landing of the Pacific War. One man drowned, but two thousand men reached shore intact before sunrise. The inevitable glitches occurred. Three boats of 3/148's soldiers missed the river mouth, landed several miles north, and had to work back to the Pundakona the next day. Two Higgins boats of Raiders became disoriented and remained afloat all night—becoming dangerously exposed to the Enogai guns the next morning—before Private First Class Alvard G. Careaga made it ashore to bushwhack across country ("in swamps up to my armpits") to notify Sam Griffith of their plight. Griffith for his part thought the landing to be "more successful than the most optimistic of us had expected."[11]

But the Northern Landing Group had run out of time. At 0559 the morning of the 6th, Harry Liversedge authorized the anxious transports to return to safe waters by speaking the prearranged radio code signal "*scram.*" Scram they did, just before daylight, barely beating the first Imperial Navy airplanes racing down The Slot towards the Kula Gulf. Roughly ten percent of the landing force supplies remained aboard the transports—typical for a hasty nighttime offload—but these odd-lots included one exceedingly critical item, the special long range radio provided at the last minute by Admiral Turner and loaded as a catch-as-catch-can expedient on a ship separate from its assigned operators. This oversight would first hinder, then cripple the Northern Landing Group.

Liversedge cajoled his soaked and sleepy troops into three columns to follow the parallel trails blazed by Corry's Boys, and by 0700 the regiment began its approach to the Dragon's Peninsula. The 1st Raiders' D Company, finally reunited with its malarial commander Clay Boyd, took the lead.

The fresh trails proved a godsend, but the heavy rain made for exceptionally rough going. "Terrain extremely difficult," the battalion diary reported for 5 July, adding, "Humidity high, men heavily loaded." Sam Griffith described the jungle's "Turkish-bath humidity while we alternately stumbled up one side of a hill and slipped and slid down the other."[12]

Thus began a remarkable three-day jungle odyssey by which the 1st Marine Raider Regiment advanced with extreme difficulty through eight miles of jungle to surprise Japanese forces along the west bank of the Enogai Inlet. In terms of human misery, the trek rivaled that of Major L. W. T. Waller's expedition across Samar in 1901–1902, and, on a much smaller scale, the march of the Japanese Army though the jungle to surprise Singapore from the rear.

"It was the wettest march we ever made," said Frank Guidone. "The troops slid, fell, picked themselves up, and kept going." Popeye Poppell shouldered his backpack radio with Able Company and followed the left-hand trace. "We are climbing hills one minute and down in the muck and mire up to our knees the next," he later recorded. "The rain is pouring down..." By 1600 the head of the regimental columns reached the Giza Giza River, dangerously swollen by rain. "Distance covered: eight miles," the 1st Raider Battalion diary clerk, Private First Class William P. Kottemann, recorded at the direction of Sam Griffith. In truth, the force had covered less than four miles "as the crow flies." Yet when Griffith tried to explain this straight-line metaphor, one of the Raiders threw it right back at him, "That may be, Colonel, but we ain't crows!"[13]

Things got worse the second day. The regiment advanced less than a mile, slowed to a crawl by hazardous crossings of the Giza Giza and Tamakau Rivers. At the first crossing Liversedge detached the 3d Battalion, 148th Infantry to proceed to the southwest to assume its assigned blocking position on the Munda-Bairoko Trail. This reduced some of the congestion along the main track, but nothing mitigated the difficulties of crossing the Tamakau, a significant obstacle.

The heavy rains had turned the river into a raging, nine-foot-deep torrent. Attempts to ferry equipment across by poncho rafts failed. Every piece of gear—and every man—had to cross the wild river over a single downed tree, massive, moss-covered, and slick. Boyd's men rigged their ever-useful toggle ropes together for a hand line. This helped, but it was not enough to protect all thirteen hundred men who edged across the log-bridge during the ensuing four and half hours. Eleven men slipped off into the cataract and would have drowned without the heroics of Lieutenant Frank Kemp, sergeants John Simonich and James F. Walsh, and native scout Eddie Wickham who repeatedly dove into the river to drag them to safety. "When the log got covered with mud plus the rain it was really slippery," recalled Frank Kemp. "I remember pulling out PFC Arnold Nadeau, packing a huge load of 60mm mortar shells, who went down like a rock when he fell off. I was lucky to grab him and get him back to the bank."[14]

At 1100 Griffith radioed Liversedge from the crossing: "Tamakau high. We are crossing on log....Difficult and slow progress....Lieutenant Kemp has already saved two men from drowning....Native scouts report no Nips, repeat, no Nips." This last point was fortuitous. Had the Japanese known of the American advance through this impassable swamp they could have put a cork in the bottle at the Tamakau. "If the Japanese had established a defense along that river we would still be there," said Frank Guidone.[15]

Conditions were no better on the far side of the Tamakau. The regiment established a tactical bivouac for the night in swampy ground, still two miles east of the Enogai Inlet. Recalled Dr. James Regan, "We slept on a muddy island in a swamp that seemed endless." Not every Raider found Dr. Regan's island. Recorded Private First Class Kottemann in the Battalion Diary for 6 July: "Swamp from calf-deep to waist deep...Intermittent rains." Sergeant Jack Tracy said, "I found a space in knee-deep water, wrapped my cartridge belt around a mangrove root and tried to relax." Popeye Poppell recorded miserably, "My feet have now turned purple from the water in my boots." The men realized their rations and water would run out well before they reached the objective.[16]

## Contact

To this point the Japanese in the neighborhood seemed oblivious of the Northern Landing Group's approach. On the morning of the 7th, Lieutenant Tom Pollard's platoon cleared the swamp, crossed the lower end of Enogai Inlet, entered the Dragon's Peninsula, and seized the small village of Marenusa. There just before noon Pollard's men first encountered the Japanese—a small patrol making charcoal from fallen logs. Private Clyde "Beaver" Wilson opened fire with his BAR, killing two, wounding several and scattering the remainder. Lieutenant Frank Kemp stared at the bodies—the first dead men he had ever seen. The regimental language officer arrived to identify the uniform markings of the slain. Instead of the expected Imperial Army chrysanthemum he found the naval anchor—*rikusentai* again. Documents on their bodies specified the 6th Kure Special Naval Landing Force.[17]

It would be the Raiders' fate to fight most of their battles (Tasimboko was the exception) against first-rate Japanese troops. They had taken the measure of the 3d Kure at Tulagi but none of the veterans ever depreciated the ferocity of these naval infantrymen.

Commander Saburo Okumura led the 6th Kure Special Naval Landing Force, a regimental-sized unit of nearly 2,000 sailors. The force had been augmented by special antiaircraft artillery units, most of which Okumura deployed in the southeast to protect Munda Airfield. The balance of his command, roughly a thousand men, remained around Bairoko and Enogai. Their weapons included the four 140mm coast defense guns positioned at Enogai (manned by the special Takemura Heavy Artillery Detachment), four 90mm mortars, thirteen Type 93 13.2mm heavy machine guns, and dozens of Nambu machine guns, both heavy and light.

When the Japanese island commander learned that the Northern Landing Group had somehow crossed the impassable terrain to the northeast and was threatening the Bairoko and Enogai facilities, he reinforced Okumura's sailors with Imperial Army units, beginning with the 2d Battalion, 13th Infantry commanded by Major Takeo Ohashi. The entire 13th Infantry crossed Kula Gulf from Kolombangara to Bairoko by barge during 9–12 July, the main body passing through Bairoko, eluding Lieutenant Colonel Schultz's trailblock, and reinforcing Munda in a matter of days. Later, after the fall of Enogai, the island commander would provide even more troops from Kolombangara to reinforce Bairoko, including the 2d Battalion, 45th Infantry and the 8th Battery of the 6th Field Artillery Regiment. These troops, clustered around Bairoko Harbor, would suffer from intermittent bombing by Allied aircraft, but they would still outnumber the emaciated 1st Marine Raider Regiment in its final attack on 20 July.[18]

Commander Okumura made one mistake early in this campaign. The intensity of Admiral Ainsworth's preemptive naval bombardment during the night of 4–5 July led the Japanese commander at Bairoko to assume his harbor was the target of the assault landing. He may have further concluded that the well-sited Enogai guns had forced the landing armada northward, requiring an alternate landing at Rice Anchorage, which, lying beyond the barrier of interminable swamps and rivers, posed no threat. A veteran of night landings himself, Okumura may have assumed that only a five-hundred-man detachment could have been offloaded at Rice in the time available, and so he reported. He was in all likelihood astounded to learn that the Americans had put four times that number ashore despite the darkness, rain, and interdictive fire from the Enogai guns.

The sudden appearance of Lieutenant Tom Pollard's platoon on the west bank of Enogai Inlet the morning of 7 July shocked the Japanese. It was too bad the Northern Landing Group could not rapidly exploit this surprise. As a snake strikes much more effectively when it is coiled—concentrated—the regiment was just the opposite, strung out along a mile and a half in "The Swamp of No Return," unable to "coil" and deliver a significant strike. Otherwise Enogai may have been had for the asking.

News of the first encounter galvanized both sides. While Clay Boyd hustled to concentrate his Dog Company near the juncture of the trails leading to Bairoko and Enogai, Sam Griffith spurred Marine Gunner Angus Goss and his demolitions platoon through the swamp to seize Triri. The Japanese got to both places simultaneously.

### The Battle for Enogai

The mission of seizing Enogai went solely to the 1st Marine Raider Battalion, and the ensuing battle would cost them more combined casualties than they had suffered since Edson's Ridge. While it must have saddened Liversedge to order one battalion to shoulder so much of the fighting, he had little choice. The regiment had been assigned too many missions for its size, firepower, and staying power. The effort to block the Bairoko-Munda "Trail" took Schultz's entire 3/148, one-third the regiment. Someone had to secure the landing point, hump supplies up the

Battalion commanders convene in Col. Liversedge's command post to plan the attack on Bairoko Harbor, about 19 July 1943. Left to right: Maj. Charles Banks and Lt. Col. Sam Griffith, 1st Raiders; Lt. Col. Michael Currin, 4th Raiders; Lt. Col. George Freer, 3d Battalion, 145th Infantry; Lt. Col. Delbert "Dutch" Schultz, 3d Battalion, 148th Infantry.

trail, and provide a reserve—that took the other National Guard outfit, Freer's 3/145.

Liversedge was plagued by terrible communications with his superior officers, Admiral Turner, Commander Task Force 31, or Major General J. H. Hester, commanding the New Georgia Occupation Force. With no word from Liversedge in three days, Turner on 7 July queried Hester, "What is Liversedge's situation?" Hester responded twenty-two hours later, "No contact with Liversedge." It took Liversedge until 8 July before he could report his slow progress and request an emergency resupply of rations and ammo by airdrop.[19]

The battle for Enogai began when Angus Goss and his well-armed demolitionists collided with a company of *rikusentai* double-timing down from their camp. The Japanese had the numbers, but Goss coolly extracted his men back to a creek bed they had just crossed. There the

Raiders took cover and opened fire. Clay Boyd, close by with Dog Company, heard the firing, and led his men off the trail and through the undergrowth. Boyd's men burst out of the brush in a timely flank attack. Goss and his men swept forward, firing and yelling. The Japanese, stung, pulled back, leaving ten dead, another mortally wounded. But the Kure *rikusentai* were far from whipped. The brief, sharp fight cost the Raiders three dead, four wounded, and a lot of ammo expended. A long three days lay ahead.

That evening the Raiders buried their dead at the base of a large banyan tree, marking their graves with the traditionally shaven logs, lashed together with comm wire as a crude cross, each wire tightly binding a single dogtag. The chaplain spoke with quiet assurance—but the Raiders shuddered. The primeval swamp seemed a hell of a place to spend eternity.

At dawn Griffith dispatched ambush patrols led by two Nicaraguan campaign veterans, lieutenants Joseph Broderick and Bennie Bunn (who had been awarded the Navy Cross for his service with Chesty Puller in the battle for El Sauce).

Broderick's Dog Company patrol had barely left the perimeter when they collided with a like-minded force of Japanese coming from Bairoko. Griffith was impatient to advance the column towards Enogai, but this small engagement blossomed into a full-scale firefight and lasted most of the day. When Broderick fell wounded, Griffith ordered Black Jack Salmon's Charlie Company to execute a complicated relief of lines, extracting the bloodied patrol. Salmon did this handily, driving back the Japanese, and Liversedge then ordered in two rifle companies of 3/145, the soldiers glad to be out of the swamp and eager to get their first crack at the enemy. The Japanese obliged.

Uneasy about this unresolved threat to his left flank, Griffith reassembled his battalion at noon and directed them towards Enogai. Tom Mullahey's Able Company took the lead, but for once Corrigan's native scouts got lost. The trail petered out in yet another swamp, leaving the head of the column immobilized by bomb-splintered, uprooted trees and mid-thigh muck. "For several hours we trudge onward," recorded Sgt. Poppell, "but as we proceed we go deeper and deeper into the water." "Disheartening," Griffith said later in a classic understatement. The Raiders reversed course and slogged back to Triri. Enogai gained a reprieve.[20]

Griffith returned to Triri to find the morning firefight raging anew and the two army companies giving ground stubbornly to a relentless attack. He summoned Lieutenant R. C. ("Ploughjocks") Kennedy to lead an assault against the enemy's rear. "Go northwest till you hear firing over your left shoulder," Griffith told Kennedy, "then do a 90-degree turn and go until the firing is heard from your left rear—then do another 90-degree turn and you'll be in their rear." Easier said then done in the jungle, but Kennedy executed the maneuver smartly, killing twenty and forcing the Japanese commander to abandon the ground.[21]

Earlier, Griffith had assigned Gunnery Sergeant Frank Guidone to guide Lieutenant Colonel "Dutch" Schultz's 3/148 to its trailblock position southwest of Triri. The Army battalion reached the junction of what they perceived to be the native scout trail and the main Munda-Bairoko trail on the afternoon of the 7th (there were several parallel trails in the jungle, and this one, to be sure, proved to be well-traveled). In addition to Guidone, Sam Griffith also provided Schulz with a team of the celebrated Navajo Code Talkers, Marines trained as radio operators whose unique native dialect could never be broken by Japanese eavesdroppers. Marine Corporal Eugene Roanhorse Crawford, twenty-nine, from near Window Rock, Arizona, a recent volunteer for the Raiders, was one of the code talkers assigned to help Dutch Schultz send secure situation reports back to regimental headquarters.[22]

There was much to convey. Schultz was in contact every day for ten days, frequently with elements of the 13th Infantry. His men suffered casualties—on one occasion his command post was penetrated—and near starvation during the prolonged mission. Schultz reported the soldiers learned to use their helmets to cook captured Japanese rice seasoned with their own salt tablets.[23]

Schultz believed he had stopped the flow of reinforcements and supplies from Bairoko to Munda, but he was mistaken. After the first intercept the Japanese merely boxed him in with a series of sharp attacks and cut a bypass route. Griffith in later years blamed the mission, not Schultz, citing the "complete fallacy of blocking positions in the jungle—the Japanese simply didn't go that way anymore, they just made a new trail."[24]

Meanwhile at Triri, Lieutenant Corrigan sent his scouts back into the brush the evening of the 8th to find a good trail to Enogai after their failure that afternoon. This they did. Griffith roused his men, now ravenous with hunger, and launched them along the new trail by 0730 on the 9th. Salmon's Charlie Company took the lead, and Private First Class Richard W. Ackerman, as the first fire team leader in the first squad of the 1st platoon, became the company scout and took the point. Ackerman would later believe he had led the entire battalion into a bloody trap, but in truth the long column effectively bypassed the initial Japanese outposts, and by the time "all hell broke loose," C Company had nearly penetrated the main line of resistance. The port of Enogai lay barely 750 yards beyond.

The Raiders encountered the now-familiar combination of Nambu machine-gun nests in the brush, well covered by riflemen in nearby trees. Ackerman, hugging the sodden earth while wicked strings of bullets snapped overhead, marveled at the intricate firelanes and wondered why they had escaped his notice. "Our platoon casualties were heavy," he said, "but I was also amazed at how many survived" that pointblank fire.[25]

Griffith quickly deployed the battalion into a firing line, Mullahey's A Company to Salmon's left, Wheeler's B Company to the right. The two companies on the left remained pinned down by withering fire, but Wheeler found an opening and pressed forward. With dusk coming, both sides broke off the engagement to consolidate their lines. The Raiders mourned the death of one of their most gifted combat leaders, Second Lieutenant Philip Oldham, killed in Charlie Company's frenzied firefight. Oldham, twenty-nine, from Philadelphia, had evinced extraordinary courage under fire at Tulagi and the Ridge, for which he had been meritoriously commissioned four months earlier.[26]

The Raiders discovered a Japanese comm wire bisecting the scout trail leading to Enogai, and Griffith dispatched Lieutenant Joe Cuetara with Marine Gunner Haines' platoon to track down the owners. Another sharp firefight broke out, and several of Haines' men went down wounded, including his runner, Private First Class Thomas "Jinx" Powers, hit in the side. Powers was a chubby, cheerful man from West Springfield, Massachusetts, one of the hard-core members of the Singing Eight Balls, a tough man to repress. He shook off his wound and took off to the rear with Gunner Haines' order to fetch help. But Powers went the wrong way, disappearing into the Japanese lines before his astonished squadmates could redirect him. Powers survived by his wits alone. At dusk, noticing many of his Japanese neighbors climbing trees for new firing positions, he did the same, remaining in his perch throughout a very long night. With the renewed advance of the Raiders the next day, and fearful he would be shot as a sniper, Powers broke into song, singing the Raiders' lyrics at the top of his lungs ("LAST NIGHT I WENT TO BED WITH MAMIE RILEY—AND MAMIE RILEY WENT TO BED WITH ME..."). It worked. Gunnery Sergeant Tony "Big Stoop" Palonis retrieved him from the tree, shaking his head in amazement.[27]

Griffith had gotten close enough to Enogai to notice that, for once, the jungle canopy thinned out. His 60mm mortars would be unencumbered by overhead obstacles, and he ordered the mortar platoon to establish firing positions for the next morning's assault.

The fortunes of war swung in reverse for the Raiders the night of the 9th. The battalion command post occupied a circle around a huge, bomb-damaged banyan tree. As Staff Sergeant Joseph Szakovics and Private First Class Harry Seymer transmitted a Morse Code message by TBX telegraph, beseeching General Hester for an emergency airdrop of food, they heard a sharp crack. A huge limb—big as a good-sized tree—broke off and landed savagely on the communicators. Szakovics, impaled, died instantly; five others were injured, and Harry Seymer's left arm was shredded. Sergeant Fred Serral scrambled quickly to assist Szakovics, but nothing could be done. Griffith ran over, cradled Seymer in his arms, and carried him to sick bay. Dr. Stuart Knox and Corpsman Thad Parker did their best but had to amputate Seymer's arm. Seymer, in shock and numbed by morphine, insisted on returning to his post to complete keying—with his good hand—the critical message over a badly damaged TBX. It was as bizarre a fatal accident as anyone could imagine.[28]

By daylight on the 10th the Raiders were faint with hunger. Most had not eaten in thirty hours. "Breakfast" consisted of rainwater drained from large-leafed jungle foliage. Griffith reminded them the Japanese had plenty of food stashed in Enogai. The attack kicked off at 0700.

Despite the frustrations of the previous day and evening, Griffith actually occupied an advantageous position for the final assault. He attacked from southwest to northeast with three companies abreast (left to right: A, C, and B), effectively cutting the Enogai garrison off from the larger forces at Bairoko. For insurance against a relief column advancing from Bairoko, Griffith posted Clay Boyd's Dog Company in reserve—but with their backs to the Raiders' assault, ready to thwart any counterattack from the west. Similarly, Tom Mullahey posted his Able Company machine-gun platoon under Marine Gunner Joe Cafarella in firing positions to cover the long sandy spur of the seaward side of Leland Lagoon in case the Japanese tried to reinforce along the shoreline. The battalion's 60mm mortar platoon, overjoyed at the chance to use their weapons after lugging them to hell and back through all the swamps, opened up a pounding barrage, especially effective in the cleared areas ahead of Wheeler's Baker Company, closest to the Inlet.

From his headquarters at Bairoko, Commander Okumura was helpless to assist his suddenly beleaguered Enogai outpost. He still could not grasp the size of this invasion force, scattered according to his own scouts between Rice, the distant roadblock, Triri, and now Enogai. He may also have believed the inflated claims of his subordinates, reporting resounding defeats of the Americans with each earlier encounter. By the time he discerned the realities of the day, the Americans had isolated Enogai for the kill.

Enogai did not fall easily. Okumura probably had two companies of his *rikusentai* there, along with the artillery crews and elements of the 1st Battalion, 13th Infantry. The machine gunners and tree snipers opposing Mullahey's and Salmon's advance were just as effective on the 10th as they had been the afternoon before, and neither company made much progress. But Ed Wheeler's line extended past the edge of the Japanese eastern defenses and B Company swept forward at a sharp clip, capturing the last village on the inlet, then reaching the Gulf. Some Japanese began to panic. Scores of them tried to escape to Bairoko along the sandy spit of Leland Lagoon directly into the beaten zones of Cafarella's Browning light machine guns. It was a turkey shoot. At least forty-five Japanese fell to this punishing fire.

Griffith chose this key moment to commit part of his reserve, sending First Lieutenant Tom Pollard and his platoon of roughnecks through C Company's lines in a direct dash for the beach. The choice was as exquisite as the timing. Pollard had three outstanding squad leaders—Corporals John King, John Carson, and Wilfred Hunt—and he arrayed them on line, ordered fixed bayonets, and led them forward, the men screaming at the top of their lungs. "That stunt was just as hair-raising to them as it first was to us," Pollard said. "By the time they opened fire, we were practically on top of them." Pollard's sudden thrust broke through to the Gulf. His men then wheeled by fire teams and attacked the machine gunners still firing at Charlie Company from the rear. A wild melee developed as the Japanese fixed defenses dissolved.[29]

As Baker Company picked up the pace to complete the encirclement, some diehard *rikusentai* made a final stand. Lieutenant Bennie Bunn, the veteran Nicaragua jungle fighter, fell mortally wounded as he captured a heavy machine-gun position. Corporal Vince Cassidy led his squad forward on the fly, avenging the loss of Bunn by snuffing out the remaining three emplacements. One of Cassidy's best wartime poems was "A Corporal's Prayer," the last verse of which read:

*And as I lead them in, my God,*
*   successful in attack,*
*I pray Thee then, protect my men—*
*   that I may lead them back.*[30]

Sam Griffith declared Enogai secured by mid-afternoon on the 10th, but one stubborn knot of Japanese machine gunners in front of Able Company never gave up, and when Clay Boyd tried to take them from behind that evening he lost twenty men before he could snap his fingers. Corporal Harold W. Smith, the pride of the Millburn, New Jersey, Police Department, died here, four days before his twenty-eighth birthday. The last-minute setback took a little luster off what was overall a hard-fought victory, but at 0630 the next morning Dog Company attacked again and swept the board clean.[31]

The 1st Raider Battalion killed at least 350 Japanese in the five-day fight for Enogai. They captured the four 140mm coast defense guns, along with rangefinders, sound locators, and spotting scopes—plus nearly two dozen machine guns. To the starving Raiders the most vital booty had to be the stocks of captured Japanese rations and bottles of *sake*. Then, when the soldiers of Love Company, 3/145, came up that afternoon from Triri bearing food and water from the day's successful aerial resupply—the direct fruits of Private First Class Seymer's heroic one-handed message—the Raiders were immersed in an abundance of riches.

Seizing Enogai had been costly. From the first firefight of Angus Goss and Clay Boyd on 7 July until Boyd's final charge at dawn on the 11th, the 1st Raider Battalion suffered forty-seven killed, four missing and presumed dead, and seventy-four wounded. The dead, all irreplaceable, included sixteen-year veteran Bennie Bunn, age thirty-six, who left a widow, Mercedes, in San Diego; Gunnery Sergeant "Swede" Erickson, who had slogged throughout the Dragon's Peninsula with Boyd's patrol and marked the Rice Anchorage landing on the night of his twenty-third birthday; as well as promising new NCOs like twenty-two-year-old Corporal William F. Cain, who left a widow, Mary, also in San Diego. Griffith renamed Enogai "Camp Cain."[32]

Thus ended a week of remarkable achievements for Griffith's stout-hearted Raiders—a difficult night landing, a herculean trek through the swamps, and their protracted and violent seizure of Enogai. It was no coincidence that to this point their missions had been fully within their unique capabilities, achievable despite their inherently limited resources. In retrospect, it is unfortunate that the Raiders' commitment to New Georgia could not have ended here. After Enogai the game changed.

Liversedge took the opportunity to bring up his landing boats from their secluded harbor at Rice Anchorage. Henceforth the regiment would be resupplied by small U.S. Navy ships slipping into Enogai's piers by night. Liversedge also called for a trio of PBY Catalina flying boats—the heralded "Black Cat" Squadron from Tulagi—to come to Enogai to evacuate the sick and wounded, which numbered an even one hundred men.

The Japanese reacted violently to the loss of Enogai. Two savage bombing raids occurred shortly after the Raiders overran the last Japanese gunners on 11 July. Caught by surprise the regiment suffered three killed and fifteen wounded, losing more invaluable combat veterans.

Platoon Sergeant Joseph L. Murphy, who had replaced Pete Pettus as chief of the Battalion Intelligence Section, was helping recover the wounded from the final attack on Enogai when the first air raid struck. A near-miss from a Japanese bomb "threw me 10–12 feet away," he said. At first he thought he had merely scraped his knees and elbows on the sharp coral. Then he felt blood running down his back from multiple fragment wounds. Corpsmen classified him as "walking wounded" and assigned him to the standby list for PBY evacuation that afternoon.

Fred Odette, B Company, and his buddy John Haxer, A Company, had learned of a Japanese well at Enogai and were eager to fill their canteens with their first clean water in a week when the bombs came screaming down. A huge explosion flattened them. "Shrapnel tore up my right jaw and right hip," said Odette. "I hollered for John but he didn't answer." Haxer had been killed instantly. Sergeant Ben Howland's squad assisted Odette to the PBYs.

The three huge Catalina flying boats made tempting targets in the harbor, and it took the Raiders a long time to ferry their sick and wounded by rubber boat out to the aircraft. Seeing no fighter aircraft flying cover, the Japanese sent two float planes to attack the PBYs on the water. Fred Odette, in a haze of shock and morphine, watched tracer bullets streaking past the porthole at his side. Murphy saw a small bomb rip through the wing of his PBY before exploding below the water's surface. The horrified Raiders along the shore reacted by firing every available weapon at the circling Japanese aircraft. Private First Class Robert Coleman, one of Tom Mullahey's A Company stalwarts, scrambled up the hill, found one of the rarely-used Boys antitank rifles, loaded a .55 caliber round in the breech, leaned against a Japanese parapet, and fired at the closest aircraft. No luck. Coleman missed the shot of a lifetime and cursed roundly. Yet his heavy-caliber bullet may have gotten the pilot's attention; shortly both planes veered away. The Catalinas lumbered into the air, bound for Tulagi.[33]

The Black Cat PBYs made three such emergency missions to evacuate sick and wounded members of the Northern Landing Group in the next several days. Liversedge had an increasing number of men disabled by disease, the result of irregular food, poor water, stress, and the usual jungle fevers. Sleep deprivation became a contributing factor after the capture of Enogai. Once the Japanese knew exactly where to find the invasion force, they dispatched Washing Machine Charlie several times each night. The Raider Regiment, concentrated largely at Enogai and Triri, presented Charlie with more lucrative targets than had been the case at Guadalcanal. Casualties mounted; worse, the men found they could not gamble by ignoring "Condition Red" alerts, so sleep became a luxury. The standard unit chronology entry for those nights read: "Charlie over six times last night, bombing. No hits, no casualties, no sleep." Often the report was more dire.

Captain Clay Boyd, racked with malaria and utterly exhausted by his patrols before the landing, was one of the sick evacuated by PBY the first afternoon. He would be sorely missed. The late Major Ken Bailey had left the Raiders a terrific legacy in his hand-picked young protégé Boyd. Few officers more fully personified the Raiders' aggressive spirit. (Sick as he was, Clay Boyd would serve the Raiders twice more—once from high overhead Bairoko, then, later that year, as a technical advisor at RKO Studios in Hollywood for a new Raiders movie.)[34]

Sam Griffith gave command of Dog Company to First Lieutenant Frank Kemp. Other changes swept the battalion. Major George Herring succumbed to malaria and had to be evacuated to Guadalcanal. Captain John Sweeney replaced Herring as battalion operations officer; Marine Gunner George McKain relieved Sweeney as intelligence officer. Griffith took a hard look at his battalion roster and realized his ranks had become so diminished he could no longer maintain four rifle companies. He reduced Mullahey's A Company and Salmon's C Company—both hard hit at Enogai—to emergency cadres and took from them to beef up Wheeler (B) and Kemp (D). The battalion would have the misfortune of entering its most violent assault at half strength.

## The Battle for Bairoko

From Enogai, Bairoko lies at the opposite side of the Dragon's Peninsula, two miles away to the west-southwest "as the crow flies." Only two main trails led towards Bairoko from the east, the main Japanese trail between that harbor and Enogai, and a native scout trail that meandered towards the southwest from Triri until it cut the main north-south Munda-Bairoko "highway." Bairoko Harbor contained numerous piers and

# Attack on Bairoko
## Aug. 20-22, 1943

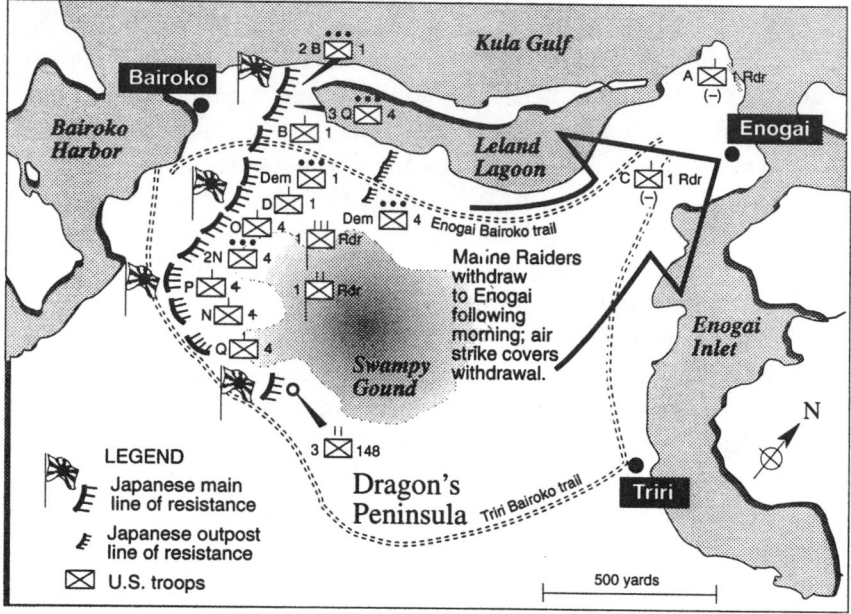

**Kula Gulf**

Bairoko

Bairoko Harbor

2 B ⊠ 1

Enogai

A ⊠ 1 Rdr (-)

3 Q ⊠ 4

B ⊠ 1

**Leland Lagoon**

C ⊠ 1 Rdr (-)

Dem ⊠ 1

D ⊠ 1

O ⊠ 4

Dem ⊠ 4 Enogai Bairoko trail

1 ⊠ Rdr

2N ⊠ 4

P ⊠ 4

N ⊠ 4

Q ⊠ 4

1 ⊠ Rdr

Marine Raiders withdraw to Enogai following morning; air strike covers withdrawal.

**Enogai Inlet**

**Swampy Gound**

E ○

3 ⊠ 148

**Dragon's Peninsula**

Triri Bairoko trail

**Triri**

N

### LEGEND

⤙E Japanese main line of resistance

E Japanese outpost line of resistance

⊠ U.S. troops

500 yards

---

beaches to accommodate the nightly barge traffic from Kolombangara. These facilities were mostly on the east side of the inlet, towards Enogai, and along this arc the Japanese began building a series of mutually supporting defensive positions. They knew Bairoko would be the Americans' next objective.

Harry the Horse Liversedge knew that he would no longer enjoy the element of surprise, the strong suit of any Raider operation. He also realized by now he faced an experienced and well-armed opponent. These factors weighed heavily on him, according to John Sweeney, who shared a joint battalion-regimental command post with Liversedge. From the first, Sweeney said, Liversedge worried that his scattered forces would be overmatched.[35]

Liversedge therefore sent his regimental communications officer, Captain Bill Stevenson (the former communications officer for Edson's Raiders) back to Guadalcanal on the first PBY evacuation flight to seek guidance and support from Admiral Kelly Turner. This was a smart move. Liversedge had two bosses. As Commander, Northern Landing Group, he still reported directly to Turner in his capacity as the amphibious force commander in addition to his regimental allegiance to General Hester as Commander, New Georgia Occupation Force. It was a ragged oversight, but it gave Liversedge a straight shot to Turner, a decisive man who could get things done. Liversedge told Stevenson to ask Turner for more troops—Currin's 4th Raider Battalion for starters—plus better radios and logistic support.

Stevenson gained an invaluable two-hour session with Turner late on the 11th. Turner appreciated Stevenson's first-hand account of the seizure of Enogai, agreed to provide the 4th Raider Battalion and a high-powered radio, and promised to inquire about army reinforcements. Naval gunfire support for the assault on Bairoko would be unlikely, Turner said, because the Kula Gulf was still a contested battlefield. All in all, Stevenson returned to New Georgia pleased with the meeting.

The timing, however, was wrong. The middle week of July was one of great turbulence for the top leadership of Operation Toenails. The campaign had entered its sixth week, and General Hester's troops showed little progress in seizing Munda Airfield from the Japanese, despite heavy reinforcements. Halsey therefore relieved General Hester in midstream, replacing him with Major General Oscar W. Griswold. The Army, embarrassed by this setback, had no interest in providing more troops for the subsidiary operation in the Dragon's Peninsula and indeed begrudged the continued assignment of the two battalions from the 37th Infantry Division. Further, Admiral Chester Nimitz had invited Kelly Turner to command the amphibious forces for his new Central Pacific drive. Halsey agreed. Turner protested—the New Georgia campaign was in major disarray—but he obeyed his orders and departed the theater four days after his meeting with Bill Stevenson. Rear Admiral Thomas Wilkinson relieved Turner. Liversedge abruptly had two new bosses, and the principal focus of both men was on Munda, not Bairoko.

All these stratospheric changes had one direct impact on the Northern Landing Force. The 4th Raiders would come to Enogai, depleted and exhausted as they were from their weeks of hard fighting on the opposite end of New Georgia, and they would give their all in a desperate fight for Bairoko. But the Turner/Wilkinson transition meant it would take a full week to move them up from Guadalcanal. This gave Commander Okumura ten days after the attack on Enogai to improve defensive fortifications for the inevitable assault on Bairoko. He put a thousand men to work preparing concentric defensive lines in an arc that bulged out five hundred yards from the inlet and extended a thousand yards along the east bank. They built five-man machine-gun bunkers—low-lying, log and coral covered, narrow firing slits, artfully camouflaged—that would prove as difficult to attack as anything any Marines would face until they assaulted Tarawa. Okumura placed his heavy machine guns in these bunkers, backed them up with the light Nambus, selected the best trees for his snipers with their scope-mounted Arisaka rifles, and cleared fields of fire. Behind the lines, along the east bank, he positioned his Type 97 90mm mortars, each capable of lobbing a twelve-pound high-explosive shell more than 4,000 yards.[36]

The delay in getting the 4th Raider Battalion redeployed to Enogai was likely unavoidable, but the consequences proved severe. The total lapsed time of ten days between Enogai and Bairoko gave the Japanese enough grace period to ensure their successful defense of the key harbor.

Liversedge consolidated his strength by ordering Dutch Schultz to terminate his inconclusive trailblock and lead 3/148 back to Triri. And he filled the airwaves with requests to Commander Air Solomons ("COMAIRSOLS") for preliminary air strikes. Surprisingly, given the turnover in campaign leadership and the lower priority of the Northern Landing Group, COMAIRSOLS responded favorably. Navy and Marine divebombers and torpedo bombers struck Bairoko hard on 15, 17, and 19 July. On the afternoon of the 19th, a matter of hours before the 1st Raider Regiment assault, nineteen torpedo bombers from Carrier Division 22 and eighteen divebombers from Henderson Field struck Bairoko with one- and two-thousand-pound bombs. Riding along as a guide on this mission in a Douglas Dauntless divebomber was Captain Clay Boyd, AWOL from the hospital. (Boyd praised the squadron for knocking out a barge pier and plastering the jungle, but one wonders at the condition of his undernourished stomach after enduring a 70-degree dive of some 6,000 feet.) Ten minutes later eight Mitchell B-25 bombers strafed Bairoko's beaches.[37]

The 4th Raider Battalion arrived at Enogai the night of 17–18 July, debarking swiftly from four APDs. This was a tough, blooded outfit, well led and well trained. Its arrival likely assuaged Liversedge's anxiety.

Beginning on the 18th and continuing through the evening of the 19th, Liversedge planned the assault on Bairoko with his four battalion commanders, the Raiders Griffith and Currin, the Army officers Freer and Schultz. As Liversedge saw it, the swampy jungles of the Dragon's Peninsula and the lack of tactical mobility assets limited the regiment's options to direct attacks along the main and southern trails. He planned a double envelopment of Bairoko, the 1st and 4th Raider Battalions

End of the road for a Japanese Type 92 heavy machine-gun crew. The open location of this weapon suggests this action took place at Enogai, where the 1st Raiders surprised the garrison by attacking from different directions. Ten days later, at Bairoko, the Japanese had positioned their heavy machine guns in substantial, well-camouflaged bunkers.

advancing in that order in column west along the main trail from Enogai, while Dutch Schultz would lead 3/148 from Triri along the scout trail to surprise the Japanese from their right flank. Sheer's 3/145 would remain at Triri, prepared to reinforce either prong as needed. Griffith's two reduced companies under Tom Mullahey and Black Jack Salmon would guard Enogai. Ed Wheeler would split Baker Company's advance on the right flank by detaching Lieutenant Christie's platoon to follow the slender northern neck of Leland Lagoon.

In hindsight, the plan had holes in it. Schultz, given the most ground to cover in the least time, was competent but conservative, the most cautious of the four commanders. Liversedge should have assigned that task to one of his Raider battalions, men trained for speed under uncertain tactical conditions and accustomed to independent operations. Further, Sheer was too far in the rear at Triri to reinforce either force rapidly. Much would depend on the Raider battalions' ability to deploy from column into line of attack in the swamps and Schultz's ability to proceed hell-for-leather along his narrow track. Liversedge also placed unrealistic expectations on a final bombing of Bairoko's eastern environs.

Liversedge ended the last conference late in the afternoon of the 19th. He directed someone to request a major air strike on Bairoko at 0900 on the 20th—but the gremlins of long-range jungle radio transmission struck again. The regiment, when it finally got through to COMAIRSOLS, could not get confirmation that the mission would fly as requested. Liversedge and Griffith assumed it would.

Typically, some nameless staff officer at COMAIRSOLS gets the blame for allegedly ruling that any request for air support not submitted by 1600 the previous day would be rejected out of hand. If there was such a ruling by such a rigid bureaucrat (and evidence of neither can be found in the COMAIRSOLS archives), then he deserves the roasting of history. On the other hand, Rear Admiral Marc Mitscher—a proven warrior, hardly a bureaucrat—commanded Air Solomons, and there were plenty of Marines on his staff who knew what Liversedge faced in the Dragon's Peninsula. Perhaps Liversedge's request came in garbled, or failed to emphasize the urgency. COMAIRSOLS had just committed more than fifty aircraft (including fighter escorts) to an "urgent attack" on Bairoko that afternoon—some of those planes were still being recovered when the new request may have arrived. Bairoko was important, but Munda was critical, and so were anti-shipping missions in The Slot to keep the Tokyo Express from reinforcing New Georgia. Such was the case on 20 July. Aircraft from Guadalcanal streaked directly over the Raiders' heads in pursuit of Japanese ships heading back to Rabaul from the seas north of Kolombangara; others pounded Munda in support of yet another army attack; still others attacked Japanese airfields around Bougainville. No one sat on their hands.[38]

Yet Liversedge clearly expected the strike mission to occur. Since he seemed to stake the success of his Bairoko assault on this preliminary event, one wonders, again in hindsight, why he did not submit his request hours earlier and insist on confirmation.

Liversedge also missed several earlier opportunities to provide a different kind of fire support for what was obviously going to be a frontal assault. Both of his army battalions had 81mm mortars and plenty of ammunition. He could have concentrated most or all of these weapons (range with an HE shell: 3,290 yards) at Enogai and peppered the Japanese lines well in advance of the Raiders' approach. Additionally, he could have demanded that the ships that delivered the 4th Raider Battalion include at least a single battery, Army or Marine, of 75mm pack howitzers. Or, as a last resort, he could have requested some artillerymen to man the 140mm guns he had just captured at Enogai. They were the biggest weapons on the Dragon's Peninsula and fully functional—the regimental journal for 12 July includes the entry, "Fuse locks found for captured 5.5-inch battery, guns in commission, ready to fire." Yet, according to Sam Griffith, although "we used captured enemy weaponry, we never did fire the big coast defense guns, there wasn't anything to fire them at."[39]

The two Raider battalions assaulted Bairoko unsupported—armed only with shoulder weapons, grenades, and cold steel.

Captain Ed Wheeler led the northern column of the Raider battalions and the regimental headquarters westward from Camp Cain at Enogai Point shortly after 0800 on the 20th. The jungle pressed in on the column; Wheeler soon lost sight of Lieutenant Christie's platoon advancing parallel to the main body along the coastal finger of Leland Lagoon. Nine o'clock came and went with no evidence of the air strike. Dr. Regan would record this day succinctly when it finally ended: "Yesterday we marched against the last Nip base in this area. We didn't get far."[40]

The first shots rang out at 1015. By 1045 the column had encountered the main outposts, and Griffith moved Kemp's D Company on line to Wheeler's left. Christie, advancing along the sandy berm without benefit of cover or concealment, ran into well-sited machine guns firing a steady, knee-high crossfire. His men went to ground, Corporal Vince Cassidy's squad quickly establishing a base of fire, but the platoon had no maneuver room. Carl Fox felt a sharp pain in his side and warm liquid soaking his trousers. A corpsman crawled to him, then chuckled. The bullet had smashed Fox's canteen, nothing more. But Christie was checkmated. The side door to Bairoko was closed.

The Raiders kept sliding left, seeking to turn Okumura's southern flank. With Wheeler increasingly slowed by heavy fire, Griffith worried about his own southern flank and ordered Angus Goss to lead his Demolition Platoon on line to Kemp's left. "Harry," wrote Griffith in a scribbled note to Liversedge, "Have committed the works." This was no exaggeration. With the exception of his skeletonized Able and Charlie Company remnants guarding Camp Cain, Griffith had "the works" on the firing line—and in the tradition of Red Mike Edson, he had his battalion command post and aid station advancing by crow-hops shortly behind Dog Company.[41]

By noon the Raiders broke through the Japanese outposts and encountered the first line of main resistance, including the heavy machine-

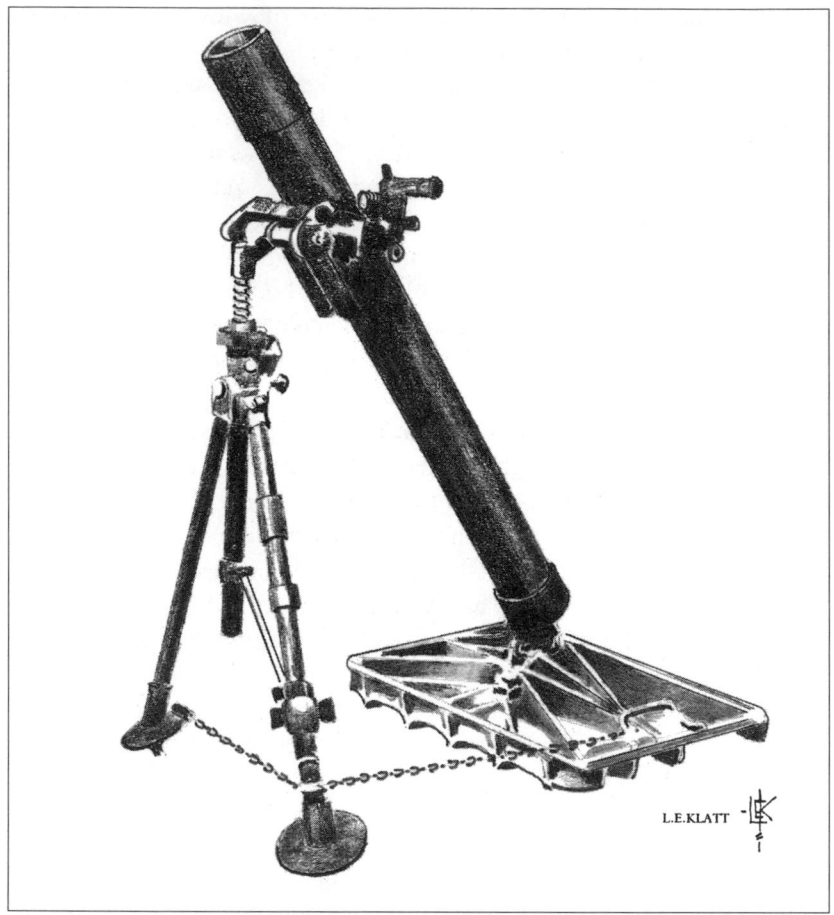

L.E.KLATT

"Japanese Type 97 90mm Mortar," by Larry Klatt. The Japanese used these weapons with murderous effectiveness against the 1st and 4th Raiders attacking Bairoko Harbor. The Type 97 could lob a twelve-pound projectile more than 4,000 yards.

gun bunkers. Lacking bazookas, flame throwers, or light tanks, the Raiders found themselves ill-equipped to tackle field fortifications. With his demolition platoon now heavily committed as infantry, Griffith even lacked the means to employ satchel charges and Bangalore torpedoes. Hand grenades helped, and smoke grenades were particularly useful in blinding a particular bunker to a desperate bayonet charge, but supplies of these munitions quickly ran low. Bloody Ridge had been different—

the Raiders had fought from static positions where each man could readily stash half a case of grenades in his foxhole. Wheeler and Kemp moved their light machine-gun platoons forward. Their rapid firing added to the cacophony in the smoking forest.

"This was an unbelievable fight," said Frank Guidone, newly promoted to lieutenant, now commanding a platoon in Frank Kemp's Dog Company. "It compared with our fight on the ["Second"] Matanikau." Other veterans believed the volume of fire exceeded that of the Battle of Edson's Ridge. Snipers were so abundant the Raiders sensed they were fighting in three dimensions. Guidone saw three men of Dog Company fall to the same sniper before other riflemen could find him and shoot him out of his tree.[42]

Griffith could feel his advance unraveling. He had heavy casualties and growing gaps in the line as Kemp and Goss kept reaching to their left to find the flank of the Japanese fortifications. Liversedge committed Currin's 4th Raider Battalion by companies, beginning with Captain Anthony "Cold Steel" Walker's P Company. This required an awkward but necessary juxtaposition of the lines. Griffith pulled Goss's small platoon and plugged it in the growing gap between Kemp and Wheeler on the right. Walker inherited Goss's extreme left flank position, reinforced quickly with Captain Earl Snell's Nan Company farther to his left. Walker embodied the spirit of all Raiders, and his nickname "Cold Steel" was genuine. With a Rebel yell he led his company in a spirited bayonet charge, angling towards the southern end of the Bairoko Inlet. The audacity of Walker's attack worked at first, and the company seized an intermediate ridge, but no one could advance upright very long against those interlocking fires. Walker and Snell were both hit; many of their men littered the eastern slope of the ridge. Griffith halted them there, meanwhile spurring Kemp to advance during the distraction. Walker, badly wounded, stayed on the job, sobered by his losses. "I never saw a dead Jap all afternoon," he said, "Only dead Marines."[43]

The regiment's main attack had slowed to a crawl. Private First Class William Kottemann, the 1st Raider Battalion combat action diary clerk, was close enough to the action in Griffith's exposed command post to observe conditions in the early afternoon first-hand: "Enemy employing many well-sited machine guns in coral emplacements. Jungle canopy prohibits use of [our] mortars....Japanese tree snipers cover positions of their automatic weapons." Similarly, Kottemann's counterpart with the 4th Raider Battalion summarized the tactical situation as "many automatic weapons, enemy well dug in and cleverly camouflaged, snipers in trees."[44]

Colonel Liversedge, still greatly agitated at the inexplicable absence of his requested air strike, now experienced another frustration. Just when he needed Schultz to lead his battalion out of the jungle to fall on the Japanese right flank he found he had lost all communications with the 3d Battalion, 148th Infantry. Nothing worked. Liversedge ordered his executive officer, Lieutenant Colonel Joseph McCaffrey, to lead a patrol and a team of wiremen back through Triri and out the native scout trail to find Schultz, assess his status and report back. This would take the better part of four hours.

Dutch Schultz, it turned out, had launched his six-hundred-man battalion from Triri at 0800, as scheduled. His route of march along the two trails to Bairoko probably did not exceed 3,500 yards, yet he found the going exceedingly difficult. The column encountered two swamps, major obstacles "where a misstep would cause a man to sink hip-deep," Schultz reported later. "Our heavy weapons men had a very difficult time to keep closed up." Schultz also encountered some "Nip positions" which were unoccupied but "required patrolling to prevent ambush," he said. At 1400, having advanced some 2,500 yards in six hours without opposition, the column ran into a Japanese trailblock on a small rise. Schultz believed he was facing four machine guns. He could also hear the sound of gunfire to his north as the Raiders battered against Bairoko's main defenses. Schultz said his lead company "immediately started to develop the situation and by 1700 had definitely fixed the enemy position along this general line." Schultz did not elaborate as to why it took three hours to "fix the position." He was just about to employ his 81mm mortars when an exhausted Lieutenant Colonel McCaffery caught up with the stalled battalion.[45]

Griffith meanwhile kept badgering Liversedge for reinforcements. He had directed a joint 1st/4th Raider patrol under Lieutenant Joe Cuetara to execute an oblique attack on the machine guns holding up Baker Company. This had some success. Wheeler finally gained a degree of fire superiority and asked Griffith for help exploiting the advantage. There was none to give. Lieutenant Colonel Currin had fed each of his remaining companies into the lines, Captain Ray Luckel's Oboe Company into a growing gap between Kemp and Walker, and Captain Lincoln Holdzkom's Queen Company to the extreme left flank. The regimental headquarters, now co-located with Griffith and dangerously far forward, had no CP protection other than half the 4th Raiders' demolition platoon. A thousand Raiders manned the firing line which now extended some eight hundred yards.

Liversedge critically needed his reserve battalion at hand, but 3/145 was far off and now being committed piecemeal. He had already ordered McCaffrey to pick up one of Freer's rifle companies when he passed through Triri enroute to find Schultz; at least one other company was needed to safeguard the supply base at Triri and be responsive to Schultz in an emergency. Liversedge ordered Freer at 1415 to dispatch Love Company to Enogai. Forty-five minutes later an impatient Liversedge asked Freer for a status report. The company had not yet departed Triri—and there was still no word from Schultz. Liversedge was incensed. In fact, Love Company would not reach the battlefield until 1830. By that time the soldiers were more welcome for the emer-

"Last Rites for Marine Gunner Goss," artist unknown. Father Paul Redmond administers last rites to the flag-draped body of Marine Gunner Angus Goss, killed in the futile attack on Bairoko Harbor.

gency supplies they brought—plasma, water, ammo—than their utility as a reinforcing rifle company.[46]

Frank Kemp's Dog Company held the single best chance for the regiment as the afternoon waned. These Raiders penetrated the second of four Japanese lines and seized a coral ridge barely three hundred yards from the harbor. The Japanese counterattacked, driving the Marines back. But Kemp was blessed with some very savvy jungle fighters in the form of Tom Pollard and Frank Guidone; Dog Company came screaming back up the slope.

The Japanese 90mm mortars launched a devastating barrage throughout the lines and the headquarters. Sergeant Poppell's spirits sank. "We are [keeping] low, but the Nips have found the range and they pound us unmercifully. Each shell seems to get five or six men....hours pass and no word from Dutch Schultz and his Army troops."[47]

Griffith sensed the crucial moment had arrived. He could hear Dutch Schultz's 81mm mortars booming sporadically far to the south. He urged his veterans on in a cold fury.

The Raiders responded as they always did. Lou Diamond back on the Matanikau had been right—"Here come the 'do-or-die men.'" For too many it became the time to die. Sergeant James Walsh, who had saved so many Marines from drowning in the Tamakau, died this hot afternoon. So did the heroic little corpsman Thaddeus Parker, shot in the spine as he rushed to succor a Raider who had just been shot by the same sniper (who then turned his cross-hairs on stricken Gunnery Sergeant Tony Palonis as he raced up to recover Parker, hitting Big Stoop in the leg). And—to the collective grief of the entire regiment—so died Marine Gunner Angus Goss, a man who best exemplified the unique spirit of the Raiders.[48]

Father Paul Redmond, regimental chaplain and World War I veteran, covered Angus Goss with an American flag and prayed for his eternal soul.

In Baker Company's battle for the northern flank, Corpsman James Boren accompanied Sergeant Johnnie Holladay (he with the unerring rifle "Old Lucifer") at the tail end of an advancing platoon. Lieutenant "Ploughjocks" Kennedy called Boren up to the head of the column. A shot rang out from the rear. Fearing the worst, Boren dashed back to find Holladay dead, killed by a patient sniper who had allowed the entire column to pass. Holladay used to gladden the hearts of the entire company, strumming his guitar and singing "John Henry." Vince Cassidy would eulogize his friend in a poem, ending with "The last string is broken, the

Evacuation of wounded men by PBY flying boats from Enogai after the Battle for Bairoko Harbor. The enemy air strike occurred just after this picture was taken.

melody dies; he is dead at Bairoko, and with him lies—'John Henry.'"[49]

At 1600 Liversedge received his first message from Dutch Schultz: "Have met Nips....Have not yet hit Munda-Bairoko trail. Strength of enemy undetermined. But know they have four automatic weapons. We are attacking. Will keep you informed." Liversedge needed more. He raised Schultz on the field phone, asked whether he could link up with the Raiders by dark. At this point, Schultz was no more than a thousand yards below the Japanese southern flank. "I answered immediately, 'NO,'" Schultz reported, persisting in this response even when Liversedge said the main attack would fail without his battalion's intervention. Schultz believed he had his own battle to his immediate front and was disappointed when Liversedge then ordered him to hold his ground overnight, then fall back on Enogai. There is no record of Liversedge requesting Schultz to support the main attack with his heavy mortars.[50]

Liversedge sent Sam Griffith along the front to determine whether the day could still be carried. Griffith went to each company position in his battalion and Currin's, appalled at the afternoon's losses. Kemp's forward salient represented the only possibility. Griffith went there last, and he and Kemp crept forward to look down at Bairoko Harbor three hundred yards away. "Do you think you can take your company down there and secure the harbor?" Griffith asked. Kemp was blunt. "I told him we might get down the ridge," he said, "but it was getting late in the day and not too many of us would make it back unless the companies on either flank could advance as well," and these faced thicker underbrush and more bunkers.[51]

Griffith's heart sank, but he had to agree with his young company commander. The day was shot, the two Raider battalions had suffered easily 250 casualties, at least half of them litter cases. Many of the original enemy bunkers remained lethally functional. Japanese mortars and machine guns continued to fire unremittingly; the Raiders were running low on ball ammunition, grenades, medical supplies, and water. The regiment was dangerously scattered; the Japanese could easily reinforce their lines at night by barge from Vila across the Kula Gulf. The Raiders had nothing at hand to counter the merciless pounding by the big 90mm mortars.

Griffith looked at Kemp and shook his head. Quickly he returned to the command post and told Liversedge they had no choice but to call off the attack and withdraw to Enogai. "I told Liversedge we couldn't take the place, that we had to have either air support or we had to have help from Schultz, and we didn't have either."[52]

To his credit Liversedge agreed immediately. They had done their damnedest. It would take most of the surviving Raiders and all of Corrigan's native scouts just to manhandle the stretchers back over the rough trail to Enogai. This was an agonizing, endless journey. Corpsman Jim Boren struggled eastward through the swamps carrying the rifles of the fallen, "including, sadly," he added, "a pocket full of dogtags that I'd taken off dead comrades." The regiment reported casualty figures among its three battalions in contact that day as follows:

| | |
|---|---|
| 1st Raider Battalion (2 Companies): | 17 killed, 63 wounded |
| 4th Raider Battalion: | 29 killed, 135 wounded |
| 3d Battalion, 148th Infantry: | 4 killed, 8 wounded |
| Total Bairoko Casualties: | 50 killed, 206 wounded[53] |

As Liversedge gave orders for defending the retreat and protecting Enogai, he paused to submit an emphatic request for an air strike on the 21st. "Request all available planes strike both sides Bairoko Harbor beginning 0900," he said, then added with bitterness, "You are covering our withdrawal." This message got top-level attention. COMAIRSOLS indeed threw every available aircraft at Bairoko throughout the 21st, dropping more than 130 tons of explosive ordnance, a new record for the South Pacific. Said John Sweeney in later years, "If we had only half of that a day earlier, I have no doubt we could have taken the place. A lot of good men were lost there. They deserved a better fate."[54]

In retrospect it is doubtful another air strike on the 20th would have made that much difference. The attack the previous afternoon had saturated the environs of Bairoko with 2,000-pound bombs—larger ordnance by far than the Marines at Tarawa ever received. But even with Clay Boyd in the lead aircraft, the aviators over Bairoko could not identify the real targets for this battle: the concentric arc of bunkers east of the harbor, hidden by the jungle canopy. Nor were the Raiders capable of marking the targets suitably. As one Marine aviator described the problem after a mission elsewhere on New Georgia, "As is usual on all jungle targets, nothing but lush foliage was visible from the air, so observation of specific results was impossible, other than the fact that the area was well plastered with bombs." Plastering the Bairoko jungle with more 2,000-pound-bombs on the 20th would have made life decidedly uncomfortable for Okumura's tree-based snipers, but nothing short of direct hits would have demolished his machine-gun bunkers. That pinpoint accuracy did not exist in the South Pacific the summer of '43.[55]

The one truly unforgivable sin committed by either COMAIRSOLS or Task Force 31 was the failure to tell Liversedge immediately his air support was not available. Knowing that as late as 1000 on the 20th would have allowed him to abort the attack and regroup. Not knowing one way or the other led Liversedge to "commit the works," and his Raiders attacked the Japanese bunkers virtually bare-handed.

Back in Pearl Harbor, Colonel Omar T. Pfeiffer, the Fleet Marine Officer and War Plans Officer on Admiral Nimitz's staff, noted in his New Georgia Running Estimate File for 21 July that the heavy air strikes directed on Bairoko "indicate the Japs are still there in force." When Pfeiffer received a full report of the defeat the next day, he was furious. The Raiders had been squandered on misguided missions, he fumed. "They are equipped for surprise operations," he stated, not prolonged inland campaigns. "Failure to relieve the Marine Raiders by regular infantry units with artillery is on a parallel with failure to relieve the 1st Marine Division at Guadalcanal."[56]

Merrill Twining for the rest of his life blamed Kelly Turner for the unwise mission—"a vague, ill-conceived, reckless foray...the identical tactics that had brought repeated ruin on the Japanese at Guadalcanal—a prolonged and debilitating march through jungle swamps with inad-

Sgt. Jack Tracy's final patrol began in New Georgia and terminated in the Raiders Cemetery on Tulagi on 7 August 1943, the first anniversary of that battle. Left to right: kneeling, Ashley Large, Jack Tracy, Henry Poppell, John Hunt; standing, unknown (possibly William Kish), Arlington Gleckner, Rex Hooten.

equate rations and supplies and supporting arms, culminating in an unsupported attack on a strong, prepared position."[57]

The Raiders returned to Enogai and assumed a life of small unit patrols and ambushes, but their spark was gone. Their corporate exhaustion led to even higher rates of sickness. Frank Guidone, the last of the prelanding expedition members, had to be evacuated back to Tulagi. So did gritty Staff Sergeant Gerry West. Liversedge considered the regiment unsuited for offensive operations. It got worse. As week after week passed under these conditions, the two senior surgeons for both Raider Battalions, Stuart Knox and J. C. Lockhart, signed a startling joint letter to Liversedge warning that the overall condition of the troops had become so depleted that "further offensive action would lead to unjustifiable slaughter." Sam Griffith had to agree. By the end of August, he said, "I had dysentery, trench mouth and malaria, all three at once, and every tooth in my head was loose, but I was in better shape than half the battalion."[58]

Munda Airfield ultimately fell to the soldiers of XXIV Corps on 5 August. Bairoko fell to army troops on 24 August without a shot being fired, the vital harbor skillfully evacuated by Commander Okumura during the night. Finally, at the end of August, forty days after the Battle of Bairoko, the 1st Marine Raider Battalion boarded ships and returned to Guadalcanal. Doctor James Regan, evacuated earlier, greeted them on the beach, along with hundreds of other Marines. The Raiders were nonplussed—they had lost a bitter battle. Yet to the Marines back at Guadalcanal they were legendary heroes for their iron-hearted exploits on the Dragon's Peninsula. Said Regan, "as those dirty, ragged, haggard, gallant men filed ashore, a soft wind was whipping the flag and a band was playing the Marine Hymn. I looked away."[59]

## Notes

1. Twining, *No Bended Knee,* 195.
2. Samuel B. Griffith, "Corry's Boys," *Marine Corps Gazette,* May 1949, 45–47; Harry Liversedge quoted in Peatross, *Bless 'em All,* 189.
3. 1st Raider Battalion Operation Order 1-43, 2 July 1943, Griffith Papers, MCHC.
4. John Miller, *Cartwheel: The Reduction of Rabaul,* Vol. VIII of *The United States Army in World War II: The War in the Pacific* (Washington, D.C.: Office of the Chief of Military History, Department of the Army, 1959), 120.
5. Carl Boyd and Akihiko Yoshida, *The Japanese Submarine Force and World War II* (Annapolis: Naval Institute Press, 1995); Samuel Eliot Morison, *Breaking the Bismarcks Barrier,* Vol. VI in *History of United States Naval Operations in World War II* (Boston: Little, Brown, 1950), 156–58. Morison mistakenly attributes the USS *Strong's* assailant to a Long Lance torpedo fired as a "Parthian shot" from one of the withdrawing destroyers, but Boyd's careful research into the *Senshi Sosho* series of original Japanese documents conclusively identifies the coastal submarine *RO-108.*
6. Jack Tracy to Frank Guidone, 5 May 1996, 2.
7. Poppell Diary, 5 July 1943, 38.
8. Frank Guidone to author, 14 and 15 February 1999; Tracy to Guidone, 5 May 1996, 2.
9. Guidone to author, 15 February 1999; Poppell Diary, 5 July 1943, 38; Tracy to Guidone, 5 May 1996.
10. Carl Fox to author, 22 February 1999; Carl Fox interview with author, 9 April 1999.
11. Samuel B. Griffith, "Operations of the 1st Raider Battalion in the New Georgia Campaign," typewritten manuscript, n.d., *ca.* July 1943 after Enogai and

before Bairoko, reprinted in *The Raider Patch,* July 1995, 12–17 [Griffith, "Enogai Campaign"]; Alvard G. Careaga to Edson's Raiders Association, 14 March 1991.

12. CO, 1st Raider Battalion, "Action Report (4 July–29 August)," 27 September 1943, 2 [1st Raider Battalion Diary]; Griffith, "Enogai Campaign," 14.

13. Guidone to author, 15 February 1999; Poppell Diary, 5 July 1943, 37; 1st Raider Battalion Diary, 2; Griffith, "Enogai Campaign," 14.

14. Griffith, "Enogai Campaign," 14; Frank A. Kemp to Frank Guidone, 25 July 1991. Records are incomplete on this point, but Lt. Kemp and at least one (possibly all) of the other three men received the Soldiers' Medal [now the Navy-Marine Corps Medal] for life-saving during the crossing of the Tamakau on 6 July 1943.

15. Griffith to Liversedge 061100L July 1943, 1st Marine Raider Regiment Message File, New Georgia, Box 49, Ser. 65A-5099, WNRC; Guidone to author, 28 February 1999.

16. James F. Regan, "No Greater Love," *The American Magazine,* June 1945, 17, 100–101; 1st Raider Battalion Diary, 2; Jack Tracy to Frank Guidone, 5 May 1996, 3; Poppell Diary, 7 July 1943, 39.

17. Frank A. Kemp to Frank Guidone, 25 July 1991; *Senshi Sosho: Nanto Homen Kaigun Sakusen, v3 (Southeastern Area Naval Operations, Vol. 3),* 199, 201.

18. *Senshi Sosho: Nanto Homen Kaigun, v3 (Southeastern Area Naval Operations, Vol. 3),* 39–42, 194–95, 221, 232, 236, 241.

19. CTF 31 to NGOF 0703 20 July 1943; NGOF to CTF 31 080121 July 1943, both cited in George C. Dyer, *The Amphibians Came to Conquer: The Story of Admiral Richmond Kelly Turner,* Vol. 1 (Washington, D.C.: GPO, 1970), 582.

20. Poppell Diary, 8 July 1943, 40; Griffith, "Enogai Campaign," 15.

21. John Sweeney witnessed Griffith's instructions to Kennedy and provided this vignette to the author. Kennedy became one of the last Raiders to be wounded in action, on New Georgia during a recon patrol on 2 August 1943.

22. Guidone to author, 16 February 1999; George Lewis to Guidone, 22 October 1991; Eugene Roanhorse Crawford obituary in *Raider Patch,* January 1994, 2–3. When Crawford and a fellow Navajo Code Talker volunteered for the Raiders on Guadalcanal just before the New Georgia campaign, an officer warned them "if we joined it would be 'hike all day, sleep little, eat little' and asked if we still wanted to join. We did."

23. Lt. Col. Delbert R. Schultz, "Narrative of 3d Bn, 148th Infantry [in New Georgia Campaign]," n.d., RG 407, Stack 270, 337-INF (148)-7-0.8, Unit Journal, Solomon Islands, National Archives [Schultz Report].

24. Samuel Griffith Oral Memoir, MCOHC, MCHC, 136a.

25. Robert W. Ackerman to Irv Reynolds, n.d.

26. Philip A. Oldham Casualty Card.

27. Griffith, "Enogai Campaign," 16; Regan, "No Greater Love," 100; Frank X. Tolbert, 1944, *Leatherneck* essay, reprinted in *The Dope Sheet,* 1975, 7. Tolbert,

a gifted combat correspondent, accompanied the 1st Raider Battalion on New Georgia.

28. Harry A. Seymer to Thomas Mullahey, 28 January 1992. According to his Casualty Card, S. Sgt. Szakovics, twenty-seven, was from Steubenville, Ohio. Harry Seymer served many years as Chaplain of the Edson's Raiders Association.

29. Frank J. McDevitt, "One Hero was Lt. Thomas Pollard," news release, New Georgia, July 1943, reprinted in *The Dope Sheet,* October 1977, 3–4. McDevitt was the second combat correspondent assigned to the Raiders.

30. Frank J. McDevitt, "Poet Cassidy Proves He's a Real Fighting Marine," news release, New Georgia, July 1943, reprinted in *The Dope Sheet,* n.d., 6–7.

31. Harold W. Smith Casualty Card. Millburn is in Essex County, New Jersey.

32. William F. Cain, Jr., Casualty Card; Casualty figures from 1st Raider Battalion Diary, 11 July 1943, 5. The 1st Marine Raider Regiment Special Action Report lists eighty WIA for the Enogai fight, the additional six wounded men presumably belonging to 3/145 from their afternoon firefight on 8 July. Dr. Regan ("No Greater Love," 100) indicates that Corporal Cain had just learned he had become a father, but there is no record of a mail delivery before 10 July, and an annotation on Cain's Casualty Card says "no children." Neither represents conclusive evidence to the contrary.

33. Joseph L. Murphy to Thomas Mullahey, n.d.; Fred Odette to Thomas Mullahey, 24 March 1992 [In the same letter Odette related the saga of Higgins boat coxswain Troy Turner, whom the Raiders "appropriated" for extended combat duty afloat and ashore in New Georgia]; Robert Coleman interview with author, 9 April 1999.

34. Col. Clay A. Boyd biographic folder, Reference Section, MCHC.

35. John Sweeney to author, 26 February 1999.

36. *Senshi Sosho: Nanto Homen Kaigun, v3 (Southeastern Area Naval Operations, Vol. 3)*, 195–236; *Handbook on Japanese Military Forces*, 353.

37. Intelligence and Mission Reports, VC-26, VC-28, and CARDIV-22 for 15–20 July 1943, COMAIRSOLS 3/43–10/43, Box 325, WWII Action and Operational Reports, National Archives; COMAIRSOLS to COMAIRSOPAC 19095 8 July 1943, Dispatches July–August 1943, 1st Marine Air Wing, Records of Aviation Commands and Units, 1942–47, National Archives.

38. *Ibid.* See also John N. Rentz, *Marines in the Central Solomons* (Washington, D.C.: HQMC, 1952), 111, especially footnote 36.

39. 1st Marine Raider Regiment Journal, New Georgia Campaign, June–August 1943, entry for 1500, 12 July 1943, Box 14, Series 65A-5188, WNRC [Regimental Journal]. The journal, hand-written on captured Japanese stationery, was recorded by Cpl. Alfred A. Haas of the Regimental intelligence staff, who the previous September had witnessed the death of the legendary Gy. Sgt. Stackpole at Edson's Ridge; Samuel Griffith Oral memoir, MCOHC, MCHC, 135. Griffith did not state why the Raiders never tried to employ the captured

coast defense guns against the enemy barge traffic crossing the Gulf each night. Nor did he mention whether he or Liversedge ever considered a mini-raid, using their several Higgins boats to insert troops with mortars and machine guns west of Bairoko the night before the attack.

40. Regan, "No Greater Love," 101.

41. 1st Marine Raider Regiment Message File, New Georgia, Box 49, Ser. 65A-5099, WNRC. Griffith sent a number of hand-written messages by runner to Liversedge during the battle. Most were optimistic until the bitter end. The best of these are quoted in length by Dr. Lee Minier in his well-documented essay, *Raider,* the second half of which was reprinted in *The Dope Sheet,* March 1990, 11–13.

42. Guidone to author, 19 February 1999, 3–4.

43. Anthony Walker quoted in Peatross, *Bless 'em All,* 226; 4th Marine Raider Battalion Special Action Report: Bairoko Harbor, New Georgia, 14 September 1943, 3 [4th Raiders Action Report].

44. 1st Raider Battalion Diary, 9; 4th Raiders Action Report, 3.

45. Schultz Report, 8–9.

46. Regimental Journal, entries for 1415, 1500, and 1830 on 20 July 1943. Love Company's departure from Triri was likely delayed by the subsequent request or decision to bring essential resupplies for the Raiders near Bairoko.

47. Poppell Diary, 20 July 1943, 44.

48. Accounts of the cause of Angus Goss's death varied. Sam Griffith and Dr. Regan said he died from the concussion of one of the 90mm mortar shells—"he didn't have a mark on him," said Griffith later—but S. Sgt. Gerry West was with his platoon leader when he died and said, "a sniper got him; he had a .25 caliber hole in the back of his head." Griffith Oral Memoir, MCOHC, MCHC, 140; Gerry West interview with author, 12 November 1998.

49. James Boren, "A New Georgia Story," *The Dope Sheet,* October 1990, 10–12. Where Vince Cassidy was a budding poet in the Raiders, Boren was a budding artist. He survived the war and became a noted painter of western scenes, elected to the Cowboy Hall of Fame. Cassidy's poetic eulogy to Johnnie Holladay appeared in *The Raider Patch,* July 1996, 22–23, after his own death in 1989.

50. Schultz's message to Liversedge is recorded in 4th Raider Battalion Special Action Report, 1600, 20 July 1943, 4; Schultz Report, 9.

51. Frank A. Kemp to Thomas Mullahey, 15 March 1994 and 1 December 1993.

52. Samuel Griffith Oral Memoir, MCOHC, MCHC, 141.

53. Boren, "A New Georgia Story," 10; 1st Marine Raider Regiment Special Action Report, Daily Summary Narrative, 20 July 1943, 5–6.

54. John Sweeney to author, 26 February 1999.

55. VMSB 114 Mission Report, 20 July 1943, New Georgia, RG 38, U.S. Navy Action Reports, World War II, COMAIRSOLS, Box 325, National Archives.

56. Extract, "New Georgia Running Estimate File (Pfeiffer for CINCPAC)," 21 and 22 July 1943, Operational History Section, Navy Historical Center.
57. Twining, *No Bended Knee,* 145. See also 184–85.
58. Statement of Doctors Lockhart and Knox dated 11 August 1943 in Griffith Papers, MCHC; Samuel Griffith Oral Memoir, MCOHC, MCHC, 143.
59. Regan, "No Greater Love," 101.

# 11

## The Enduring Legacy, September 1943–August 1945

*We were small, but we had a time.*

Colonel Samuel B. Griffith, 1945[1]

ONCE AGAIN the 1st Marine Raider Battalion sought solace among New Caledonia's benign climate and friendly natives. The men were sick, emaciated, dog-tired, and bitter. Most believed the first leg of their New Georgia campaign had been worthwhile—the night landing at Rice, the arduous jungle trek, the seizure of Enogai. At that point, having lost the element of surprise and being so far removed from the sources of fire support, the troops believed they should have been replaced by a regular infantry battalion. The attack on Bairoko had been snake-bit by poor support and bad luck that had cost too many of their best men. Dying on The Ridge in desperate defense of Henderson Field was one thing—a certain comforting glory—but dying on the Dragon's Peninsula while assaulting fortifications with rifles and grenades was something else. The Raiders would not soon forget Bairoko.

Lieutenant Lee Minier wrote his family that, for him, New Georgia had been "easier than Guadalcanal," but Minier missed the Bairoko assault because Able Company had been sidelined after its costly fight for Enogai. Most other survivors considered the fighting at Bairoko to have been at least the hellacious equivalent of The Ridge. But Minier did not escape the jungle's toll. "Your wandering son," he wrote, "has been in a naval hospital for the past three weeks," afflicted with "malaria, yellow jaundice, fungus...and bad temper." He was not alone.[2]

"I think about half the battalion wound up in hospitals," recalled Sam Griffith. "I got back [to New Caledonia] and I was turned in by the doctors to the base hospital in Nouméa right off the bat. I'd lost about forty pounds." A week later Griffith feebly attempted to report the campaign to General Vandegrift, commanding the I Marine Amphibious Corps. "Vandegrift took one look at me," Griffith related, "and he said 'You are going back to the States.'" Griffith relinquished command to Major George W. Herring on 9 September and departed on a stretcher, ending his long stewardship of Edson's Raiders. The U. S. Army would bestow its Distinguished Service Cross on Griffith for his conspicuous leadership throughout the Dragon's Peninsula.[3]

George Herring, a veteran of six of the seven Raider battles, took command because the battalion executive officer, Major Gus Banks, was hospitalized. Herring was barely more fit. Two months earlier he had been evacuated from Enogai with malaria. Fewer than half of the five hundred men in his command were fit for duty.[4]

Banks eventually recovered and assumed command from Herring on 3 October. By then the battalion was in a turmoil of old timers departing and new men coming aboard. The popular Tony "Big Stoop" Palonis was one of the departees. Wounded (for the second time) at Bairoko while he attempted to rescue Corpsman Thaddeus Parker, Palonis had been evacuated to the Nouméa hospital. While still a patient, he received a meritorious promotion to Master Gunnery Sergeant. Big Stoop, twenty-one years old, became the youngest Marine to attain that exalted rank.

Replacing veteran combat leaders of such renown as Palonis and Griffith was difficult, yet many of the newcomers gave promise of perpetuating the tradition, especially the irrepressible young lieutenant, Leonard E. Fribourg (who years later would follow Clay Boyd's example in Hollywood when he served as technical director for the movie *Sands of Iwo Jima*).[5]

Once again New Zealand offered its healing graces to the Raiders. The battalion spent a glorious month in Auckland during October-November 1943. Some men engaged in the obligatory street brawl with those New Zealand servicemen lucky enough to be home from the European Theater. Following the donnybrook, the locals taught the Raiders new verses to their celebrated drinking songs. Other troops followed different paths. Sergeant Popeye Poppell looked up former Raider and fellow communicator Horse Collar Smith at the nearby Fourth Base Depot, then took off for Wellington to renew acquaintances from the battalion's first visit. Lee Minier attended to life's more basic pleasures. "I got pretty fat down there," he wrote home. "They have wonderful chow—steak and eggs with every meal!"[6]

For all these reasons the Raiders left Auckland reluctantly. Their grim steaming accommodations did little for troop morale. The battalion had sailed to New Zealand aboard the spic-and-span hospital ship *Rixey*. They rode home on the aged auxiliary ship *Maui*. "Ship old and dirty," recorded Pharmacist's Mate Second Class Byron H. Eller, a veteran of the Dragon's Peninsula campaign, "no water to wash or shower."[7]

Major Banks knew what his veterans had lived through, and he took his time squaring away their wildcat ways. Nevertheless, the battalion displayed ragged discipline that had never been tolerated under Merritt Edson or Sam Griffith. Scores of AWOL Marines scurried up the rat-lines of the *Maui* just before the ship departed Auckland. Indiscriminate shooting broke the peace at Camp Bailey on Christmas Eve and New Year's Eve. The camp brig seemed never empty of Marines confined on bread and water for infractions of the Rocks and Shoals. Private First Class Charles L. Capron guarded the stockade and recalled that the prisoners received three loaves of bread a day. "But their buddies on the out-

The Raiders loved a good songfest such as this one in Auckland, New Zealand, in November 1943.

side were looking after them," he said. "They would intercept the loaves, cut them open, and stuff them full of meat, fruit, and other goodies. One could go to the brig and come out fatter than he went in."[8]

Major Banks and his senior NCOs tightened the screws after the holiday outbursts. Once again the Raiders found themselves enduring long conditioning hikes, night training, and field firing. No one knew for sure where the next campaign would take place, but there was much talk about an assault on Kavieng, New Ireland, one of Rabaul's final outposts. "Two weeks of very tough training," recorded Popeye Poppell. "We now realize that our time is very short and every person tries to learn as much as possible." Lee Minier wrote his family that he "spent the last week running a special school for machine gunners of the entire battalion."[9]

The Raiders left Camp Bailey, said goodbye to their native friends, and sailed once again for Guadalcanal on 24 January 1944. This time they established a bivouac at Tassafaronga Point on the northwestern coast, eight miles beyond the dark Matanikau. Poppell took note of the ruins from the earlier battles: "The shoreline is dotted with wrecked Nip beach craft and...huge hulks of partially sunk transports."[10]

The veterans in the ranks hardly recognized Guadalcanal. "Starvation Island" had been transformed into a major staging base for the final reduction of Rabaul. The place was damned near civilized. Great changes were in the winds.

## The End of the Raiders

While the 1st Raiders enjoyed the hospitality of New Zealand, their brothers in the 2d and 3d Raider Battalions had formed the 2d Provisional Raider Regiment under Colonel Alan Shapley and sailed for Bougainville with the 3d Marine Division. There on 1 November the Marines executed a forcible landing at Cape Torokina, then held on against violent air and surface counterattacks—even a Japanese night counterlanding within the force beachhead. Lieutenant Colonel Joseph McCaffrey, second in command to Harry the Horse Liversedge during the New Georgia campaign, commanded the 2d Raiders at Bougainville and died at their head on D-Day.

The 2d Raider Regiment fought valiantly at Bougainville under absolutely dismal conditions, yet their mission was identical to the infantry regiments of the division. Only once did some of them operate as raiders. On 29 November Mike Company, 3d Raiders teamed with the

1st Parachute Battalion to disrupt Japanese communications at Koiari, ten miles east of the beachhead.

The night landing produced the inevitable confusion; the troops came ashore in two widely separate points, dangerously divided, yet their initial luck seemed good. The main body of parachutists landed squarely amid an unguarded Japanese supply dump—similar to the Tasimboko Raid fourteen months earlier. Unlike Tasimboko, however, the Japanese counterattacked in great strength, and for the balance of the day the issue at Koiari remained in doubt, even when the Raider company fought its way into the perimeter from up the beach. Once again Japanese 90mm mortars raked a force of lightly armed Marines. Well-placed machine guns drove off the Higgins boats each time they tried to approach the beach to rescue the landing party. Finally, by means of an emergency recall of three destroyers from convoy duty and under the protective, long-range 155mm artillery fire from the 3d Marine Defense Battalion at Cape Torokina, the parachutists and Raiders extracted from their beleaguered beach after dusk. The Marines sustained 121 casualties in the aborted raid, including seven men missing. Koiari left a bad taste with those who survived—and among those who evaluated the raid from afar.[11]

Only one Marine Corps special mission succeeded in the Bougainville campaign, the brilliant deception operation on Choiseul Island executed by Lieutenant Colonel Victor H. Krulak's 2d Parachute Battalion during 27 October–4 November. Krulak's Marines rampaged throughout Choiseul with such abandon that the Japanese regional commander believed this to be the main American attack and fatally thinned his defenses in south-central Bougainville.

Choiseul and Koiari occurred during a significant crossroads in Marine Corps operational and organizational planning. The Pacific War was changing rapidly. Many senior Marine Corps officers took this opportunity for a hard-nosed reassessment of the special Marine units that had proliferated during the opening months of the great conflict— the Raider and parachute battalions, the barrage balloon squadrons, the glider group, and the defense battalions. After two years the Marines were emerging as a major offensive force in the theater. The gritty defense battalions could better serve as artillery or antiaircraft units; the barrage balloons could go to the Army. And now that the Marines had been committed in virtual totality to the Pacific Theater, there was little rationale to retain the parachute and glider units. The jungles and mountains of their island objectives did not lend themselves to airborne operations.

But what about the Raiders?

No Marine could disparage the valor the Raiders displayed at terrible costs during Tulagi, Makin, Guadalcanal, New Georgia, and Bougainville. Both regiments and all four battalions exemplified the utmost offensive fighting spirit of the Marines. Yet most of their greatest victories occurred while fighting as regular infantry outfits. Their amphibious raids had been few and far between, and, like Koiari, not always successful. Moreover the Raiders often sustained appalling casualty rates, the result of pitting lightly armed, high-mobility forces against an increasingly lethal and fortified Japanese enemy.

Many of the original concepts of employment for Raiders had either proved invalid or been usurped by other forces as the war progressed. Evans Carlson and James Roosevelt had proposed that Raiders serve as long-range guerrilla forces in occupied Japanese territories. The best application of this mission in the Pacific War would have been in Burma or the Philippines, but neither area evolved as a reasonable objective for Marines (British and U.S. Army units served well in that capacity in the former and army forces in the latter). The primary mission for Raiders rather quickly became linked to amphibious warfare, much as Holland Smith and Merritt Edson had envisioned in 1941.

Combat missions assigned to Marine Raiders during 1942–1943 commonly took the form of what may be called either "Stiletto" or "Spear Head" operations. Both required amphibious mobility, stealthy delivery, surprise, and a certain lion-heartedness. "Stiletto" operations were pure hit-and-run raids, executed to stab and distract the enemy and destroy some of his supplies and equipment. Such missions could be achieved by small units—a company, for example, certainly nothing larger than a light battalion. Makin, Tasimboko, and Koiari were "Stiletto" operations.

"Spear Head" missions involved larger Raider units engaged at greater risk and for higher stakes. The challenge was to lead an amphibious assault, land early, preferably by surprise at dark, and seize the beachhead and its critical terrain features to facilitate the landing of larger, follow-on forces. Tulagi serves as one example of this type mission. The best example comes from the U.S. Army's recapture of Attu Island in the Aleutians. The 7th Division landed its scouts from the submarine *Nautilus* by night prior to D-Day to seize the hills ringing the proposed beachhead. This worked well. Likewise, the 1st Marine Raider Battalion served admirably as a "Spear Head" in their New Georgia campaign by leading the regiment ashore at Rice Anchorage, penetrating the flooded jungle swamps, and seizing Enogai. At that point, had Commander Task

Force 31 reinforced the Raiders via the captured port with a conventional infantry battalion supported by even a battery of artillery, the 1st and 4th Raiders might have been able to sweep the board clean at Bairoko.

In the same context, Colonel Alan Shapley's 2d Raider Regiment served in part as a "Spear Head" at Bougainville. The 2d Raiders landed on the right of the Koromokina River; the 3d Raiders stormed Puruata Island. But the 3d and 9th Marines formed equal parts of the Bougainville "Spear Head," again begging the question as to the continued necessity for special assault units.

Undeniably the Raiders achieved their highest value to the nation and their Corps during the Guadalcanal campaign of 1942, a desperate struggle in which the availability of superbly trained Raider Battalions with their aggressive, indomitable spirit proved so vital to the 1st Marine Division. The Raiders best manifested their special value at Edson's Ridge, one of the epic battles in American history.

After Bougainville, however, the nature of the Pacific War—and the Marines' role within it—changed drastically. Watchful Raider leaders discerned four major factors bearing on their future.

The Pacific War entered a distinctive new phase around the middle of November 1943, the "fault line" occurring between Bougainville and Tarawa. The Bougainville landing followed the old pattern in the South Pacific sub-theater: another half-step up the long ladder of the Solomons towards Rabaul; a site carefully selected within range of land-based aviation; a maximum emphasis on surprise and speed of execution; a minimal preliminary bombardment by four destroyers; an abject inability to transport the landing force's new Sherman 75mm medium tanks to the objective; and a hasty, pell-mell offload before the inevitable counterattacks appeared. The 3d Marine Division and its attached Raider Regiment made it work, despite the drawbacks.

The Tarawa assault in the Gilberts three weeks later stands in vivid contrast. Although still executed in a hurry, still mindful of an intervention by the Japanese Combined Fleet in nearby Truk, the Central Pacific Force surrounded the atoll with a formidable armada of its own, pounded the island with battleships and cruisers, launched Sherman tanks in the assault waves from a weird-looking new amphibious ship called an LSD (dock landing ship), and intercepted most Japanese aircraft and submarines that sortied from the Marshalls. Despite many mistakes, heavy casualties, and a determined Japanese defense, the 2d Marine Division seized tiny Betio Island—known till then as "The Gibraltar of the Pacific"—in three days. The rest of the Gilberts fell within a week. The great Central Pacific drive thereby achieved enough momentum to march across the ocean in seven-league boots towards Iwo Jima, Okinawa, and Japan itself.

The new *Essex* class of fleet carriers made the biggest difference in the Gilberts campaign. The leading ship had been commissioned while the 1st Marine Raider Battalion enjoyed its liberty in Wellington nearly a year earlier. Now the new ships had reached the Pacific in numbers sufficient to give Chester Nimitz and his fleet commanders an insurmountable edge over the Imperial Navy. Their fast carrier task forces would figuratively sweep the seas.

The need for surprise in amphibious landings consequently diminished, and so did the value of light, hit-and-run, raiding forces. Landing force commanders, facing increasingly fortified island objectives, came to favor prolonged, preliminary, daylight, naval bombardment over hasty, surprise landings at night. Bougainville's one hour of preparatory fire gave way to three hours at Tarawa, then to thirteen days at Guam. And while amphibious commanders continued to conduct diversionary landings to confuse the enemy, the scale increased significantly from Krulak's Choiseul model. The entire 2d Marine Division executed successful "bogus" landings at Tinian and Okinawa.

Moreover, the proliferation of specialized new amphibious ships diminished the need for Raiders. A landing force commander who could count on beaching a battalion of medium tanks on the heels of the assault waves had therein his own "Spear Head." Even the 1st Raiders' trademark mobility, the APD fast transports, fell from grace. The newer APA attack transports, while not as fast, possessed more defensive firepower, carried eight times as many assault troops and boats, and were built with much better damage control features. The last factor was not the least concern. When a Japanese bomber torpedoed the faithful old warhorse USS *McKean* (APD 5) enroute to Bougainville the night of 17 November, the ship sank in twenty-eight minutes. Fifty-two of the 185 embarked Marines and sixty-four sailors were lost.[12]

Each new transport could deliver an entire reinforced infantry battalion with all their weapons and vehicles. A Marine Raider company, severely constrained in numbers and weapons by the limited lift of its APD, paled in comparison, despite its undeniable fighting heart.

The scope of amphibious warfare, in other words, had outgrown the customary role of Marine Raiders by 1944.

A second factor that foreshadowed the demise of the Raiders was the emergence of the standard Marine infantry battalion as a multi-mission

The war had changed by 1944. Now redesignated as the 1st Battalion, 4th Marines, the former Raiders debark to assault Emirau Island. Guam and Okinawa would follow.

combat force. Increasingly, Marine riflemen began taking on roles once considered achievable only by the Raiders. As early as September 1942 on Guadalcanal, Colonel Bill Whaling formed a "scout-sniper group," an elite and skillful band of jungle-savvy sharpshooters. By the time of Tarawa, the 2d Marine Division had highly trained scout-sniper platoons in each infantry regiment; indeed, the scout-snipers of the 2d Marines under Lieutenant William Deane Hawkins were the first to engage the enemy, landing a storming party at the head of Betio's long pier five minutes before the assault waves touched down.

Similarly, the regular infantry battalions co-opted the Raiders' role as rubber boat landing parties. Major General Julian Smith in 1943 directed that the first battalion in each regiment of his 2d Marine Division maintain proficiency in rubber boat landings. Major William K. Jones took this responsibility to heart, training his 1st Battalion, 6th Marines in rubber boat operations so industriously he garnered the nickname "The Admiral of the Condom Fleet" (with due respect to the late Gunnery Sergeant Gerald B. Stackpole, killed a year earlier at Edson's Ridge). As a consequence, the most successful rubber boat landing of the Pacific War came not from the Raiders, long identified by their ubiquitous black "condoms," but from Jones' 1/6, whose sunset landing with 880 fresh troops over Betio's Green Beach at the close of the second day of the fighting provided the indisputable turning point of the battle.

The firepower gap between infantry and Raider battalions grew exponentially after Guadalcanal. By 1944, with the Raiders still constrained to their light machine guns and 60mm mortars, the standard infantry battalion could storm a fortified island armed with flame throwers, 81mm mortars, and bunker-busting rocket launchers. Assault battalions were frequently reinforced with 37mm anti-tank guns and self-propelled 75mm guns ("Half-Tracks") from the regimental weapons company.

The typical infantry battalion commander by 1944 had become a master at coordinating his supporting arms. If his troops became stymied by a thorny Japanese pillbox, the battalion commander merely had to look over his shoulder and motion for the services of his attached artillery forward observer team, the naval gunfire control team, the tactical air control party, or the tank liaison officer—or all of them together. Raider Battalion commanders rarely had such a luxury (with the notable exception of the 11th Marines' forward observers who stood by Edson so valiantly at Bloody Ridge). While few infantry battalions could match the Raiders' ability to kill the enemy with superb marksmanship, disciplined light machine-gun fire, or their bare hands, the evolution of Japanese counterlanding tactics towards fortified caves favored the infantry's combined arms of longer range and higher velocity.

A logical new mission for the Marine Raiders in 1944 could have been amphibious reconnaissance, but specialized new forces along these lines were already in place. Navy Underwater Demolition Teams, so dramatically needed along Betio's fringing reefs, first appeared in the Marshalls. Augmented by regular Marines, these "half fish, half crazy" naval swimmers proved instrumental in preparing the difficult landings at Saipan, Peleliu, and especially Iwo Jima. Similarly, Holland Smith's experimental reconnaissance unit had emerged as the Fleet Marine Force Reconnaissance Company (later Battalion), commanded throughout the war by Captain (later Major) James Logan Jones. The Force Reconn Marines performed many missions that would have been suitable for the existing Raiders with a little postgraduate training. They launched in rubber boats from the submarine *Nautilus* to seize Apamama Atoll during the Tarawa campaign, acquiring a site that soon provided the most outstanding airfield in the Gilberts. Their stealthy reconnaissance of potential landing beaches at Tinian provided invaluable intelligence. They landed at night to seize offshore islands around Okinawa for field artillery outposts or early warning radar sites against incoming kamikaze attacks. The Raiders had the valor and elan for such missions—but the Force Reconn Marines got there first.

The third factor bearing on the Raiders' demise involved fundamental changes within the Marine Corps itself.

The Corps had emerged from World War I in dire need of a distinctive new mission. Their service in France, glorious as it had been, duplicated the role of the U.S. Army. The visionary leadership of Marines like "Pete" Ellis, John Lejeune, and John Russell led the Corps to the brink of a revolutionary new mission, offensive amphibious warfare, but the doctrine remained unproven and suspect, the capability crippled by lack of assault ships and landing craft. The Marine Corps in 1940 was still a backwater outfit of ships' detachments, patchwork brigades, and static defense battalions. A weaker Commandant than Thomas Holcomb might have rolled over and accepted President Franklin D. Roosevelt's well-meaning suggestion to convert the few operating forces of the Corps into commando units along the British lines. This was a major turning point for the Leathernecks. Had the Corps dutifully followed the commando path they probably would have fought World War II with a maximum strength of about 30,000 men (as opposed to 500,000). Their commando forces— gallant, outgunned, and increasingly marginal—would have contributed little to the overall war effort, and the Marine Corps would quite likely have been legislated out of existence in the postwar cutbacks.

Instead, to the everlasting credit of Holcomb, Vandegrift, and Holland Smith, the Marines embraced the amphibious mission and rose to unprecedented prominence by virtue of their service throughout the Pacific. Along the way, especially during the first two lean years of the war, the Marines complied with the spirit of their commander in chief's request by conducting a wholesale test and evaluation of amphibious Raiders (not commandos). It was a noble experiment, and the Raiders gave the nation a terrific psychological boost by their swagger and valor during the darkest days in the South Pacific. But by 1944 the Marine Corps had bigger fish to fry. General Vandegrift at Guadalcanal had planned his defensive campaign in terms of battalions. Now as Commandant he concerned himself with the four Marine divisions and four Marine aircraft wings already in the field—plus the two additional divisions needed for the Central Pacific drive just underway.

In the end, the Corps secured its future usefulness to the nation not just on the brilliant incandescence of Tulagi, Makin, and Tasimboko, or even the Marines' ghastly beach-front toeholds at Tarawa or Iwo Jima, but mainly on its demonstrated ability to wage a complete campaign with combined arms from the sea, the staying power to fight from D-Day to total victory—three weeks at Saipan, thirty-six days at Iwo, eighty-two days at Okinawa. Doing so demanded immense firepower, large-scale logistic support, and standardized training. Within such a massive concentration of effort there was no longer any room for small, specialized units, with their own peculiar weapons and equipment, unique training camps, and inherently high casualty rates.

The fourth major factor bearing on the future employment of Raider battalions was the abiding prejudice against them held by many senior Marines. As Holcomb had feared from the first, creating "elite units within an elite Corps" caused disruptive animosity from non-Raider units. His successor as Commandant shared similar views. As General Vandegrift remarked in 1962, "I had always felt—and I knew General Holcomb felt it to a degree, too—that a well-trained infantry battalion could do anything that these other specialists could do. Of course they couldn't be parachutists or gliders...but they could certainly be raiders."[13]

"You don't have a Marine Corps within the Marine Corps," said Colonel Alan Shapley, who had relieved Evans Carlson in command of the 2d Raider Battalion. Shapley recommended the units be disbanded even after commanding the Raider Regiment in Bougainville. "I believed, as General Edson believed, that there wasn't much a Raider battalion could do that a good Marine battalion couldn't do."

Citadel history professor (and Marine colonel) Dr. John W. Gordon concluded that the Raiders' style of operations "became an anachronism belonging to the dark days after Pearl Harbor, and their elitism an embarrassment to the standard, work-horse infantry battalions which now began the drive across the Pacific."[14]

The regular infantry battalions were earning their own combat spurs. In September 1942 every rifleman in the Corps stood in awe of Edson's Raiders for their legendary defense of Bloody Ridge. A year later, the Marines on Guadalcanal turned out to cheer the Raiders as they returned from their courageously failed attempt to storm Bairoko Harbor. Yet most infantry battalions by the end of 1943 had experienced their own epic battles. Those Marines who had fought for Bougainville's Hellzapoppin Ridge, or Cape Gloucester's Aogiri Ridge (with Lew Walt), or crossed the reef under fire at Betio were no longer inclined to suffer the condescending cockiness of the Raiders, nor anyone else.

In retrospect the Raiders could have been used more effectively if the theater commander had assigned more frequent missions with troop-carrying submarines. The navy had three such craft available in the Pacific at the war's beginning. Two were used successfully in the Makin Raid. Then the propensity to use submarines to insert and withdraw Marine Raiders disappeared. Yet the concept was not new to Edson's Raiders. Major Ken Bailey, for one, had executed night landings by rubber boats from a submarine in the Caribbean in early 1938 when he was a second lieutenant in the 5th Marines. Sam Griffith had suggested this mode of tactical mobility during his tenure in command of the 1st Raider Battalion. Nothing came of these overtures. As we have seen, the Japanese sank the transport sub *Argonaut,* and the Force Reconn Marines used the *Nautilus* to seize Apamama. [15]

Had there been a continued link with the transport submarines, the Raiders might still have retained a certain operational value after Bougainville. Admiral Nimitz, for example, might have deployed sub-launched Raiders to sting isolated Japanese-held islands like Wake or Marcus, or even the Kuriles, north of Japan. But these at best would have been "Stiletto" operations, more like a pinprick. By 1944 pinpricks were insufficient. The time had come to bulldoze the Japanese from their island outposts by brute force.

Each of these factors led senior Marines to the decision to abolish the Raiders.

Colonel Omar T. Pfeiffer, the former senior Marine officer for Admiral Nimitz now serving in the War Plans Division for the Chief of Naval Operations, paved the way for this decision in late December 1943. Pfeiffer was both an astute force planner and an artful negotiator. During the Christmas season he brokered a compromise agreement between General Holcomb (Vandegrift would not become Commandant until the first of the year) and Admiral King concerning the disbandment of the Raiders.

"The Marine Corps has always felt that its infantry elements are essentially raiders," Pfeiffer wrote in a memorandum to King, "and that Pacific conditions are different from the European which resulted in the establishment of commandos. [The Marine Corps] would like to end its raider program so as to make all infantry organizations uniform and to avoid setting up some organizations as elite or selected troops." Pfeiffer then added the sweeping claim long favored by the Commandant: "Any operation so far carried out by raiders could have been performed equally well by a standard organization specifically trained for that specific operation."

Seeking a middle ground between Holcomb's antipathy towards the Raiders and King's lukewarm support, Pfeiffer suggested the Raider Battalions be disbanded, then combined to form a conventional infantry regiment, trained and equipped for raiding operations if necessary. In a flash of brilliance, Pfeiffer suggested the new regiment take the same name and lineage of the 4th Marines, captured by the Japanese at Corregidor in May 1942. To further reflect their roots and residual capabilities, the Commandant allowed the new regiment to call itself "the 4th Marines (Raiders)." King agreed. Holcomb announced the decision in a 29 December message to the Commanding General, I Marine Amphibious Corps in Nouméa. The effective date would be 1 February 1944, sixteen days shy of the second anniversary of the establishment of the 1st Raider Battalion in Quantico.[16]

The Raiders could see the end coming. Some railed against it. Said Captain Anthony "Cold Steel" Walker of the 3d Raiders, "Our failure at Bairoko was used as an argument for eliminating the Raider organization, but, in fact, if we had been provided the gunfire of one destroyer we may well have won." Lieutenant Lee Minier believed the Raiders' own publicity had been their undoing. "The Raiders are no more," he wrote home. "There was too much publicity and false and exaggerated stories and movies being published about Raiders and other special units and the Marine Corps doesn't like that sort of thing. So we have become a regular line regiment."[17]

Captain Art Haake, one of the original platoon commanders in Edson's Raiders before transferring to the 3d Raider Battalion, waxed poetic about the changeover:

*Here's some news to make you hot;*
  *They're doing away with the best they've got*
*And throwing us in with the common lot,*
  *For we're the last of the Raiders.*

*So put away your boots and knives,*
  *As souvenirs of the Raiders lives.*
*And do your fighting with your wives.*
  *For we're the last of the Raiders.*

*Our chow was poor, we had no sacks—*
  *Just ammunition in our packs.*
*We've never seen the WAVES or WACS,*
  *For we're the last of the Raiders.*

*So throw away your Raider schemes,*
  *And throw away your Raider dreams.*
*We're going to join the Fourth Marines.*
  *For we ARE the last of the Raiders.* [18]

Frank Guidone, an original member of Edson's Raiders who had made every landing, could see the commandant's logic. "I have always maintained we were not unlike any other infantry battalion," he wrote in a 1991 letter to historian Jon Hoffman. "Our engagements with the enemy were largely conventional with the exception of the Tasimboko Raid." What made Edson's Raiders different, Guidone believed, was the battalion's unique leadership and spirit. "We were blessed with exceptional junior officers and good upper brass leadership." The same could be said for the quality of the unit's squad leaders and platoon sergeants. [19]

There were new leaders now, but it would soon be evident that the same spirit prevailed. Edson's Raiders became the 1st Battalion, 4th Marines on 1 February 1944 with surprisingly little gnashing of teeth, and the traditions continued.

## The Fourth Marines

The Headquarters compromise title "Fourth Marines (Raiders)" did not last a day on Guadalcanal. "This is going to be a Marine regiment," Colonel Shapley announced to all hands as he assumed command, and from that point forward the parenthetical "(Raiders)" disappeared from the regimental letterhead.

Alan Shapley's war had begun on 7 December 1941 in Pearl Harbor when a Japanese bomb blew him off the battleship *Arizona*. He swam to Ford Island, stripped off his oil-soaked clothes, then stalked the island buck naked, searching for a weapon with which to fight back. He now had that weapon in hand. Under his strong leadership the 4th Marines would achieve a sterling combat record throughout the next eighteen months, and Shapley would avenge Pearl Harbor several times over. Although he had forcefully suppressed the last vestiges of the Raiders, he was unabashedly proud of his veteran regiment. "You'll never convince me," he said later, "that the 4th Marines wasn't the best regiment the Marine Corps had in World War Two. I certainly had the material." [20]

On 20 March 1944 the 4th Marines landed unopposed on Emirau Island in the Admiralties. In August, as part of Major General Lemuel C. Shepherd's 1st Provisional Marine Brigade, the regiment stormed ashore on Guam. Shepherd's brigade became the nucleus of the 6th Marine Division, the only division formed entirely overseas. Colonel Shapley led his regiment ashore at Okinawa on April Fool's Day 1945, and the regiment fought with distinction at Mount Yae Take, Horseshoe Ridge in the Sugar Loaf complex, and the Oroku Peninsula. Those veterans of the 1st and 4th Raiders still in the regiment enjoyed a grim satisfaction in the amphibious seizure of Oroku Peninsula. There General Shepherd's division outfoxed and ultimately destroyed the forces of Rear Admiral Minoru Ota, the last great *rikusentai,* who had commanded the 8th Combined Special Landing Forces in New Georgia and Kolombangara during the Raiders' assault on Bairoko. After ten violent days, Ota—colorful to the end—donned his dress uniform, radioed a final salute to the Emperor, and committed hari-kari.[21]

On 30 August 1945 in Tokyo Bay the 4th Marines formed a combined landing force with the Royal Marines and blue-jackets from both nations to execute the initial ship-to-shore movement in defeated Japan. Landing in the Yokosuka Naval Base, the allied force fanned out to liberate prisoner-of-war camps. This was heart-rending work. Many of the POWs represented the survivors of the original 4th Marines captured more than three years earlier. In a memorable ceremony, the new 4th Marines marched in review to honor the enfeebled survivors, who somehow struggled to their feet, crying unashamedly, as the regimental colors streamed past.

The road to Tokyo through the Central Pacific exacted a high toll among the former 1st Raiders in the 4th Marines. Fifty-two died in the fighting on Guam; fifty-nine on Okinawa. Perhaps because they had once been Raiders they became marked men, distinctive veterans of whom so much more was expected. In the heavy fighting on Guam and Okinawa, it did not particularly matter whether a man had been a cook, a baker, or a candlestick-maker in the 1st Raiders; if new troops discovered they had "fought with Edson or Sam Griffith" they were supposed to lead from the front.

Lieutenant Lee Minier rejected the opportunity to return to the States after his second anniversary overseas passed. He wrote his family on 11 May 1944 that he would be "staying on for another campaign. This one should be most interesting and I didn't want to miss it." A month later he wrote again: "Have been aboard ship for two weeks. Going into action again....This is going to be an all-Marine show. Thank goodness. Give everyone my love, Lee."

On 21 July the 4th Marines landed on the right flank of the brigade beachhead on the southwest coast of Guam. That afternoon, as the 1st

Battalion fought to control Hill 40 during their violent advance towards Alifan Ridge, Lieutenant Minier crossed an open field to locate improved firing positions for his machine-gun crews. Japanese gunfire struck him in the head, killing him instantly. Lee Minier had celebrated his twenty-seventh birthday aboard ship four days earlier. His troops mourned the loss of this perpetually cheerful and thoroughly professional young Raider.[22]

Captain Frank Kemp, Dog Company's stalwart young commander at Bairoko, fell on Okinawa, badly wounded by a Japanese artillery shell. Lieutenant Leonard Fribourg received two Purple Hearts during a nineteen day span in that campaign. Corporal Richard E. Bush, who had joined the 1st Raiders in October 1943, served as a squad leader in 1/4 on Okinawa. There, on 16 April 1945, he ferociously led his squad up the steep slopes of Mount Yae Take. Seriously wounded and evacuated, he kept his presence of mind when a Japanese soldier lobbed a hand grenade into the forward aid station. Bush grabbed the grenade and crushed it to his body to shield his fellow wounded Marines. Gravely wounded in the blast, Bush became one of only a precious few Marines to live through an act of such incalculable unselfishness. After the war, President Harry S. Truman draped the Medal of Honor around his neck.

Merritt Edson, assigned as chief of staff of the 2d Marine Division before Tarawa, visited the hospitals throughout New Zealand and Australia looking for former Raiders recuperating from the New Georgia campaign to beef up his new outfit. More than 150 answered his call, providing an invaluable core of well-trained veterans to the 2d Division. Eleven former 1st Raiders died at Tarawa, including two "plank-holders" from Quantico days, Sergeants Wallace J. Clark (previously wounded on the first day at Tulagi) and William C. Culp. Sergeant Culp died on D-Day in the assault on Red Beach Two, virtually the eye of the storm. Sergeant Clark died in the fighting for Buariki at the bitter end of the atoll on the last day of the campaign.[23]

Among former 1st Marine Raiders who went on to serve elsewhere in the Pacific rather than with the 4th Marines, eight died at Iwo Jima, four at Saipan, and one each at Tinian and Bougainville. Not all Raiders died in combat. Sergeant John Simonich, whom Lee Minier regarded as the toughest Marine in the battalion, died in an accidental explosion of TNT during a training exercise in Camp Pendleton, California, on 12 December 1944. Simonich, who had survived all seven of the Raiders' battles and severe wounds at Edson's Ridge, left a widow and a four-month-old daughter. He was twenty-six years old when he died.

Lieutenant Colonel "Jumping Joe" Chambers recovered from his Tulagi wounds in time to return to combat in command of the 3d Battalion, 25th Marines, 4th Marine Division. Merritt Edson's unique and unremitting combat training at Quantico and Samoa had left a deep impression on Chambers, and he prepared his green outfit for battle with a fury. Some of his troops began calling themselves "Chambers' Raiders" half-jokingly. "They all knew I had been with the Raiders and a lot of the training was along the same lines," Chambers said.

At one point staff officers told Chambers to prepare his battalion for a rubber-boat landing on Wotje Island in the Marshalls. Chambers told them they were crazy. "Rubber boats were for small unit hit-and-run operations, not a full infantry battalion. We'd be wiped out." When the requirement stuck, Chambers sought out Major Tony Antonelli at his Raider training camp in Camp Pendleton's Horno Canyon and borrowed all his rubber boats. "About drowned half my men in the high surf," he said. "Then the planners finally wised up."

Chambers led his 3/25 through sequentially difficult landings (in LVTs, not rubber boats) in the Marshalls, Saipan, Tinian, and Iwo Jima, all in less than one year. "After the Marianas," recalled Chambers, "some joker interviewed some of our wounded, and they got to talking about 'Chambers' Raiders.' He wrote it up in a magazine. Later on I was called before General Franklin Hart, the assistant division commander. He informed me that there were 'no goddamned raider battalions in the 4th Division!'"[24]

Chambers' battalion landed on the extreme right flank on D-Day at Iwo Jima. In leading his men off the beach and over the cliffs of the heavily defended Rock Quarry, despite the loss of five hundred casualties, Chambers received the Medal of Honor. Two days later a Japanese Nambu machine gunner shot him through the chest. He survived by the thinnest of margins and, like Corporal Bush, received his medal at the hands of President Truman.

## The Legacy of Edson's Raiders

Three hundred and twelve men who served in the ranks of the 1st Marine Raider Battalion died in combat. Twenty-five others died in training accidents or from sickness. Although they typically fought against seasoned Japanese veterans, the 1st Raiders inflicted a disproportionate number of casualties in the ranks of the Imperial Army and the Special Naval Landing Forces at Tulagi, Tasimboko, Edson's Ridge, the Matanikau River,

**Twenty-year-old Cpl. Richard Earl Bush, who fought with the 1st Raider Battalion on New Georgia, received the Medal of Honor for conspicuous gallantry as a squad leader in the 1st Battalion, 4th Marines on 16 April 1945 at Okinawa.**

Enogai, and Bairoko Harbor. They also qualified for a disproportionate number of the nation's highest awards for individual valor, the Medal of Honor, Navy Cross, Distinguished Service Cross, and Silver Star. Twenty-four U.S. Navy ships were named in honor of 1st Raiders (including one "alumni" serving with another Raider unit). Both the 1st and 2d Raider Battalions qualified for the Presidential Unit Citation awarded the 1st Marine Division for the Guadalcanal campaign.[25]

Merritt Edson was undeniably the "Alpha Raider." By training his Raiders how to think as individuals but fight as a battalion, Edson created a unique organization, one useful to field commanders within a broad spectrum of combat capabilities. His high-spirited Raiders stirred the hopes and fired the imagination of a fearful nation with their early victories and gallant defeats during the war's first year. Although designed solely as an offensive weapon, the 1st Marine Raiders won their most notable battle in the rock-ribbed defense of Edson's Ridge, a conflict that has become one of the indisputable touchstones of Marine Corps history.

The 1941 selection by Generals Holcomb and Smith of Lieutenant Colonel Merritt Edson to command the initial U.S. Raider outfit was fortuitous for the Marine Corps and the nation. Edson was uniquely qualified to command such a bold new battalion. He knew Marines and their weapons. He knew jungle operations. And he knew the Japanese. Within a few short months Edson by force of will converted a disparate group of salty regulars, long-time reserves, and starry-eyed volunteers—lawyers, farmers, soda jerks, roustabouts—into a superbly trained, highly cohesive fighting force. Edson's training program set the standard for generations of future Marines. No one is likely to improve on his formula of physical conditioning, night operations, field craft, cross-training, and marksmanship—*combat* marksmanship.

Edson excelled in combat. "He was completely unflappable—completely unflappable," said Sam Griffith, no slouch in battle himself. Indeed, in Red Mike Edson and Chesty Puller the Marine Corps may have found its all-time greatest combat leaders. The two men were markedly different, but both led from the front, faced the enemy with ice water in their arteries, and—from Nicaragua to the South Pacific—represented hell on wheels to Sandinistas and Japanese alike.[26]

Edson left a quieter but equally significant legacy with his battalion. He passionately believed in recognizing meritorious performance, especially among his enlisted men. He never hesitated to nominate a man for an award, as evidenced the first week of the Tulagi battle when he recommended both Private First Class Ahrens and Gunnery Sergeant Goss for the Medal of Honor. More importantly, he established a system within the 1st Raiders to recognize, screen, and meritoriously promote any man who demonstrated exceptional leadership capabilities in combat. The proportionate number of meritorious promotions and commissionings within the enlisted ranks of the battalion during 1942–1943 surely exceeded those in any other battalion in the Fleet Marine Force. "We commissioned some absolutely outstanding people," said Griffith. Edson ensured that his battalion would perpetuate their initial successes by "growing their own leaders."[27]

Although Edson was handicapped by his reserved personality, there was little doubt in anyone's mind that he loved and valued his troops. As Sam Griffith wrote Lew Walt after Edson's death, "He had an iron will but not an iron heart. He was loyal to all of us, and I know that he placed more store in being a Raider than in the many rewards and decorations he received."[28]

Red Mike Edson's abiding influence on the 1st Marine Raider Battalion is impossible to exaggerate. In the process of establishing an organization of former members in 1949, Lew Walt and Sam Griffith proposed—against Edson's objection—that the outfit be known for its first commander instead of its numerical designator. Thus was born the Edson's Raiders Association, a tightly knit group which in 1999 conducted its fifty-first consecutive annual reunion at Quantico, its surviving veterans evincing a bonding spirit so intense as to be almost tangible to outside guests.[29]

Historian Jon Hoffman's well-researched Fiftieth Anniversary monograph of the Raiders' service in World War II concluded with the observation that "the commanders in the Pacific Theater may not have properly used the Raiders, but the few thousand men of those elite units bequeathed a legacy of courage and competence not surpassed by any other Marine battalion."[30]

Courage and competence. The spirit of the Raiders persists today, not in the form of elite special units, but in the reincarnation of those Marine infantry battalions of 1944–1945, inspired by the Raiders' example, that demonstrated so convincingly they could perform any mission with professional expertise. Modern infantry battalions provide the ground combat element of today's Marine Expeditionary Units (MEUs) that routinely engage in forward deployment operations with the fleet. A hallmark of these well-trained, air-ground task forces has been their qualification as "Special Operations Capable." The certification does not come easily. Candidate units must demonstrate their proficiency in a wide assortment of missions, from hostage rescue to boarding uncooperative ships during a maritime quarantine. During the Allied bombing campaign in Bosnia in the 1990s, to cite one example, such qualified Marines executed a complex "TRAP" (tactical recovery of aircraft and personnel) operation to rescue a downed U.S. Air Force pilot within an hour of receiving his distress signal. "Thank God for the Marines," said the rescued pilot.

Red Mike Edson would have flashed that "so-and-so" grin!

## Epilogue

In northern Guadalcanal in 1989 a farmer dug a hole to plant a tapioca tree at the jungle's edge below a grassy ridge and discovered human remains and a snarl of barbed wire enclosing a blackened dog tag. The medallion bore the faintly discernible name of Frank Russell Whittlesey, USMC. Working with a mere handful of old bones, the Army's Central Identification Laboratory would take three painstaking years to validate the identity and track down the next of kin. The remains proved to be indeed those of Russ Whittlesey, the aspiring poet and Yale student who had volunteered for the Marines, then volunteered again for the Raiders—the unselfish Marine who shoved his wounded buddy Edgar Shepard off the path, then died at the hands of approaching Japanese soldiers at the onset of the second night's battle. By sheer destiny, the farmer had dug his hole exactly in the spot where Captain Sweeney's patrol discovered and buried Whitt's body in the jungle after the battle of Edson's Ridge, a site recorded by Sweeney at the time to be "about 1,000 yards south of the Guadalcanal airfield, just forward of the support line of the 1st Marine Raider Battalion."[31]

On Memorial Day, 25 May 1992, the family of Private Frank Russell Whittlesey brought his remains home from Edson's Ridge for reburial in the family cemetery in Pittsfield, Massachusetts. At the ceremony, Raider Ken Peters read a compassionate salute from Colonel John Sweeney, Raider Ted Eleston delivered a eulogy, and the 25th Marines provided an Honor Guard. A full half century after his heroic death, attended by full military honors, Raider Whittlesey had finally come home.[32]

Memorial services for other Edson's Raiders became a common fact of life as time began to take its toll where Japanese bullets had failed. Colonel John "Tiger" Erskine attended Ben Howland's funeral and was struck again by the bond between each of the veterans. "This affection, tolerance, and genuine interest in each other reinforces the sense of kinship between the Raiders, living and dead," he wrote in 1984. "The whole scene makes me want to be a witness in my own funeral."[33]

Similarly Father Paul J. Redmond, the beloved chaplain of the 1st Raider Regiment in New Georgia, observed on the occasion of his ninety-first birthday, "The men of the Raider Battalion were men tried in the cauldron of adversity—a family so knit that when one died, some part of each one died. When one was wounded all felt pain—a family so close that each one would risk his life for another."[34]

In the end, Raider Vince Cassidy, poet, rifleman, and nonpareil squad leader, seemed to speak for the service and sacrifice of all the Raiders in these sparse verses written after the terrible losses at Bairoko Harbor:

REQUIEM
by Vincent Cassidy

*Sleep well, ye dead*
*Who fought and bled*
*   neath southern skies.*
*Safe in our minds*
*Your memory finds*
*   eternal life.*
*No longer fear,*
*Nor start to hear*
*   wild battle cries.*
*Such things are past*
*You've peace at last,*
*   and no more strife.*
*Oh, ye who died*
*   there at our side*
*   though great your loss*
*By dying you*
*   gave meaning to*
*a Southern cross.*[35]

The five stars of the Southern Cross, a constellation visible only in distant lands below the Equator such as the Solomon Islands, form part of the Raiders' distinctive insignia patch. The white skull on the red Sandinista flag catches one's first impression; the five stars abide, forever.

Rest in peace, Raiders.

## Notes

1. Samuel B. Griffith to Historical Division, HQMC, 6 October 1945, Griffith papers, MCHC.
2. Minier to family, 30 August 1943 and 25 September 1943, from Dr. Minier, *Raider,* 235.
3. Griffith Oral memoir, MCOHC, MCHC, 145.
4. Peatross, *Bless 'em All,* 232.
5. *The Dope Sheet,* 1990, 7–1; *Fortitudine,* Fall 1993, 27. Palonis retired in 1969 as a lieutenant colonel; Fribourg in 1974 as a brigadier general.
6. Poppell Diary, 26 October–4 November 1943, 54–55; Minier to family, 24 November 1943, from Dr. Minier, *Raider,* 236.
7. Dr. Byron H. Eller to Edson's Raiders Association, 17 February 1992.

8. Charles L. Capron, "Brig Time in New Caledonia's Camp Bailey," undated memoir, author's possession. Capron joined the battalion in December 1943. He was wounded in action in Okinawa on 15 April 1945, two weeks after the landing.

9. Poppell Diary, 16–23 December 1943 and 2–15 January 1944, 58–59; Minier to family, 9 January 1944, from Dr. Minier, *Raider*, 239.

10. Poppell Diary, 24 January 1944, 60. Poppell records departing Nouméa on 21 January 1944 and arriving on the 24th, counter to the battalion's chronology. Henry C. Poppell left the old outfit a week later, transferred to the new 3d Battalion, 4th Marines. Both he and his valuable journal survived the war intact.

11. Henry I. Shaw, Jr., and Douglas T. Kane, *Isolation of Rabaul: History of U.S. Marine Corps Operations in World War II,* Vol. II (Washington, D.C.: HQMC, 1963), 271–72.

12. *Dictionary of American Naval Fighting Ships,* 302.

13. Vandegrift Oral Memoir, MCOHC, MCHC, 967–68.

14. Gordon, "The U.S. Marine Corps and an Experiment in Military Elitism: A Reassessment of the Special Warfare Impetus, 1937–43," 370.

15. 2d Lt. Kenneth D. Bailey to Col. S. M. Harrington, "Night Reconnaissance, report of," 5 March 1938, Serial 65A-4552, Box 2, Exercises and Operations, WNRC. Bailey conducted at least two submarine-launched reconnaissance operations during Fleet Landing Exercise #4, first off Vieques Island, then near Ponce Playa, Puerto Rico.

16. Charles L. Updegraph, Jr., *U.S. Marine Corps Special Units of World War II,* (Washington, D.C.: HQMC, 1972), 34–35; See also Commandant of the Marine Corps (by this time Gen. Vandegrift) to CG, Fleet Marine Force, San Diego Area, "Marine Corps Parachute and Raider Units," 8 January 1944, Box 1806, RG 127, National Archives. Paragraph four reads: "The 1st Raider Regiment and the 2d Raider Regiment (Provisional) have been ordered reorganized as the 4th Marines (Raiders)....Johnson LMGs will replace the BARs as far as practicable." The next paragraph advised that the Raider Training Battalion had also been disbanded and its personnel [including Major Antonelli] transferred to the new 5th Marine Division.

17. Anthony Walker, "New Georgia Revisited," in Sexton, *Our Kind of War,* 89; Lee Minier to family, 20 February 1944, from Dr. Minier, *Raider,* 241. Minier may have been sad at the breakup of the Raiders but he was proud of the lineage of the 4th Marines.

18. A. A. Haake, "Last of the Raiders," n.d., reprinted in the 1994 Marine Raiders Association Reunion Packet, copy in author's possession.

19. Frank Guidone to Jon Hoffman, 1991.

20. "This is going to be a Marine regiment," attributed to Alan Shapley in Charles L. Banks Oral Memoir, MCOHC, MCHC, 22; Alexander, *A Fellowship of Valor,* 73, 244; Alan Shapley Oral Memoir, MCOHC, MCHC, 82.

21. Alexander, *Storm Landings*, 169–70, 206.

22. Lee Minier to family, 11 May 1944 and 11 June 44, from Dr. Minier, *Raider*, 243–44; Author interview with Dr. Minier, 9 April 1999; Lee Neil Minier Casualty Card.

23. Peatross, *Bless 'em All*, 281; Casualty Cards for sergeants Wallace J. Clark and William C. Culp.

24. Paul H. Chambers, ed., *The Third Battalion, Twenty-Fifth Marines: An Oral History of Col. Justice Marion Chambers, USMCR (Ret.)*, unpublished manuscript, 1987, 8.

25. Fatality figures based on the Edson's Raiders Association "Lest We Forget" roster. Combat deaths combine the three categories of killed in action, died of wounds, and missing in action presumed dead.

26. Samuel Griffith Oral Memoir, MCOHC, MCHC, 86.

27. *Ibid.*, 87.

28. Samuel Griffith to Lewis Walt, 16 February 1956, Box 15, F21, Griffith Papers, MCHC.

29. "Edson's Raiders Association," *The Dope Sheet*, November 1957, 1–2.

30. Jon T. Hoffman, *From Makin to Bougainville: Marine Raiders in the Pacific War* (Washington, D.C.: History and Museums Division, HQMC, 1995), 40.

31. Kevin Klose, "Lost Marine Comes Home," *The Washington Post*, 25 May 1992, A-1; Death Certificate, Private Frank R. Whittlesey, copy in author's possession.

32. Klose, "Lost Marine Comes Home," A-1; Memorial Service leaflet and eulogy provided courtesy Col. John Sweeney.

33. John C. Erskine, "In Memoriam," *Leatherneck*, April 1984, 6.

34. Father Paul J. Redmond, quoted by Fred A. Serral, *The Dope Sheet*, May 1992, 10.

35. Vincent Cassidy, "Requiem," written in 1943 after the New Georgia campaign, reprinted in *The Dope Sheet*, July 1988, 7. Dedicated in that issue at the request of Edward Drziak in special memory of Marine Gunner Angus Goss.

# Appendix A

## Battle Honors and Commanding Officers, 1st Marine Raider Battalion, 1942–1944

### Official Battle Honors

7–9 August 1942: Tulagi-Guadalcanal Landings

10 August–13 October 1942: Capture and Defense of Guadalcanal (Presidential Unit Citation, 1st Marine Division)

5 July–28 August 1943: New Georgia Occupation

### Battle Chronology

7–30 August 1942: Tulagi Assault

8 September 1942: Tasimboko Raid, Guadalcanal

12–14 September 1942: Battle of Edson's Ridge, Guadalcanal

27 September 1942: Matanikau I, Guadalcanal

8–9 October 1942: Matanikau II, Guadalcanal

5–10 July 1943: Seizure of Enogai, New Georgia

20–21 July 1943: Battle for Bairoko Harbor, New Georgia

### Commanding Officers

16 February–21 September 1942: Lieutenant Colonel (later Colonel) Merritt A. Edson, USMC

21–27 September 1942: Lieutenant Colonel Samuel B. Griffith II, USMC (WIA)

27 September 1942–13 January 1943: Major Ira J. Irwin, USMCR

13 January–8 September 1943: Lieutenant Colonel Samuel B. Griffith II, USMC

8 September–3 October 1943: Major George W. Herring, USMC

3 October 1943–1 February 1944: Major Charles L. Banks, USMC

# Appendix B

## Ships Named after 1st Marine Raiders

| Ship | Individual Raider Honored | Remarks |
|------|---------------------------|---------|
| DE 575 | PFC Edward H. AHRENS | KIA, 7 August 1942, Tulagi |
| DD 713 | Maj. Kenneth D. BAILEY | KIA, 27 September 1942 Matanikau I |
| APD 39 | PFC Woodrow W. BARR | KIA, 7 August 1942, Tulagi |
| APD 136 | PFC Louis J. CARPELLOTTI | KIA, 7 August 1942, Tulagi |
| DE 450 | Cpl. Joseph E. CONNOLLY | KIA, 9 October 1942, Matanikau II |
| APD 130 | Sgt. Dallas H. COOK [A Co. "Alumni"] | KIA, 18 August 1942, Makin [2d RDRs] |
| DD 946 | Maj. Gen. Merritt A. EDSON | MOH, 12–13 September 1942, The Ridge |
| DD 829 | 1st Lt. Myles C. FOX | KIA, 8 August 1942, Tulagi |
| DE 367 | Cpl. Neldon T. FRENCH | KIA, 9 October 1942, Matanikau II |
| DE 508 | Pvt. John J. GILLIGAN | KIA, 8 August 1942, Tulagi |
| DE 444 | Marine Gunner Angus R. GOSS | KIA, 20 July 1943, Bairoko |
| DD 712 | Pvt. Edward E. GYATT | KIA, 7 August 1942, Tulagi |
| DE 449 | Pvt. William T. HANNA | KIA, 9 October 1942, Matanikau II |

| Ship | Individual Raider Honored | Remarks |
|------|--------------------------|---------|
| DE 510 | PFC George HEYLIGER | KIA, 9 October 1942, Matanikau II |
| DE 583 | Pvt. George A. JOHNSON | KIA, 10 August 1942, Tulagi |
| DE 348 | 1st Lt. Eugene M. KEY | KIA, 7 August 1942, Tulagi |
| DE 577 | Pl. Sgt. Alexander J. LUKE | KIA, 7 August 1942, Tulagi |
| DE 183 | Lt. (jg) Samuel S. MILES, MC, USN | KIA, 7 August 1942, Tulagi |
| DE 587 | Pvt. Thomas F. NICKEL | KIA, 7 August 1942, Tulagi |
| DE 578 | Pvt. Robert I. PAINE | KIA, 7 August 1942, Tulagi |
| DE 369 | Ph. M. 2d C. Thaddeus PARKER, USN | KIA, 20 July 1943, Bairoko |
| DD 863 | PFC Donald B. STEINAKER | KIA, 9 October 1942, Matanikau II |
| DD 721 | Sgt. Woodrow R. THOMPSON | KIA, 9 October 1942, Matanikau II |
| APD 129 | Sgt. Donald W. WOLF | KIA, 9 October 1942, Matanikau II |

# Appendix C

## Postwar Milestones

THE 1ST MARINE RAIDER BATTALION lost many leaders in combat, but enough survived to fill the top ranks of the Marine Corps in later years. Silent Lew Walt rose to four-star rank and retired as the assistant commandant. Merritt Edson, Tony Antonelli, Gus Banks, Leonard Fribourg, Sam Griffith, Foster LaHue, and Ed Wheeler became general officers. Clay Boyd, Jumping Joe Chambers, Ed Dupras, Tiger Erskine, Tom Mullahey, Black Jack Salmon, Houston Stiff, Bill Sperling, and John Wolf Sweeney, among others, became colonels. John Carson became a sergeant major, while Ralph Level, Edward Wojciekowski, and Robert Anielski made master gunnery sergeant, among a great number of former Raiders who reached the highest enlisted ranks.

Merritt Edson might well have become commandant. He served overseas in World War II longer than any other general officer, and he earned his Medal of Honor the hard way at the ridge that still bears his name. Yet during the reunification battles that raged between the services and the Truman administration in the late 1940s, Edson typically launched a preemptive spoiling attack, retiring from active duty as a major general so he could be unrestricted in telling the Marine Corps story to the American people. He died in 1955 (the same year, ironically, that Chesty Puller was forced to retire from the Corps due to medical disabilities). Edson was only fifty-eight when he died, and the circumstances of his death (found asphyxiated in his garage with the car running) created a suspicion in more than a few people that he might have taken his own life. Most of his admirers—and they were legion—dismissed the possibility. Former Raiders around the world grieved over his premature passing. Bill Stephenson, Edson's feisty communications officer at Tulagi and Guadalcanal, wrote in a Florida newspaper, "It is with a heavy heart that one of his old Raiders learns that Red Mike Edson has been ordered to 'permanent duty beyond the seas.'" Regardless of the circumstances, Merritt Edson departed this world as one of the greatest combat leaders in American military history.[1]

Major General Kiyotake Kawaguchi died in Japan on 16 May 1961 at age sixty-eight. The Allied war crimes tribunal sentenced him in 1949 to six years confinement at hard labor for the murder of the Filipino chief justice in Cebu in May 1942, four months before his orders to Guadalcanal.[2]

Commander Saburo Okumura escaped from Bairoko with the remnants of the Kure 6th Special Naval Landing Force during late August 1943. In December he took command of the 88th Naval Garrison on Manus Island in the Admiralties. Okumura and about half of his force held on for several months after the American landing on that small island. On 1 May 1944 Okumura sent one final message to Imperial General Headquarters, "No men have equipage or provisions. We ask for directions." There is no record to indicate the date he perished.[3]

In September 1961 former Raider Marvin D. Butterfield, badly wounded on Guam while serving in Captain Tom Mullahey's C Company, 1st Battalion, 4th Marines, returned his souvenir Japanese battle flag to the elder brother of the slain Japanese soldier from whom it had been taken in 1944.[4]

In 1979 Queen Elizabeth II knighted retired Sergeant Major Jacob C. Vouza, distinguished Solomon Islander scout who accompanied the 1st Marine Raiders during their surprise raid on Tasimboko, his native village.

On 6 August 1989 General Al Gray, the twenty-ninth commandant of the Marine Corps, and Association president James V. Mallamas officiated at a ceremony unveiling the Edson's Raiders Memorial at Quantico National Cemetery. Designed by landscape architect Eric Groft, son of veteran Marlin F. ("Whitey") Groft, the memorial was unveiled by two recent widows of former Raiders buried in nearby graves, Mrs. June Walt and Mrs. Sue Howland. A full dozen past presidents of the association attended: Charley Pacini, Ken Peters, Thomas Powers, John Apergis, John DiSalvia, Bob Youngdeer, Frank Fitz, Jack Tracy, John Carson, Henry Poppell, Dr. Bob Skinner, and James "Horse Collar" Smith.

On Flag Day, 14 June 1990, the city of Tampa dedicated Palonis Park in memory of the late Lieutenant Colonel Anthony J. "Big Stoop" Palonis.

On 8 August 1992 Major General Charles Wilhelm, former coastwatcher Martin Clemens, and several surviving Raiders unveiled a new marker on Edson's Ridge on Guadalcanal featuring a bas relief copy of

*Night Attack, Edson's Ridge,* the dramatic painting by Solomons veteran Donald L. Dickson.

On 27 October 1995, fifty-three years after the fact, Secretary of the Navy John Dalton authorized the award of both the Navy Cross and the Silver Star to former Raider corpsman Delbert D. Eilers for extraordinary valor under fire at Edson's Ridge and the "Second" Battle of the Matanikau.

Also in 1995, retired Major Gene C. Martin donated the distinctive samurai sword he captured in the second night's action on Tulagi to the Marine Corps Museum for display in the facility's World War II "Time Tunnel" exhibition.[5]

On 6 August 1999 (7 August in the Solomon Islands), former Raider Robert Youngdeer unveiled a granite memorial in the back yard of his Cherokee, North Carolina, home inscribed to "Red Mike and his Gallant Men, Edson's Raiders, South Pacific, WWII, Semper Fidelis." Youngdeer had survived being shot in the face as he tried to rescue a wounded Marine at first light on 13 September during the Battle for Edson's Ridge. Youngdeer, who named his firstborn son Merritt Edson, served as Principal Chief of the Eastern Band of Cherokees in the mid-1980s. Nearly 100 people attended the private dedication, including many Raiders or their widows who traveled a great distance to stand in honor of their comrades one more time.[6]

## Notes

1. William Stevenson, "Fighting Marine, Gentleman, Patriot," *Titusville Herald,* 16 August 1955. The best account and assessment of Edson's controversial death is contained in the closing chapter of Jon T. Hoffman's superb biography, *Once a Legend.*

2. Ikuhiko Hata, *Nippon Rikukaigun Sogo Jitin* (Tokyo: Daigaku Shuppankai, 1991), 45.

3. *Senshi Sosho: Nanto Homen Kaigun Sakusen, v3 (Southeastern Area Naval Operations, Vol. 3),* 490–92. The Americans declared Manus secured on 5 May 1944. The Japanese IGHQ announced their assumption that their Manus garrison had died to the last man on 31 May 1944. CDR Okumura was posthumously promoted to captain.

4. Dick Fagan, "Mill Ends," *The Oregon Journal,* 21 March 1962, 11.

5. Kenneth L. Smith-Christmas, "Sword Here May be First Taken from Japanese by Marine," *Fortitudine,* Fall, 1995. Major Martin earlier engraved the blade with "Platoon Sergeant Gene C. Martin, USMC, 1st Raider Bn, Tulagi, B.S.I., 8 August 1942."

6. "Monument Honors WWII Marine Battalion," *Asheville Citizen-Times,* 17 August 1999.

# Notes on Sources

PRIMARY SOURCES CONSULTED for this book included the official correspondence between the commandant of the Marine Corps and his general officers; operational message traffic between Admiral Chester Nimitz, Rear Admiral Kelly Turner, Admiral Ernest King, and the commandant; training and evaluation reports from the 1st Battalion, 5th Marines, 1st Separate Battalion, and the 1st Marine Raider Battalion; Reports and Analyses issued by the Commanding General, Amphibious Force, Atlantic Fleet; and the various action reports submitted by the Raiders and their associates during and after the Tulagi, Guadalcanal, and New Georgia campaigns.

Other primary sources included the wartime letters and diaries of participating Raiders; oral memoirs from the Marine Corps Oral History Collection; original Japanese accounts translated from the *Senshi Sosho* war history series; the original battalion Muster Rolls and Casualty (fatality) Cards; and personal correspondence and memoirs from the Edson Papers in the Library of Congress, the Griffith Papers in the Marine Corps Historical Center, and key operational reports held in the National Archives and the Washington National Records Center.

Secondary sources include the fifty-year collection of *The Dope Sheet*, the newsletter of the Edson's Raiders Association; official biographies and award citations maintained by the Reference Section, Marine Corps Historical Center; a rich assortment of wartime and postwar magazine articles (especially those by Sam Griffith, Richard Tregaskis, R. M. Mattingly, and Jon Hoffman); and the hundreds of postwar interviews conducted with surviving Raiders by my predecessors and myself.

Among the related books and monographs, Jon Hoffman's *Once a Legend* (Novato: Presidio Press, 1994) provides the most comprehensive and best-researched biography of the enigmatic Red Mike Edson. On the subject of Raiders and other special Marine Corps units in the Pacific War, see Oscar F. Peatross, *Bless 'em All: The Raider Marines of World War II* (Irvine, California: Review Publications, 1995); Charles L. Updegraph, Jr., *U.S. Marine Corps Special Units of World War II* (Washington, D.C.: HQMC, 1977); Martin J. Sexton, *The Marine Raiders' Historical Handbook* (Richmond: The American Historical Foundation, 1983); and Jon T. Hoffman, *From Makin to Bougainville: Marine Raiders in the Pacific War* (Washington, D.C.: HQMC, 1995). I found Richard Frank's *Guadalcanal: The Definitive Account of the Landmark Battle* (New York: Random House, 1991) to be the most useful work on that enormous campaign. Also insightful and pertinent is Samuel B. Griffith, *The Battle for Guadalcanal* (Philadelphia: Lippincott, 1963). Action on the Dragon's Peninsula in New Georgia in July 1943 is less well covered, but a solid account is contained in John N. Rentz, *Marines in the Central Solomons* (Washington, D.C.: HQMC, 1952), the original monograph. I also recommend two unpublished manuscripts, Herbert R. Edson, "The Do or Die Men: The Development and History of the First Marine Raider Battalion," 1954, and Lee N. Minier, "Raider: An Account of the 1st Marine Raider Battalion," 1989.

The most convincing fictional account of Raiders in the South Pacific is the novel, *The Right Kind of War*, by John McCormick (a 4th Raider Battalion veteran), published in 1992 by the Naval Institute Press. Turner Publishing Company's recent anthology, *History of the Marine Raiders: More than a Few Good Men* (Paducah, Ky.: Turner Publishing Company, 1999), contains useful photographs and anecdotes from all four battalions. Also, the Marine Raider Museum in Richmond, Virginia, and the Marine Raider Room in the Command Museum at the Marine Corps Recruit Depot, San Diego, are both well worth visiting.

As evidenced by the citations in the chapter endnotes, my most common sources were the individual Raider's narrative descriptions of the events that took place within the ten-foot circle around his fighting hole—from Quantico to Bairoko.

# Index

## About the Author

Joseph H. Alexander served on active duty in the Marine Corps throughout 1960–1988. He served two tours in the Republic of Vietnam and five years at sea on board amphibious ships. Colonel Alexander was Chief of Staff, 3d Marine Division, and a distinguished graduate of the Naval War College. Retired in Asheville, North Carolina, he is the award-winning author of *A Fellowship of Valor: The Battle History of the U.S. Marines* (1997) and three books published by the Naval Institute Press: *Storm Landings: Epic Amphibious Battles in the Central Pacific* (1997), *Utmost Savagery: The Three Days of Tarawa* (1995), and *Sea Soldiers in the Cold War* (1994, with Merrill L. Bartlett). He is chief military historian for Lou Reda Productions and has appeared in fifteen documentaries aired on The History Channel and the Arts and Entertainment Network.